Educational Game Design Fundamentals

A Journey to Creating Intrinsically Motivating Learning Experiences

Educational Game Design Fundamentals

A Journey to Creating Intrinsically Motivating Learning Experiences

George Kalmpourtzis

CRC Press
Taylor & Francis Group
Boca Raton London New York

CRC Press is an imprint of the
Taylor & Francis Group, an **informa** business

CRC Press
Taylor & Francis Group
6000 Broken Sound Parkway NW, Suite 300
Boca Raton, FL 33487-2742

Printed on acid-free paper

International Standard Book Number-13: 978-1-138-63154-0 (Paperback)
International Standard Book Number-13: 978-1-138-63157-1 (Hardback)

Library of Congress Cataloging-in-Publication Data

Names: Kalmpourtzis, George, author.
Title: Educational game design fundamentals : a journey to creating
intrinsically motivating learning experiences / George Kalmpourtzis.
Description: Boca Raton, FL : CRC Press, 2018. | Includes bibliographical
references.
Identifiers: LCCN 2017060414| ISBN 9781138631571 (hardback : alk. paper) |
ISBN 9781138631540 (pbk. : alk. paper)
Subjects: LCSH: Educational games--Design and construction. | Educational
games--Evaluation.
Classification: LCC LB1029.G3 .K34 2018 | DDC 371.33/7--dc23
LC record available at https://lccn.loc.gov/2017060414

Visit the Taylor & Francis Web site at
http://www.taylorandfrancis.com

and the CRC Press Web site at
http://www.crcpress.com

To Nikos, Voula, and Tilemachos, who would always be there

Contents

Acknowledgments

Every journey is unique and has its own great challenges and quiet moments—moments when you constantly test your resolution and your way of thinking. Every journey also starts with one or more people, who, over the course of time, meet new wanderers with similar or different ideas, interact, and come out stronger, wiser, and with greater resolution to continue their journey. Writing this book was no exception. When I initially conceived this project, I didn't imagine the extent of dedication required to pull it through. There were moments that I was tempted to stop, and it was mainly due to the support of family, friends, colleagues, and all those amazing educators and game designers that you hold this book in your hands. Though I could write a book about writing this book (and this is no exaggeration!), instead I will briefly thank those who really impacted its course and creation. This book would not be as it is if it weren't for the following people:

George Ketsiakidis, Lazaros Vrysis, Fragi Katsimpas, Christoforos Nalmpantis, and Tilemachos Kalmpourtzis, for their continuous revision of the manuscript, and for challenging of my way of thinking, providing endless support, and being greatly understanding of me being lost in my "book universe" during all this time; Ifigeneia Tsolaki, for her epic support, focus, meticulousness, and for pushing me forward toward the end of the tunnel, especially during the last stages of writing this book. Sophia Spirliadou, for her mind-blowing work on the book's illustrations, continuous understanding, positive energy, and creativity; Marcus O'Connor, for his great support in proofing the manuscript on different occasions; Margarita Stogia, for her support during interview transcriptions; Professor Marianna Tzekaki, for her great impact on my way of approaching play and games; Michael Berthoix and all the amazing people at Maskott for giving me the space and opportunity to experiment and create;

Rick Adams, Jessica Vega and all the wonderful team of CRC Press, without whom this book would never be published; Jen Helms, Thomas Planques, Klaus Teuber, Francois Boucher-Genesse, Pr. Francesco Mondada, Pr. Kylie Peppler, Utku Kaplan, Laura Malinverni, Pr. Gundolf Freyermuth, Benjamin Kym Hyun, Nick Winter, Pr. Julian Alvarez, Pr. Damien Djaouti, Jesse Himmelstein, Simon Egenfeldt-Nielsen, Stephane Cloatre, Pr. Eric Sanchez, Ryan Gerber, Pr. Drew Davidson, Stephen Coy, Pujiarti Alim, and Celia Hodent, for their interest, participation, and contribution of views and perspectives to this book and for making me feel that I am not alone in this journey for exploring educational gaming; and Dr. Petros Lameras, Pr. Eric Sanchez, and Pr. Zack Hiwiller, for reviewing this work, challenging my thoughts, and making me wiser and this book better.

Author

George Kalmpourtzis is an award-winning game designer and educator. Finding himself between the fields of education, game studies, and user experience, he has been founder, director, and board member of several European design studios. He has designed and produced numerous games for computers, consoles, and virtual and augmented reality, and he is constantly on a journey to discover new opportunities to play! George has been working as a consultant for corporations and non-government institutions around the world, identifying play as a key aspect of human expression and communication. George also holds BSc degrees both in education and engineering, a MSc degree in information systems, and a PhD in design pedagogy.

Introduction: The Journey Begins

SEARCH FOR THE EDUCATIONAL GAME DESIGNER: WHO SHOULD READ THIS BOOK

Many aspects and activities of one's life can be viewed as journeys. Some are straightforward, some are long and hard to complete, and some are still in progress. Designing educational games is no exception to this notion. Designing educational games is a journey, and an amazing one! It begins with realizing what learning and game design is and progresses to coming up with complete, playable games and communicating with one's players. When I first dreamed of writing this book, I realized one thing:

Every journey must have a destination.

So, I brought forward the greatest challenges I always experience when I design games for learning contexts:

Can games be used in learning contexts in a meaningful way?

If so, how can we design games that manage to both attract players' interest and help them to evolve?

These questions are the answer! This book follows the amazing, challenging, and continuous journey of educational game designers in creating games that do not just entertain, but have a profound learning impact on their players. After discovering the destination, I realized one more thing:

There is no journey without a hero.

But who is the hero of this journey? Or, in other words, **who is the educational game designer**?

This question kept haunting me, my friends, colleagues, and peers for a while. Eventually, I reached the conclusion that, like in many of our favorite stories, there is not one single defini- tion of what we call a "hero" for this book. Heroes rise from the needs and challenges of their environment. They do not always know from the very beginning the whole set of obstacles they will encounter, and they also do not know they are the ones who will bring balance to the universe! In this sense, I cannot give a definition of the educational game designer. But I can say that educational game designers share some of the following characteristics, challenges, and difficulties:

They are dedicated, interested, or simply curious to explore how games can be used and designed in learning contexts. Some of them have already found a way to integrate games into their work but want to go deeper; some of them have occasionally used games in learning contexts but are still trying to find a way to use educational games in their own particular teaching contexts; and others can see the potential of educational games but do not yet feel comfortable introducing them to their deliveries.

They constantly think of innovative and novel ways to design learning experiences in their school, work, family, and daily life. In other words, they are those insomniac, constantly active individuals who try to challenge their medium, their deliveries, and their learners. They are those people who always have a new idea and want to create more and more interesting learning experiences; in this case, through games.

Even though they may already create their own games, from board and card games to highly complex video games, they are not always sure about their practices and design decisions and how effective they will be in learning contexts.

They have countless ideas for educational games that are both fun and have an impact on their players, but they are not aware of the resources and processes required to make them real. Coming from very diverse backgrounds, it is highly likely that educational game designers may have an overview of only a fragment of the educational game design process. They may understand pedagogy but lack technical or logistical skills, or they may have great technical understanding but miss those aspects that are necessary to make their games educational for players.

Their nature is agnostic to their background. They are teachers ranging from early childhood to university and lifelong learning, vocational trainers, human resource managers, psychologists, instructional designers, game designers, developers, parents, friends and, in fact, come from any profession, have any background, or engage in any activity that directly or indirectly has a learning impact on those around them.

They have an impact on the use and design of educational games. Most of the time, educational games are created by teams of people. These people come from very different backgrounds. Still, each and every one of these people, whether they know it or not, has a tremendous impact on the final learning experience. In other words, an educational game designer is each and every person who makes up an educational game team.

They are creative minds who are interested in helping their field of work evolve and have a meaningful impact on their peers, friends, and society.

If any of the above aspects describes you, you are the hero of this book.

THE DESTINATION: WHAT YOU WILL GET BY READING THIS BOOK

So, let's set out on an amazing adventure to design meaningful learning experiences through games. Like any adventure, things won't always be smooth. There will be interesting and intensively inspiring moments where you will unleash your creativity and breathe life into your creations, but you will also challenge both your perception on learning and gaming, identify obstacles and design challenges, and will find or create your own tools to cope with them. At the end of the adventure, you will have a different perspective on educational game design.

More specifically, at the end of the book, you will:

Have a better understanding of the fundamentals of educational game design. This includes an understanding of learning theories, game mechanics, aesthetics, storytelling, designing interfaces, identifying technical limitations, and platform specificities and evaluation.

Engage in a continuous process of harmonically combining game design and educational contexts. As we will see later, games are not the answer to every learning situation. Understanding how games can impact players in a meaningful way is one of the first steps to a successful and effective educational game design approach.

Be able to better assess your ideas in terms of feasibility, enjoyment, and learning impact. It is natural that creative minds may come up with both mind-blowing and also not-so-intuitive ideas. Some of them may be great but could require a huge amount of resources, time, or money; others may not be as effective as they should be. Being able to filter one's ideas is an invaluable asset and great virtue of educational game designers.

Be able to take vague and loosely defined ideas and transform them into concrete educational game projects.

Have a better understanding of the needs, tools, materials, people, and procedures needed for the implementation of educational games so that you are able to handle issues, avoid pitfalls, and overcome obstacles that may arise throughout the process of creating your own games.

Be able to harness your creativity, knowledge, and ideas, and be able to create tools and mechanisms that will help you critically examine your own and also any other educational games.

Make the first steps to designing your own games, from **tic-tac-toe** to MMO RPG games.

THE STARTING POINT

Like with any aspect of our lives, losing track of one's path is a possibility. It is on these occasions that educational game designers return to what they consider fundamental for them and the field they work in. So, before we begin, let's lay some ground work and, more importantly, let's set some things straight!

Educational games are about principles, not rules.

There is not one single recipe for success and there is not a magical perfect way to design educational games. It is natural that not everyone likes the same games and that not all games have the same learning impact and appeal for every player. It is even possible that the same games may have a different impact for the same players at different moments.

So, there are no golden rules in educational game design. But there are patterns, principles, theories, and approaches that can help educational game designers make their decisions. Games like **Classcraft**, **Code Combat**, **Math Mathews**, **Zoombinis**, and **Geocaching** may be very different from each other, but they do share several design principles that have made them excellent examples of their genres. The selection process to choose which aspects are left in or out and in what measure is definitely not easy; otherwise, games could be created by highly sophisticated algorithms without needing the creative and unique impact of the human touch of game designers.

It's highly possible that the same type of game may not be effective for helping players to learn both pottery and advanced calculus, in the same way that one single game may prove to be ineffective at teaching both early childhood students and adults about sustainable development. It is through constant reflection, the challenging of one's beliefs and perceptions, team spirit, and understanding of those principles that effective and meaningful educational games are created.

The history of pedagogy has been written by brilliant minds who defied existing theories. They understood the needs of their societies and they broke what others viewed as "rules," setting their own paradigm and impacting those around them. This is the case from the philosophers of ancient Greece to Confucius and from Comenius to Fröbel and Montessori.

Educational games address eternal and universal needs, but also individual human ones.

Play and games are not limited to one's culture or geographic region. They are part of human nature. People do not play because someone told them to or showed them how. They play because they want and need to do it. The same happens with learning, even if we do not always realize it. In fact, play emerges in learning and learning can be facilitated through play. Kids, for instance, love to learn. They show keen interest when discovering something new. They get excited when they first see a vacuum cleaner or when they see a new animal. Learning acquires a substance of play. On the other hand, if we observe the way that baby animals play with each other, we can see that their play contains elements of hunting and evasion of attacks. So, without realizing it, they learn through play.

So, the question is not if play and learning go together. They have done, still do and will always do, as fundamental parts of our human nature. Rather, it is how and under what circumstances those two elements can be used together to help people evolve even more. Even if these needs are universal, they are not expressed and perceived in the exact same way by everyone. We do not like the same games and we do not learn in the same way or at the same pace. Even if games address the needs of every human being, they also need to focus on each individual through a different style, tone, and approach in order to help them reach their own potential.

Educational games are about dedication, not the shortest path.

A big problem with education games is that their designers often downplay some of their aspects in favor of others As a result, those games may not feel right or have the expected learning impact on their players. There are cases where educational games are not educational. There are other cases where they are not fun and even others where educational games offer neither learning value nor fun! Several of those games may be unpolished, unchallenging, and inaccurate in terms of their learning aspects or may not present experiences that help players to learn.

Most of those games will have taken the shortcut. On one hand, there are games that focus on beautiful graphics without a consistent educational perspective. On this occasion, the games were used to "trick" students into receiving learning information in the same way that they would have without the fancy graphics. Believe me, players are extremely smart and have a keen sense for discovering "disguised" learning activities presented as games. On the other hand, there are educational games whose learning aspects may be accurate, but all other game-related aspects are disregarded. Those games are most likely boring, and eventually, even their own designers won't play them.

When designing educational games, there is no easy path. Educational games are not just about learning or about play and games. They are about the whole experience. Meaningful and memorable experiences come from complete game concepts, masterfully implemented. This is the only way. Deciding to go any other way will guarantee that your games will lack in one or more aspects and will not manage to provide players with the amazing learning experiences that you expect.

Educational games are about respect and deep understanding of their audience.

I tend to find that when creative and skilled educational game designers create games that do not work as expected, they are usually blinded by their need to prove a point, idea, or pedagogic perspective. Hence, they get distracted from their main target: their audience. On the other hand, I have realized that educational games that work well were usually designed with the needs of the audience as the main driving force of the design.

Even if it's really fun designing games, we don't make them to be showcased in museums or exhibitions. Educational games are made to be played with. They target their players' needs, meet their expectations, and challenge their current state of mind. In order for this to happen, though, they need to present worlds, characters, and circumstances that players are familiar with, can understand, and can empathize with.

Consequently, educational game designers are not and should not consider themselves as beings from another dimension! They need to understand their players, feel their needs, and understand their way of learning. They need to design games that players are going to dedicate a portion of their lives to completing. More importantly, players are going to explore those worlds; discover new information; challenge their own perspectives, ideas, and misconceptions; question their views on the world; and, eventually, make their lives better. In order to achieve this, designers need to spend time with their players, observe them, understand them, and interact with them.

Ignorant educational game designers blame their audience for not being able to understand or figure out their games. Masters of the craft try to see where they lost contact with their players and work on rebuilding this connection.

Educational games are about meaningful change and fun, not just tests, exams, and performance.

Undoubtedly, for the majority of people, school is permanently connected to tests, exams, and measurement of performance. As a result, several games have focused specifically on those aspects, disregarding whether players have actually learned something. I do not suggest that assessment isn't important. On the contrary, it is a key aspect of education and educational game design—when it is meaningful. But what is the real reason behind education and facilitating learning? It's change!

Change is about altering players' perception, developing their skills, helping them understand their own self and the world around them. It's about being inspired, wanting to their environment, becoming motivated to learn and finding enjoyment in the process. So, educational game designers are bestowed with the challenging task of finding meaningful ways of assessing their games' impact on players' learning without negatively affecting the learning and play experience.

If talent can get you far, craft can get you farther.

There are some lucky people to whom brilliant ideas, innovative mechanics, and amazing stories come easily and without any effort. There are also those who are very skilled at a particular art or craft, like painting, building things, or playing music. This comes handy! In all my years as a game designer and educator I have met several of those amazing people, who were creating their own games and playing them with their students, friends, and colleagues. But let's take a look at this common example:

A highly talented educator with many wonderful ideas tries to make a game. She is excited and wants to make an impact on her students, so she comes up with a strategy video game about math. She uses all her skills, and at the end, produces a game that does not fascinate her students. Its mechanics, level of polishing, and final experience simply aren't quite there. On the other hand, another educator comes up with a very simple idea: an outdoor treasure hunt game about history. This is a game that students have played several times. But, since it is designed and executed properly, students like it and find themselves learning the content that the educator wanted them to.

If players have the choice between brilliant and novel ideas that are badly designed, executed, and presented, and simple ideas that are not, they will always choose the second. You may be a creative genius but if you cannot explain and make your ideas real, it does not matter. This is why learning and developing your craft, is important.

If you think you know how to make great games, then by mastering the craft you will be able to make even greater ones and if you are in doubt about your game design skills, developing the craft will give you the confidence and experience to make more informed design decisions. Craft is partly agnostic to the medium in the sense that the same principles apply to all games, from card and board games to MMO RPG video games. Still, being able to understand the resources, challenges, and limitations of the medium you are going to design for, along with the necessary teammates you will need on your way, is also part of mastering the craft of designing efficient and meaningful educational games.

1 Designing Learning Experiences

This chapter covers the following:

- Exploring the notions of learning and education.

- Understanding why people are motivated to learn.

- Identifying the different forms of knowledge.

- Designing intrinsically motivating experiences.

- Building experiences that captivate your audience's attention.

In this chapter we examine the nature of learning and its importance for our players and identify the attributes and qualities that make people want to learn and, subsequently, grow and evolve. We also examine how learning can take place and how designing intrinsically motivating experiences can give you a kickstart when designing your games.

I consider helping people learn to be among the hardest paths one can choose to follow. From kindergarten to university and from pottery lessons to lifelong learning, education requires the combination of countless skills in order to have a real impact on someone's mind. This is because educators need to contribute to the fostering and creation of environments that indulge people's curiosity, increase their passion for a topic, encourage them to explore the world around them, and help them evolve. This is starting to sound complicated already!

However, the solution is rather simple. The greatest tool in completing this demanding challenge can be described with four magic words:

Intrinsically motivating learning experiences.

This chapter is about the design of intrinsically motivating learning experiences, the wondrous feeling that will mesmerize your audience and keep them hooked in the magic realms of the worlds you create—all while helping them to learn. In order to fully understand the depth and importance of designing intrinsically motivating learning experiences, we will examine the nature of learning, experience, and motivation, and lay some groundwork that will help you understand how you can achieve them through games.

WHAT IS "LEARNING"?

A very common question that people ask me when I tell them that I design games for education is whether games are an effective tool for learning. My answer to their question starts always with another question:

What do you consider to be learning?

If we look back over our lives, we can all recall special moments where we were presented with a problematic situation or a dilemma, the outcome of which was unknown. These experiences took place at home, at work, at school, during weekdays, during holidays. We have experienced situations like this almost everywhere and at any time. During these situations, our knowledge, skills, beliefs, and decisions affected the way history unravelled, leading us to a new adventure or to the elimination of a problematic situation. These moments remain etched in our memory as they had an impact on us:

They changed us, they expanded our depth of knowledge, and they helped us to achieve a goal or brought us closer to achieving it in the future. It is in situations like this that learning occurs.

But what is learning? It could be said that learning is achieved as a result of participating in events that were designed to teach us something. Every day, millions of students go to school and are presented with a diverse curriculum of courses and activities, each of which aims to help them learn a different subject. Students participate in curricular and extracurricular activities for a large amount of their weekly time. But still, have all these students completely mastered the areas of literature, physics, mathematics, or arts? Simple observation would suggest otherwise. Consequently, mere participation in any form of activity does not guarantee learning. So, the question still remains:

What is learning?

Learning is a process. Learning is a process of acquiring or reconstructing existing knowledge leading to our internal change. This change is the result of living experiences that ultimately affect our knowledge, skills, values, behavior, or stance toward a topic. Let's take a moment to examine this definition. We say that learning is a process. Learning does not happen instantaneously. Instead, people who take part in learning activities require an amount of time to truly comprehend a concept. Being able to play the violin is not an achievement that happens in an hour or a week. On the contrary, potential violin players need many years of training in order to master this art, a continuous process of studying, practicing, and performing.

Learning is personal. This amount of time is also not the same for everyone. It is connected with a variety of factors that can be internal, like the way each person learns, or external, like the complexity of the task. We have all met people who tend to grasp a particular concept quicker or slower than others based on the way it was presented and taught. Learning to play tic-tac-toe requires less time and effort compared to chess because the latter presents a more complex set of rules. So, we can also see that learning is an individual process that changes from context to context. This is an interesting point to keep in mind as in later chapters we will see how you can evaluate the nature and complexity of your games in order to teach your subject better.

Learning is continuous and part of our every day lives. Learning is continuous and ongoing. Learning comes from within us, as an inner and personal procedure, and it is not something superficial that just happens to us. Additionally, it is not related simply to how good we are at mathematics or physics. On the contrary, it is related to every aspect of our lives, from the way we decide to dress to our view of the universe. Learning defines our personalities, our relationships, and our ways of expressing happiness and sadness. There are situations where learning happens spontaneously, without us even realizing it, like discovering the attractive and repulsive attributes of magnets while playing with them or by exploring social identity through roleplaying games, even from early childhood. There are other times that learning comes as a result of participating in structured environments, facilitated by a teacher or not, like attending cooking classes or joining a massive open online course.

There is not just one single way of learning. As it turns out, there is not just one single way of learning. For example, some animals know things thanks to their instincts. This means that the information they need to know is already preprogrammed in their heads. That would seem to be a very appealing idea for some students!

However, instinct can provide us with only a specific and limited set of information. Spiders are capable of creating complex webs and using them in amazing ways, but they would never be able to solve mathematical problems or compose music. Their capabilities are limited and specialized toward specific tasks important for their survival. On the other hand, humans, like all mammals, are able to learn from their peers and extend their depth of actions and capabilities, helping them to survive and evolve. In this way, they were able to search for shelter, create clothes from the skin of animals, and master fire. Consequently, since ancient times, people have needed to find a way to facilitate the learning process efficiently. This is why education was born!

ABOUT EDUCATION AND PEDAGOGY

We can say that education is the process of helping ourselves or others to learn. I consider **education as the art of facilitating learning**. On the other hand, the science that studies the theory and practice of education is pedagogy. By incorporating various tools and techniques, educators aim to support the process of other people's learning. Even if the term is more often used to describe formal education, like primary school, high school, and universities, education can take many forms. Since its purpose is the design and establishment of learning environments, it cannot be limited to specific contexts. Education can be about mathematics, chemistry, physics, and arts, but it can also be about values, communication, expression of ideas, and personal perspectives. Those who facilitate those learning circumstances, called educators or pedagogues, can be teachers, trainers, social workers, psychologists, our friends, or ourselves. Since learning happens everywhere, education can also be found in any aspect of our lives. This fact also makes the selection of proper teaching tools a challenge.

Later on, this book, while incorporating educational tools that you already possess, will examine some common educational tools and approaches and evaluate the impact of integrating them into your games and in different learning contexts.

At school

In his book **Futuredays: A Nineteenth Century Vision of the Year 2000**, Isaac Asimov published several designs of artists, who, at the beginning of the 20th century, tried to imagine how the world would be in the year 2000. One of the designs was dedicated to the future of education. The artist envisioned classrooms where students would not need to study but instead knowledge would be automatically embedded in their heads through the use of technology. Specially designed machines would read books and pass their information to connected students instantly and without effort. It's been over a century and such a technology still hasn't been invented! Until it is, learning and teaching will require both effort and time to achieve. Learning is an individual process, different for each person, requiring the understanding of how people perceive their environment and evolve in it. In order to facilitate learning, educators are entrusted with the very challenging task of designing experiences that support learning. This is also the reason why educators must be humans and not machines.

Every person has the potential to help others to learn. This might be with knowledge, skills, arts, crafts, whole scientific domains, values, or even a personal ideology. Whatever your educational objectives are, you need to have an understanding of the particularities of your very specific field that you want to teach, since this is an area that cannot be covered by just one book! It is obvious that training someone to become a ballet dancer requires particular knowledge of the human body, gymnastics, and dancing, which wouldn't be quite so necessary when teaching computer programming, which requires the development of algorithmic and mathematical skills. These particularities, along with the different approaches to teaching your topic, are also the only requirements necessary to enter the magical world of educational game design with this book. Based on your expertise and understanding of your subject, we will later find the appropriate tools to design and create games that will address the topics and students' individual needs.

Types of Learning

During the continuous process of learning we evolve by assessing new or existing knowledge, leading to internal change. But learning doesn't only take place in schools. There was learning long before school was invented, as learning is an integral part of human nature. Most of our communication skills, for example, are a result of learning through interaction with other people, inside or outside a school environment. There are various areas that are not covered by the school curriculum. If we want to learn about these areas, we need to join a club or seek the help of an expert, such as a potter, juggler, or shoemaker. But there are also times when we learn without any obvious external aid. Let's look at some cases from everyday life and see if learning took place during them:

- Trying to open the safety cap of a pill jar.

- Changing a spare tire on the highway.

- Participating in salsa dance lessons.

- Singing in a local choir.

- Playing a board game.
- Attending a chemistry course.
- Presenting in front of an audience.
- Consoling a sad friend.

In which of those situations did learning take place? The answer is all of them. Each of these situations offered new knowledge that had an impact on the people who participated in them. Changing a spare tire is obviously not a skill one has from birth. In order for someone to change a spare tire, they need to possess a specific toolset and know how to use it. So, a situation like this is a great opportunity for someone to learn this skill, sometimes through the help of somebody else or through exploration, trial, and error. Any of the above situations raise an opportunity to learn a new skill. It also becomes apparent that there are different ways that learning occurs. In some cases, there is a defined structured that intends to help us learn, such as school or a dance class, and in others we learn by interacting with the world around us. In this sense, there are three ways that people learn: formally, informally, and non-formally.

Formal learning is the type of learning that takes place inside a structured and well-defined framework, with learning objectives, with the intention that students gain knowledge. Formal learning is found within our initial education, such as school, college, university, or through the training structures of our workplace, such as conferences, workshops, and seminars. We participate in formal learning sessions because we intentionally want to learn by expanding our perspective on one or several topics. Since formal learning is based on a well-defined structure, its effectiveness and outcomes are easily monitored. This is the reason why it is usually followed with some certification or degree. However, formal learning environments do not always guarantee optimum learning conditions. The most characteristic example in this case is school. Without doubt, its importance is crucial for shaping any nation's society and culture and it is responsible for the education of hundreds of thousands of students, but at the same time school does not have the same impact on all students. The nature of formal learning also makes it easier to address both small and large audiences and assure the use of particular procedures or methodologies in learning contexts.

Informal learning, on the other hand, does not consist of set objectives in terms of learning outcomes, it is never organized, and it is not intentional from the side of the learner. Informal learning is based on the premise that during our lives we are constantly exposed to learning situations. These situations can be at home, at work, or during leisure time. Learning is everywhere and by experiencing different situations, we evolve. On a cold winter's night, the fact that we will dress warmer shows that, based on our experience, we know that if we don't, we may get ill. In another case, if we see that somebody is sad, we hug them, offer advice, console them, or just don't interfere because we know they don't want to be disturbed. These are decisions based on experiences that are not usually part of the curriculum of a formal learning context. There are countless circumstances where informal learning takes place, inside or outside school environments. Still, the nature of this type of learning cannot be manipulated by educators.

Non-formal learning is the type of learning between formal and informal learning. This type of learning includes a variety of learning situations and approaches that are not usually covered by school but are presented in an organized framework and have learning objectives. Non-formal learning contexts combine spontaneity, diversity of teaching methodologies, and a focus on the interests of the learner. Non-formal learning does not usually conform to specific norms but aims to have an impact on learners. There are various examples of non-formal learning. Several adult learning activities, such as continuing education courses or corporate training workshops, apply non-formal techniques in order to facilitate learning. Several non-governmental organizations use non-formal learning to inform and motivate local communities about intercultural learning, human rights, cultural diversity, or disease prevention. The interesting point about non-formal learning is that participation can be intentional or unintentional, since non-formal learning contexts usually take place naturally and spontaneously during other activities or on their own.

But which type of learning takes place while playing games? Actually, by playing games, players can be introduced to all types of learning. Games are merely tools in the hands of educational game designers. They can be used in different ways and different contexts, learning or not. There are games that are already part of official curricula, being designed and structured under a particular learning framework, thus being part of formal learning. There are situations where players can learn something spontaneous that the creator of the game had not actually planned to teach. This could be anything: from the name of a location in **Tomb Raider** to identifying a new genre of music by listening to the radio stations in **Grand Theft Auto**. In this case, players are learning informally. Last but not least, games can be used in non-formal learning contexts by proposing learning environments that do not necessarily follow a particular norm and are based on the particularity of a group. Custom games (geography bingo, shape domino, etc.) created by teachers to present a topic or the use of existing games with specific learning objectives in mind are examples of the use of games in non-formal learning.

The impact and extent of the use of games in learning contexts has been a topic of fierce discussion for several decades and will be for many more. There are those who view games only as informal learning tools that may or may not be of significance to players' development of skills and acquisition of knowledge. There are others who view educational games as tools that facilitate learning only in formal learning environments. Then there are those who view games as opportunities for learning, regardless of the difficulty the topic presents through the basis of being a game or despite the age of players, like the designers of serious games. As we will see in Chapter 2, play encompasses every aspect of our lives, whether we realize it or not. From the easiest to the most complex subject and from our early childhood till our final years, we both play and learn. So, we are presented with a very interesting question: Should we differentiate those aspects or should we bring them closer?

Starting from Chapter 3, we will see various examples of incorporating different types of learning into existing games and how you can introduce them in yours. At the same time, it is a good point for you to start reflecting on the nature of learning you want to facilitate in your games. Are your games going to be used in formal, informal, or non-formal learning contexts? Could your games also be used in different kinds of teaching situations? In fact, the existence of one of these different types of learning contexts does not prohibit the existence of another. On the contrary, we encounter situations of different kinds of learning in our lives, many of which differ a lot from each other.

Educators who want to have an impact on their students incorporate different types of learning into their teaching methodologies. We could identify non-formal learning situations in school environments as well as formal learning contexts outside of school. One of the very first steps toward setting up your game is to identify what types of learning you want to incorporate into your designs and how you can combine them together. Games, as a tool for learning, can be found in both formal, informal, and non-formal contexts. But even if a perfect learning environment has been set up, the participation and interest on behalf of the learner remains one of the most important elements of the learning process. This is why we need to also understand why people want to learn.

REFLECTION POINTS 🔍

Try to identify previous personal experiences, where you felt that learning took place and identify the elements that had an impact on you. Which of those elements would you like to keep in your game and which ones would you prefer to avoid?

- Among those situations some belong in formal, informal and non-formal contexts. How did those different situations affect your learning experience?

- What is the context in which you expect your game to take place? Is your potential game going to be used in a formal or a non-formal context?

- What type of learning would you expect to facilitate through your game? Would you go for something very structured or would you base your design on spontaneity?

THE INFINITE POWER OF MOTIVATION: WHY DO PEOPLE LEARN?

Some years ago, I was part of the design team for the mobile arcade game **Puji's Shootout**. From the early stages of the design, I presented the game to some close friends and relatives, one of which was my friend Bob. After some days, I realized that Bob's six-year-old daughter, Sonia, liked to play the game and kept asking her dad to open the game for her on his tablet. Bob, who had recently bought the tablet, hadn't fully come to grips with it yet. This led Sonia to learn how to do this by herself. Sometimes her dad would even ask her for help to open some other applications, which was an interesting turn of events. Sonia learned how to operate a complex piece of technologic machinery just because she wanted to play. She developed an interest in learning how to operate the tablet and subsequently, she developed the necessary mechanisms to achieve her goal. In other words, Sonia was motivated to learn!

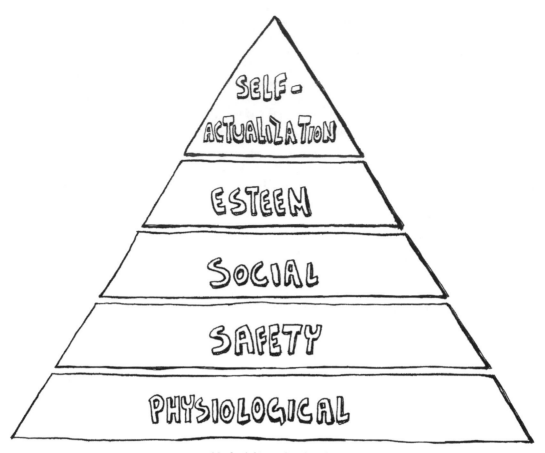

Maslow's hierarchy of needs.

Motivation is a strong force that guides people's actions, decisions, and views toward achieving their goals. This motivation can be expressed in many ways and for different reasons and it can be different for every person. Motivation psychologist Abraham Maslow proposed a theory on the premise that people are motivated by their unsatisfied needs. For this reason, he devised a hierarchy schematic, usually represented through a pyramid that represented those needs. According to Maslow, in order for someone to be motivated to complete a particular need, all needs that are placed below it in the hierarchy need to have been fulfilled [1]. Maslow's hierarchy includes the following needs:

Physiological needs are connected to someone's survival. These needs include securing water, food, air, or sleep. The needs consist of the basic requirements for someone's body to function normally.

Safety needs are related to any requirement for the survival and well-being of the human body and mind after the physiological needs have been fulfilled. After securing the absolutely necessary requirements for their body to function, humans search for a safe place to settle, take care of their health, and try to find the necessary means to ensure the stability of that situation, like seeking financial independence through working. Someone's deprivation of safety can lead to frustration as well as physical or mental trauma.

Love and belongingness needs express the human desire to have a stake in any group they are members of. Acceptance from one's peers is an important aspect of a person's life as it affects the way they interact with their environment. People need to love and be loved and deprivation of circumstances where these emotions take place can have a strong impact on their personalities.

Esteem needs are the reason people want to be respected. These types of needs are related to the way people accept and view themselves, as well as to the respect and recognition they receive from their peers. Failure to fulfill these needs can lead to low self-esteem or lack of confidence, making people feel inferior to others and thus affecting their decisions, priorities, and motivation.

Self-actualization needs are at the top of Maslow's hierarchy. They are linked to someone's desire for self-fulfillment and personal growth. Through those needs, people seek the peak of an experience, the fullest of their potential, a better understanding of themselves. Needs like this include someone's desire to become the best teacher or the exploration of the meaning of life.

A quick look at human history presents us with several achievements that were based on the basic needs of Maslow's pyramid: The discovery of fire, construction of shelters, designing aqueducts, metalworking, and hunting are just some examples of the impact of motivation arising from the human desire to fulfill needs. In order to have a need fulfilled from a higher level of Maslow's pyramid, we need to have covered those from all the levels below. This makes sense if we consider that it's highly unlikely that somebody will seek to perform ground-breaking cancer research if they have not first secured a place to live and eat. Needs affect our motives. Motives affect our preferences and behavior. Preferences and behavior in turn affect our learning choices, consciously or unconsciously. Since any need we have requires some knowledge, skill, or decision-making to be fulfilled, understanding someone's needs can help teachers to motivate their audience. Intentionally or unintentionally, we learn so that we achieve our goals. Learning is our best tool to adapt to new environments and situations and achieve what we long for. Whether that is being able to afford a place to stay, find food, protect ourselves from changing weather conditions, become famous, find true love, or make our mark in the world, humans need to develop skills, be able to collect the necessary information, and make decisions based on this information. This is the essence of learning and this is its goal. This is also why people learn!

Attention is needed! Maslow's pyramid offers an interesting and comprehensive way of approaching motivation. However, if there was a known formula of motivation, it would have already been applied in our activities and everybody would be filled with energy, excitement, and joy. Is this currently the case? Obviously not! The reason is because each individual is different. We think differently, we approach life differently, and the priority of our needs may vary by region, age, or culture. We may prioritize needs differently in various instances. It's also possible that some of our needs may be considered to be in more than one category of needs. Like most situations regarding human learning, there are no perfect formulas and nothing is black or white.

When designing games, game designers try to appeal to the needs of their audience. There are players who want to explore the world around them, players who want to love and be loved, players who want to be part of a group, players who want to find their true potential. From **Far Cry: Primal** to **The Sims**, there are human needs that are fulfilled physically or virtually. By appealing to or fulfilling those needs, games become interesting and offer a motivating environment where players want to evolve.

Motivation can derive from different kinds of needs. It is quite usual for people to try to address needs that were artificially or intentionally created by their environment to help them learn. This is the case with using rewards to attract the attention of students and introduce them to a learning topic. Students, for example, study to get a higher grade, college students prepare themselves by aiming to get certification, and professionals train to get a promotion. In all of these cases the motivation is born in order to achieve a goal proposed by someone else, which could be the school, the university, or someone's employer. There are also moments where motivation arises from somebody's desire to accomplish a personal goal, set only by themselves. Playing a video game, watching a football match, collecting stamps, and hanging out with friends are activities that people enter not because someone else told them to or tried to increase their interest toward. People choose these activities because they find a personal, internal interest that completes one or more of their needs.

Based on whether motivation comes from someone's personal, internal need or an artificially created need of their environment, motivation can be categorized as follows:

Intrinsic motivation is an internal desire to acquire more knowledge, take on new challenges, and evolve in order to fulfill someone's needs. Intrinsic motivation arrives from one's inherent interest in a particular activity or task itself. Someone who likes dancing or wants to become a dancer will be likely to train harder than someone who doesn't. This training will not be limited to dancing classes but will continue while at home, at work, or while walking in the street because the person dancing finds pleasure in this activity. This kind of motivation lasts for a long time and has a strong impact on someone. On the other hand, it is not easy for an educator to develop this within students as it is based on variable internal factors for each individual. Intrinsic motivation does not rely on external factors, such as certification and grades, but is built on someone's unique interest in a topic, their autonomy, and their belief that they can achieve a particular goal. One of the main arguments of using games in learning contexts is that they can offer intrinsically motivating experiences. People don't play because someone asked them to. They play because they find an interest in the activity of playing itself. They don't expect to get a reward for playing as playing itself is the reward.

Extrinsic motivation, on the other hand, is related to actions one takes to achieve a particular goal or have a specific outcome. Extrinsic motivation is based on the premise of understanding what elements or situations create motives for individuals or groups. In this sense, extrinsic motivation can be a reward, such as grades, gifts, or acknowledgment, but it can also be punishment. As the incentives of extrinsic motivation are not always aligned with one's priorities, extrinsic motivation can have a smaller impact in comparison with intrinsic motivation. But at the same time, activities and sessions where educators try to foster extrinsic motivation are easier to achieve and organize compared to intrinsic motivation.

There are several examples of extrinsic motivation regarding learning. Students could be extrinsically motivated to study for university because their parents promised them a car. Others could be participating in many school activities in order to receive the esteem of their peers. However, in both cases students' motives were related to an external stimulus rather than the pleasure of the activity itself.

Let's consider the case of a student coming back from school and needing to do her homework. Unmotivated to do the homework and feeling tired, the student wants to play her favorite game on a console. The student's parents, wanting to motivate her to do her homework, tell her that she can play the game when she finishes. The student has an external motive to do homework. When the homework is finished, she gets the reward and starts playing the console. The game she likes offers an interesting environment and she wants to become better at it. Her desire to evolve in the game's context is internal, thus making it stronger. The student is intrinsically motivated to develop her playing skills. Wouldn't it be amazing if her homework was somehow integrated into that game or if the homework could propose an environment just as interesting?

The magical power of games is that they can be both intrinsically and extrinsically motivating experiences. Apart from the fact that games can be used as a reward to motivate learners to study, the very process of play can be inherently interesting for players, motivating them to explore a game universe just for the fun of it. This is also the key point of using games in learning contexts. If the game environment features elements that an educator wants to teach, the purely interesting exploration of a game world can lead to the facilitation of learning. Being able to design activities that motivate players to learn is a topic we will continuously consider throughout the book. From design to implementation and evaluation phases, we will be examining your core game elements for their impact on players' interest, trying to create intrinsically and extrinsically motivating experiences.

REFLECTION POINTS 🔍

Try to identify personal experiences where you were intrinsically or extrinsically motivated. Try to use these experiences as reference when you want to attract the interest of your audience.

- What type of motivation do you invoke in your game? What needs of your players do you want to address, in order to attract their attention and motivate them to learn through your game?

- In what ways could you use the following in your game?

  - Intrinsic motivation

  - Extrinsic motivation

- Do you want to use your game as a reward that could extrinsically motivate learners to participate in a learning activity or do you want to present an intrinsically motivating experience that players find pleasurable just by participating in it and integrate learning concepts there?

KNOWLEDGE IS POWER

Knowledge itself is power.

–Francis Bacon

One day, almost two-and-a-half thousand years ago, Archimedes, a Greek mathematician and physicist, was preparing for his bath in Syracuse. While entering his bathtub, he observed that the level of water was rising the more he moved into it. He then realized that this would be a great way to measure the volume of irregular objects, like his body. Excited by his discovery, he ran out of his house, naked, shouting "Eureka!"—at least that time he had an excuse! Using this discovery, Archimedes was able to examine if the crown of the king of Syracuse was made out of pure gold by calculating its density. Actually, his method showed that the crown did not contain only gold but was the result of a mixture of other metals. Being sure about his discovery, he bet his life when the king actually decided to destroy the crown in order to examine its purity. Archimedes was right. He had used his analytical skills to process the knowledge he had already received and discovered something new.

Knowledge and the way to acquire and analyze it is very important in any aspect of human life. Imagine life without knowledge. The wheel would not have been invented, making transportation extremely difficult. Imagine a world without telephony, connecting the farthest places of the planet and making exchange of information possible around the globe. Imagine humans without social skills. People with no moral values and ways to behave would constantly struggle and live a life with many hardships, where no friends and loved ones would be by one's side. Imagine humans with no respect for their environment, where no one cared about the sustainability of their society and the future of their species. These are just a few examples of the importance of different kinds of knowledge to us and the ones around us.

On the nature of knowledge and how it can be applied, there have been various analyses. In 1956, prominent educational psychologist Benjamin Bloom and his team published an analysis on the **Taxonomy of Educational Objectives**. Even if the application of this analysis has been the center of several debates, Bloom proposed an interesting way to categorize knowledge. Following this we have three main categories of knowledge: cognitive, affective, and psychomotor [2].

The **cognitive domain of knowledge** includes the recollection and identification of facts, patterns, and concepts that help the development of intellectual skills and abilities. This domain is connected with our understanding of the world; remembering terms, facts, or concepts; applying and analyzing the knowledge we receive; and evaluating that knowledge and constructing more. The cognitive domain is related to a variety of tasks, such as solving mathematical problems, setting up our tablet, or flying a rocket ship. It encapsulates all these complex processes that require us to recall our experience, filter it, evaluate its significance to a specific situation, and make a decision. Whether we will eat a mushroom in the forest or we will enter a specific area in a video game labyrinth is a matter of choice, which is affected by our emotions, experience, and definitely our knowledge of the current situation.

The **affective domain of knowledge** describes the way we interact with the ones around us. This means that through the affective domain we develop our values and the way we apply them in our lives. The way we respond to comments, receive feedback, internalize our thoughts, and interact with our society is the result of the development of our affective skills. In other words, this type of knowledge defines the way we listen and respond to other people or phenomena that happen in front of us, our participation and stance toward social events and actions that will improve the way of life for us and others, as well as the way we work, cooperate, and communicate.

The **psychomotor domain of knowledge** is related to the mastery of our movements. This includes physical movement, coordination, and the use of motor skills. This domain requires work and effort in order to achieve high precision, technique, and speed in several psychomotor skills. These skills include all areas from walking and dancing to typing on a keyboard or playing the piano. The development of fine motor skills is a process that starts as soon as early childhood. Fine motor skills, contrary to our gross motor skills, are connected to the mastery and use of small muscle groups, like our fingers. These skills are enhanced through practice and training. Since we live in a physical world, mastery of this domain is as important as all others, since our body is one of our main tools for expressing ourselves and interacting with our environment.

What we get from Bloom's analysis is that knowledge can take different forms and can affect us in various ways. Through the evolution of pedagogic principles and perspectives, the taxonomy of knowledge will be revised and extended. The important part to keep in mind is that knowledge can take different forms, and opportunities for learning can be found everywhere. Nature does not usually express itself in singular tasks. Instead, human interaction with the environment requires multi-tasking, observation, and assessment of several stimuli, expressed in varied forms and requiring different competences to deal with. In order to have a better perspective of how people learn and can use the knowledge they receive, we must identify the impact of knowledge on us.

DEVELOPING SKILLS

Every day we encounter new situations where we need to apply our knowledge in order to find solutions to problems that arise. Sending an email, solving a puzzle, driving, or presenting in front of an audience are just some of the countless cases where we need to apply our cognitive and physical abilities to complete tasks or provide solutions to problems. These abilities are called **skills**. Skills are human tools for achieving particular goals.

Thymio is an educational robot with several applications in educational game design. Using and controlling it requires the development of a diverse skillset from mathematics to programming and literacy. (Used with permission of Mobsya.)

Every day, by using their skills, people construct buildings, cook food, drive to and from home, read books, sing, dance, and communicate. Every task that we perform depends on skill. This is the reason why learning environments aim to help learners develop their skills. There are attributes that can be found in every situation of human life. Picasso and Einstein might not have worked in the same areas and probably did not need the same skills to explore their fields, but they were both able to adapt their thinking and actions to their environments and create and innovate. In other words, they had learned how to think.

Critical thinking is the human ability to form a perspective based on the use of rational thinking. People who possess critical thinking can draw conclusions based on their own observation, analysis, and interaction with a topic. They do not depend on the opinions of others and have the great advantage of being able to critique other people's views, evaluating their opinion. Critical thinking is the main goal of modern pedagogy: Helping learners to develop their own system of collecting, assessing, and producing information, making them active and competent members of society. Critical thinking cannot exist without the development of skills. In fact, it is the result of mastering the use of several skills and understanding their use in order to become mentally independent.

Skills development does not focus only on labor but on a variety of aspects of human life. Social skills are also a prominent part of any human interaction. Collaboration, expression of ideas, conflict resolution, and leadership are some of these social skills. But learning and teaching are not only about the development of skills. Being part of a vast universe, where any of our actions affects the lives of others, people need to have a holistic view of the environment that surrounds them and develop as a part of it.

Social development has been studied throughout the ages, from Socrates to Freud, and has been part, to greater and smaller degrees, of the majority of educational systems. Humans are by our nature social beings. To understand our role in society, we first need to understand who we are. Self-awareness is among the first and most important steps in a person's life and is linked to the way we present ourselves, behave, and reflect on our personality. Societies try to raise people with self-respect and confidence so as to evolve and grow. Collaborating with one's peers, receiving and giving feedback, resolving conflict, and being able to identify and control one's emotions are important skills that people develop inside a learning environment but also throughout all their lives. Humans, as social animals, need to be with other humans. They need to be able to accept and be accepted, and to express their happiness and sorrow, as well as their ideas about complex issues. The ability to solve a complex problem might not have a lot of meaning without being able to explain and present it to our society, since solutions only have an impact when they are applied to problems of our own or others.

DEVELOPING VALUES

The United Nations defines **sustainable development** as development that meets the needs of the present without compromising the ability of future generations to meet their own needs [3]. In other words, sustainable development leads to a better quality of life for everyone now, and for future generations. It presents a global vision of progress and prosperity through short- and long-term goals that lead to the shaping of attitudes, stances, and behaviors, with regards to social, economic, and environmental issues as integral components of human progress.

In order to better examine sustainable development, let's see some examples of unsustainability. Economic development of local areas or whole countries and uncontrolled use of natural resources with no concern for the environment is a very typical example of the need for education about sustainable development. A factory that opens near a river has the potential to offer great economic growth to the local society by offering jobs. If the factory executives do not take the necessary measures to ensure that the produced waste is filtered and stored properly, the toll on the river ecosystem could be devastating, rendering the area uninhabitable. In this case, the current generation has lived with prosperity and growth for a period while the consequences of leaving behind a contaminated land will be felt in the future.

Sustainable development is not only related to environmental preservation. It is also connected with the social structures and values of people. Examples like this have been highlighted in literature throughout the ages. Concepts likes jealousy, discrimination, or ignorance are a part of human nature and the way people have handled them defines their personality and position inside their society. In the Japanese art of Aikido, one of the principles is that in order to bring peace to the world, we first need to start bringing peace to ourselves, thus affecting the others around us. Change for something better initially comes from us. Based on this idea, the European Union proposed the Erasmus+ program. This program supported the exchange of students and young people among different areas of Europe and organized training sessions about various social issues. The aim of the committee that created this program was to help young people and future citizens meet, explore, and discover the different cultures of the continent, helping to create an atmosphere of understanding and active participation.

REFLECTION POINTS 🔍

- What are the types of knowledge you want to present through your game?

- What are the types of skills you want to help players develop while playing your game?

- Are there any particular values that you want to promote through your game?

- Is there any social or communication aspect that is important in the game and that you would like to help players develop while entering your game?

BUILDING EXPERIENCES

The only source of knowledge is experience.

–Albert Einstein

Some years ago, I was part of a training team in Sicily, Italy. The subject of the course was how social workers could use clownery as a tool for social inclusion. It was actually a very interesting topic, treating a variety of cases, such as substance abuse, immigration, and working with people with disabilities. Part of the training team was an expert on clownery, Alessio. During the six days, participants would work on themselves, build their own clown personas, and then perform in several institutions or spaces around Sicily. This would include hospitals, care centers, and public squares. Through the use of various tools and activities, involving drama, games, and clownery, Alessio succeeded in creating an intense atmosphere, where 20 people became tightly bonded, overcame their fears, and performed in front of different audiences. This course is still etched on my memory. It was an amazing, life-changing event that had a great impact on me. This was a learning experience.

Any game that you are going to design, build, or use aims to offer a unique and particular experience to your players. As we will see in the next chapters, all the elements that you will work on while creating your games, game mechanics, aesthetics, narration, technology, and education focus on the same thing: providing your players with intrinsically motivating experiences that help them learn. But how are experiences perceived by players? What are the qualities of experiences that are memorable and have an impact on players? Are all experiences educational and what elements do you need to have in mind when designing your games? Let's try to answer those questions!

THE ART OF DESIGNING EXPERIENCES

The most important attitude that can be formed is that of desire to go on learning.

–John Dewey

We live experiences every day. Actually, almost every action of our lives leads to or comes from an experience. Experience is linked with what we listen to, see, feel, and think. However, among these experiences there are some that particularly stand out. Those experiences can be both good and bad in the same way that we have a memorable experience playing both an amazing and a very boring game.

Everything we design, implement, and present intends to create an experience for other people. Even if we like to call ourselves game designers, I would rather say that we are actually experience designers, since games, movies, and theater are tools and ingredients we use because we want to create a specific atmosphere through which our audience experiences something unique.

Experience can come from any aspect of our daily lives. But when they are designed by us, they have our personal signature, bearing our history, experiences, and mindset. Experience is the result of the combination of materials, imagination, narration, game mechanics, technology, and aesthetics. It is the result of human interaction with the world around us. This is the reason why game designers need to have a comprehensive perspective of their actions. Games like **Super Mario**, **Grand Theft Auto**, and **pinball** affect us in various ways, like the need to use our skills, the freedom to explore a virtual world, or the need to combine physical ability with speed. The impact of the experience of playing such games does not differ from the one of playing **hide-and-seek**, **poker**, or **Reversi**. Each game uses different means to provide us with a unique experience that serves the purpose of its creator and leaves a mark on us.

In order for an experience to have significance for someone, it needs to bear some value, to present something of importance at a specific time that will excite, surprise, soothe, or challenge something inside people's minds. Consequently, experiences are connected with people's daily lives and have meaning through those. In his book, **Art as Experience**, philosopher and educator John Dewey reflects on the notion that works of art and the activities of people's lives are connected, and to perceive the aesthetic of a work, people must first comprehend the context of events and scenes of daily life [4]. Dewey also suggested that experience arises from the interaction of two basic principles: continuity and interaction.

Continuity describes the aspect of experience as this is perceived by an individual—in this case, your learners. Its proposal actually explains that the impact of an experience depends both on pre-existing experiences and the quality of those that come after. This notion will help you to prepare the necessary environment for your games. For example, knowing that players already have experience playing a specific genre of games, you know that they have an understanding of game controls and interactions and have specific expectations from the game they will be presented with. In this case, you could design your games based on those facts. The final game will be a new experience. If they find it interesting and play it, this game will have an impact on them, affecting their existing experiences and leading them to seek out new ones. Continuity is just one of the various reminders that game design is a tool for the creation of amazing experiences, which are not always perceived in the same way by every player.

According to Dewey, an experience is always what it is because of a transaction taking place between the learner and what, at the time, constitutes their environment. In other words, people are not passive objects during an event that constitutes an experience but play a part in it. This is called **interaction**. Of course, watching a movie does not incorporate a lot of interaction but if we examine the presentation of a movie inside the context of a classroom presentation about the Amazonian rainforests, the choice of presenting a movie and then creating an essay might have a particular impact. Games, however, are closely linked to interaction. In fact, interaction is an integral attribute of play and games, making them a great tool in the hands of educators. Through gaming contexts, the environment becomes transformed through the prism of rules and situations, during which players need to take decisions and arrive at solutions. The transaction between player and game is obvious in this case.

Through interaction and continuity, your audience will have the opportunity not just to be passive observants of events but to take part in them and affect their course. Through experience, players have the opportunity to observe, experiment, and reflect on their action. The fact that students know a mathematical formula does not necessarily guarantee that they are able to use it! Creating experiences that captivate players' interests and involve them in the discovery of something new can bring you closer to a new and interesting teaching tool. As game designers, you need to harvest this potential and use it to create experiences that are both fun and constructive for the human mind.

GAMES PROVIDE IMMERSIVE EXPERIENCES

Albert Einstein, in an effort to explain the idea of special relativity, proposed an analogy that described how when a guy sits with a nice girl for two hours he may think it's only a minute, but when he sits on a hot stove for a minute he may think it's two hours. This, according to Einstein, is relativity. This is just one example of the countless cases where the space–time continuum is affected by the experience one has entered. Einstein based his example on a characteristic of the human mind: **Immersion**.

There is a point in time when we play a game or perform a task where we lose sense of time and space. Other people may be talking to us or several events may be happening on the radio or TV but we don't seem to pay attention to them. When speaking later with those others, they seem surprised that we hadn't been paying attention to what they were saying. This means that we were so deeply focusing on the activity we were working on that we could not focus on anything else. We have all experienced moments like this. This is immersion.

Immersion is a state of mind where one's focus is so directed toward a topic that everything else passes unnoticed. It's like a Zen state where we seem to know what to do and are actually flowing with the story or sequence of events of a task. During an immersive state, we lose track of time. People come and go, clocks are ticking, and we are still playing. For us, however, time passes like before. We also lose awareness of the real world. We don't seem to notice things that are happening around us and at the same time we do not interact with anything else apart from the task we are absorbed in. In fact, we are so involved with this task that we have the feeling that we are a part of this task environment.

The notion of being absorbed and engaged inside experiences is not new. It is actually an aspect that game designers and educators usually take into consideration, empirically and unconsciously. Fascinated by the behavior of artists, chess players, and athletes, Hungarian psychologist Mihály Csíkszentmihályi proposed the concept of flow [5]. Csíkszentmihályi initially observed that artists get so absorbed in their work that they forget to eat and sleep. So, he proposed that flow describes the state in which individuals are so involved in an activity that nothing else seems to matter. During flow, people have intense and focused concentration on what they are doing at the moment, they lose their awareness as social actors, they seem to know how to react to any situation that may arise, they feel that time has passed faster than normal, and the experience of the activity is intrinsically rewarding. In other words, players that are in a flow state while playing a game love to play the game and use the end goal (winning the game) as an excuse to continue playing.

Games have this amazing quality of presenting us with our own special worlds. These worlds are isolated, physically or mentally. They are not always bound by the rules of reality. On the contrary, game worlds may present new rules, where actions and objects may have a totally different meaning or use. A tea party with dolls would seem a futile activity in a real context, but in the context of children's symbolic play, it acquires an absolutely different essence. A virtual sword or shield are absolutely useless in the real world, but they may be priceless for the players of an RPG game. So, games present temporary worlds, inside our ordinary ones, with the sole intention of facilitating play. Johan Huizinga, in his book **Homo Ludens** [6], called any world of this kind a **magic circle**.

Immersion also exists in educational contexts. The fostering of immersive activities leads to greater learner engagement and thus to greater learning impact. More or less everyone has participated in learning activities that were boring and time would not pass no matter how intensely we stared at our watch. But there have also been moments that we loved participating in an activity and time passed so fast that we didn't really notice it. Whether these sessions were games or not, they were intrinsically motivating and engaging. Usually, we understand if activities are intrinsically motivating when we play or present them to others. This means that usually you are not able to assess the intrinsic value of a game until you present it to your audience. As we will see in Chapter 5, this is one of the greatest reasons why prototyping has such an important role in the game design process.

THE IMPACT OF INTRINSICALLY MOTIVATING LEARNING EXPERIENCES

Tell me and I forget, teach me and I may remember, involve me and I learn.

–Benjamin Franklin

The biggest talent of an educational game designer is the power to create experiences that captivate people's attention and foster an environment where they acquire new knowledge, develop skills, and reflect on situations that will later lead them to evaluate their attitude towards a topic. This task is, understandably, not easy. In fact, it is a complex process, where the designer needs to calculate several factors and make decisions that will support both learning and making the game intrinsically motivating to players.

Experiences are the essence of people's interaction with their surroundings. Still, not all experiences are educational. Also, not all experiences are intrinsically motivating. It is the game designer's task to identify these attributes and design experiences or sequences of experiences that will help players learn. Mastering the design of learning experiences is probably the most important and difficult challenge of any artist and educator, since the understanding of the concept of the learning experience encapsulates most of the aspects of pedagogy and game design.

If we try to remember which activities captivated our attention and actually helped us to learn, we will see that in most of them we were engaged in participating, investigating, experimenting, solving problems, being curious, taking responsibility, and being creative. We can easily see why games fit this description and why they are an interesting tool for the creation of intrinsically motivating learning experiences. By designing games, designers intend to create experiences that bring out certain emotions, images, and textures, and help their audience travel to or reconstruct in their minds a particular moment, place, or time. In order to achieve this, designers need to provide the right amount of stimulation that will captivate the attention of the audience, guide them through the experience and, at the same time, avoid confusing, tiring, or distracting them from the message they want to convey. So, an interesting question is raised: How detailed must an experience be so that it has an impact on players?

Let's take, for example, a video game that wants to inform players about the topic of sustainable development for the oceans, seas, and marine resources. The game features explorers on a ship, living adventures around new aquatic ecosystems. The role of the designer of the game is to use the necessary means: aesthetics, technology, game mechanics, and narrative elements to make players feel the excitement of travelling the seas while also being informed about sustainable development. From one side, the designers have the option to present life onboard as accurately as possible, presenting all the procedures required to navigate a ship as well as getting ready to dive into the water (putting on equipment, testing functionality, etc.). On the other side, they can present only the elements that are absolutely necessary to make players experience particular emotions, presenting specific elements of the environment and story.

In the first case, however accurate the game is, the designers risk overloading the experience with information that the player will not be able to process, risking a shift of focus from the actual objective: Informing players about sustainable development of aquatic ecosystems. Similar examples can be presented in all forms of art. Film directors are not going to present us with the full 15-minute walk of a character from one location to another. Instead they present only those scenes that are necessary to capture a moment that gives us an experience. In other words, designers of experiences try to capture the essence of what they want to present and give it to us through their medium—in our case, games.

Throughought this journey, our aim is to elaborate on the creation of intrinsically learning experiences through the use of games. By examining the elements of play and games individually and globally and their relation to learning, we will see the best practices and approaches that work and ones that don't work; and we will examine case studies and get insights from leading figures of educational game design that will help you to critically view your ideas, evaluate them, make them concrete and, finally, bring them to life.

THE DIGITAL AND PHYSICAL EXPERIENCE

A healthy mind in a healthy body.

–Juvenal

While designing classrooms in the French countryside some years ago, I fell into a case where we had to propose two different designs for two classrooms of the same grade, because their respective teachers were either very pro or very anti the use of digital or physical teaching objects. One teacher was a technology fanatic and wanted to incorporate several new tools, such as interactive whiteboards, tablets, interactive tables, and motion sensor devices, while the other one wanted to base his entire teaching methodology on physical objects, like building blocks and board games. Since this was a very interesting case, where we designed two entirely different classrooms for students of the same age in the same school, we would frequently visit the school and interview the students to see what their impression was. What we saw was that students of the high-tech classroom strongly desired to be involved in the activities of the traditional classroom and vice-versa.

There is no perfect way to create a learning environment, just like there is not a bigger preference between digital and physical objects. The use of technology in a classroom is definitely an interesting asset but does not replace the need for interacting with physical objects. We live in a material world, where every day we need to interact with physical objects. Developing skills to do so is part of our nature and thus we need to participate in games like chase or hide-and-seek that are connected to our gross motor skills, attention, and agility; we also need to participate in games like **Monopoly**, **Scrabble**, or **Jenga**, which require the use of fine motor skills, calculations, and mental representations. At the same time, digital games present us with a new way to represent and interact with the world, delivering new features and capabilities that were not possible before. Players are able to perform in-depth inquiries using the Internet, enter distant or ancient worlds by using virtual reality goggles, or enrich their perspective using augmented reality.

As we already saw, the success behind learning experiences lies in the interaction with learners, their ability to make decisions and see their outcomes, and the impact it has on our minds at a specific moment. Something that game designers should always remember is that we should not restrict the impact of our experiences by using only specific tools. Except in a case where we wish to achieve a specific learning or aesthetic result, our experiences should be characterized by diversity in the resources we use to create them. A good balance between digital and physical could possibly ensure a more global perspective in our experiences.

The success of learning experiences is not based on whether our means are digital or physical. It is a grave mistake of game designers to count only on the appeal of their medium. There are several video games that do not attract the interest of players, are boring and, most importantly, don't help them to learn. It is exactly the same for physical games. Experienced educational game designers do not rely on the attractiveness of their materials but use and combine elements in order to achieve optimum learning environments. On top of this, physical and digital can perfectly coexist in learning situations and deliver amazing learning experiences. With the development of digital means, their integration into daily lives becomes seamless, helping new mediums to arise, like those of augmented and virtual reality.

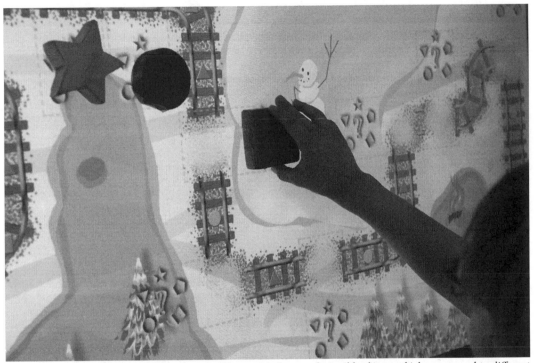

ChooChoo Maths is played on an interactive tabletop with the use of tangible objects, which correspond to different geometrical shapes. The game was designed to introduce players to identifying and comparing geometric shapes and is an example of how digital and physical worlds are blended in order to provide particular learning experiences. (Used with permission of Maskott.)

If we try to identify games that have endured the test of time, we can see that they have some similar attributes. Of course, games like **Go**, **Scrabble**, and **The Settlers of Catan** have different rules and are based on different materials from outdoor games like hide-and-seek, tag, or video games like **The Legend of Zelda** or **Angry Birds**, but all of those games still succeed in awakening particular feelings. While playing we feel excited, afraid, happy, sad, or inspired. All those emotions that are there when we play games that we enjoy are not limited to whether a game is physical or digital. That's why this book does not focus only on video game design but on the design of learning experiences through any form of game. Games are about principles, about understanding these core attributes of play that help educational learning designers convey their message to their audience.

REFLECTION POINTS 🔍

Try to find experiences that are memorable to you and understand what made them special. Try to see what emotions were present during these experiences. Try to identify experiences that made you feel:

- Motivated
- Excited
- Inspired
- Happy
- Angry
- Sad
- Indifferent

- Evaluate the impact of those experiences on learning and non-learning contexts so that you can later have a reference when designing your game.

- Have you felt immersed in learning experiences? What were those situations and how did they lead you to a flow state?

- What types of experiences do you want to offer to your players?

- Do you want to go for a physical or digital experience?

THE EXPERIENCE GOGGLES

There are no facts, only interpretations.

–Friedrich Nietzsche

Experiences are not felt, perceived, or reflected upon the same way by all people. The sentiment of living an experience and the reflection toward it depends on various factors that, combined together, create the complex and brilliant mindset of our audience. For instance, several studios that publish games featuring dragons in Western countries change the representation of those dragons when they publish the same games in Asia. This is mainly because of the representation of dragons in different locations: In Western countries dragons are usually dinosaur-like creatures with a big body and a smaller head, while in an Asian context they tend to have a larger serpent-like body. Elements like this affect the experiences we design, which are also based on players' expectations and cultural preferences.

In the 1970s, IBM wanted to understand why their production plans in different countries performed differently. IBM was an international corporation with thousands of employees all over the world. They had set up the same procedures globally and employees of various countries had the same level of training. For this reason, they asked for the help of social psychologist Geert Hofstede.

Hofstede, after the analysis of a large sample of employees from different areas, concluded that the diversity between various regions was based on the culture of the local country [7]. So, how do we define culture?

Defining culture is not easy, mainly because it engulfs almost every aspect of our lives. It is like software that defines the basic assumptions, values, and norms that people hold. But is culture a human attribute set in stone? And which elements define culture?

As with human life and mentality, culture is an ongoing process. It is not static and it is flexible enough to absorb new elements that will help it to evolve. Of course culture also works the other way, by filtering out incoming elements. This phenomenon is called **uncertainty avoidance** and is related to how a society reacts to situations that bring something new, and thus makes it uncertain. In some cases, introducing a totally new concept or phenomenon is met with enthusiasm while other times it is met with skepticism. In 2013 Google introduced **Google Glass**, a revolutionary augmented reality head mount device. Google Glass was an interesting tool that would evolve the way people used mobile technologies and be a new medium for which to design games. But the way the technology was presented and the consumer culture of the time lead to the technology's failure to become established in the market.

In trying to identify the elements of cultures we come across many questions. Is culture about language? Is it about games? Is it about the way we dress, or behave in social situations, the books we read or the movies we see? Probably it's all of them plus many other elements. In fact, culture is like an iceberg: Only a small portion is visible, and that piece is supported by a much larger piece under the water that stays invisible. This invisible part is the foundation and corresponds to norms, values, and basic assumptions about the world. The visible part can be more easily perceived and is an expression of the foundational part of culture.

To design games that will eventually have an impact on other people's lives, you need to have a perception and idea about their culture. Even if this sounds fundamental, many times we forget that even in our local areas, there are people with different habits and customs, people who come from different backgrounds. In order to design gaming activities that include them as well, we need to perform research and understand and respect their preferences.

We can describe someone's culture by using a metaphor where everyone is wearing fantastic colorful goggles. Players always examine an experience through their own goggles.

Let's imagine two neighboring cities: Redville and Greentopia. Citizens of Redville wear red goggles and thus see the world reddish, while residents of Greentopia wear green goggles and see the world greenish. By visiting Greentopia, citizens of Redville fail to see the world as greenish as the Greentopians do. And by buying green goggles, it is possible that they will see the world in a brown color instead of green, since they always wear their red goggles.

It is good to always have culture in the back of our minds and reflect on our decisions in order to ensure inclusive experiences. This will make your games more accessible and interesting to larger audiences, creating a bigger impact on your audience. Since culture is an integral part of the notion of play, it will be an element that we will encounter various times throughout the book.

PERSPECTIVE: INSPIRING DISCUSSIONS ABOUT WORKPLACE DIVERSITY THROUGH GAMES

Jesse Himmelstein

Game Lab Director
Centre de Recherches Interdisciplinaires (CRI)

Encouraging players to reflect is a central goal of a game for learning or social impact. In the IncLudo project, we are creating games to promote diversity in the workplace. The project setup is a bit peculiar—our team is based in Paris, but our games are made for an Indian audience. We work with a nonprofit in Delhi called ZMQ, who have reached out to organizations willing to experiment with our games, as well as bringing their experience in designing for those environments.

The project is structured around running workshops with organizations such as companies, nonprofits, and government teams. At the workshops, the participants play our games and then discuss issues around diversity that are specific to their organization. It is therefore key that the games inspire discussion and reflection, or else they only distract from the subject rather than supporting it.

Diversity is a complex and delicate issue, and people are hesitant to talk about it openly, for fear of ridicule or conflict. Perhaps for this reason, few games exist that address diversity directly. In the face of this challenge, we decided to experiment widely, and test a number of different concepts and forms. We dedicated about a third of the project, one year, to this prototyping process. We made 13 different prototypes, including single and multiplayer games, card games, debate games, board games, interactive stories, platformers, flying games, caption contests, trivia games, and social network analysis.

Through playtesting in Indian organizations, we whittled our set of prototypes down to those that worked the best with our target audience and environments. We found that the designs that were the most successful were those that encouraged players to consider different points of view, and evaluate the point of view of other players.

Let's take three of these designs as examples, for **Another Day**, **Pirate Partage**, and **Parley**:

Another Day is a piece of interactive fiction that has grown into a visual novel. The player takes on the role of a human resources manager near the top of an Indian company. In the absence of company leadership, the player must negotiate workplace conflicts around diversity. In the first chapter, older men are upset by the "revealing" clothes that a younger woman is wearing, and want to forbid them. In the second, a religious conflict erupts when one Muslim employee tires of praying in the bathroom and wants a dedicated space in the office for religious practice. Those in the Hindu majority oppose this idea, arguing that they don't have a special space of their own. The remaining two chapters address discrimination against women and homosexuals.

As **Another Day** is a single-player experience, we had to make special arrangements to accommodate a workshop discussion format. We decided to keep the format short (under 15 minutes of play time per chapter) so the participants can play a chapter within the workshop and discuss it immediately afterwards. We also designed role-playing activities for each chapter, in which participants take the role of the characters and must try to convince the other characters. Because the roles are assigned randomly, a participant is likely to get a role that they might not entirely agree with, and yet must assume that point of view in order to play well.

Pirate Partage is a very different sort of game. It's a rambunctious and loud cooperative game for four players about pirates. Each player assumes the role of a pirate that has a different "handicap." One can't see, another can't hear, another can't talk, and the last can't use their fingers, only chopsticks. The players must work together to move treasure from one chest to another. A tablet in the middle of the table counts down the remaining time, but also announces periodic attacks of the royal fleet that they must fend off together. A defining feature of the game is our use of wooden cards, made with a laser-cutting machine, that allow the "blind" pirate to play by feeling the cards with their hands.

Playtesting revealed that new players have a very hard time at first, as they are confronted with seemingly impossible communication barriers—how does a "blind" player communicate with a "deaf" one? And yet they become proficient quite quickly as they develop strategies to communicate between themselves and to succeed as a team. We have designed workshops in which participants are separated into teams early on, and can watch other teams play in order to adopt the best strategies used by others. Later, we show videos of how real people with physical disabilities can not only navigate a "normal" day-to-day life, but even do incredible feats in athletics, music, and art. After having taken on a handicap for even a short period, participants are much more appreciative of what such individuals are capable of.

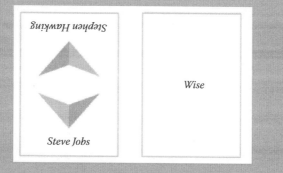

Parley is a debate game, with rotating teams. At the start of each round, one player is the moderator, and the players to the moderator's left will debate against the players to the moderator's right. The debate topic is decided upon by two random cards, one that pits two people or fictional characters against each other, such as "Superman vs. Wonder Woman" or "Steve Jobs vs. Stephen Hawking," and another that provides an adjective, such as "wise" or "strong." Each team is assigned to defend one of the two characters. For example, one team must make the case that Steve Jobs is wiser than Stephen Hawking, and other must argue that it is Stephen Hawking who is the wiser. In the spirit of classical debate rules, the teams have a few minutes to discuss among themselves, and then each will have to present their arguments and rebuttals in just a few minutes before the discussion naturally opens up into a less formal exchange. Finally, the moderator will decide which team made a better case, and award them points.

Because the players don't get a choice of which side to defend, the game forces them to adopt a certain point of view, at least temporarily, in order to make a strong case and find flaws in the argument that they would normally support. Making verbal arguments in this way sharpens our reasoning and stretches our knowledge. In fact, some scholars believe that humans evolved an ability to reason primarily to create and evaluate arguments and persuade others, rather than to make better decisions [1].

In this game, more than with the previous two examples, we chose to adopt a "stealthy" approach to our choice of debate subjects. The Tiltfactor lab at Dartmouth College has demonstrated that insisting too much on the social message of a game not only tends to make players less likely to want to play it, but it is also **less** effective at shifting player's attitudes and perceptions [2]. Following their suggestions, we balance the number of subjects that are clearly about diversity with those that are about other subjects. We also use fictional characters as subjects for debate, which allows players to make strong arguments without offending each other as easily.

These three game designs are different from each other in form and technique, but all three attempt to provoke thought and discussion on the subject of diversity in the workplace, which is otherwise challenging and sensitive to talk about. The designs work by making players adopt and exercise a different point of view, through making difficult choices, assuming handicaps, or arguing a side of debate that is not their own.

We believe that games can be used to great effect in provoking social change, if we are willing to bring them into unexpected environments such as schools and workplaces, and experiment to find what designs excel in these new places.

All our games for IncLudo are open source. To play the games or learn more about our project, visit our website.

Contact details:

@himmelattack

https://cri-paris.org/gamelab

REFERENCES

1. Mercier, H., & Sperber, D. (2011). Why do humans reason? Arguments for an argumentative theory. *The Behavioral and Brain Sciences*, *34*(2), 57–74. https://doi.org/10.1017/S0140525X10000968.
2. Kaufman, G., Flanagan, M., & Seidman, M. (2016). Creating stealth game interventions for attitude and behavior change. *Transactions of the Digital Games Research Association*, *2*(3), 173–193.

SUMMARY

So, what topics did we cover in this chapter?

- Learning is an ongoing process of acquiring existing knowledge that leads to internal change. Learning is continuous and involves every aspect of someone's life.

- Any situation can be an opportunity for learning. Learning happens outside school as well.

- One way to identify learning categories is by categorizing it in formal, informal, and non-formal contexts. Games can be used or designed in any of these contexts, but their use and nature will be different, depending on the nature of context.

- People learn because they want to fulfill their needs. By identifying those needs and appealing to them, we can create games that have individual value for our players, thus motivating them to participate.

- Motivation can be intrinsic or extrinsic. Intrinsic motivation is related to inherent interest in a task while extrinsic motivation is related to external rewards. Understanding how you want to motivate your learners, will help you to shape your game concept later.

- Knowledge can take different forms. It can be related to our cognitive, affective, and psychomotor activities. The way we acquire and process knowledge affects the development of our skills and values.

- When designing games, we are actually experience designers. Intrinsically motivating experiences that captivate our audience's attention is our ultimate goal.

- Experience is about continuity and interaction. Continuity is related to understanding your audience's background and building experiences around it and interaction is related to the impact of players on your game and vice-versa.

- Creating experiences through games is not about digital or physical materials. It is about understanding principles and identifying the core attributes of play.

- Culture is a very important element of games. Games are a part of culture and culture is a part of games. Not everyone lives an experience the same way and this is an important point to keep in mind when designing your games.

REFERENCES

1. Maslow, A. H. (1943). A theory of human motivation. *Psychological Review, 50*(4), 370–396.
2. Bloom, B. S. (Eds.) (1956). *Taxonomy of Educational Objectives. The Classification of Educational Goals, Handbook I: Cognitive domain.* New York: Longman.
3. United Nations. (n.d.). Sustainable development. Retrieved from http://www.un.org/sustainabledevelopment/.
4. Dewey, J. (1994). Art as experience. In S. D. Ross (Eds.), *Art and Its Significance: An Anthology of Aesthetic Theory* (3rd ed) (pp. 205–223). Albany, NY: State University of New York Press.
5. Csikszentmihalyi, M., Abuhamdeh, S., & Nakamura, J. (2014). Flow. In M. Csikszentmihalyi (Eds.), *Flow and the Foundations of Positive Psychology* (pp. 227–238). London: Springer.
6. Huizinga, J. (1955). *Homo Ludens: A Study of the Play Element in Culture* (R. Hull, Trans.). Boston, MA: The Beacon Press.
7. Hofstede, G. (1984). *Culture's Consequences: International Differences in Work-Related Values.* Berkeley Hills, California: Sage Publishing Inc.

2 The Magical Powers of the Game Designer

This chapter covers the following:

- Exploring the different roles involved in game design.
- Understanding the roles and challenges of game designers.
- Elaborating on the qualities and skills of educational game designers.
- Exploring the notions of play and games.

It's very important to properly understand what you need to design before designing it! In this chapter, we are going to explore the different roles involved in the game design process. On top of this, we are going to examine the roles, responsibilities, and challenges of educational game designers and shed more light on the notions of play and games in learning contexts.

How would you respond if somebody proposed a game where an elephant is dropped from the sky with a parachute?

While designing a game for a local NGO, I was brainstorming with a team of young college volunteers about the game they wanted to create. During this session, several ideas came up, each one more interesting than the last. One young woman then came up with an idea that eventually made the biggest impression on my mind. She proposed that an elephant, wearing a parachute, would be thrown from a helicopter as part of the game. At the beginning, it seemed odd and impractical. But was it?

This idea of a parachuting elephant as a game element still affects me as a game designer and educator. The reason is that it represents two sides of the same coin: imagination and reality. Game designers are bestowed with the task of constantly creating novel, intuitive, and meaningful experiences. For this reason, they are always trying to locate the boundaries between the possible and the impossible and push them. They challenge our way of thinking and help us to grow. In this aspect, games are only as limited as their designers' imagination.

On the other hand, game designers are analytical, practical, and pragmatic. They make sure that their ideas become reality and their concepts will eventually become playable games and will lead to learning experiences. In this aspect, game designers need to understand what they can and cannot achieve with the resources they possess and strive for the optimum result possible. They are both the heart and brain of the design process.

Game designers strive for balance. Balance between the possible and the impossible, reality and imagination, the objective and the subjective, the fantasy and the feasible.

I don't know if I will ever play a game with a live parachuting elephant. However, every new game that we aspire to create presents its own challenges, both big and small. So, this chapter is dedicated to the magical powers of those who want to make the impossible possible and the logical fantastical.

AN INTRODUCTION TO GAME DESIGN

Let's get one thing straight. **Playing and making games is awesome!**

Yet it's also important to realize that it's not an easy task! Based on the same principle that eating cake doesn't make someone a cake chef or watching movies doesn't make someone a film director, there are many aspects that need to be taken into consideration when someone decides to create a game. Whether you want to design an outdoor, board, or video game, there are different elements that designers need to analyze, anticipate, and master in order to create interesting experiences that players enjoy and through which they learn.

A game should captivate players' attention, motivate them toward a specific topic, and interact with them in a way they enjoy. But even before this, the game needs to be implemented by specifying its core mechanics, programming some of its components, drawing or sketching some of its visible parts, and presenting and evaluating its impact on players. In order to achieve this, game designers need to have an understanding of the resources they need, the specialists they need to consult, and the process that is necessary to produce a final game.

In order to succeed in creating games, an understanding of the requirements, needs, and your current resources is crucial. A very common mistake made by novice designers is underestimating the process of game designing. Asking for things that are difficult or impossible to implement, or things that require a lot of programming time, can result in conflict, friction, the slowing down of the whole game design pipeline, and may, ultimately, lead to a bad game or no game at all.

On the other hand, some designers tend to overestimate the design process, being skeptical of proposing new elements or moving away from their own previous creations. It is with experience and constant playtesting that game designers can understand and assess situations related to the design and implementation of a game and make the necessary decisions that will lead to amazing games.

This multidisciplinary nature of games requires the cooperation of different people and a broad perspective and understanding of various game aspects. Depending on the type and style of game, game design teams can consist of few people, like the ones of **Braid** and **Limbo** or can include hundreds, like the ones for **Grand Theft Auto** or **Call of Duty**. The roles of people involved in games are many. Some of the most important ones are presented below:

Programmer: The programmer is the person who is responsible for the implementation of a video game in terms of programming. The role of the programmer is to talk with all members of the team and have a concrete vision of the game. Programmers are the ones who will propose the platforms and tools through which a game will be implemented and will maintain the game's functionality as soon as it gets released.

Artist: The artists are responsible for the aesthetic appeal and style of a game. Whether the game is a 3D shoot 'em up game or a board game or the history of a museum, the involvement of artists is crucial to represent the elements of the game through a pleasing aesthetic. Their role is to propose a look and feel that will make a game unique and will highlight its mechanics and learning objectives. Depending on the size of the project, there can be one or lots of artists involved in a game project. Some roles, like the ones of the lead and concept artist, offer the general vision of the game and their designs represent elements from the world of the game and its characters and objects that will not necessarily be integrated into the final game graphics. Other artist roles, like those of 2D, 3D, and technical artists, are related to the implementation of graphics that will be used inside the game.

Producer: The producer is the person who oversees the whole production of a game. This role includes involvement in almost every aspect of game creation, from creative choices to development and marketing. Producers are the people who usually form a game team, manage its workload, and represent it in internal and external studio affairs, like talking to management or promoting a game. This role is especially important in big studios, where the number of people involved in the process can be quite large.

Music and Sound Effects Specialist: These two roles are related to the sound or music of a game. Since ancient times, people have understood the importance of music for the creation of specific atmospheres. Ancient Greeks would use drums during wars to increase the morale of soldiers and bring rhythm to coordinated attacks on enemies. In the same way, music in games creates a particular atmosphere, giving life to a specific experience. Sound effects are the small sounds that represent specific events, like that of jumping, clicking buttons, or shooting. The existence of music and sound effects has a particular importance in video games, since they increase and facilitate interaction with players.

Tester: The role of the tester is to play games and find problems. Problems can be of varying natures, like technical implementation, game mechanics, the wrong representation of an incident, spelling, and so on. Testers try to play games in different ways and explore the various cases through which a bug could arise. Depending on the size of a game creation team, testers can be in-house but they can also be friends, relatives, and the wider gaming community.

Game Designer: Is this person responsible for designing the game. Does this mean that they need to program? Do they need to create graphics? Do they need compose music, test the game, and present it? The answer to these questions is: Maybe yes and maybe no! In order to answer the question of what a game designer is and what they do, we need a whole chapter and not just a paragraph!

THE ROLE OF THE GAME DESIGNER

In order to understand the role of the game designer, let's imagine an orchestra. The orchestra consists of various instrument players, like trumpeters, pianists, violinists, and bassists. Each one of them has a specific role: to play their instrument in the best way they can in order to produce a particular piece of music with a specific style. Each instrument player has explicit instructions on the melody and time to enter the symphony, specified by the music sheet, created by the composer. On top of this, a specific performance can be executed in various ways, which differ in style, tempo, force, or choice of instruments. The force that binds all these elements together, giving a particular perspective to this musical work of art, is the maestro.

Similar to the orchestra example, game designers are both composers and maestros. They are the people who devise the idea of a game, explain how the game is played, and are present throughout the whole creation process in order to make sure that the game they proposed is implemented in a way that presents the experience they wanted. Game designers are the people who take an idea and transform it into a game. The work of a game designer starts at the very beginning of the game design process and ends at the very end, when the game has been published, and often the role continues even after this phase. During this amazing journey, the game designer reflects on specific ideas, proposes ways the game could be played, tests these proposals, and explains to everyone else how the game will be played.

In order for a game designer to be able to design a game, a good understanding of the team's resources is necessary. Like a maestro who knows the individual sound and capabilities of each instrument in an orchestra, game designers need to know the attributes, capabilities, and restrictions of their medium. Game designers who have a good grip of these elements can use them in amazing ways to create intrinsically motivating experiences. On the other hand, a fuzzy understanding of these elements will inevitably lead to games with defects that do not serve their purpose.

The decision to create a card game, for example, for a group of fifteen players could pose restrictions on the way those players are going to communicate. Additionally, in a case like this, the waiting time for each player would be quite long, meaning that players might get bored. In another case, deciding to create a 3D shooter with amazing graphics could cause performance issues if the game designer initially envisioned the game to be played on mobile devices, and more importantly, the character control would be very difficult, since there is usually no other input device apart from the touch screen. By knowing their resources and understanding how they work, game designers know what ingredients they have at their disposal to cook up a great game.

But what skills and knowledge are needed for someone to be a game designer?

The answer to this question is, a little bit of everything! As the heart and soul of the game, you need to take into consideration various aspects in order to bring your ideas to life. In some cases, knowledge and experience that might initially seem irrelevant could be helpful sources of inspiration, for understanding a subject better, or organizing one's thoughts. Since games have a multidisciplinary nature where various artistic skills and perspectives are met, you will need to be able to understand some technical jargon or individual points of view and evaluate them through your own perspective. These are just some of the areas involved in the art of game design:

- Anthropology

- Psychology

- Aesthetics

- Music

- Storytelling

- Technology

- Management

- Testing

Are all those different fields really necessary for a game designer? The truth is that they are. The more that game designers create, the clearer it becomes that every little aspect matters and that everything they know offers them a clearer and broader perspective on what they can accomplish and how. Throughout the book, we will try to address several of those aspects and examine how they can be used as tools for the creation of intrinsically motivating learning experiences.

THE EDUCATIONAL GAME DESIGNER

If designing games requires the understanding of different and various fields, educational game design is game design on steroids! In educational game design, designers are asked to design games that are both intrinsically motivating and have learning impact. Educational game designers need to identify learning objectives, research training methodologies, have an understanding of how people learn and, on top of this, possess the game design fundamentals to propose games that are fun to play while also having a particular learning impact on players.

Taking into consideration the number of aspects a game designer must anticipate in order to design a normal game, designing an educational game presents a new set of challenges. Designing educational games requires the combination of learning and game design. Even if this combination sounds easy or relatively easy, the mixture of these two ingredients is a matter of great debate, as we will thoroughly examine in Chapter 4. A bad combination of these two elements can lead to a simple game with no learning value, a learning activity with no intrinsically motivating value, or may frustrate and confuse players while not helping them to evolve. As we will see later on, there is not a single recipe for successful educational games. Good games are the result of experience, continuous effort, dedication, and creativity.

Designing games is like exercising a muscle. Muscles are complex structures that help our body complete particular tasks. Muscles can have different flexibility and size depending on the task we need them for. But the more we use one muscle, the more it grows and, thus, the more efficient it becomes. In the same way, by exercising and applying your game design skills, you will design more interesting games. Even though there is no magic way to create intrinsically motivating learning experiences, there are **several skills** and principles that are rather handy when entering the world of educational game design. Let's study some of them!

Skill #1: Listen and Observe

The first and greatest virtue of educational game designers is the ability to listen to and observe their environments. Any artist, teacher, or designer who doesn't possess these two abilities are prone to creating games that do not touch the hearts or minds of their players. If you want players to like your games, your games need to target subjects and themes that they find interesting and to which they can relate. Understanding what is important for your players, what they like, what they don't like, what they miss or wish for, which elements to pay greater emphasis to, and which topics are sensitive are among the primary priorities of educational game designers. We will examine this aspect thoroughly in Chapter 9, when we will examine a game's audience.

If listening and observing are important in game design, in educational game design it is twice as important. Educational games intend to entertain and help players learn. If your games are detached from reality, presenting worlds and situations that players cannot relate to or empathize with, it is likely that the learning impact of your games will not be what you expect. You cannot be unfamiliar with your audience and you cannot be ignorant of the environment surrounding it if you want to have an impact on them.

Since games and education are both addressing the needs of the human mind, they are part of a society's culture, and thus they are affected by it. As we have already examined, culture encapsulates an immense part of our daily life and consists of elements we see and that we don't see. A good game designer listens and observes everything at every point. Every event, incident, or routine of human life captures an essence of an experience. It is on these details that good games stand out. In the film **Pulp Fiction**, there is a famous scene where the characters of John Travolta and Samuel Jackson talk about how people in different countries call the same burger different things: a quarter pounder with cheese in the United States is a royale with cheese in France. Simple though this scene may be, it is memorable. In the video game **Splatoon**, the visual style incorporates elements of industrial design which add a particular tone and style to the game, which makes it original. Uniform attempts to describe situations or concepts you don't have a good understanding of will be easily identified by users, and even if they won't be able to point them out, they will have a feeling that something in your game is not natural.

Skill #2: Games Are Not the Solution to Everything

Even if the use of play and games in learning contexts is a very powerful tool, it is not the solution to everything. As a learning tool, like all others, games can have amazing effects in specific situations and zero effect, or not the expected one, in others. A skilled educational game designer needs to always have in mind that playing games does not differ from practicing theatre, playing music, doing exercise, or facilitating a discussion. In fact, this statement has two sides: from one side, games present a diverse set of capabilities to teachers as a tool for learning, and if used correctly, they can increase student engagement and interest toward learning. It is in the hands of educational game designers and educators to address possible skepticism on the use of games, like our predecessors did when introducing revolutionary tools that are now indispensable parts of the school curriculum.

On the other hand, like any learning tool, the use of games in learning contexts needs to add value to the process of learning and not make it harder. When designing educational games, one of the first things you need to consider is whether your learning objectives can be met by doing so. Additionally, reflection on the impact of using games in order to achieve those learning objectives should happen. There are cases where the use of games is an excellent choice and there are others where introducing games could complicate the learning process and have the opposite results. The use of games, for example, as a tool for teaching science can increase the motivation and participation of a classroom, but on the other hand, it could be a difficult and challenging task if teaching advanced calculus in university. Even if there is not always a correct recipe to indicate where it's better to use games and where it's not, you should always keep in mind that the use of games comes with benefits and challenges similar to those of any other learning tool.

Skill #3: Game Designers Communicate and Present Their Ideas

Even if human imagination has no limits, there are times when it becomes restricted by someone's lack of expression and communication skills. You may be able to envision great games that will have enormous impact on your players, but if you want to make them real and well-perceived, you will need to be able to present and explain them to your colleagues, producers, or players.

Communication skills come with experience and practice. The more we practice them, the more skilled we become at their application. These skills consist of both listening and understanding the needs of others, but also being able to structure our thoughts and present them in a way that others will understand. Presenting ideas varies from person to person and is relevant to someone's character, style, and objectives. There are designers who prefer talking about their ideas, there are others who prefer to write them down and present them in a structured presentation, and there are still others who just make doodles and elaborate on them while presenting them to their peers. Any form of expression is suitable as long as it serves its purpose: explaining to others what you have in your mind and giving them a taste of the experience that you want to create. In order to see what works better for you, you need to try different ways of presenting your ideas.

It is important to keep in mind that presenting our ideas in the same way to everyone won't always have the same effect. There are people who prefer to listen, people who prefer to read, people who want to know many details before shaping an idea, and people who jump right to the point. It is part of the work of game designers to be able to adapt to different situations and present their ideas, pitches, and games to different audiences.

In this aspect, game designers may eventually come to use performing skills in order to present a concept to their audience. Especially in educational contexts, where experts of different fields meet in order to create a game, attracting the attention of one's peers and being able to explain someone's ideas in a simple but concrete way is crucial to the project's success.

When entering a game design process, you need to keep in mind that not everyone has the same background or the same experiences as you and does not use the same terminology. It is very possible that some members of the team do not even play games. Vague explanations, not presented well, lead to frustration and possible conflict, delaying the development of a game and affecting its quality.

Skill #4: Game Designers Are Constantly Learning

I know that I know nothing.

—Socrates

The ancient Greek philosopher Heraclitus used the phrase **ta panta rhei**, which means "everything flows." Nothing remains the same in the universe. Everything changes and evolves. So does our perception of the world and our understanding of learning and education. Educational game design and its expressions cannot escape from this constant evolution. Whether change derives from internal, personal, or psychological factors, or from changes in the environment, your games need to be able to adapt to the needs of your players. Educational game design, being a complex and demanding art, presents game designers with an opportunity for personal development, through which they can examine their surroundings and interact with them through play.

Successful game designers see any incident during the game design process or any comment they receive as an opportunity for development. They listen to what their peers have to say and then assess that feedback in a way that helps them overcome new obstacles. Experience is built on successful moments but is mainly based on failures and reflection on how to avoid them or work through them in the future. Research on the presented learning topic, the game's context and one's audience always helps. It is also certain that nobody can be prepared for everything that will happen along the way, so being flexible and keeping an open mind comes in very handy.

Being connected with human nature, game creation can be expressed both through individual and collaborative work. But since very few people are highly skilled in all aspects of game design, the art of educational game design becomes more interesting, and more feasible, through cooperation. Another great virtue of educational game designers is the ability to identify their own weaknesses or lack of expertise on a particular topic and seek the help of another expert. By forming teams like this, you will be able to focus on the areas where you are most skilled and avoid distractions, while maintaining a higher overall quality for your games.

Skill #5: Educational Game Designers Have an Impact on Their Society

Whether it is direct or indirect, good educational games have an impact on players. In order for game designers to achieve this impact, they need to be in close contact with their players and understand their mentality, needs, and expectations. A common issue appearing in educational game design is that game designers or educational experts, however well they know a topic, can forget to consult their audience about a game they present. Through this, they risk proposing a game experience that does not reflect the needs of their target groups or lacks the atmosphere and approach required to captivate their interest.

Educational game designers are active members of their society. They create games that can change lives by informing and motivating people to adopt particular values and views on life. Games like **Super Mario**, **Minecraft**, and **Angry Birds** have become landmarks in the development of our culture. So, designing games that others will play and decide to spend some time from their lives with comes with great responsibility. Game designers need to be very careful addressing the topics they want to present, respect their audience, and empathize with it. Games with impact are the games that your players will love and play. Whether you or your team like the games you make is not enough if your players do not find them interesting. It is by seeing the game through the eyes of the society you design for that your games will have an impact.

Skill #6: Educational Game Designers Understand the Context around Which Learning Takes Place

It is difficult or impossible to design educational initiatives without understanding the context where learning takes place. Context describes any cultural, historical, technical, logistical, or living aspect related to the space and people that are involved in the game playing process. Context gives meaning to players' actions. The digits 0 and 1 acquire a totally different meaning in the teaching of mathematics in kindergarten than they do as digits of the binary system in university computer science. Historic figures, landmarks, and events can be viewed from very different perspectives depending on the context of different cultures, countries, and civilizations.

The relationship between context and learning is mutual. Context gives meaning to learning and learning gives meaning to context. From one side, learning cannot be defined without context. We already saw that learning acquires meaning only inside specific contexts. However, by learning, players enter a process of change and they develop skills and competences. They challenge their previous beliefs and they evolve. Consequently, they have an impact on themselves, their culture, and their surroundings, therefore giving another meaning to their **learning context**.

Skill #7: Educational Game Designers Have a Perspective on the Learning Game Triangle

Educational games require the designer's attention at many levels. Great debate has emerged from this complex structure and the different aspects of educational games and the questions that educational game designers need to give answers to are countless.

- Would a really engaging game, without any focus on teaching a topic, help people learn?

- Would a structured approach to learning with few gaming elements captivate the interest of players and engage them for hours?

- Would a mobile game, requiring delicate and precise finger movement, be effective for players in early childhood?

- Would games be a more efficient way of teaching calculus to university students?

- How will the members of a classroom or a social group approach and use educational games as learning tools in comparison to other learning tools?

Of course, there is no single correct answer to all those questions. As we already saw, games and learning acquire meaning in specific contexts. So, in some contexts, games might prove to be very efficient and in others, not so much. Possibly there will be some players who would respond positively to some games and others who would not. It is also possible that with the resources players have at their disposal, some games can be efficient learning tools and some not. Game designers who do not take into consideration all those different aspects of educational game design risk creating experiences that do not fulfill their initial objectives.

Educational game design is among the most important and challenging tasks for game designers. Various factors correlate with each other, creating a complex, yet magical, opportunity to facilitate learning. We could try to think of educational game design as a magic triangle, at each corner of which is an important aspect of the design process: Players, Game, and Learning Aspect. This triangle represents the structure and relationships among the basic elements that are needed to create an educational game. Let's inspect them individually:

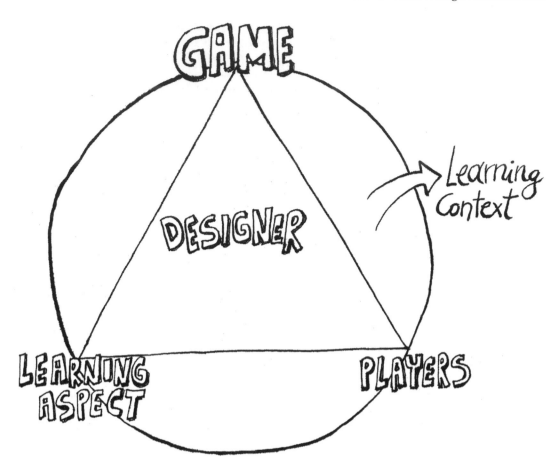

Players: A learning or gaming experience does not exist without someone to live it. Understanding the needs of players both in terms of their preference in games but also in their learning styles is a key point for a successful game design process. Players enter a game world, interact with its elements, and learn through an approach designed through the learning context.

Game: Another side of the triangle consists of the element of a game. Without doubt, we could not imagine a game design approach without games, but the game's influence on the learning experience as a whole can strongly vary depending on the objectives of the educational game designers. Games like **Lego Mindstorms, Scrabble**, or geocaching have very different approaches on the way their gaming aspect can be used to deliver learning content. Apart from this, the form and nature of games is directly related to the needs of players and the learning context, through which games will be used.

Learning aspect: The learning aspect encapsulates the necessary elements that are related to players' learning. This includes educational objectives, methodologies, tools, and approaches toward teaching a topic and assessing feedback. In other words, learning aspect is the educational perspective of a learning experience. Learning aspect affects the nature of games and the experience of players, but it also changes depending on learner profile and gaming style. The interaction and interconnection of learning context with game and players is strong and mutual.

As we saw before, learning acquires meaning in different contexts. Hence, it is difficult or even impossible to define educational games without being able to identify the context around which they are designed for. So, the magic triangle is defined inside specific learning contexts.

Game designers who want to design games that are both educational and fun need to understand that all three elements of the triangle are equally important. Moreover, these three elements do not stand alone and are not separate from each other. Each one of the learning game triangle's elements is affected by any change on the other two elements. If a game rule changes, for example, players are going to have a different gaming experience, while learning context will be affected, since it is possible that this rule was put in place in order to emphasize a specific learning topic, make students reflect on an idea, or fulfill a particular learning objective. The role of an educational game designer in this sense is to bring balance to this triangle in order to create engaging learning games.

In the center of the triangle, as the force that maintains balance in the system, is the educational game designer, the heart and mind of the game design process. Positioning educational game designers in the center of the triangle is not a coincidence. Designers, whether they are teachers, practitioners, or corporate trainers, are central to the nature of the experience since they need to understand their learners, blend learning and gaming elements, design and implement their ideas, present them to their players, and possibly be a part of the games they present to help players reflect on what they have learnt and assess them in order to make them better.

Skill #8: Educational Game Designers Take into Account Learning Scenarios

Creating educational games is a great challenge. But creating games is just a small part of creating intrinsically motivating learning experiences. Apart from creating them, designers need to have in mind that educators will need to introduce them to their learners, implement or facilitate them, help them realize what they have learnt, and assess their use. This process is not linear and shouldn't necessarily be described only by those steps. What is important to remember, however, is that there are situations where your games may be integrated in a broader delivery scheme, called a **learning scenario**.

Learning scenarios are descriptions of learning situations based on each educator's pedagogical approach. Learning scenarios describe learning goals, define different roles of educators and learners, and suggest resources and tools required. Learning scenarios also describe the process of organizing and facilitating learning situations or may even define particular phases that may facilitate and drive the learning process. Learning scenarios may include any type of activities or services, including, of course, games.

So, it's very likely that your games may be part of a much broader scheme, aimed at helping players learn more efficiently. Even if there are several ways to break down learning scenarios, we can, in most cases, identify three phases, which include introduction, activity, and debriefing.

The **introduction phase** aims to introduce the game to players and ensure that they feel comfortable participating in the activity. Are players going to refuse to participate in a game? Let's consider that a university class consists of 100 business administration students who are used to participating in very formal lectures. Let's now imagine that a very energetic speaker is asked to deliver a speech, enters the room, reaches the podium, and asks 20 students to stand up and play a game. Is it certain that all 20 students will want to play? They are going to be exposed to a new, possibly uncomfortable situation, where 80 other students will be watching. So, is it guaranteed that all potential players will be interested in your games? Absolutely not! It is part of your design and planning to make sure that players will be properly introduced and informed about your games and feel comfortable participating in them. During introduction you can also provide players with hints, both about the game and the learning context, in order to make the game's presentation even easier.

During the **activity phase**, players participate in the game. They act and react inside its context. They explore, they invent problem-solving strategies, and they arrive at conclusions about how to advance in the game's context. But is this enough? Does the fact that players managed to advance in a game and come up with a solution to the presented problems guarantee that they learned? The answer is no. It's very possible that learners may not create the connections between the skills or information they acquire while playing and the knowledge of how to use them outside the context of the game. This is why the last phase is very important.

The **debriefing phase** aims at helping players reflect on what they learned while playing. Even if this step may sound trivial, it's definitely not. The nonexistence of debriefing and time for reflection may render the whole gaming process of low educational value, since players may not have the opportunity to realize what they have learned. It's during debriefing that players realize that skills they acquired while playing can be used in other contexts and the knowledge they received may be applied in different ways.

We are going to address each of those phases by examining their components throughout the book. It is important to always consider that your games may be part of a bigger learning process. Some educators may need to adjust some aspects of your games so that they better address their learning objectives and others may need to find a way to integrate them in their learning scenarios.

REFLECTION POINTS 🔍

- This is a great opportunity to consider some aspects of your preparation toward the design of your games. Educational game design can be educational for anyone involved in it. Understanding your environment, objective, and audience is the first step toward designing amazing learning experiences.

- Try to observe your audience and interact with them. Try to identify their needs and desires and use them as a point to reflect your game design concept. Are your ideas going to address those needs?

- One of the greatest questions that educational game designers should constantly consider is whether the use of games or playful activities can support learning and fulfill your learning objectives.

- Try to clarify the elements of your learning game triangle. Who are your players? What is your game? What is your learning context? How do these three elements interact and what do you want to achieve?

EVERYONE CAN WORK ON GAME DESIGN

During a workshop in Italy, I was part of a training team with the objective of preparing social workers to design and create gaming activities, related to immigration and human rights. These social workers would then use these activities as learning tools in educational institutions in their local areas. After five days of workshops and training, the participants were finally confronted by a great challenge: They had one day to design their own games and present them during the following day to more than 100 students who would visit the training venue. In order to complete their task, they were divided into groups of five people and were allowed to use any material they could find. After an intensive day (and night), the new game designers were ready to welcome more than 100 high school students and introduce them to their newly conceived worlds.

When students entered the training venue, they were very surprised. Here were adults who had prepared games for them about two very serious topics. They participated, they talked, and they felt engaged. Teachers were also impressed by the large participation of students in the gaming activities. On top of that, the new game designers were happy seeing students playing their games. This training was a great experience for different people for very different reasons. This is the magic of educational game design! Furthermore, people with no particular background in game design who still wanted to have an impact on their students managed, after being trained, to design and create games that students later actually played. Whether or not the proposed games were engaging, fun, or educational, they were the product of reflection and cooperation of motivated people who just wanted to make a difference. And this is the main ingredient of every game designer.

A game prototype created by a group of preschoolers during a game design workshop.

Creating games is like speaking a language. Everyone can learn how to speak a new language. Some people will reach a high level faster than others, but at the end, everyone who makes an effort is able to communicate with their peers. When people speak, their tone of voice, rhythm, and style change. Everybody's speech is different, it is personal and characteristic to their character and personality. Similarly, in game design, people don't design the same games. This is because game design is someone's form of expression and is strongly attached to someone's experiences, views, and aesthetics.

In his work **Homo Ludens**, Johan Huizinga observed that play is not only a characteristic of human beings. Animals play as well. They play, they are trained, and they increase their skills in several areas of their lives. Play among lions is a way for them to train in combat with other animals or become more agile and efficient while hunting. So, as we have already seen, play is a form of expression of ideas and can be used by nature in order to pass information from peer to peer or from one generation to another. In this sense, by creating games, game designers create their own representation of information and thus express their ideas through a very unique form. Creating games is a very special form of expression that everyone can use.

Just like any form of art, educational game design addresses an important topic for educational game designers or the societies they live in. Being a part of a society, educational game designers have the opportunity to talk about subjects they prefer and express their views and opinions about a topic they care about.

THE CHALLENGES OF EDUCATIONAL GAME DESIGN

Even if anyone can become an educational game designer, it doesn't mean that this is an easy task. Much like painting, acting, and composing, educational game design requires dedication and continuous effort in order to create games that will captivate players' attention and help them to learn. A very common mistake from people who want to be involved in game design is underestimating the importance and challenge of this art. Everyone has the freedom to do so, at their own peril! Here are the most important aspects that anyone who wants to become an educational game designer needs to keep in mind.

Challenge #1: Respect existing norms.

Like any form of art, games are connected with the sociocultural aspects of their times. Players have already played other games, they have seen other movies, and have already formed a particular taste for what they like or dislike. This means that it is highly likely that your audience already has specific expectations and needs from the games they want to play. This doesn't mean, of course, that you need to create replicas of games your players already like. On the contrary, players always long for new experiences, original gameplay that will surprise and amaze them. But you need to know what works and what doesn't, what players tend to enjoy and what they find boring, what is immersive and what is frustrating. That is why norms exist.

Norms are the set of attributes and relations among the game elements that tend to offer a particular result. Norms that result in interesting games endure the test of time and thus are there for you to identify and take into account when creating your games. Successful games usually consist of such norms while games that frustrate players usually do not respect them or overuse them. **Mario Kart**, for example is a family game, with a great focus on family audiences and multiplayer gameplay. The game focuses a lot on the experience of interactions among players inside the game and offers simple and easy-to-use gameplay. It offers a less-tense atmosphere, as players can play the game with company. The game designers of Mario Kart chose this direction for their game as they identified that specific patterns, elements, and game relations have better results for specific genres.

Anxious, inexperienced writers obey rules. Rebellious, unschooled writers break rules. Artists master the form.

–Robert McKee

If the use of norms would always lead to games with a great impact, games would be designed by computer algorithms! Norms exist in order to offer a perspective and help you guide yourself through the game design process. In his influential book **Story**, Robert McKee discusses the use of norms for script writers, which I also find very relevant for the work of educational game designers. McKee observes that unique pieces of art, in his case movies, are characterized by both a respect for universal norms but also the freedom of the creator to defy and modify them when necessary. So, successful games are the result of striving for balance between following and defying those norms, understanding what your players want and what they don't know they want yet, what they need to learn and how to achieve this.

Challenge #2: Pay attention to your learning objectives.

A common mistake of educational game designers is that they tend to overemphasize the impact of gaming elements in their experiences. Games can be powerful tools for learning when designed with attention and dedication but can also prove to be rather ineffective if their learning aspect is not properly and adequately presented. Educational games do not just intend to amuse or entertain but also to help people grow and develop their knowledge and skills. Games that are only slanted toward entertainment, without giving proper emphasis to players' learning, fail to help them learn.

In this aspect, learning objectives should not be just an additional element of your games but a core element of their gameplay.

In order to properly adopt a particular pedagogic approach or achieve your learning objectives, you need to thoroughly research your topic. If you are an expert on your topic, you can always look for novel new approaches to teaching your subject, and if you lack knowledge of a field, you can seek the help of an expert. In any case, consulting your peers is always a good idea, as this will help you diversify your thoughts and examine the topic you want to address from different perspectives.

Challenge #3: Respect the art of game design.

In contrast to the previous point, another mistake of inexperienced educational game designers is understating the gaming elements in a learning experience in favor of educational objectives. In this case, game designers tend to focus on educational objectives, leading them to become anxious about achieving them, sacrifice gaming elements, or to not pay great attention to them. This leads to learning activities with an obvious learning outcome where gaming elements are clumsily integrated and could very easily be removed without any impact on the activity.

If you don't want your efforts to go to waste, you will need to respect the art of game design and the capabilities of this medium. In order for you to create games that are fun to play and have impact and meaning, you need to understand both the nature of play and conquer the meaning you want to teach. If you don't respect the art, you risk creating activities that only you will consider to be games.

Challenge #4: Games are magical and complex structures.

Even if games create a magical atmosphere where time flies quickly, creating them is not as easy as playing them. In fact, behind each game element lies the labor of one or several people who have probably spent hours studying and thinking about how to achieve just that feat. Complexity and sophistication in both design and implementation varies from game to game. But underestimating the complexity and great effort that is required for the creation of games will undoubtedly lead to situations that you haven't anticipated and will cause frustration to you and your team.

Creating the simplest video game, for any device, requires the existence of at least one person who will program it, someone who will work with the visual aspects, and someone who will be responsible for the music and sound effects. This team can grow up to several hundreds, depending on what you want to achieve. Good game designers have a good perspective of every part of the game creation process in order to understand the capabilities and limitations of their medium and anticipate problems that will arise from the complex but amazing process of creating games.

Understanding that any feature and attribute of a game requires the work of a particular specialist is among the first tasks of an educational game designer. If you want your characters to perform an animation while moving you will need an artist with animation skills who will be responsible for animating each and every different character in the game. If you want your game to have high-quality graphics, you need to check the capabilities of the devices that will run your game and optimize the game's performance with your developer team. Changes in some rules or functionalities of your game might be impossible after development has started if you have not anticipated several elements due to the cost that would be necessary to reprogram your game engine or time restrictions. These are just some of the countless examples of underestimating or not taking into consideration the complexity of creating games.

If, while designing a game, you consider that a feature, a rule, or an attribute is easy to implement, think twice! That feeling might not be the result of confidence but may have more to do with a lack of perspective on a particular aspect of game creation. It is always preferable to consult experts of an area of game development in order to clarify a fuzzy idea. It is even better to admit that you do not know something and ask for help rather than assuming that you know it and reaching a point where you and your team will be blocked. After all, creating games is a vast and challenging topic and it is through team work that educational game designers create real impact on their societies.

GAME DESIGNERS PLAY GAMES

In the same way that you can't cook a delicious Chinese meal without having tried Chinese cuisine, you should expect that it's rather difficult to make games that others will love without having played games yourself. Playing games is game designers' food for thought! Designers who don't play are detached from the industry culture, from players' needs, and from all the stimuli and creative processes of their peers. This is actually a common mistake that I see when some educators decide to create their games. With no particular experience playing games and with a lack of interest in playing, educational game designers risk proposing activities that have no appeal or they reproduce a concept that has already been presented before, without the creator even realizing it.

By playing games we are part of the continuous and ongoing evolution of our society and culture. We share the same questions, problems, and fortunes of our players and we can better understand their needs. In this way, we can propose learning experiences with an intrinsic value. By understanding our audience, we can better approach it and affect it. The bigger the understanding, the bigger the impact. Even in cases where the theme of your game is not related to current sociocultural events, like history of sci-fi games, the use of language, events, and characters can be determinant on where the focus of players is set. This may not be a great issue when designing games for science, but it might become rather sensitive when working on subjects like history, religion, or human rights.

But through this process we also discover ourselves. We see what games we like and don't like. What amazes us and bores us. What helps us learn and what doesn't. Consequently, we construct a critical approach to games that helps us structure our own personal opinions and be able to defend our choices when necessary. Also, by playing games, we have references through which we can give examples to our colleagues. When educational game designers try to explain their concepts to other members of their team it's rather handy to be able to make references to existing games. It is also normal that people who listen to others' ideas try to classify them through references to what they have already played. A common response to presenting one's concept might be, "This sounds like **The Legend of Zelda**" or "That perspective is like in **World of Warcraft**." Imagine not having heard of any of those games! That's something you would definitely want to avoid.

Also, playing games can give an insight into existing trends and attributes that can help you design more interesting experiences. You can additionally see what works and what doesn't. Among your first steps when deciding to go toward a game direction and a learning topic is to identify what already exists. In this way, you are able to avoid mistakes that have already been made by other designers and anticipate problematic situations that will either hinder your design, the development of the game, or the presentation and learning aspect of the game. Without a doubt, you will not like all the games you play, just as you don't like all the books you read. However, every game is a new experience and can always teach you something. Playing games is part of a game designer's work. So, get started!

The Game Designer's Perspective

Wherever you go, go with all your heart.

–Confucius

As we analyzed in Chapter 1, game designers aim to create intrinsically motivating learning experiences by designing games. But is there a specific and definite way that can guarantee that your games will be interesting or intrinsically motivating? While designing games, designers will encounter players that may like, dislike, or are just indifferent to their game concepts. Educational game designers will be asked to make decisions based on their interaction with players while knowing that those decisions might have a positive effect on one part of the player population while affecting the view of the game for others in another way. In addition to this point, games are works of art, strongly linked to a designer's perspective of the world. Consequently, educational game designers need to be able to assess various factors and combine them with their own views and ideas in order to create games.

There are countless factors that affect the direction of the development of a game. In an attempt to group them in bigger components, the following are four filters on a game designer's perspective.

Filter #1: The Filter of Your Inner Self

This filter is related to the way game designers view games, the environment around those games and players. There are always topics that we like and don't like. There are games that we prefer to play and games that we don't. There are educational topics, tools and approaches we like to use and ones that don't fit in a particular context. Through the filter of your inner self, you judge your game through your own personal preferences and experiences. For example, if you have participated or organized a game activity about teaching coding through an outdoor activity, you would be positively or negatively influenced to take on a relevant project based on the success of this activity. Additionally, there are things that, based on your personal experience or existing literature, work better in specific contexts.

The filter of your inner self can also work negatively though. Keeping to one's personal preferences might risk the possibility of missing or avoiding paths that would be interesting for the development of the game. Since games are tools for the creation and fostering of experiences that the players will live, as we will see later, it's not only the personal preferences of the designer that matter. The filter of your inner self can be developed with experience and experimentation. Cooperation, communication, and interaction with designers, educators, and students, as well as continuous engagement in games and new stimuli are some of the best tools to expand one's perspective and understanding of their own needs. Additionally, even if this might not always be the case, it's important that you like what you do!

Filter #2: The Filter of Players' Expectations

When designing educational games, it is important to know and understand your audience. This step will help you to anticipate several problems that might arise later in the development process. Some time ago, I was part of a research project on the design of educational games for people with visual and auditory problems. The design team initially started designing games that seemed interesting to students who would visit the laboratory occasionally. However, none of those students had difficulty seeing or listening. When the games were presented to this target group, several technical problems did appear: The contrast of visual elements was not that high, thus creating frustration for players with visual impairment, and the controls were rather complex for a target group that was not very experienced in playing this type of video game.

It is important to understand what players expect of the game and what their needs are. Even though this might not always be clear, it is an important element to base design decisions on. The filter of players' expectations requires that you have an understanding of your audience. This understanding needs to characterize the majority of your audience and not individual cases, which is something that you can achieve by interacting and communicating with players.

Filter #3: The Filter of Designer's Ethos

Educational game design is a very sensitive area because the choice of learning tools, approaches, and topic might have a serious impact on a player's mentality. Educational game designers, like any stakeholder in the teaching process, bear the responsibility of delivering learning experiences that are accurate and support a learner's critical thinking. Without doubt, a game concept and design will be affected by the game designer's personal point of view. Even though this might not be obvious in the fields of physics, chemistry, or mathematics, it has a greater impact on the teaching of history or social issues, like human rights and intercultural learning.

The filter of a designer's ethos always raises the question of whether the teaching of a topic, and its delivery through a game, are clouded by the educational game designer's personal beliefs.

Filter #4: The Filter of Teaching Accuracy

No tool, however powerful, can guarantee learning conditions if educators don't have a good idea of the topic they want to teach. Even if this statement sounds pretty straightforward, it is very easy to get carried away from the game design process and focus less on learning aspects. This is, of course, a big mistake. In order to be sure and confident about the learning potential of your games, you need to have a good understanding of the topics you want to teach. If the game is designed by a team, the learning expert needs to be able to communicate and explain the approach that is used and the importance of using it so that everyone understands its impact on the learning experience.

The filter of teaching accuracy aims to help you constantly evaluate the correctness, accuracy, and consistency of your game in terms of the topic you want to teach.

REFLECTION POINTS 🔍

- The game designer's perspective is one of the various filters that you can use while designing games. Try to filter your thoughts through some of the filters mentioned before.

- What are your personal opinions and expectations of your game? Try to examine the game through different perspectives.

- Do you have a good understanding of your audience? If yes, what will be the impact of your game on them?

- Are you impartial to the subject and have you tried to present the learning context in a way that offers a global perspective to students and supports their critical thinking?

- Have you done sufficient research on the teaching of your learning subject?

THE ELEMENT OF CREATIVITY

In their book **Breakpoint and Beyond: Mastering the Future Today**, George Land and Beth Jarman discuss an experiment they performed on more than 1,000 students where they presented them with a paper clip and asked them to propose how they would use it [1]. The researchers wanted to examine the resourcefulness of the same students during their development in a school environment. So, they performed the same test on the same students when they were five, ten, and fifteen years old. Students that would surpass a specific amount of possible answers to the paperclip question were considered "divergent thinking geniuses." After analyzing the results of the tests, the researchers found that 98 percent of five-year-old students who took the test were classified as geniuses. As it turned out, the same students while growing up performed worse and worse on the test, and only 30 percent were classified as geniuses when they were ten; at fifteen, only 12 percent of them could propose a sufficient number of answers. As it turns out, creativity can be both learned and unlearned!

But what is creativity? Usually the first answer that comes to mind is the production of novel answers to problems or situations that arise. And that is definitely an element of creativity. Whether it is in the field of science, art, or athletics, people need to find solutions to problems that often differ from experiences they have previously had. Proposals that are unique, which we have not seen, heard, or experienced before are characterized by creativity. But is this all that makes a person creative? Are students who propose that the answer to $1 + 2$ equals 10 or that the formula H_2O represents fire considered as creative? Probably not. Novelty makes sense as a creative quality only when the proposed solution has a meaning in a given context. Additionally, creativity is linked to influencing and inspiring other people. Pieces of art, technologic achievements, and scientific discoveries are the result of creative people who, in turn, inspire and motivate future generations to have a diverse impact on their communities.

Creativity is an important feature of any game designer. Especially in the field of educational game design, the use of creativity has a particular importance: from one side, games are the result of creative thinking, and from the other side, these games should be a tool for helping players develop their own creative skills. This means that your games should provide players with experiences that inspire, motivate, and encourage creative thinking, or at least they should not discourage it. Also, it is always important to remember that educational game design has special challenges, compared to casual game design, as educational game designers have specific learning objectives they want to achieve. At the end, though, any product you propose will still be a game and, consequently, this is how players will view and judge it. If your game fails to captivate their attention and motivate them toward exploring its world and contents, it's highly likely that after a few minutes, they will try another game that will quench their thirst for fun.

Creativity is related to any aspect of your game design, whether this is gameplay, aesthetics, or the way you present the content you want to teach. During every instance of educational game design, you will be required to be resourceful, flexible, and capable of expressing your ideas to other members of your team or, in several cases, to your players. But creativity is not a gift that comes without effort. Even if there are people with a predisposition toward a particular field, their creativity is a result of hard work and open-mindedness. Below are some tips and exercises that can help your creative thinking process:

Generate more than one solution to a problem. By trying to figure out various ways of solving a problem people explore novel ways of understanding a given situation. Usually, in real life situations, there are no perfect solutions. Specific decisions come with their benefits but also a price to pay. Reflection on these possibilities and making decisions is a great exercise for creative minds that comes in quite handy during game design contexts.

Avoid premature judgement and filtering your thoughts. It happens very often that thoughts that come to our minds are filtered by our judgment. This is definitely a handy mechanism for various occasions but in the case of designing games, filtering and suppressing your thoughts can be a big problem. It is always better to unleash your creativity and explore the deepest parts of your mind by expressing and then analyzing your thoughts, rather than filtering and suppressing ideas at their birth. Good ideas can come from anywhere and their validity and power are not always obvious unless you picture them inside your game context.

Find relationships between things that are seemingly unrelated. This is always a great activity related to imagination. Like the paper clip example, it is a fundamental part of a game designer's work to think outside the box and to create new stimuli for players that will impress, motivate, inspire, and help them develop their own imaginary universes. Not everything in your worlds needs to be real. It just needs to serve a purpose. Books like Dr. Seuss's **Green Eggs and Ham** and Roald Dahl's **Matilda** or games like **The Curse of Monkey Island** or - were not successful because they followed reality but rather because they twisted it and used it to provide a particular experience to their players. Great contrast and connections between elements that are seemingly unrelated is a great tool for the generation of creative and original ideas.

Work collaboratively and exchange ideas. Cooperation and interaction with our peers can be a very creative task. From one side, you try to express and communicate your ideas, helping you make them concrete, while you develop your communication and expression skills. On the other side, you have the opportunity to see your vision from other perspectives, offering you a valuable chance to explore your imaginary universes through the eyes of others.

WHAT IS A GAME?

One of the longest and most tiring topics of discussion when designing games for educational contexts is the nature of the produced game. Even if we consider that we have an understanding of what games are, in practice multidisciplinary game design teams tend to have difficulties agreeing on the final outcome. During my experience as an educational game designer, I have had the opportunity to listen to phrases like "This is not a game," "This is an activity," "This is not educational," and my personal favorite, "This is too much of a game." At the end, the question is still the same:

What is a game?

PLAY AND GAME

Unlike many other languages, the English language makes a distinction between play and game. Let's take some examples of play:

- Someone plays the guitar.

- Two kids are playing by chasing each other in the park.

- Two teenagers at the park play with their eyes while flirting.

- A teacher plays with a puppet while presenting the map of the United States to his class.

- Someone is playing with their food, drawing faces with ketchup on their dish.

- Someone is exploring a new software platform by playing with its different components.

- A family plays **Jenga** during the evening.

- Someone plays **Monument Valley** on their tablet.

As we can see, there are cases where play is part of a concrete process, with goals and expected outcomes, like the case of playing **Jenga** or **Monument Valley**, which we call games. But there are also cases that would not sound right to identify as games, like experimenting with a new software platform or making ketchup faces on our dish. In this sense, there are activities during which we play that are not necessarily games. In this sense, there are several activities in our daily lives that we could classify as play. So, which activities are called play and which not?

EXAMINING PLAY

According to Swiss psychologist Jean Piaget, the several theories and different opinions on the nature of play show that as a phenomenon, it is difficult to understand [2]. He argues that even if in general we tend to study and identify play as an isolated function, play could be imagined as an aspect or expression of any activity. This is interesting. So, anything we do could be considered as play. Does this make sense? Let's take some examples from daily situations:

- Wiping the floor.

- Wiping the floor and identifying figures created on the wet floor.

- Eating shrimps.

- Sorting the shrimps on someone's plate and eating them in order of size (from smallest to largest).

As we see, the same activities with simply a different direction or a different context can be considered play or not. But how can we understand this direction and aspect of playfulness in our activities? Let's try to imagine play as a pole. Activities that are closer to this pole are more easily considered as play. But is there actually a way to estimate this proximity of an activity towards play?

Piaget proposed that the proximity of an activity toward play depends on the balance of the individual elements that play consists of. And that raises a whole new question! What are the elements of play? So, let's examine what play is.

Play is pleasure. People play because they have "fun." This profound and simple aspect is one of the fundamental elements of play. But not all activities we enjoy are related to play. Drinking a cocktail or having a shower might be activities we enjoy but we don't consider them as play. These activities become pleasurable when we put effort into them: Exploring different ingredients and making a new cocktail, for example. So, pleasure is also related to a person's involvement and effort toward an activity. Are there cases of play like this? A lot! In fact, while playing, players are able to invest as much energy as they want at a given point and enter a state that they consider enjoyable, leading to pleasure.

Play is about surprises. As Jesse Schell proposes, we can consider play fun because it includes pleasure and surprises, thus presenting an interaction between play and the user [3]. This suggests that in play there is always something at stake, a question we need an answer to: Will someone be able to make all their shots in basketball? Will someone be able to build a lasting castle in the sand? Will this move in **Bejeweled** lead to a winning state? Even in cases like an unorganized activity, where a young child plays with building blocks, there are several unexpected outcomes: The house the child builds could collapse or all the blocks might not fit together. So, this element of uncertainty on the outcome of play offers an interesting perspective on the notion of play.

Play is autotelic. People engage in play because they find interest in the activity itself. The word **autotelic** means that the goal of entering an activity is the activity itself! Let's take an example: Students can do their homework because they will receive a reward from their teachers. In this case, students decided to engage in the activity of doing homework not because they love the process of doing homework itself but because through it they will achieve another goal. In contrast to this case, play indulges curiosity, which consequently increases the interest of students toward an activity, making them interested in the activity itself.

Play is spontaneous. There several situations where play arrives as a spontaneous expression of an activity. People can doodle while listening to others talk, organize a made-up game in the school yard, or make up nicknames for their classmates (not all play is kind!). Play can arise in a great variety of situations. On the other hand, there are several situations where play can take place in organized situations. There are several examples like this, the most obvious of which are games: existing forms of play. The spontaneity of play, though, remains an interesting aspect when studying play in learning contexts, since it is very often important for facilitators of an activity to avoid suppressing spontaneous expressions of play during a teaching activity.

Play is free from conflicts. An interesting aspect of play is that it can be adapted to the particular needs, expectations, and desires of players. During play, action figures can fly, defying gravity; narrative elements can be bent in order to satisfy the desires of the narrators; and rules can change in order to express the mood and decisions of a player. This magical ability that play offers players allows for the possibility of experimentation with different situations and roles, as well as the expression of the player's opinions and sentiments. If, for example, a rule or convention does not satisfy players, they can change it in order for them to be satisfied. On the other hand, we can find several cases where conflict exists in play. Again, a common example is games, as we will see in the following.

As we already saw, the nature of play is related to the context, personal preferences, and perception of a particular instance of an activity. Even if play consists of the elements presented previously, it doesn't mean that the existence or not of one or more of those elements can guarantee that an activity will be considered as play. It is always important to consider that those elements are valued differently by different individuals, groups, and cultures. Accordingly, the nature of play and games can vary from context to context. The best way to see if people play or not is to identify it while someone is engaged in an activity. It is down to the educational game designer to identify the particular needs of players and bring an equilibrium to the activities that will be considered as play. Having a better understanding of play, it's time to explore the nature of games.

PLAY AS AN INDISPENSABLE ELEMENT OF LEARNING

Every maker of video games knows something that the makers of curriculum don't seem to understand. You'll never see a video game being advertised as being easy. Kids who do not like school will tell you it's not because it's too hard. It's because it's boring.

–Seymour Papert

As we established before, play is an expression of any activity someone can engage with. In this sense, education and learning can be strongly related to play. Or, in other words, education and learning can be play. We can all recall cases where a teaching session was interesting, engaging, and would be considered like play. The relationship between play and learning is not something new. Plato reflects on the notion that education should be fun and fun is a state that arrives from playing. Additionally, he proposed that play is a preparatory step for someone's career in the sense that by playing a symbolic role, for example the one of a carpenter, people can be motivated to learn more about a skill. Eric Klopfer, Scot Osterweil, and Katie Salen suggest that play itself incorporates learning by offering learners the ability to exercise freedom in five particular axes [4]:

Freedom to fail. During play, students have the possibility to enter situations that would seem like failure in other contexts. Without the supervision of someone else, players, from children to adults, have the opportunity to structure their play the way they want without the fear of entering situations that would be considered wrong. Players who play tennis can fall, get back on their feet, and move forward, or they can play crazy shots in a game and see what will happen. Through this process of trial and error, players have the ability to learn and explore the world around them.

Freedom to experiment. Play offers the opportunity to experiment with one's environment. Through ludic environments, players have the chance to explore their environment without restrictions and possible insecurities that would come with the notion of failure. Let's take, for example, children playing with blocks. Placing them irregularly while creating a structure could lead to the collapse of the construction, a result that in other contexts would seem incorrect. However, these cases arrive very often while playing with blocks. Children are not discouraged. Instead, they enjoy this process, while continuing to build something else from the beginning. Cases like this can arrive in different types of environments, like formal, informal, and non-formal learning contexts.

Freedom to fashion identities. Since play can take different forms, players have the opportunity to explore their position toward their world through various perspectives. Symbolic play, for example, offers the opportunity for players to explore different identities inside their society. Through symbolic play, children can become a mother, father, doctor, or blacksmith. They can try different communication styles and control their emotions, like being angry, sad, or happy.

Freedom of effort. An interesting aspect of play is how much effort players want to put into an activity. Play does not force students to constantly invest all their energy. On the contrary, players are free to go all out at specific points and at any point they want to, change their pace or completely stop. This magic aspect of play affords the freedom to students to manage their pace according to what they desire at a specific moment.

Freedom of interpretation. One of the biggest challenges of educational game designers is that no experience is perceived in the same way by all students. The same happens for play. In fact, every student experiences gaming contexts differently, also being able to give a meaning to their learning experience based on their previous understanding of a taught concept.

Of course, like any analysis of play, there are situations where parts of this analysis might not apply to a particular context. But does play incorporate learning only in this aspect? Of course not. Learning through the prism of play acquires another value and interest for learners. Let's take, for example, young children. During early childhood, children try to explore their environment and understand it. They experiment, they ask questions, they observe. This concentration and investment of energy is intentional, intrinsic, and brings pleasure to them. For them, observing a praying mantis, playing with marbles and watching how they move, or identifying the attributes of magnets on their toys is a game.

But when they grow up and go to school, this connection between learning and pleasure ceases to exist. One of the main reasons for this is that this intrinsic motivation to explore the universe that would give birth to all those emotions of surprise, pleasure, and suspense is replaced with extrinsic rewards, like grades, gifts, or recognition. Consequently, the process of learning is detached from its original playful nature.

So, since play is one aspect of the process of learning, we conclude that the discussion is not if play and learning can exist but how we can better use the elements of play in order to optimize learning. Understanding this idea, at the beginning of 20th century, pedagogue Maria Montessori suggested that play is really work, especially for children [5]. This is the reason why Montessori placed great emphasis on integrating play in her classrooms. However, her games were purposeful and with specific objectives, trying to use play towards the completion of her learning objectives and the development of her students' cognitive skills. Even if Montessori mainly focused her work on children, the direction that she established applies to any age, raising a great argument for the use of play in a learning context: that play, with the appropriate direction and guidance from an educator, can lead to amazing learning results and the development of learners.

GAMES

So, we established that play can be part of any activity, depending on the way we actually execute it. However, not all of those activities can be characterized as games. So, what are games? An interesting approach to the nature of games is the one of Csíkszentmihályi: According to him, games are culturally prepackaged sets of experiences that allow players to experience play [6]. What Csíkszentmihályi actually says is that being part of a culture, we were introduced to existing ideas of games. Let's take a moment to reflect on this. Are there games that we were introduced to when we were kids? When we think of it, there are several! From traditional games, like hide-and-seek or the game of tag; to notable board games like chess, Uno, or cards; to symbolic games, like playing doctor or cops and robbers—those games have been introduced to us through our society and culture.

Still, this proposal does not clarify the nature of games. So, let's see how some people who have studied the field of games view them:

First Definition

Games are an exercise of voluntary control systems, in which there is a contest between powers, confined by rules in order to produce a disequilibrial outcome.

—Elliot Avedon and Brian Sutton-Smith [7 , p. 405]

This very interesting definition by Avedon and Sutton-Smith presents several important elements of game analysis. First of all, games are voluntary activities. This means that players enter them because they want to. Even if there are cases where someone could be forced to play a game, participating, for example, because friends or school pressed them to, games are primarily voluntary activities. Games are also activities where there is exercise of control systems. In other words, players act inside games. This action can be physical, like in badminton, or it can be mental, like in Uno.

As the definition suggests, games involve a contest between powers. This means that players enter an artificial conflict during games, which might lead to a competition. On top of this, this game context is defined by specific rules and at the end of the game, the outcome of the game will not be the same for all players.

Second Definition

A game is an interactive structure that requires players to struggle toward goals.

–Greg Costikyan [8]

In this definition, Greg Costikyan emphasizes the interaction among players and games. In **I Have No Words & I Must Design**, Costikyan tries to identify the difference between games and other forms of art and communication, like stories, toys, and puzzles. He argues that the main element that differentiates games from those activities is the interaction between players and games. The outcome of a gaming context is not defined but it is affected by players' choices and at the same time the feedback that players receive impacts their decisions. Costikyan also observes that games require struggle toward goals. So, games have specific aims and objectives and players need to fulfill them by putting effort into them.

Third Definition

Game is the set of positions from among which the player can choose in a given state of the game, and by extension, in mechanics for example, the set of possible positions and thus movements of a system, of an organ, of a mechanism that has furthermore been subjected to certain constraints.

–Guy Brousseau [9, p. 49]

In this definition, mathematics didactician Guy Brousseau offers another perspective of analyzing games. According to him, games can be viewed as a set of different positions that a player can choose among at a given instant. Let's take **Monopoly**, for example: At any given point, players have the option to buy the unowned tile they land on, build a hotel, sell their property, play a card, and so on. These are all different options that correspond to different outcomes later on in the game. However, those options are not infinite. Someone cannot buy all street tiles of the game at once. They need to either land on them or exchange them with another player. These are constraints, as Brousseau suggests.

Fourth Definition

A game is:

- A closed, formal system that

- Engages players in structured conflict and

- Resolves its uncertainty in an unequal outcome.

–Tracy Fullerton, Chris Swain, and Steven Hoffman [10 , p. 43]

This definition presents games as systems, formal and closed. In fact, games are already structured contexts, defined by rules, created by designers. There are several elements inside games that make sense only inside their framework. Erection of settlements in **The Settlers of Catan** makes sense only inside this particular game, offering no particular value outside of the game. In this aspect, they are closed and formal. Another interesting aspect of this definition is the term of engagement. Players do not just enter a game world, they are intrinsically motivated and thus immersed in it, making them engaged. Players enter conflict situations and need to make decisions that will lead to an unequal outcome that is not certain. At the end, some players will win, some players will lose, but this outcome is not certain from the beginning of the game.

Fifth Definition

A game is a problem-solving activity, approached with a playful attitude.

–Jesse Schell [3, p. 37]

An interesting aspect of this definition is that games are presented as problem-solving activities. This notion is actually suggested by some of the definitions presented before. Decision-making among different states and obstacles can be considered a problem-solving process. But of course, not all problem-solving activities are considered games. Trying to find a solution to lighting a fire while camping in the forest or raising a sturdy and robust sky scraper don't sound like games. Let's now consider a pie-eating contest where contestants have their hands tied and have to eat a whole pie. This is a problem-solving activity. Contestants can't use their hands. Still they need to find a way to make the pie disappear into their bellies. Most possibly, they know they are going to get dirty and it's highly likely they are going to approach this activity in a playful attitude. So, this is a simple and interesting definition of games.

If we examine the definitions above, we will observe that games are viewed as closed systems, the context of which has a meaning only inside their own scope. As we already saw, Johan Huizinga proposed the notion of a playground, isolated from the real world, bound by specific rules, the rules of the game that someone plays. This playground is called the **magic circle**. According to Eric Zimmerman and Katie Salen, the magic circle of a game is where the game takes place [11]. When people play, they enter this magic circle or they create a new one. Let's take, for example, two children playing doctor, performing surgery on a doll. The children know that they are not doctors. They also know that the doll is not alive. But within the boundaries of the magic circle, they are bound by its rules and conventions. The idea of the magic circle shows the particular and immersive nature of games and emphasizes their potential in learning contexts.

In any case, the great complexity and immense connection of play and games with our everyday lives make them rather difficult to describe and define. So, let's try to give an overview of the aspects and qualities that the definitions above cover. Considering play as an expression or aspect of every human activity, as Piaget suggested, play can also be viewed as an expression or aspect of learning. From the other side, when people play games, they are also prone to learning. They are presented with artificial problems that they need to find solutions to and through their interaction with the games, they may receive new information, develop their skills, or form different perspectives on topics related to their lives and society. Players' decisions and actions matter in gaming contexts, since the development of a game is very connected to them. Many would say that decisions and actions are important for simple activities that are not characterized as games too. Any type of exam requires solvers to make decisions. Are they games? The vast majority are not! The main reason for this is that they are not intrinsically motivating by themselves. In this sense, we could try to describe educational games as:

Interactive problem-solving structures, presenting players with a set of positions or options, the decision among which may result in different outcomes, both positive or negative for players, the advancement through which aims to create intrinsically motivating learning experiences.

This definition tries to cover the aspects that were examined in this chapter. Whether you agree with this definition or not, each individual perspective that is being presented will be examined thoroughly in the next chapters. So, the journey continues!

It becomes apparent that defining games and play is not an easy task. Actually, the more we try to define these notions, the more it becomes clear that they are connected to a vast number of aspects of human life. In fact, even if we can understand what play and games are, their great connection with every aspect of our lives make them difficult to define, in the same way that it's not easy to describe notions like experience or fun. Another important point in game analysis is that, as not everyone lives an experience in the same way, games are not viewed or identified in the same way by everyone. This is also the reason why this field has been studied by such a wide variety of scientists, researchers, and professionals and there are definitions that conflict with each other.

PERSPECTIVE: THE CREATION OF NEWSGAMES AS A TEACHING METHOD—EMPIRICAL OBSERVATIONS

Damien Djaouti
LIRDEF—Montpellier University
Julian Alvarez
CIREL—Lille I University/Play Research Lab, CCI Nord

INTRODUCTION

The name **serious game** indicates "games that do not have entertainment, enjoyment or fun as their primary purpose" [1]. These games, which are being developed in increasing numbers, have useful applications in various market segments, including education, health, communication, politics, and defense. These different applications give rise to an organization of serious games into subcategories [2]. "Newsgames" are serious games that address current events or, as defined by [3]: "[G]ames that utilize the medium with the intention of participating in the public debate." While professional journalists, of course, use these games, sometimes individuals also use Newsgames to express their own points of view on current events [4].

As part of an introductory video game design course intended for engineering students, we opted to move away from the design of games for pure entertainment and focus on designing Newsgames. Although conducted empirically, introducing Newsgames into our course seemed to enrich the teaching. In addition to teaching a method for video game creation, these classes introduced other elements to our students as well. In this article, we will first present how our course is organized, then discuss the Newsgames created by our students and what they learned from this experience.

EDUCATIONAL APPROACH

Since 2005, we have given a course on video game design to students with different majors at different training centers. The educational goal has been to encourage learners to design and execute small video game projects with a message. Games like these are known as **serious games**. For example, serious game themes focus on teaching about proper nutrition or introducing different sectors of industry. In 2010, we began focusing on designing Newsgames with engineering students majoring in computer science, civil engineering, chemical engineering, civil aviation, and meteorology. For three consecutive years, the classes were given at two different establishments, each with its own approach. The first establishment was a French engineering school called the INSA of Toulouse. This course was given as a one-week (35-hour) introductory module to students in their fourth year of their engineering master's. The second establishment was the computer science department of the French Toulouse III University. This course was only open to students in their fifth year of a computer science master's. A total of 30 hours of class time divided into two-hour sessions was spread out over one semester. The courses were structured in five phases:

1. **Introduction**: The learners basically had not heard of serious games at this juncture. We began by presenting concrete examples of games to captivate the learners and pique their curiosity. **Darfur is Dying** (2004) addresses the humanitarian crisis situation in Darfur and **September 12th** (2003) broaches the subject of responses to terrorism. These were the games that elicited many student questions: **Who produces this game? Why did they design a game on this theme?** Answers to these questions enabled us to introduce the serious game concept while presenting the various phases of the course.
2. **Discovery of serious games**: We then invited students to perform their own web search to identify other examples of serious games. The objective of this phase was for the learners to observe the wide variety of themes discussed through video games. This approach also inspired learners to design their own serious games.
3. **Video game design methods and tools**: We then introduced students to the fact that they would need to discuss a current event of their choosing through a video game, thereby designing a Newsgames-type of serious ggame. To do this, we held a class on entertainment video game design methods and tools adapted to serious games. We based this on our own design methodology, which is derived from the DICE model [5]. This generic design model, built by analyzing and summarizing a dozen different serious game design methodologies, outlines four major steps:

   * Defining the serious content of the game.
   * Imagining a game concept.
   * Constructing a prototype.
   * Evaluating the efficacy of the prototype.

   The last three steps form an iterative cycle that repeats until the designer is satisfied with the assessment of the serious game.
4. **Serious games design and execution**: The students divided themselves into groups of four to five people and began working on their serious game project. Throughout this phase, which represented the majority of the course in terms of hours, the teacher abandoned his "magisterial" role to adopt the role of a mentor accompanying students during the execution of their project.
5. **Presentation and evaluation of executed projects**: Finally, for evaluation purposes, the students presented their serious games to the rest of the class. A student who was not a member of the group was designated to test the game in front of everyone. This student was invited to give his or her opinion of the game, thereby eliciting discussions within the class. These presentations sometimes gave rise to real, in-depth debates among the students. We will see this in the next section.

To ensure that they successfully completed their serious game projects, our students were offered the tools they needed to do so. The engineering students attending our classes had different levels of computer expertise. There were two main groups. The first group included students familiar with a programming language, generally Java or C++. These were all engineering students majoring in computer science. The second group included engineering students from other areas. They usually had no special programming knowledge. In the latter group, which dominated our classes, we offered simple-to-use entertainment video game design software, like RPG Maker or The Games Factory 2. We call this type of application "game creation toolkit" [6] because they incorporate all the functions needed to design video games. In general, a two-hour game creation toolkit presentation session was enough to enable learners to start using the toolkit to create their own serious game.

RESULTS: STUDENT PROJECTS

From 2010 to 2012, we had approximately 80 engineering students in our Newsgames software design courses. These students designed a total of 17 games.* The current events discussed and the software used to design these games are described in the following table. Details of the Newsgames Designed by Students: Current Events Addressed and Design Software Used

TABLE 1
Details of the Newsgames Designed by Students: Current Events Addressed and Design Software Used

Year	Current Event Addressed	Design Software Used
2012	The explosion in the number of millenarian sects predicting the end of the world in 2012.	The Games Factory 2
2012	The *Costa Concordia* shipwreck (two games).	The Games Factory 2
2012	The Megaupload closing (two games).	The Games Factory 2 (Group #1) Java (Group #2)
2012	Scandals in the British press.	The Games Factory 2
2012	The potential stripping of France's AAA credit status.	The Games Factory 2
2011	Sharp fuel cost increases.	The Games Factory 2
2011	The Mediator legal proceedings (mediator is a French medication which lead to many unexpected deaths).	The Games Factory 2
2011	The Wikileaks saga.	The Games Factory 2
2011	The Arab Spring in Tunisia.	The Games Factory 2
2011	The HADOPI law (a French law against Internet piracy).	Java
2010	The Haitian earthquake.	RPG Maker XP
2010	The Influenza A epidemic (two games).	Flash CS4 (Group #1) Java (Group #2)
2010	The surge in suicides at Orange/France Telecom.	Flash CS4
2010	The wave of expulsion of illegal immigrants by the French government.	Flash CS4

As illustrated in the table, the current events cover many themes. The students were able to choose the current event they wanted to develop. Using journalistic resources available

* All Newsgames designed by our students are available at http://www.ludoscience.com/EN/ressources/projet /index.html.

on the web, the students found the documents they needed on their current event of choice. Subsequently, designing a video game based on news often encourages students to have in-depth debates on the current event in question.

For example, in 2010, the influenza A epidemic was the topic of a Newsgame called **Superflu**. The group of students who designed this game thought that the only way to eradicate the pandemic was through worldwide cooperation despite the differences in financial resources from country to country. The serious game of this group of students was a multiplayer game. Each player was assigned a part of the world with cities and vaccine or antiviral production sites. The players could choose to supply their own cities with the medications produced or supply cities managed by other players. The game was knowingly designed so that the only way to eradicate the pandemic was for all players to distribute all of the medications they produced to the first outbreak sites, even if these sites were outside of the player's own territory. This serious game conveyed the vision of one group of students in the class.

However, not every group had the same approach to a given current event. Another group from the same class designed **Flucorp Inc**. This group adopted a radically different view of the problem. Here, players represented directors of pharmaceutical production companies. The goal was to sell different products (protective equipment, vaccines, antivirals) with efficacy that varied according to how much was invested in medical research. If players invested massively in research, they could rapidly help contain the epidemic, but would not reap significant financial profits. In contrast, if players chose to invest only modestly in research, they would have the time to sell several different vaccines of ever-increasing efficacy. Subsequently, players were encouraged to manage the epidemic while maximizing profits. These students employed a nearly militant approach to the current event. Their game indirectly criticized the attitude adopted by pharmaceutical companies during this crisis. In the end, the different ways of addressing the same current event using Newsgames raised a lively debate between the two groups of students.

Some Newsgames designed by our students broached current events that were so sensitive they sometimes upset the players. The **Tunisian Oppression** game was about the 2011 Tunisian Revolution from the point of view of dictator Ben-Ali. Several small action games chronicled the epic of the dictator overthrown by his people. First, by playing the dictator's guards, players needed to contain the masses by shooting real bullets at them. The game was designed so that the people will always win. Players then needed to try to escape with as much gold as possible to a country willing to provide refuge. Despite its satirical undertones, this game sometimes offended. When students presented their game to the rest of the class, an energetic debate ensued on the way the game portrayed these events. Although the designers of this serious game wanted to express that "the people will always win despite the fury of the dictator," the discussions raised demonstrated that there is a certain difference in interpretation in the final message by the users.

This phenomenon occurred again with the **Escape from Port-au-Prince** game, the subject of which was the especially sensitive, horrific earthquake that hit Haiti in January 2010. Players represented catastrophe survivors who needed to leave the city and stay alive. The group of students who designed this serious game voluntarily decided to be fairly blunt regarding this current event. During their struggle to survive, players ran into pits filled with cadavers and were faced with Cornelian dilemmas to obtain food and conserve it. All this occurred while players were under the constant pressure of hunger and the risk of dying from it. When this project was presented at the end of our class, several students were literally shocked. In addition to the catastrophe itself, students questioned the way in which the topic was addressed.

Although they were video game lovers, and had themselves designed Newsgames, some students found "this subject to be too serious to be addressed in a video game." The fact that "this violence was real and existed for people in the world, in contrast with what is found in entertaining video games" bothered these students. In contrast, other students defended the validity of video games as media for addressing any subject, just like any other media. As a result, a spontaneous debate lasting about 30 minutes followed the presentation of this serious game.

In addition to everything they learned about video game design and the current events discussed, all students in this class reflected upon the possibilities and limitations of video games as a means of expression. This phenomenon is reminiscent of the **Darfur is Dying** serious game, which elicited similar reactions when we presented it to students at the beginning of the course. They were often shocked to play children who could be kidnapped by militia as they sought water in the desert during a war ongoing in real-life.

CONCLUSION

Given the various projects carried out by our student groups, we observed that designing Newsgames seems to stimulate debate on issues that go beyond the simple scope of video game design techniques. On the one hand, learners reinforced their knowledge about the current events they incorporated into their games thanks to the research they conducted, mainly via the Internet. On the other hand, it seems that by imposing "serious" subjects for a video game project, these learners exercised and developed their reasoning skills. For the purposes herein, a learner's "reasoning skills" means precisely documenting a subject to develop a point of view, and then comparing, contrasting, and defending this point of view vis-à-vis the point of view of other people. To this end, we identified three dimensions that seem to be interesting from a pedagogical point of view:

- **Development of an approach for addressing a given current event with support from journalistic information sources**. Designing a Newsgame based on a real subject requires learners to document the subject and acquire knowledge that can be used both to design the game and to elicit discussions during debate. Here, we observed that designing a video game, and a serious game in particular, encourages learners to read. This reading is generally thorough because the learners must be able to use the information they read in their video game.

- **Exchange of points of view on a given subject using video games as a medium for "discussion."** The fact that learner groups design Newsgames on a given subject using very different approaches shows them that not everyone sees current events in the same way. The example of the two influenza A games exemplifies two very different, fairly representative views of this subject.

- **Organization of student debates on the validity of video games as media for discussing current events**. We only observed this kind of debate for video games that incorporate very sensitive current events, such as the 2011 Tunisian Revolution or the 2010 Haitian earthquake. Although designing different video games for the same current event encouraged debate among our learners, the discussions moved away from the current event and moved toward the communication potential of video games. Therefore, in an informal way, there were discussions on issues related to media education.

Nevertheless, we observed that different learners do not subsume these three academic dimensions in the same way. Although all students took part in the first dimension (motivation to perform documentary searches), the same was not true for the second and third dimensions.

Only the groups of learners in a given class designing Newsgames on a given subject took part in debate on the current event incorporated into the video game. To promote debate on the communication potential of video games, we simply needed to identify at least one Newsgame that elicited a certain discomfort among a few learners in a given class.

To offer learners in a given class the opportunity to incorporate all three of these identified academic dimensions, perhaps it would be wise to require current event subjects to be sensitive and have different groups address the same subject in parallel.

According to our empirical observations, such an approach could certainly help develop the learners' reasoning skills. However, we can also question the potential of the educational scope of such an approach. For example, if we asked learners to create serious games other than Newsgames, such as learning games or edugames, would we observe the learners assimilating knowledge coming from an academic program?

When we refer to previous experiments conducted on the use of serious game design in classrooms [7–9], we do think that this teaching method has a real pedagogical potential that is yet to be fully explored. We will pursue our experiments with other students and other kinds of games, and we hope that this article will inspire you to try this method with your own students!

REFERENCES

1. Michael, D., & Chen, S. (2005). *Serious Games: Games that Educate, Train, and Inform* (1st ed). Boston, MA: Thomson Course Technology PTR.
2. Sawyer, B., & Smith, P. (2008). Serious games taxonomy. In *Serious Game Summit 2008, Game Developer Conference* (pp. 1–54). San Francisco.
3. Sicart, M. (2008). Newsgames: Theory and design. In Stevens, S. M. & Shirley. S. (Eds.), *Proceedings of the 7th International Conference on Entertainment Computing* (pp. 27–33). Berlin, Heidelberg: Spinger.
4. Frasca, G. (2006). *Playing with Fire: The Little Game that Could*. Retrieved from http://serious gamessource.com/features/feature_101806_little_game_1.php.
5. Djaouti, D. (2011). *Serious Game design: Considérations théoriques et techniques sur la création de jeux vidéo à vocation utilitaire* (PHD Thesis). Toulouse, France: Université de Toulouse.
6. Djaouti, D., Alvarez, J., & Jessel, J. P. (2010). From "mods" to "gaming 2.0": An overview of tools to ease the game design process. In *Games: Design & Research Conference*. Volda, Norway.
7. Kafai, Y. B. (1995). Minds in play: *Computer Game Design as a Context for Children's Learning.* Mahwah, NJ: Lawrence Erlbaum.
8. Rieber, L. P., Luke, N., & Smith, J. (1998). Project Kid designer: Constructivism at work through play. *Meridian: Middle School Computer Technology Journal, 1*(1), 1–9.
9. Robertson, J., & Howells, C. (2008). Computer game design: Opportunities for successful learning. *Computers & Education, 50*(2), 559–578.

SUMMARY

So, what topics did we cover in this chapter?

- Game designers strive for balance. Balance between the possible and the impossible, reality and imagination, the objective and the subjective, the fantasy and the feasible.

- Game designers can come from any background and need to combine aspects from different fields in order to create games that attract a player's interest.

- Educational game designers are characterized by several skills and qualities, some of which include the ability to listen and observe others, communicating and presenting their ideas, and constantly learning.

- Even if games are a really powerful learning tool, they are not the solution to everything! Understanding when and how to design and use educational games is a great skill.

- Educational game designers try to maintain balance between their players, the learning and game aspects of their games, as well as have a good understanding of the contexts they are designing for.

- Defining play and games is not easy. We examined several definitions and approaches for play and games and their impact on learning.

REFERENCES

1. Land, G., and Jarman, B. (1992). *Breakpoint and Beyond: Mastering the Future Today*. New York: Harper Business.
2. Piaget, J. (1952). Play, dreams and imitation in childhood. *Journal of Consulting Psychology, 16*(5), 413–414.
3. Schell, J. (2014). *The Art of Game Design: A Book of Lenses* (2nd ed). London & New York: CRC Press.
4. Klopfer, E., Osterweil, S., and Salen, K. (2009). *Moving Learning Games Forward: Obstacles, Opportunities and Openness*. Cambridge, MA: The Education Arcade.
5. Montessori, M. (1949). *The Absorbent Mind*. Madras, India: The Theosophical Publishing House.
6. Csikszentmihalyi, M., and Bennett, S. (1971). An exploratory model of play. *American Anthropologist, 73*(1), 45–58.
7. Avedon, E. M., and Sutton-Smith, B. (1971). *The Study of Games*. New York: John Wiley & Sons.
8. Costikyan, G. (1994/2006). I have no words and I must design. In K. Salen & E. Zimmerman (Eds.), *The Game Designer Reader: A Rules of Play Anthology* (pp. 192–211). Cambridge, MA: MIT Press
9. Brousseau, G. (2002). *Theory of Didactical Situations in Mathematics* (N. Balacheff, M. Cooper, R. Sutherland and V. Warfield, Trans.). Dordrecht: Kluwer Academic Publishing.
10. Fullerton, T. (2008). *Game Design Workshop: A Play-Centric Approach to Creating Innovative Games*. New York: CRC Press.
11. Salen, K., and Zimmerman, E. (2004). *Rules of Play: Game Design Fundamentals*. Cambridge, MA: MIT Press.

3 Pedagogy and Games

This chapter covers:

- The aspect of solving problems in gaming contexts.

- The ways and extent that educational game designers can impact players' learning.

- A study of the most prominent learning theories.

- Creating and assessing learning objectives.

- Designing games, taking into account learning curricula.

This chapter aims to provide an overview of the most prominent learning theories that can greatly affect the way that educational games are designed. Additionally, we will examine how educational game designers can approach and impact the way their players learn. Finally, we will work on setting accurate and measurable learning objectives and examine how to design educational games that are aligned with official curricula.

Pedagogy is a science that has been developing for thousands of years. During this amazing process, many great pedagogues have come up with various perspectives and practices on education. From the idealism of Plato to the pragmatism of John Dewey, and from the realism of Aristotle to the democratic education of Neil, we can see a mosaic of different views on how people learn.

This great diversity of views and perspectives is strongly connected to the fact that everybody perceives the world differently. Learning takes place during particular periods of time and in specific locations, and affects specific people. Knowing the theories and ideas those people presented does not mean that we need to follow them to the letter, as many would believe. Understanding them makes us more informed and prepared to deal with situations that will occur during educational game design and helps us to make decisions based on the practices, examples, and experience of our peers and predecessors.

Even if there are several books more suitable to introduce you to pedagogic science, this chapter aims to present some of the most important learning theories and ideas related to educational game design.

SOLVING PROBLEMS

The more I work in education, the more it becomes obvious that learning is not just about acquiring knowledge but also about being able to properly use it when necessary. Information or skills we acquire and develop become useful when problematic situations appear in our lives that need to be solved. Problems are not only about mathematics. On the contrary, we encounter numerous problems every day. From figuring out which is the quickest route to work or figuring out a way to fix our washing machine, people need to find answers to problems every day. So, problem solving skills are in fact rather important for learning.

What makes games interesting in educational contexts is that they are a very efficient way of presenting problems. Let's see some examples.

• In card games, like **Magic: The Gathering** or **Yu Gi Oh!**, the main premise of the game is that players inflict damage to the life points of their opponents with the cards that they possess in their hand, helped by how they have designed their card decks.

• In the tower defense game **Plants vs. Zombies**, players need to form the best inventory of zombie-fighting plants and arrange them effectively throughout the field in order to protect their house from being invaded.

• In the board game **Risk**, players need to form different strategies in order to expand their domination over a world map, trying to complete particular quests that were assigned to them at the beginning of the game.

As we can see, all of these cases present problem situations that require solutions. As game designer Jesse Schell suggests, games are problem-solving activities presented with a playful attitude [1]. This argument was also raised by scholars Johan Huizinga and Karl Groos in their analysis of play. When lions play, apart from engaging in a pleasurable activity, they unintentionally develop several skills, like stealth, agility, or hunting, that are required for them to survive [2]. So, problem solving requires the use and development of several skills and disciplines, including the following:

• Reasoning

• Communication

- Observation

- Analysis

- Assessment

- Identification of existing knowledge

As we have already discussed, solving problems is not limited to the fields of mathematics or science. Problem-solving skills are required and applied to almost every aspect of our lives. A team of five people facing another team of five in basketball need to come up with a solution that will help them shoot the ball through the opposing team's hoop. A game design team needs to come up with an efficient way of successfully pitching their idea to a game producer, which requires attracting the producer's attention and presenting their idea correctly. A young couple moving to a new home have to try to figure out how to move all their stuff in the most efficient way possible. These are all problems. There are always some people who can solve problems more easily than others. Why is that? Because they have worked on developing their relevant problem-solving skills.

The Zoombinis is a characteristic educational game where players are asked to find solutions to problematic situations. (Used with permission of TERC.)

Problem solving can be rather challenging. This is what often makes the development of problem-solving skills a challenging task. Problem solving is addressed by several learning curricula with priority usually given to formal learning environments. The complexity and difficulty of solving problems is usually accompanied by anxiety or a lack of confidence in learners. Games have an amazing ability to change the presentation and delivery of problems to players, making them invisible to players' eyes, while they are still engaged in the game context. Students who play dominoes, for example, do not consider it a chore to have to count dots and match them with their own pieces, which contrasts with other activities where counting problems are presented without a playful aspect.

If games can be considered problem-solving activities presented with a playful attitude, then educational game designers are provided with a wonderful opportunity to structure learning experiences that help players evolve their problem-solving skills. This process can be improved by introducing players to ways of approaching problems and by creating their own problem-solving strategies. In his book **How to Solve It**, mathematician George Polya proposed four steps for the analysis of problem solving [3]. Those steps are:

Understanding the problem. When I was studying engineering, I had a professor who liked to give us problems with more information than was necessary to actually solve those problems. Among this information, most of the givens were useless and only a few values of specific variables were actually necessary. The point he wanted to make is that life is not about applying formulas but rather it is about understanding the situations we are in. In the same sense, every solution to a problem starts with understanding what its givens are, its context, and what the solver is asked for. This requires solvers to understand the instructions and resources they have at their disposal in order to reach a solution. From a designer's perspective, games as problem-solving contexts should offer the necessary information to players in order to help them understand the problem they need to solve. We have all played games where the rules were not clear from the beginning, causing misunderstandings, frustration, and confusion.

Devising a plan. Most problems come with multiple solutions, each of which has its own cost. Problem solvers need to take into account the different parameters and make decisions that may have consequences later on as the game develops. A common example of this point are tower defense games. In several games of this genre, raising buildings or training soldiers with different costs and attributes is crucial for players' ability to defend their territory. In such cases, there is not always one correct way of achieving victory while players must make estimations, devise strategies, and test hypotheses, taking into account their current situation and available resources.

Carrying out the plan. There is a grand distance between concept and actual implementation. Having previously devised a plan, players are faced with the task of actually enforcing it. Let's imagine a chess match. Considering that the problem presented by the game is outmaneuvering the enemy army and capturing the opponent's king, players devise and carry out plans. In order to achieve this, in each round players take into account their own and their opponents' resources. But nothing guarantees that a plan will be successful. A miscalculation or a different move from the opponent may call for reconsideration of the plan, which leads the problem-solving process to the next step.

Looking back. Polya considered that taking time to look back at how problems were solved can be a very valuable process. By looking back at what they did, solvers can identify what they could have done differently and question their choices in order to achieve a better outcome next time they encounter similar problems. As we will see later in the book, this process, called reflection, is of great importance to educational contexts. Not to mention life itself!

Polya's problem-solving analysis can work iteratively, allowing solvers to perform problem-solving approaches, evaluate them, and reapply them or reject them in favor of other ones. Apart from presenting a model of solving problems, this analysis can be a very useful tool for those who create problems, and consequently fir those who design games. Each of those steps in problem solving is also an opportunity for teachers to support the development of players' problem-solving skills.

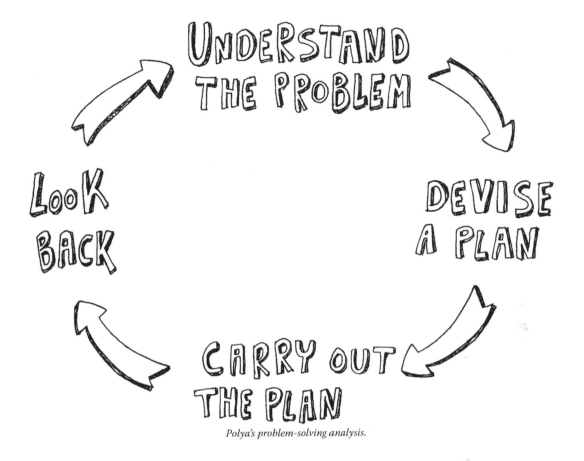

Polya's problem-solving analysis.

But how can this problem-solving analysis be used in game design? Let's apply this analysis to a game. The first level of **Super Mario** presents the basic game elements: Enemies, power-ups, point systems, controls, landscape. From the very first time that players play the game, they are presented with the problem of completing the first level. After they understand what they need to achieve and the ways to do so, they can form their own strategy for achieving their plan. Not everyone completes the first level of Super Mario in the same way. Some try to finish the level quickly by finding the secret "warp pipes" and others find their own sequence of movements in order to achieve their objectives. Some others may not even be able to finish the first level. This may mean that their approach or problem-solving strategy was not that successful and they need to devise another plan to secure victory. Whether or not players lose at times, they have the time and opportunity to think on what they did and play the game again successfully.

This analysis becomes easier if designers can identify and understand the problems they pose to their players. Game problems may be directly or indirectly related to the game's learning objectives. Games that fail to present their goals and rules quickly and efficiently frustrate players, who will most likely prefer to play other games. In those cases, the first step of facilitating problem solving was already unsuccessful. In the same way, there are games where it is very difficult to come up with a winning strategy or others where the solution is too simple. The former may be found very difficult and intimidating while the latter will probably be considered not challenging enough. At the same time, both the second and third steps, planning and implementing, of the problem-solving analysis were unsuccessful. In fact, viewing games as problems is the first way of evaluating one's games!

REFLECTION POINTS 🔍

Viewing game design as a problem creation activity can offer great insight into the designed games. You can take into consideration some or all of the following thematic questions:

- Is the information you want to pass on presented correctly in your games? In order to answer this question, take into consideration the following points:

  - Is the necessary information for the game presented in the correct way?

  - Is the question you want the players to answer correctly formed?

  - Do you provide enough information to explain the problem?

  - How complex is the problem you present?

- How does your game support players' problem-solving skills?

  - Have players encountered similar problems before?

  - Should the players be presented with similar problems beforehand?

  - Do your problems offer multiple solution possibilities?

- Does your game provide the opportunity for players to evaluate their decisions?

PERSPECTIVE

Kylie Peppler

Associate Professor of Learning Sciences, Director of the Creativity Labs
Indiana University

Can games be used in educational contexts and, if yes, what learning theories do you use?
I think games are really useful in many occasions, from preschool through adult learning settings. They make learning a more playful experience, and this process makes clear what the learning goals and objectives are.

Furthermore, when it comes to such contexts, I like to see how **designing** games, not just playing them, can reveal what students have learned. I use a range of learning theories for this, one of which is **constructionist theory**, which focuses on how people externalize their thinking by creating "objects to think with" that are both personally meaningful as well as shared with others for feedback and iteration. Through this process of design, learners reformulate what they know and grow their understanding over time. Games learning often connects to other larger concepts, like systems thinking and computational thinking. When we use tools like games or simulations, we can actually introduce those ideas to very young children instead of delaying them until high school or college, which is usually when they are introduced. A few examples of games that are in this direction are **Sims**, **Minecraft**, or other popular games that have more of a constructionist orientation. We have built games about architecture that have introduced big ideas about this topic in ways that allow students to create and design buildings, for example, and share them with others.

Considering that games require the collaboration of several people, how would it be possible for them to cooperate effectively in order to design educational games that could have a meaningful impact on players?

The design of games brings diverse groups together; we see it time and time again in our work, in both children and adults. I think that the most important thing is to start designing and playing the game in an iterative fashion that later allows people to figure out what they would do differently, share their opinions, and learn from one another. So, I would encourage diverse groups to build an early prototype or just play some games together that they think are provocative. When you try to build a new group, it is nice to do your research together, share games, explain what you are thinking about the game and learning perspective, and share the same language. Then you can go on to building an early prototype that you can design and play. In fact, you can iterate between those two things. This makes the collaboration more robust.

For example, in our work, we wanted to design high-quality games to help young children understand complex concepts, like biology and systems thinking. For this, it was important that we work iteratively with biologists, young children, and classroom teachers. The biologists were able to distill the content into its most powerfully succinct form, young children offered us feedback on what was exciting about the game (which isn't always what we'd assume), and the classroom teachers helped us view the game from the perspective of the users, ultimately adapting the game for their specific settings. So, we worked together with our colleagues, after-school groups, and classrooms to design such experiences, taking into account the complexity of the topic and the learning theories we'd apply to understanding what youth are learning when they experience the game.

How do you combine the learning and the gaming elements together in order to make the games?

We have a backwards design approach where we think of the objective we want to learn in a particular context. So, we usually start by brainstorming rather widely with those objectives in mind. For example, we may want the kids to learn about systems thinking and complexity. Those decisions set up our design constraints. This could then lead us to designing games based on specific themes, which, in our case, were the complex systems of bees, ants, blood circulation, or ecologies. We then evaluate those different ideas in terms of how hard it would be to build them, as well as how much kids would really like the system. So, we are looking for ideas that attract children's interest as well as really good examples that help them learn and grow. The learning contexts that we work on are usually the things that aren't often well-presented in schools, yet we strive to make an impact on how children understand domains like math, science, language, or the arts, long term. Gaming can embody key ideas that can be difficult to capture traditionally in other media such as text, diagrams, or animations alone.

Do you have any advice that you would like to give to potential educational game designers?
I would say that getting to know more about learning theories and methodologies such as design-based research is important. You should add a person to your team who is knowledgeable on these areas, which can improve the game as well as the overall learning outcomes. It can make clear the learning objectives and get rid of all the distracting elements, clarifying the game mechanics in the process for the game designers. Once all this is clear and you know what your objectives are, it ultimately allows you to be more creative. I would also advise trying not to put too many objectives into one game, as the core mechanics of the game will end up suffering as a result.

What are your sources of inspiration and your influences?
I try to get influences from different places; my background as an artist is often helpful. For example, when I think about games I think about interactive design as a kind of human-to-human interaction and how I can get people to interact differently. So, I look for games and experiences that are interesting, that attract players' interest. Game players don't want to stop playing because it is exciting. I like games that put learners in a lifelong learning trajectory, where the learning can deepen with repeated play over time. In this way, games actually grow with the learner.

THE ROLE OF THE EDUCATOR

The Zone of Proximal Development

As we previously discussed, learning takes place everywhere. It can be formal, informal, or non-formal; it can be spontaneous or organized; it can take place indoors or outdoors. Our ancestors understood that in several cases, knowledge and skills can be transferred more efficiently inside organized environments, setting the foundations of pedagogy and education. But who can be an educator? Who can be a teacher, an instructor, a trainer?

Let's see some examples of educators:

- Teachers from kindergarten to university.

- Designers of massive open online courses on platforms like Coursera or EdX.

- Designers of virtual and augmented reality experiences in museum exhibitions.

- Human resources trainers in corporate environments.

- Vocational trainers.

- Someone's peers, such as classmates, colleagues, or elders who offer advice and guidance.

- Our parents.

In all these cases, some people intentionally or unintentionally design environments where learning is facilitated. We can learn from our teachers, from our families, from our friends, from digital or augmented reality experiences. From this perspective, it becomes apparent that it would be more helpful to try to understand what educators do instead of who they are.

So, what is the role of an educator?

The response to this question can be given by studying one of the most influential pedagogical theories of the 20th century, the notion of the **Zone of Proximal Development**.

At the beginning of the 20th century, psychologist Lev Vygotsky, being critical of the use of standardized psychometric tests to measure the achievement of students, argued that in this way educators were not taking into consideration the students' individual potential [4]. By only identifying the present capabilities of students and not taking into account their potential to develop, educators only measured the development that had arisen from an educational context. In other words, Vygotsky believed that the level of development that can be achieved by someone without any external help indicates the development they achieved from their past experiences. On the other hand, performance that is the result of assisted guidance indicates the potential development of a student. Complicated? Let's see an example.

Among the students of a classroom, Dorothy can sing a song nicely without prior instruction. Dorothy was able to listen to the song, synchronize with its tempo, and sing in the right tone. The music teacher of her school, identifying her skills, understood that they could help her develop those skills. By organizing activities that would help Dorothy to develop her singing skills, she was able to sing other songs as well and develop her own personal style of singing. What happened in this case is that with the help of her teacher, Dorothy was able to push the limit of her skills a little forward. This result would possibly never have been achieved without external guidance. This gap between what someone can do at a particular instance, based on their own experiences, skills, and competences, and what they could do with the guidance of an educator is the Zone of Proximal Development.

The Zone of Proximal Development indicates the true nature of educators, which is stretching the limits of learners' development by designing and facilitating learning experiences. From this perspective, educators identify the potential of each individual student and try to help them to expand their skills, competences, and understanding of a taught concept. But how is the notion of the Zone of Proximal Development implemented in teaching contexts? Let's imagine that learning can be represented as an under-construction building and let's also imagine that educators are builders. In order for educators to be able to reach all the areas of the building, they need to raise scaffolds around it. By being able to reach every corner of the building, construction workers can identify where they need to pay greater emphasis when building it and organize their efforts. When they finish, the scaffolds are gradually removed. The final result is a beautiful building without any signs of construction work around it, ready to serve its purpose. This analogy was used by psychologists Wood, Bruner, and Ross in order to expand the notion of the zone of proximal development in learning contexts [5]. They called it **scaffolding**.

As its name suggests, scaffolding represents several teaching mechanisms that, when applied in learning contexts, can help students to evolve and "stretch" their skills in a way that wouldn't be possible without the help of an educator. These mechanisms disappear gradually while students progress and are able to apply the knowledge they acquired. At the end, students are capable of conquering a concept without external help. Scaffolding works best when applied to the individual needs of each student, allowing teachers to differentiate their support. Scaffolding becomes more efficient under the following processes:

Attracting learners' interest. It is only natural that people want to learn about things they are interested in. Educators need to incorporate a learner's interest into the requirements of the task or concept they want to teach. One of the greatest arguments of the use of games in education is that games can actually become very efficient in attracting people's attention when designed and presented properly.

Simplifying and facilitating learning processes. Through the scaffolding perspective, efficient teaching requires that learners are gradually introduced to the taught concept. If learners are presented with all materials of the learning environment from the beginning, without any guidance, it is possible that they will either feel frustrated or use those materials in ways that the educator did not intend. In both cases, learners will likely not develop the skills the educators hoped to help them develop. If learners were introduced to the environment through a set of simplified activities, each of which was designed for specific purposes, their introduction to the aims of the environment would be smoother while they would also be closer to developing the skills educators expected. In other words, nobody can fly an airplane from day one! First, they need to be introduced into the basics, then fly a simulator, then fly with the assistance of an instructor, and then set out to conquer the skies! Successful scaffolding makes sure that all those steps were prepared in the most efficient way possible.

A usual comment I hear is that simplifying and restricting players' options in order to achieve particular learning outcomes may have a negative impact on the gaming experience, which is true if the notion of scaffolding is not applied properly by designers. The main aim of using scaffolding when designing games is to introduce players to their gameplay and learning objectives. The more players evolve throughout the game, the less support they should receive. Games like **World of Warcraft** or **Skyrim** apply scaffolding mechanisms by featuring introductory quests in order to introduce players to their game mechanics. And still, players do not feel restricted.

Let's take for example the game **Slice Fractions**. Slice Fractions aims to teach the mathematic concept of fractions to players. In order to do so, players need to help a mammoth cross to the other side of each level by slicing ice cubes and dividing them into smaller pieces that will eventually be used to extinguish the lava obstacles that block the mammoth's path. In order to facilitate scaffolding in the game, the designers created a set of introductory levels, each of which presents a functionality or a particular logic required for the player to advance through the game. Through this process, designers made sure that they presented the necessary points for the game to be played while indirectly facilitating the learning experience.

Providing feedback. Feedback is very important in learning situations. Meaningful feedback can help players identify their misconceptions, see what they did wrong, optimize their performance, and discover solutions to their problems. As we will see in Chapter 13, feedback can have different uses throughout the game design process.

Frustration control. Learning should be less stressful with a tutor than without. The security and confidence provided by the guidance of an instructor or a learning platform should be used in order to make players feel confident during learning experiences.

As we can see, educators are those people who can help other people grow and develop their skills and understanding of the world. Raising scaffolding structures that are based on the individual needs and skillset of each student, educators try to expand those skills in the Zone of Proximal Development. These scaffolding structures can take various forms like games, classroom presentations, lectures, online courses, outdoor activities, and any other tool that the educator may prefer to incorporate in the course delivery. The selection and combination of those tools, however, is connected to the approach the educator chooses to apply while teaching. But what are those approaches and how are they applied in teaching contexts?

PERSPECTIVE

Eric Sanchez

Professor
University of Fribourg

In your opinion, what is the role of educators in educational game design?
When we talk about educators, the use of games is crucial. It's also important to clarify that we do not necessarily talk only about teachers. We also talk about museum curators and other people who are involved in the implementation of game-based learning approaches. I think that educators play several and different roles in such experiences, depending on different moments. First, as stakeholders in the game design and application phases, they should be able to participate in the game design process. Additionally, it is very important that they have an active role in the implementation of the game. I think that the success of educational games depends a lot on the capacity of teachers to integrate the learning aspect in those practices. For example, in **Classcraft**, there are lots of parameters that can be modified by teachers in order to provide particular learning experiences. The success of Classcraft is related to the capacity of teachers to change and adapt the game to the needs of their practice.

Of course, teachers play an important role during the time that a game is presented in the classroom and the game-based learning scenario that the game was part of. We have discussed this aspect a lot with teachers. It's hard for some of them to escape from playing a presented game and help students both learn and play. Consequently, we need to find a role for teachers at this phase and often this role is orchestrating the game. By orchestration, I mean giving points, badges, or participating as game masters. Teachers also play a role in the advancement and climaxing of games. I have worked previously with teachers in projects where they worked and contributed to this aspect.

Finally, another role of teachers is debriefing. Game-based learning is about integration of contextualization and decontextualization of knowledge. During games, students develop implicit knowledge based on the games they play. Hence, it's important that during debriefing, educators make sure that this knowledge is decontextualized, leading to transfer.

What is the most efficient ways that games can be introduced in learning contexts?
Regarding the use and introduction of games in learning, let's first consider that during ancient times the word distinction of play and learning were not that far. So, it is more of a barrier in people's minds to connect learning with play. Second, I think that more and more educators are interested in game-based learning practices. For instance, in France, government bodies and institutions are very open to pushing forward the idea of integrating games in teachers' courses. So, it's also an issue for administrators in education to facilitate and enable educators to implement such practices. A third barrier is related to the way that game-based learning is approached and used in learning situations. There are several occasions where such techniques are used in order to conceal existing approaches, like putting chocolate on broccoli. So, teachers can see the motivational power of games, but they don't see the intrinsic characteristics of games that are important for the success of such approaches, like contextualizing the knowledge in the game contexts or the freedom to make mistakes during playing and so on. Another barrier is about the knowledge we have on the impact of game-based learning. Research is important for this aspect. Teachers should be participating in this process as well. Finally, we need good games!

You have been working a lot with teams on educational game design (teachers, game designers, developers). In your point of view, what are the greatest challenges of such teams?
There are many challenges in creating these kind of teams because if we want something good, we need to make it possible for people from different fields to be able to collaborate. And these people have very different approaches. All those people are educators, designers, computer scientists, researchers, and making sure that they can work together and succeed in their missions is undoubtedly a great challenge. To address this challenge, we need people who are able to understand what each person involved in the team does and create links and communication channels between those people. The second challenge is time and money, because the process of making games means that games need to be conceived, designed, and tested in different phases. So, the difficulty is about the agenda and scheduling and dealing with constraints in the development of the game. Additionally, there is always the issue of the success of games. Education may not be the best market for games and it's very challenging to design, develop, test, and sell games in different contexts.

There is a long discussion about evaluation, but being able to assess game impact correctly may be a challenge. What points should be tested and evaluated in educational games?
There are different means of assessment. A common way consists of performing tests after having completed a game to try and see what has or hasn't been learned. I think that this way is not very efficient. What is missing is that designers often forget to check if players were actually involved in the game assessed. It's possible that players participated without being involved or having played. For instance, players could still be just clicking anywhere on a game screen without purpose and produce analytics that may have no real value for a proper and meaningful assessment. This is the reason why a deeper examination is needed. I call this process **playing analytics**. Playing analytics is the result of collecting data during game

sessions. Playing analytics do not just show the effect of games on players but can also reveal insights about how games are approached and played, what strategies were used by students, and can help create links between those strategies and the learning process. Playing analytics also offer the opportunity to capture the learning process. This is what we do in different games in our lab. Through this experience we had the opportunity to see that players approach games very differently; they apply different strategies, and all of them were relevant for learning. Through this process, for instance, we have also observed that the way teachers introduce and present games may have a great impact on how players approach those games and learn. So, it's important to clarify that we don't evaluate only a game but the whole didactical situation, including the learning context, the way it was presented, how students perceived it or how it was implemented, and so on.

How can collaboration and competition be used in educational contexts?

Competition is often a debatable aspect on education, mainly out of educators' fear that their approaches should not be based on competition. In every game, competition is there. In games, competition can be against adversaries or against the game itself. The game presents an antagonistic system while the students learn through their interaction (failure and success) with it. So, on one hand it's important that some competition exists in the game, and on the other hand it's important not to base one's whole pedagogic approach on competition among players. Some balance should be maintained and found in this aspect. Research findings present two aspects about competition. From one side, it motivates students to evolve and grow through their participation in such activities, and from the other side it may cause stress and lack of confidence for them. So, it's a challenge to maintain some balance between those two aspects.

Another aspect that is important to pay attention to is the general interaction process between players and educators. There are cases where players communicate with educators while playing and other cases where players collaborate and communicate with each other. We call this **epistemic interaction**, an aspect that is very important for learning. There are two categories of epistemic interactions. The first one is related to the communication and interaction of players with the games and their adversaries, and the second one is related to their communication and collaboration through play, the exchange of information, sharing of knowledge, and challenging each other's views. When we designed the educational game **Tamagocours**, we added a chat functionality to the game so players could discuss and exchange information with each other. We observed that this process played a key role in helping them understand the learning aspect of the game and develop new types of strategies by giving and receiving feedback.

BIBLIOGRAPHY

1. Sanchez, E. (2017). Competition and collaboration for game-based learning: A case study. In P. Wouters & H. van Oostendorp (Eds.), *Instructional Techniques to Facilitate Learning and Motivation of Serious Games* (pp. 161–184). Cham: Springer International Publishing.
2. Sanchez, E., Young, S., & Jouneau-Sion, C. (2016). Classcraft: From gamification to ludicization of classroom management. *Education and Information Technologies*, 22(2), 497–513.
3. Sanchez, E., Monod-Ansaldi, R., Vincent, C., & Safadi-Katouzian, S. (2017). A praxeological perspective for the design and implementation of a digital role-play game. *Education and Information Technologies*, 22(6), 2805–2824.

IMPACT OF PEDAGOGIC APPROACHES ON EDUCATIONAL GAMES

Now that we have a better picture of the role of the educator, we can see that there is not one particular and efficient way to help people learn. The tools, styles, and approaches of people who educate others depends on their audience and their own personalities. This makes more sense if we take into account that, from our personal experience, we have all met different types of educators: Teachers who would mainly stick to presentations and lectures, teachers who would lean toward outdoor activities and exploration of the surrounding environment, teachers who would add more interaction to their delivery, and many others who would have a particular perspective on how to structure their courses. Educators have their own styles, based on their personality and experiences, and thus we should expect that the same would apply to educational games. Consequently, there is not only one way to design educational games.

Educators have always been influenced by the culture, perspective, and theories of their times. Some of those perspectives were eventually shaped into theories. As educational game designers, we are directly or indirectly affected by those learning theories. Having an overview of those learning theories gives us an insight into how other educators around the world approached education and how our modern understanding and perspective of education has been shaped. On top of that, these theories offer a common starting point for discussion in educational game design, which is a valuable asset for game designers.

A common issue of educational game design teams is that a colossal amount of time is lost purely because the members of the team do not speak the same "language." People with technical backgrounds tend to put greater emphasis on implementation, people with an arts and design background tend to pay greater attention to the game's external appeal, and pedagogues tend to focus mainly on learning, disregarding other aspects. Let's get one thing straight. Successful games are about all of those things. This means that no matter what one's specialty is, being able to understand their peers' perspective is not just helpful, it's mandatory if they want their games to be efficient and successful.

A common understanding of basic learning theories can prove to be an invaluable asset for any educational team member, since it will help everyone come a little closer. So, I suggest that you take a deep breath and read the following sections, as they will prove quite useful when designing your own games! In this section we will briefly examine some of the most important learning theories that have influenced modern education and are closely related to educational game design.

BEHAVIORISM

Some years ago at a primary school, I met a teacher called Jeremy. Jeremy believed that students were like "empty boxes" that you could fill with knowledge and experiences. He was very passionate about his role. Every day he would prepare presentations, gaming sessions, and activities that he would present to the whole classroom. Jeremy rewarded his students when they completed their homework, performed good deeds, or were actively engaged in classroom activities. On the other hand, Jeremy was strict on what he considered inappropriate behavior by discussing it with his students and even resorting to some sort of punishment. It's highly likely that most of us have encountered a teacher with characteristics similar to those of Jeremy. Whether or not he realized it, Jeremy had adopted elements of behaviorism in his teaching.

The pedagogues who proposed behaviorism at the beginning of the 20th century considered learners as blank slates, or **tabula rasa** in Latin. In other words, they believed that only our environment determines our behavior. Consequently, behaviorism did not account for someone's inner thoughts, emotions, or particularities in order to assess knowledge. On the contrary, behaviorists only paid attention to behaviors and actions that were observable. Based on this premise, behaviorists considered someone's behavior to be the result of habits and actions that are formed in response to specific events, called **stimuli**. In order to understand it better, it would be helpful to examine the work of physiologist Ivan Pavlov.

While conducting research on the digestion of dogs, Pavlov observed that when the dogs of his lab were about to be fed, they would produce saliva. Pavlov then observed that his dogs would even salivate just on the sight of their food's dish or just by listening to the sounds of the guard who was feeding them. This behavior attracted his interest because the dogs would respond not only to see-ing or smelling their food, but they would also produce saliva in reaction to other stimuli that were related to it. In a way, Pavlov's dogs learned that those particular images or sounds were connected with them being fed. Fascinated by this discovery, Pavlov continued to experiment in this direction. For example, he used light bulbs that would turn on just before the food was about to be served. After a while, the dogs of his lab would produce saliva just by seeing the light bulbs turned on.

However, Pavlov also observed that if the lights were turned on randomly, without being followed by the delivery of food, eventually the dogs would not salivate anymore, disconnecting this stimulus from their reaction.

Pavlov observed that natural reactions can be linked to unrelated stimuli through a specific process. In the dogs' example, when being fed they would see or smell their food, causing them to salivate. Seeing and smelling the food was a stimulus that would unconditionally cause an unconditional response, in this case, salivation. But if neutral or unrelated stimuli become associated with those unconditional stimuli, they become conditional stimuli and can have the same impact as unconditional ones. In the previous example, turning on the lights would cause dogs to salivate in the same way that they would by smelling and seeing their food. So, conditional stimuli can lead to conditional responses. This type of learning is known as **classical conditioning**. As behaviorism matured as a theory, another approach to learning emerged known as operant conditioning.

Operant conditioning, proposed by Professor B. F. Skinner, expanded the concept of classical conditioning by proposing that the environment, including someone's parents, educators, and peers impact our behavior by either reinforcing or weakening particular traits [6]. Following experiments, Skinner observed that both humans and animals would repeat actions that lead to pleasant outcomes while they would try to avoid actions that lead to unpleasant ones. For example, Skinner would present rats with a button. When the rats pushed the button, a food pellet would fall, rewarding them for pressing the button. Behaviorists named any stimulus that happens at the right moment in order to enhance a particular behavior as reinforcers and considered the act of using them as reinforcement. Reinforcement can be positive or negative.

Positive reinforcement is connected to stimuli that increase the probability of a specific response. Examples of positive reinforcement are congratulating students on their performance or offering stickers to students who completed their homework; in the field of video games, this could be offering badges, unlocking hidden content, or gaining experience for someone's character.

Negative reinforcement is related to stimuli that increase the probability of a specific response when these stimuli are decreased or removed. Let's see an example. Imagine that a guest in your house plays very loud music. If you close the door to your room, the volume will be decreased. In the future, closing your door when the noise is loud will be an interesting option, since it is connected to noise reduction. So, in this case decreasing sound volume by closing the door leads to negative reinforcement. Negative reinforcement is not rare in games. A very common example can be seen in racing games. In order to highlight that vehicles should stay on the road, vehicles that deviate to the sides move at a slower speed. Eventually, in order to avoid moving slower, players try to avoid going off road.

In behaviorism, **punishment** is connected to stimuli that reduce the likelihood of a behavior taking place. Punishment can take two forms: either a pleasant outcome, a reinforcement, is removed or an unpleasant outcome is introduced. If some students, for instance, lose game privileges because they fought during recess or if students get more homework because they did not complete the previous day's homework, they received punishment. Punishment is not the same as negative reinforcement. Punishment is a mechanism that suppresses particular behaviors while negative reinforcement is used to increase behaviors of learners.

Game designers, intentionally or unintentionally, apply behavioristic learning techniques in their games in several ways. If, for example, players discover Easter eggs or hidden areas in a game that offers gifts, they will be alert to the possibility of more Easter eggs or hidden areas. This is an example of positive reinforcement. On the other hand, negative reinforcement can be found in several role-playing games, where players are only able to use specific gear or vehicles when they reach a particular experience level. In a case like this an unpleasant situation (not being able to use the cool gear) disappears when reaching a particular state. Apart from reinforcement, we come across punishment very often in games. A great example are sports games, where inappropriate behavior or disrespect for the game's rules can leave a specific player or a whole team with a disadvantage against their opponents.

Behaviorism rose to prominence and heavily affected pedagogic perspectives of the 20th century. In the second half of the 20th century, however, several educators, psychologists, and researchers expressed their concern that behaviorism did not pay any attention to the internal mental processes of learners or their individual characteristics. Actually, even if behaviorism did show considerable results in some cases, as a theory it could not account for several questions about learners' thinking processes. Especially during and after World War I, new technologies were constantly being introduced and the need for training personnel in their use was becoming increasingly large, a period when a new learning theory started to shape.

COGNITIVISM

In his famous experiment, called the **War of the Ghosts**, psychologist Frederic Charles Bartlett wanted to explore the role of memory in the learning process [7]. Bartlett presented participants with exotic folklore stories and asked them to remember and retell them at different times. He then observed that readers tended to present the story in a way that would fit their cultural background and familiar elements. Readers would forget or omit elements which they were not used to and the longer the intervals at which they were asked to recite the story, the more elements they would omit. Thus, they would narrate the story in a structure more familiar to them despite the form of the initial storytelling. Bartlett realized that the story was processed by the readers in a way that would "fit" their previous experiences and perceptions.

As we saw before, a criticism of behaviorism as a learning theory was that it didn't take the mental processes of learners into account. As behaviorism was growing, there were several scientists who were interested in the study of memory, attention, perception, language, and their impact on learning. This lead to the birth of cognitive psychology. One of the most important concepts of cognitive psychology is the one of schema.

A **schema** is a mental structure that organizes or transforms the knowledge we receive in order to fit our experiences and preconceptions. Schemata are structures that we either inherit from our parents or we dynamically construct through our interaction with our environment. We construct and use schemata all the time. For example, when being presented with a new video game, most of the times we already know how to navigate around menus or we can already assume how part of the game is played because we have previously played other games and have built a mental structure that can help us to comprehend this game. Though if a game presents many interface changes or the gameplay is very different from what we have previously experienced, it is possible for us to get lost, since we do not possess a mental structure that helps us to assess this knowledge.

But how can schemata be used in learning? Swiss psychologist Jean Piaget considered that people learn through expanding their personal schemata by incorporating two cognitive processes: assimilation and accommodation [8].

• **Assimilation** is the process through which people receive and internalize incoming information by using existing experiences or preconceptions. For example, by reading this book, you receive information about educational game design, which you try to comprehend through your own experiences, ideas, and perspectives. Since you have already developed schemata that help you to comprehend these concepts, it's very possible that your understanding of this book may be different from someone else's, as other people have developed their own mechanisms in order to process such information. Those mechanisms are the schemata.

• **Accommodation**, on the other hand, is the process through which people alter and develop their existing schemata in order to be able to process new knowledge that they receive. Using again the book example, by reading this book and assimilating its information, your opinions and perspective on educational game design will change. In other words, your schemata will be altered as a result of accommodating the information of this book.

Piaget believed that people learn through a continuous and iterative process called equilibration. **Equilibration** is achieved when people can perceive and understand the world around them using their existing schemata, which is what we call assimilation. However, there will always be situations and concepts that cannot be explained or comprehended using only existing schemata. Being introduced to a new language, using a new piece of machinery, or playing a new game may lead to an unpleasant state of disequilibrium, where we will need to develop mechanisms in order to process the new knowledge. There are countless situations where someone may not be able to understand a concept in mathematics, build a drawer from IKEA properly, or figure out best way to play pinball. Disequilibrium is dealt with through accommodation. Through accommodation, people change their schemata in a way that helps them deal with the new knowledge they receive, reaching a state of equilibrium, where we can sufficiently process the situation that created the disequilibrium in the first place. The work of Piaget has been constantly revisited and expanded and is connected with several learning theories, one of which is the one we will see next.

Along with the evolution of cognitive psychology, the role of the educator was revisited several times, always trying to create optimum learning conditions. This lead to the birth of another great learning theory called **constructivism**.

CONSTRUCTIVISM

During a game design session in a primary school, I asked two students, Denis and Nadia, to present to the classroom the rules of hide-and-seek. When Nadia was presenting the rules, Denis interrupted her and said: "That's not how you play hide-and-seek!" He then continued, explaining the rules of the game as he knew them only to have Nadia interrupt him with her own version. Which of them knew how to play hide-and-seek? Probably both of them. But the versions of hide-and-seek each one of them knew were not the same. Was this unusual? Not at all!

Cases like Denis and Nadia are everywhere and they are related to how learning takes place.

• What is our perception of the world and is this an absolute and specific truth about all elements of our world?

• Do we all seek justice in the same way?

• Do we all agree on social issues?

• Do we all share the same point of view on topics about our everyday life?

Obviously not!

In constructivism people are considered as creators of knowledge in their own unique way based on their experiences. Consequently, there is not one single objective "truth," since any knowledge is interpreted through the prism of the past experiences of a person. Constructivism suggested several radical changes to modern pedagogic approaches, bringing learners to the center of the learning process. In constructivist environments learners are active participants in the teaching process. They can impact the way teaching is organized and delivered by expressing their interests and particular needs. The role of the educator changes as well. Constructivist educators construct learning environments and facilitate learning processes aiming to help students reach an understanding of some given information. Learning is a personal and individual process, adapted to prior knowledge, interests, and skillsets.

As a result, educators who follow constructivist approaches need to prepare various ways of delivering their courses, adapted to the needs of their students, contrary to the traditional classroom presentation for all students. Teachers have a dual role as well. From one side, they teach, and from the other, they explore and learn along with their students, dealing with real-time problems and questions raised throughout the learning process. Psychologist Jerome Bruner also encouraged learners to discover what they needed to learn and induct this knowledge to their cognitive structures. He called this **technique discovery learning**. In discovery learning, learners are encouraged to explore their environment and find answers to problems posed by the teacher or pose new ones themselves, based on their interests.

Constructivists also focused on the importance of culture and context in the construction of knowledge. They considered that there are no generalized mechanisms to apply knowledge to every context, but learning takes place in each context individually. An example of this is that practice usually differs from theory. University students who want to become doctors will find that rules of textbooks may differ from a real surgery, where various, and unaccounted for, factors will affect their performance. Another example is that learning to drive in the countryside may differ from driving in a big city with heavy traffic and challenging parking spots.

Culture is a key aspect of learning in constructivism. Vygotsky considered that through interaction with one's peers, through observation and the use of language, learners would develop mechanisms that would help them overcome limitations in understanding different concepts. This interaction and collaborative nature of learning can help learners make sense of their world through the prism of their culture and society. For example, when we look at the wall and see a circle with two lines moving on it, we understand that it is a clock. Similarly, people who first enter the world of video games have difficulty at the beginning mastering those games or understanding game-related jargon such as "afk" (away from keyboard) or "gg" (good game!). It is through interaction with our peers and through the context of our society that those words take on meaning or that we know that the device on the wall can measure time.

Constructivism continues to have a strong impact in pedagogic thinking. For several decades, many educators contributed to the development of the theory by either expanding it or borrowing some of its main principles. It is also important to remember that different social and cultural needs require adaptations in teaching approaches. It is natural that pedagogic perspectives in the United States may vary at some level from the ones in Europe or Asia. So, educators from different contexts have, at different times, proposed constructivist theories that are closer to their societies' needs and perspectives.

Two constructivist approaches that are interesting for educational game design are inquiry and project-based learning. Let's examine them and see how they could be used in educational game design.

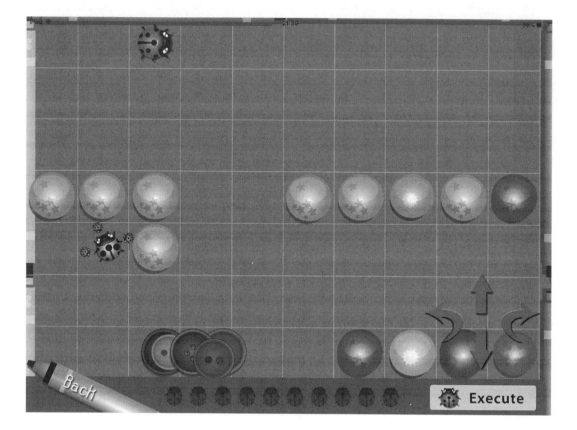

Through their interaction with the world of the mobile game **Ladybug's Box**, players can develop their spatial thinking skills by controlling a ladybug and helping it to meet its family. Players can explore the virtual space and experiment with the different types of interactions that are offered, observing their results.

PERSPECTIVE: TRANSFORMATIONAL GAMES

Drew Davidson

Professor of Interactive Media
Carnegie Mellon University

At the ETC, we challenge our student teams to create transformational experiences in which they work to design experiences that will have a positive social impact. We're interested in how these could be used for education and learning, health and medical, civic engagement, and more.

When creating transformational games with learning goals, I think it's important that instead of focusing on fun, you should consider how both games and learning can be hard. In fact, games can be challenging to the point of frustration (along with broken controllers, even). Also, games aren't fun if they're too simple and we quit because we're bored, or too complex and we quit because we give up. The trick is that a good game keeps us pleasantly frustrated.

Csikszentmihalyi's notion of flow, in which a person achieves an optimal experience with a high degree of focus and enjoyment, is an apt method for discussing this pleasantly frustrating experience. We're in a flow state as we enjoy the challenges and feel rewarded as the game's increasing difficulty matches our increasing mastery of the gameplay, and vice-versa.

I believe games help to enable an experience of flow not by being fun, but by being well-designed in how they challenge a player. Similarly, I think learning is comparably challenging. We all know that we learn some of our most valuable and important lessons from our failures, and games reward players for experimenting and failing on our way to getting it right. As we tackle the challenges in the game, we're engaging in problem-based learning, pushing at the system of the game to figure it out. Constance Steinkuehler has noted how players engage in the scientific method to test out their various ideas and see which ones work the best, developing a form of literacy and mastery.

This is one of the many reasons why teachers are so important in the learning process. Teachers provide the context within which kids learn, shaping the challenges, and helping them make connections across topics to best transfer their mastery into a literacy of learning.

I believe that a good learning game is explicit about its constraints and learning goals and uses its gameplay mechanics to help engage and motivate players to rise to the challenges of a game, trying again when they fail, and developing a mastery through a well-designed and scaffolded challenge and reward cycle. This occurs because a game is hard, and the fun is found through tackling the challenges and gaining a sense of accomplishment as we develop a literacy and mastery of the experience.

And this can't be done through gamification. We can't just gamify learning; adding badges, levels, achievements, and rewards. That's focusing on making it "fun." Instead we should focus on the challenges of learning, and how to increase the difficulty to match our mastery and motivate us to succeed. And we will be rewarded through our accomplishments of meeting and exceeding the challenges and developing our literacy.

So, instead of focusing on the fun of learning games, we should look at how they're challenging. The trick is to help make it a pleasantly frustrating one like Alan Kay's notion of "hard fun" where we enjoy the challenge. Our sense of accomplishment is a hard fun that we earn as the increasing difficulty matches our increasing literacy and mastery. Games are hard, learning is hard, but players and learners will rise to the challenge and have fun as they succeed.

INQUIRY-BASED LEARNING

Judge a man by his questions rather than by his answers.

–Voltaire

Exploring someone's environment and discovering new information is a crucial process in constructivist learning. Asking questions and trying to find answers to those questions is part of this exploratory process. In traditional education, however, asking questions is not always encouraged. On the contrary, students are expected to memorize facts and learn specific answers for specific problems.

Inquiry-based learning is a learning approach that encourages the formulation of questions in order to explore a concept or idea. Instead of simply presenting facts during a presentation, educators design learning environments, through which students pose questions that they later need to find answers to. This process of inquiry can either be simple or complex, requiring educators to facilitate the whole research process by trying to keep students excited and motivated about solving their own problems. Inquiry-based learning is usually presented in an iterative cyclical form, describing a sequence of procedures such as formulating questions, performing relevant investigation, discovering answers to those questions, and reflecting on those results. Inquiry-based learning strongly encourages collaborative work between peers through the exchange of ideas, resources, and tools among partners.

Inquiry-based learning consists of the following steps:

Ask: Students are presented with problematic situations, during which they are encouraged to pose their own questions. These situations can be organized or spontaneous. For example, by watching steam forming liquid drops on a pot lid presented by the teacher, kindergarten students may wonder how it is possible that water is both liquid and gas, starting a discussion about the water cycle. In another case, a non-provisioned software crash during a presentation in a computer science university department could initiate an inquiry into why software solutions may crash.

Investigate: The natural step after asking questions is that of investigation. During this step, learners enter an adventure where they need to collect information, filter it, and experiment. The process of investigation should be a self-motivating experience, driven by the curiosity of learners.

Create: After or during investigation, learners start reviewing the collected information. They compare it and shape it in a way that gives answers to their questions. This creative process, where learners generate new ideas and theories that are not directly related to their own perceptions, is creation.

Discuss: As we already saw, inquiry-based learning strongly encourages collaboration through exchange of information, resources, and ideas. During this step, students share information they have collected and discuss it with their partners. Comparing their findings and experiences during the previous steps, they acquire a greater perspective of the concept they examine.

Reflect: Reflection is the process of looking back. During reflection, learners revisit the whole inquiry process and try to see if they offered a solution to their problem and if the process they used in order to reach their conclusion was efficient or correct.

Inquiry-based learning is an iterative process. This means that after learners finish their reflection, they are back to step one. Inquiry-based learning, like all constructivist approaches, does not view learners' mistakes as something bad. On the contrary, mistakes created by learners are useful signs that help educators identify misconceptions about specific concepts. Mistakes can, in fact, be a very good starting point for initiating an inquiry or revisiting an inquiry that was already complete.

So, how can games be used in this context?

Actually, there are several ways that this can happen. These are just some of the ways that you could incorporate or facilitate inquiry-based sessions with games:

Games as tools for initiating an inquiry. Since games are effective at attracting people's interest, they are excellent tools for the introduction of inquiry-based sessions. Games can present a situation or idea and be used as the first step toward the initiation of questions on the subject matter. It's not even necessary that the same games will be used later on during the inquiry process as they will have already fulfilled their purpose: They introduced learners to the taught subject and helped them to reflect on it.

Games as tools of exploration. Working in the countryside, I was once asked to help a teacher friend who wanted to teach students about the herbs of a nearby forest. She had already presented the subject to her students, who were interested in exploring the forest and finding those herbs. The main problem was that the forest was rather big and splitting up the students without any guidance could make the activity take longer, making them feel bored, and lose track of its learning purposes. What we came up with was a game based on the use of a geographic information platform that allowed her to define points of interest in the forest, guiding students toward the herbs they needed to identify. Players were divided into teams that needed to find a particular set of herbs, identify them, and take photos of them using the school's tablets. The teams that succeeded in finding all herbs required would win. The tablets were equipped with an app that indicated the areas where those herbs grew. In this way, the game actually facilitated the discovery process by offering feedback to players and helping them to develop a better understanding of their local forest by facilitating the process of discovery.

Games as tools for discussion. A very common argument against the use of games in educational contexts is that they isolate players and do not help them develop their social skills. Like any tool, if designed and used properly, games can be very beneficial in collaborative work and the facilitation of discussions. We have all witnessed situations where the objectives of a game brought us closer to our peers in order to find strategies to solve problems. This can be the creation of a diversion for players to reach the "home base" undetected in hide- and-seek, the discussion about which answer is correct among teams of players in **Trivial Pursuit**, or whether the team splits up or sticks together in order to find its designated herbs in the exploration game mentioned previously. Discussion and collaboration can be encouraged or necessary if the mechanics of games are built toward it. As we will see in Chapter 9, there are different ways to achieve this, based on the priorities and objectives of the game designers.

Games can support inquiry-based learning either by fulfilling one or several of these cases. There are games that can be used solely as a means to present a subject and there are games that manage to present and facilitate the whole inquiry process. There are cases where educators find complete gaming solutions convenient for their teaching processes and there are other cases where they look for flexibility that will help them to adapt their courses to the individual needs of their audience.

REFLECTION POINTS

If you are going to apply some of the principles of inquiry-based learning in your games, try to identify which elements you would like to include in your game and how they will affect the game and your teaching approach.

As specified in this section, games can have different uses in the context of inquiry-based learning. What will be the function of your game? Will it be used as a tool for

- Initiating an inquiry?

- Exploration and facilitation of the learning process?

- Facilitation of discussion?

PROJECT-BASED LEARNING

Project-based learning is another constructivist approach that focuses on facilitating learning experiences through participating in and implementing projects. This approach has been advocated by several psychologists. Those educators considered that students can learn more efficiently when they are creating their own problems, while guided by the common goal of completing a project and being immersed in the challenges this task requires. Project-based learning incorporates procedures that require the use of knowledge in order to solve complex and challenging tasks, promotes collaborative work in small teams, and encourages students to take responsibility for completing the goals they have proposed.

Project-based learning combines various skills and learning approaches, such as inquiry-based learning, problem solving, experimentation, and exploration of one's environment. The main characteristic of this approach is the focus on the completion of a common goal: the project. The subject of the project can be either proposed by the educator or the learners. It can be spontaneous or organized. After the subject is proposed, learners decide on their audience and the nature of their end-product, and define the steps through which they will achieve their final goal. As the project moves forward, learners encounter problems that they need to solve. Usually they work in small teams that meet and discuss their progress frequently. During this process, educators act as facilitators. They prepare learning environments that will help learners to collaborate and raise as many questions as possible, and by observing teams, they offer help and guidance to help them find solutions to their problems.

Primary school student working on a project focused on forest life. (Used with permission of Maskott.)

During a training session on game design that I was facilitating, I had difficulty selecting a learning subject to work on. In our brainstorming sessions, however, I realized that some participants were interested in the topic of human rights and immigration. It was then clear what our topic would be! Moreover, it was chosen by the group. Initially we discussed the idea, we checked our resources, and the group was divided up into smaller teams. Each team would investigate a particular aspect of immigration and at continuous intervals all the teams would exchange information in order to finally set their mind on their final game. After fierce debates and a lot of discussion, the teams decided to come up with two different games, each of which would address immigration from different perspectives: One with an outdoor game played in a local square, and a set of board games played in a local café that the students knew. After three days, we had two finished games. The game were presented to the local community with a lot of discussion among the players and the game designers.

This was a project-based learning case. The project was set around the topic of immigration. The topic was not initially clear to the participants of the session, but they showed interest in it. That was the initial reason that we started this project. The participants later set their goals, took responsibility for them, and tried to complete them by solving each problem that arose during the process. There will always be problems that are not anticipated, and this is the interesting and challenging aspect of project-based learning.

Project-based learning is also connected to another constructivist approach, called **constructionism** [9]. In constructionism learners acquire more knowledge by using information they already know. Constructionists consider that through engagement in meaningful projects that students like, they will explore and discover new knowledge based on the skills and competences they already possess. Game design always has an aspect of project-based learning. This is primarily because designing and developing games are both parts of completing a game project. Project-based learning and game design is usually an interesting combination. That's why several tools have been introduced for this area. Programming languages like **Logo** and **Scratch** are very characteristic of this field and if you haven't have the chance to play with them, this is a good opportunity to do so!

PLAYERS' MULTIPLE INTELLIGENCES

Having worked in children's summer camps for several years, I had the opportunity to observe the development and evolution of several children that came every summer. Since I would also have the opportunity to meet their parents, I would frequently listen to complaints about their kids' performance during the school year. Some complaints would be about not paying attention in class, not doing their homework, not performing well in tests, being aggressive or indifferent, and the list goes on. It turned out that many of those particular kids turned out to have very interesting careers later on. Some of them became craftsmen, artists, or professional athletes; several others proved to have potential that was not covered by the curriculum offered at school, but that they discovered and developed after finishing school. These students were no less intelligent than the ones who performed better in curricular activities. They just processed knowledge in different ways.

In his book, **Frames of Mind: The Theory of Multiple Intelligences**, developmental psychologist Howard Gardner proposed the theory of multiple intelligences [10]. According to Gardner, instead of considering that our brain consists of one super computer responsible for our intelligence, the process of knowledge may happen in different parts of our brain, responsible for different types of intelligence. The development of each of those different types of intelligence may differ from person to person and this gives each individual the ability to understand and give meaning to the world through their own perspective.

Attention is advised! Gardner opposed the idea of labeling learners according to specific intelligences. He preferred to use this theory as a tool that would offer another perspective in learning environments by offering more diverse resources to learners. The theory of multiple intelligences advocates for diversity in learning, providing an alternative perspective on traditional learning approaches. It would hence be futile to use it just as an alternative way to simply categorize learners. As we already pointed out, there are no fixed formulas in learning. Consequently, it is strongly suggested that you use this theory wisely.

So, one of the most important points of the theory of multiple intelligences is the emphasis that not everyone learns in the same way and that teaching approaches should take this into consideration. If you have the opportunity to design your game in a way that your learning resources are presented in a diverse way and will be better perceived by a variety of learners, then you have already moved one step toward creating games with greater learning impact. The theory of multiple intelligences also offers the opportunity for designers to consider combining learning topics in their games. Considering that a game resource can have a different impact on different players, combining or developing particular cognitive areas is always an interesting topic. The intelligence modalities proposed by Gardner include the following:

Verbal-linguistic: One's sensitivity to the sounds, rhythms, and meanings of words as well as the different functions of language. People with evolved verbal-linguistic intelligence are good at reading, writing, or narrating stories.

Logical-mathematical: Related to one's capacity to understand the underlying patterns of causal systems, scientific reasoning, and deduction. People with evolved logical-mathematical intelligence are able to handle long chains of reasoning.

Musical-rhythmical: Related to one's appreciation, awareness, and use of music or any type of sounds. People with evolved musical-rhythmical intelligence have a higher sensitivity to rhythm, pitch, and timbre.

Visual-spatial: One's capacity to perceive the visual-spatial world with accuracy and perform mental transformations.

Bodily-kinesthetic: The ability to control one's body movements and handle objects with skill.

Interpersonal: One's set of capacities to respond appropriately to the moods, temperaments, and desires of other people. People with high interpersonal skills can empathize easily and communicate effectively with other people.

Intrapersonal: One's ability to identify their own strengths, weaknesses, desires, and feelings, and analyze them efficiently in order to regulate their behavior.

Naturalistic: Related to people's ability to connect with their environment, recognize flora and fauna, as well as make other consequential distinctions in the natural world.

Gardner's theory is highly influential in educational game design for two main reasons. First of all, it becomes evident that not everyone approaches their environment in the same way but, instead, that people use their own individual learning mechanisms in order to give meaning to the world around them. This means that games should also be able to address those individual mechanisms of players. In practice this usually happens when games are introduced as an alternative means of education that accompanies formal learning environments. Another way is that game designers take into account the individual particularities of their audience and either design games that can be adjusted to those particularities or specialize their designs from the very beginning of the design process in order to address them. We will examine this point again in Chapter 7, which is dedicated to understanding your audience.

The second reason is that the theory of multiple intelligences indicates a great diversity and variety in the ways games can address learners. Since not everyone learns in the same way, each game can address one or several of these multiple intelligences and create learning experiences that focus on the development of related skills.

THE BEST LEARNING THEORY

As a player, I am a fan of trading card games, like **Magic: The Gathering and Hearthstone**. In such trading card games, players are asked to create their own decks of cards in order to enter duels against other card holders. In order to win, players need a combination of skill, luck, and good selection of cards in their deck, as several of those cards can be combined in order to enhance their abilities. The more I was playing this type of game, the more I realized that there is no single deck that will always win. Some decks work better over particular decks, let alone that the combination of cards in a deck should match the personality and combat style of each player. Similarly, in almost every case in game design and education, there is not always one correct path to success.

There is no single best theory that can be applied to any context. My personal advice to any aspiring educator or game designer is that a good understanding of learning theories is very important only as a means of developing one's individual teaching skills and perspective. It is very common for students of pedagogy, after studying about learning theories, to tag themselves as behaviorists, constructivists, cognitivists, and so on. Even if this is one way to go, it is important to emphasize that even some of the great minds that proposed those theories shifted their focus and ideas as those theories matured and were applied in classrooms. Jean Piaget's work spans from cognitive psychology to constructivism. Lev Vygotsky, who died several years before constructivism was formed as a theory, proposed several constructivist approaches. The theory of Albert Bandura, who is considered a behaviorist, consists of several constructivist elements. If these great thinkers kept an open mind to their approach on learning, I strongly advise that you do too!

The best way to work with the theories presented previously is to be inspired and identify which of their elements can be used in your games. Not all audiences have the same needs and priorities. Also, not all players learn in the same way. On top of this, game designers are constantly facing practical challenges, like technical limitations, limited resources, and specific learning objectives, posed by clients or national curricula. In our personal experiences we have all met various kinds of teachers who have affected us in different ways. These people had different teaching approaches. In the same way, your games need to reflect your personal design and teaching approach that keeps the motivation of players high while helping them to conquer the concepts you want to teach.

REFLECTION POINTS 🔍

There are always several options concerning learning theories that can be used in one's games. This is a nice opportunity to reflect on those options and figure out the direction that you will apply to your games.

- Are there particular elements of learning theories that you consider important for your game's nature? What do you want to achieve by integrating those approaches in your games?

- Are there any learning aspects of those theories that you would like to avoid and why?

- What is the role of the educator or the educational game in the learning process?

- What is the role of the learner in the learning process? Are the individual needs and priorities of learners taken into account?

LEARNING OBJECTIVES

Understanding and shaping pedagogic perspectives based on learning theories is a very important aspect of educational game design. Learning theories provide general frameworks and guidelines that provide educators with tools and resources in order to better facilitate the design of learning environments. However, those concepts need to be applied to your designs when creating educational games. In order to achieve this, you need to have a concrete idea of the things you want to teach and what you want to achieve by designing and presenting your games to potential players. This is why learning objectives are so important in educational game design.

A very common problem in educational game design appears when designers don't have a clear idea of what they need to teach. "Teaching science or history" at this stage of game design is a vague statement and does not provide you with a concrete and sturdy basis to proceed with developing your project. If you lack perspective on educational design at this point, it's highly likely that you will return to this stage later in the development process, requiring more resources, development time, and budget. This means loss of time, money, and patience!

So, let's examine two concepts that have proved to be helpful in educational game design: learning aims and objectives. **Learning aims** are general statements set to describe the main outcome of your game. For example, let's say that you were asked to design a video game focused on training players how to drive cars. The learning aim of this game would be to enable players to operate a driving vehicle. This statement is general. People who will read it, can understand the general outcome of playing the game, but they do not have an idea of how this is going to be achieved. If you start designing your games with only a learning aim, you will start with many questions still unanswered. That's why aims need to be accompanied by objectives.

If learning aims present the general idea and learning outcome of your game, **learning objectives** are small steps that will help you achieve those aims. Learning objectives are smaller statements regarding specific performances and their completion. These objectives in fact articulate the different skills that need to be conquered by the end of your game and the necessary knowledge that is required to achieve them. Setting learning objectives helps designers to have a better understanding of the direction of their game and how to reach a final product that will be both entertaining and educational. The process of putting learning objectives on paper will also help you and your team reflect on what you really want to teach your players, which is not always that clear at the beginning of the design process.

Learning objectives are immediately related to the nature of your game. They will directly or indirectly influence its design, mechanics, implementation, and delivery to players. On the other hand, the nature of the game can also have an impact on your learning objectives. These two elements will always affect each other throughout the whole design process. In the next chapters we will see how you can prioritize the impact of these two aspects. In any case, though, as designers you want to deliver immersive learning experiences. And in order to be sure that you deliver such experiences, you need to monitor and assess them. Through assessment throughout your game, you will be able to see if your learning objectives are fulfilled with the current gaming activities you propose. Since assessment is a very important aspect in educational game design, we will cover it in a later chapter as well. For the moment, your first goal is to propose your learning objectives. Here are some tips that will help you to articulate your learning objectives:

Tip #1: Learning objectives need to be clear and simple.

As we already saw, learning objectives are little steps that will help your players reach your main learning goal. A tip that I usually propose is that learning objectives should be clear and simple.

Nine out of ten times, if you cannot express your learning objectives in short sentences, your objectives can be broken down into more steps. Of course, this is not always the case; there may be situations or concepts where you will need to present complex concepts or become rather precise by using larger word structures. However, try to keep simplicity as a main element in setting your objectives. The more vague and generic your learning objectives are, the cloudier your design options will be.

Another important aspect of writing learning objectives is that each objective should focus on the development and application of a specific cognitive process. If, for example, the objective of your game is to help players learn the Korean language, you will probably have three different objectives for speaking, reading, and writing. By doing so and breaking down your aim into learning objectives you will be able to design relevant game mechanics that will help players to develop those competencies.

Tip #2: Learning objectives should be measurable.

We briefly talked about assessment before and we are going to examine it thoroughly in Chapter 13. In brief, assessment helps educators and game designers monitor the performance of players in the way they learn and play. Assessment is possible when the criteria that were set through the learning objectives are being met. This is why learning objectives should be formed in a way that can be measured. As we will also see later, in order to ensure that learning takes place those learning objectives need to be included in considerations correctly! Let's see an example in the following learning objective of a math game:

Players will understand counting.

This seems like a simple learning objective. But was it correctly formulated? In order to reply to this question, let's try to see if it is easily measurable. If, for example, students are asked to count from one to 100, did they master counting? What about beginning to count from other numbers, like starting from 12 and counting forward? Or what about counting by twos or fives? We can see that this learning objective becomes rather vague in this context. It is important to keep in mind that elements that fail to be specified in your learning objectives make their assessment more difficult, causing potential problems in measuring a game's impact later on. The more concrete and specific you are, the better you will be able to later measure the impact of your game towards your learning objectives.

Tip #3: Learning objectives should be player-oriented.

Even if learning objectives reflect the educator's perspective and teaching goals, they acquire a more interesting perspective when they put players at the center of the learning process. By placing players at the center of your learning objectives you will have the opportunity to explore the needs and particularities of your target group and better reflect on the nature of your objectives. If, for example, you were again to design a game that would help players learn Hangul, the Korean alphabet, instead of presenting your learning objective like this:

I want to present players with material that will help them learn Hangul.

It is better to present your learning objective like this:

Players should be able to read and write the characters of Hangul.

REFLECTION POINTS 🔍

Identifying your learning aims and objectives is one of the most important phases in the process of educational game design. The first questions that you should be able to answer are

- What are your learning aims?

- What are your learning objectives?

Were your learning objectives formulated and presented in an efficient way? Learning objectives that fail to be simple, clear, and concrete will likely cause confusion, friction, and loss of time. In order to analyze and review your learning objectives, try to answer the following questions for each objective you propose:

- Is your learning objective clear and simple? Can you explain your learning objective to your peers in a way that is easily comprehensible to them? If they can't understand it or if you need to offer additional clarification, it's highly likely that you need to revise your learning objective.

- Is your learning objective measurable?

- Does your learning objective take into consideration your audience and its particularities?

INCORPORATING CURRICULA

It is natural that educators have their own teaching approaches. So, even from the Renaissance period it became apparent that if education is not coordinated from a universal body or institution, students from different regions or schools may learn totally different things. Having the freedom and ability to shift the focus onto topics that they considered important, educators might focus more on one topic and omit another. Different nations understood that there should be a global coordination on the concepts taught in school in order to ensure that students who finish different education levels have studied the same learning fields. This need gave birth to curricula.

The nature of a curriculum can vary depending on context and place. In any case, though, curriculum refers to a general framework that offers directions regarding students' learning experiences in a learning environment or guidelines about delivery of learning content in learning contexts. Usually, curricula are intended to ensure standardized content across different institutions or provide guidance about the sequence of learning activities. Their nature varies for different situations and the learning theories that have inspired their authors. Consequently, there are curricula that are firmly organized, leaving very little space for educators to improvise, and there are others that offer great autonomy inside the boundaries of a teaching framework. There can be curricula for any topic, such as math, language, arts, science, history, and so on.

Even if it sometimes proves to be a challenging or frustrating aspect, understanding, and incorporating curricula within educational games is necessary. The most important reason is that in several countries, resources that do not encapsulate national curricula are either not proposed as relevant learning resources and in some cases are restricted in public institutions. Another important reason, especially for game designers with young audiences, is that when it comes to education, parents will prefer learning resources that are connected to their national curriculum. So, understanding the curricula of your target audience becomes an indispensable asset for your design.

A great challenge so far for the educational game design industry is that national curricula vary in approaches, focus, and content from area to area. Australia, for instance, has the Australian Curriculum, the United Kingdom has the National Curriculum, France has the Programme

Nationale, and the United States puts forward Common Core even if, in the end, individual states can propose their own curricula. This means that games that are in line with the curriculum in one country might not be in another. For example, the topic covered for a particular age or class may be taught later in another curriculum. This is one of the greatest challenges of educational game design when it comes to projects with large audiences. Even if integrating aspects of a curriculum while designing games for a classroom, a school, or a local community might not be such a big issue, doing the same for a game aiming to sell in different countries might prove very difficult.

If you consider that you need to work with national learning curricula for the game you want to design, it is best that you start your research at the earliest stages of game development. In this case, your learning objectives should also reflect the impact of the curriculum in your design. If different curricula apply to your main audience (if for example you want to sell your game both in the United States and Europe), you should examine if there are common points between them and, more importantly, if there are differences in the teaching approaches they propose. In cases like this you can design games that encapsulate the common points and later expand your learning objectives based on the freedom you get from the curricula you are addressing. There are also many cases where two or more curricula are not aligned or they are rather strict, and in that case, you should consider reducing the scope of your audience. Sound complicated already?

PERSPECTIVE

Q&A with Jenn Helms
Co-Founder of Playmation Studios

How do you combine learning and gaming elements in order to create your games?
Learning becomes a game when you use a systems-based approach to game design. By starting with the system you want the player to explore, whether it is the system of English syntax or the system of algebra, you can immerse the player in your educational objectives. The outcome of this approach is that there is no longer a chasm between the learning and the gameplay. For instance, in **Sleep Furiously EDU**, one overall objective is for the player to learn what patterns of words result in a structurally correct sentence. Players learn this through the gameplay. By consciously putting together words within the game, players can learn how those words come together to form a sentence and when they do not. Other game elements are added in to reinforce that learning such as a point system and stars.

The important distinction with this approach and many other attempts at educational games is that those game elements aren't just used in an attempt to make dry textbook material game-like. Instead, the learning itself becomes playful when the academic system is turned into a world the player can explore.

How do you evaluate your games' impact on players?
Evaluation is a major hurdle for small development studios. In the beginning, we had to rely on qualitative feedback and observation during playtesting sessions. We have found playtesting to be incredibly valuable in our design iteration process. We have been able to uncover when players are stuck, what is confusing, and how the difficulty level is responded to. From observation and from qualitative feedback, we were able to conclude that our games were having significant educational impact on players.

Over time, we have also had our game **Stagecraft** tested as part of a PhD student's thesis. We were excited to have our game be a part of their work, but even in this study, the sample size was too small to be conclusive. We are now giving access to Sleep Furiously EDU to a non-profit in exchange for usage data, which is great. Paying for an independent, third-party study has not been something we could afford. My advice to small studios is to playtest often and to look for creative partnerships that can get you access to data that will allow you to evaluate your game further.

How important are prototypes in your design process? How do you use them?

Prototypes are essential to our process. Prototypes allow us to answer essential questions early on, such as the following: (1) Is the gameplay fun? (2) If there is something difficult technologically, can we pull it off? (3) Can the entire team be brought into the vision? (4) What concerns do we need to address before we can commit to developing this game further? It is important to remember that prototypes need to be made as simply as possible to address the above questions. The longer your team spends on a prototype, the more time you might be wasting on a game concept that does not go anywhere. Our first prototype of Sleep Furiously was made in three days. It was very rudimentary but it allowed us to answer all of the above questions, giving us confidence as we moved forward.

Any advice for potential educational game designers (ideas, examples, suggestions to structure their thinking and work)?

A great place to start is to focus on a subject area that you are already an expert in. Once you have narrowed down your expertise, what systems are there to explore? How can you create a world in which the player can inhabit that system? What could the player's goal be interacting with that system? Once you have an idea, prototype the basics and ask yourself if it is fun to play. It can be helpful to play other successful systems-based games for inspiration such as **Kerbal Space Program** and **Sim City**. Keep in mind, however, that it can be easy to fall into the trap of trying to emulate what has already worked. What our field needs is new innovative designs and the best way to uncover those is to explore new ideas within your field of expertise and then prototype and iterate.

One final recommendation is to reach out to communities of other game designers for support and inspiration. I believe this is important enough that I founded a new conference in the San Francisco Bay Area in 2016 to bring together professionals on the topic of games for learning and meaningful purpose: The Intentional Play Summit.

What is the most important virtue of an educational game designer?

There are a few essential virtues. The first is curiosity. An educational game designer needs to be someone who is constantly learning new things. The second is a willingness to experiment. As a game designer learns new things, how can what is being learned be expressed through new game mechanics and environments? The third is to be observant. It is essential to be in tune to the feedback you receive from playtesting sessions. The fourth is to be humble yet confident. As a game designer, you have to be humble enough to take constructive feedback and recognize when your game needs an improvement, even if that challenges your prior beliefs. At the same time, you have to be confident enough to discern when the feedback makes sense or when there is a different problem or solution at work.

It is important to note that these are virtues of all great game designers. Too often we make a weightier distinction between educational game design and other game design than there really is. The big difference between educational game design and other game design really comes down to objectives. What sort of learning is it that you want your player to take away from your game? If your educational game is being used in schools that question becomes, how can your game support the teachers' objectives in their classrooms?

Even if working with curricula can be a painful process, it is part of an educational game designer's role. The more games you will design and the more interaction you will have with educators, districts, or national institutions, the more comfortable you will be integrating curricula into your game designs.

SUMMARY

In this chapter we covered the following topics:

- Games can be approached as problem-solving activities. Viewing game design as a problem creation activity can offer great insight into the designed games.

- We explored the role and qualities of educators in educational game design and examined the notions of the Zone of Proximal Development and scaffolding.

- We examined some of the most prominent learning theories, such as behaviorism, cognitivism, and constructivism.

- Not all players learn in the same way. Players learn in different ways and rhythms, and approach games differently.

- Games can be interesting tools for facilitating and organizing inquiry and project-based learning activities.

- Being able to define and express your games' learning objectives is a crucial aspect of your designs. Learning objectives need to be clear, simple, measurable, and player-oriented.

- Games are usually parts of broader learning scenarios or curricula. Hence, being able to align your games' learning objectives with those curricula can make them more efficient and approachable to a bigger range of people, professions, and institutions.

REFERENCES

1. Schell, J. (2014). *The Art of Game Design: A Book of Lenses* (2nd ed). London & New York: CRC Press.
2. Groos, K. (1976). *The Play of Animals* (K. Groos & E. L. Baldwin, Trans.). New York: D Appleton & Company.
3. Polya, G. (1945). *How to Solve It*. A New Aspect of Mathematical Method. Princeton, NJ: Princeton University Press.
4. Vygotsky, L (1978). *Mind in Society: The Development of Higher Psychological Processes*. Cambridge, MA: Harvard University Press.
5. Wood, D., Bruner, J. S., and Ross, G. (1976). The role of tutoring in problem solving. *Journal of Child Psychology and Psychiatry, 17*, 89–100.
6. Skinner, B. F. (1948). "Superstition" in the pigeon. *Journal of Experimental Psychology, 38*(2), 168–172.
7. Bartlett, F. C., & Bartlett, F. C. (1995). *Remembering: A Study in Experimental and Social Psychology*. Cambridge: Cambridge University Press.
8. Lapsley, D. K. (2006). Moral stage theory. In M. Killen & J. G. Smetana (Eds.), *Handbook of Moral Development* (pp. 37–66). Mahwah, NJ: Lawrence Erlbaum Associates Publishers.
9. Papert, S., & I. Harel (1991). Situating constructionism. In S. Papert & I. Harel (Eds.), *Constructionism: Research Reports and Essays* (pp. 1–11). Norwood, New Jersey: Ablex Publishing.
10. Gardner, H. (1983). *Frames of Mind: The Idea of Multiple Intelligences*. New York: Basic Books.

4 The Game Core

This chapter:

- Elaborates on how to approach and start game design projects.

- Explores the notion of the game core.

- Examines the need for planning and anticipating the resources for a game's creation.

Game design can be a very challenging and complex process. Being able to anticipate and solve design and communication issues from the beginning of the design process can be a crucial step toward the creation of final games. From this need, the notion of the game core is born and examined.

THE MAGIC RECIPE

Have no fear of perfection—you'll never reach it.

–Salvador Dalí

One of Albert Einstein's greatest challenges was the explanation of all the fundamental forces in the universe through a single theory. The unified field theory, as it is called, aimed to describe the behavior of any element on a macroscopic and microscopic scale in the universe. Einstein died without finding an answer to whether such a theory was possible. A similar question to Einstein's constantly arises in educational game design. **Is there a successful formula that leads to intrinsically motivating learning experiences through gaming?**

Before we answer this question, let's take a look at some interesting cases of using games in teaching contexts.

Case 1: An educational game focusing on the development of players' spatial thinking was presented in a school in a rural area. The game presented players with hotspots in their local area, each of which would feature a special challenge. The game was played on tablets and smartphones and required an Internet connection in order to download some of its content and allow players to chat with each other. The game was also based on global positioning systems in order to detect players' locations. The team that created it had already tested the game in other schools and its evaluation so far was quite positive toward the development of spatial thinking skills. However, the game design team did not anticipate that the location of this particular school was in the countryside, surrounded by mountains and the Internet connection was weak or at times nonexistent. In the end, many of the game's functionalities could not be used and players felt frustrated or tired at not being able to play the game properly.

Case 2: A group of trainers, wanting to introduce the topic of cultural diversity in their seminar, organized a board game that would get players to discuss the topic and build upon the different participants' perspectives about culture. The group of trainers had already played this game in training sessions, where the participants were a mix of Asian and European citizens, with great success. In this case, the trainers played the game with only a group of Asian players. However, the game was not very successful this time. Participants did not share very different opinions and avoided confrontation, contrary to previous cases of more culturally mixed groups. A game that was very successful on previous occasions, in this case, proved to be not very effective.

As we can see from these cases, games that have great results under one set of circumstances won't always have the same impact in others. There are several reasons for this. First of all, as we saw in the previous chapter, not everyone approaches knowledge and the world around them in the same way. Consequently, you cannot expect that all players will react to your games in the same way. Secondly, experiences acquire value and meaning under particular contexts and circumstances and are connected to elements like the correct timing of presenting the game, preparation of players or proper preparation in terms of equipment and materials.

In fact, building upon the appeal and learning experience of your games is a challenging and constantly evolving task that usually does not happen instantaneously. There are cases where reading a book, looking at a painting, or watching a movie will impact some people by appealing to their contemporary emotional state or events happening around them in society. But the same situations may fail to have the same effect on others who did not share the same emotional or experiential state. In the same way, games can have an impact by building immersive learning experiences based on the combination of factors revolving around your players.

It is highly possible that players who play a game at a specific point in their life may not have the same experience playing the same game at a different time. This is because players and their environments constantly evolve. Consequently, any element of your potential game should adapt to the needs of a particular teaching situation. Elements like rules, narrative, aesthetics, technological implementation, and even learning objectives are not absolute but are subject to change in order to achieve a particular experience.

Until a magic theory that accounts for all those aspects is discovered, game designers are entrusted with the amazing and challenging task of finding the correct recipe that will serve up an immersive learning experiences for different situations. Still, there are tools that can seriously help the game design process—some of which we will present in this chapter.

THE EDUCATIONAL GAME DESIGNER'S JOURNEY

I consider making games like heading off on a great adventure. During this journey you explore new territories, overcome obstacles, and learn more about yourself. At the end, you come back stronger than ever! Like every journey, the game designer's destination and the path to reach it are not always clear from the beginning. Several elements regarding learning objectives, audience perspective, game mechanics, aesthetics, narrative, and technical restrictions will very possibly arise during this journey, sometimes all at once! Not knowing one's final destination is not necessarily a bad thing. On the contrary, in some cases, it can be an opportunity for the creation of something great.

However, a sense of direction and an overall perspective is always helpful in designing intrinsically motivating learning experiences. There are mainly two reasons for this: First, it is common that game designers shift their focus toward particular game elements such as learning objectives, evaluation, mechanics, or aesthetics, paying less attention to other ones. Hold on a second! Shouldn't educational games put greater emphasis on educational aspects? The answer is simple. Educational games that only develop the educational aspect stand out like an orchestra with only one good trumpet player. The trumpet player may be exquisite, but the whole experience seems off. In the same way, you should avoid producing games where it is obvious that a few elements were very well thought out and others were underdeveloped.

The second reason is that multidisciplinary teams usually consist of experts from very different fields, such as game design, graphics, programming, pedagogy, or the game industry. Without proper preparation and a facilitation of the work process, those teams can easily become trapped in endless loops, where experts from individual fields will focus on the field they know about and feel safe with, trying to build solely around that. In some cases, due to deadline restrictions or budgetary reasons stemming from this lack of communication, game projects may get scrapped or postponed.

I was once part of a group responsible for the creation of a game for teaching language to primary school students with visual and auditory impairment. The group consisted of experts in the fields of education, developers, designers, artists, and instructional designers. Completing this game proved to be one of the greatest challenges in my life! Each partner in the group had their own vision of the game, focusing on the aspect they knew the most. For some the game was about teaching language, for others it was a game about working with students with auditory impairment, and for others it was a game focusing on students with visual impairment. On top of this, the team could not agree on the nature of the game. Some partners insisted on designing a set of quizzes that could be presented with a playful attitude. On the other hand, the game designers of the team were furious about this idea and came up with their own versions of what they thought would be more suitable. By the end, the whole design process was a disaster for everybody, having a great impact on the final result.

This story presents a common situation in educational game design. The main issue of this team is that its members did not have or share the same vision of the final game outcome. When game designers do not have a clear perspective of the final learning experience they want to create, the final result will end up causing friction, losing time and money, and producing a final game with no impact on players. In order to start with a concrete basis when initiating new game design projects, I use the tool of the game core. Let's see how it works.

THE GAME CORE

One of the first questions I ask to aspiring game designers that come forward with a new game idea is to describe the absolutely essential elements that are required to create their games. The main reason behind this question is to offer designers the opportunity to reflect on the nature of their game and consider what elements are fundamental for the learning experience they want to create. This question is not always easy to answer, since it requires designers to reflect on their game ideas, analyze them, break them into pieces, and try to give answers to questions that were previously unclear in their minds. The fruit of this labor is a list of elements that are indispensable for their game. This set of elements is the **game core**.

The game core comes in very handy in game design situations for many reasons. First of all, it provides designers with the opportunity to reflect on their concepts and critically examine their ideas by identifying which elements of the game are fundamental to the experience they intend to design. Whether this is the establishment of a particular atmosphere or the communication of a message, proposing one's game core is a great opportunity for thinking about the game as a whole entity.

A SENSE OF DIRECTION

More importantly, though, the game core is a concrete basis for the design of any game. While designing games, I tend to hear more comments and suggestions on what the designed game should not be. I strongly disagree with this approach! I believe that trying to define a game based on what it should not be is rather inefficient. This is because comments of this sort are not usually accompanied by suggestions or solutions. So, at the end, the team ends up with restrictions but not solutions! Hence, teams can be trapped in great loops, defining what their games are not like but not actually working on the form of their games.

On the other hand, I am a great fan of the "The game should be …" phrase! Even if the proposed idea may not be used at the end, it offers a perspective that can be evaluated and either be scrapped or give birth to something interesting.

By designing the core, designers reflect on the elements that absolutely must exist in their concept. Since this is not a procedure that takes place instantaneously, the designers will need to give answers to questions that will come up during the proposal of their core. It's better to bump into those questions at this phase of the design process than to stumble upon them later on.

On top of this, the game core can be used as a way of analyzing and examining existing games, allowing designers or educators to identify the elements that characterize the essence of a proposed game. In any case, the game core is just an approach on initiating game design concepts that should be adapted to the individual needs of each designer and teaching situation. Consequently, it can either be used as a jumping-off point for an initial discussion about the nature and direction of a game project so that game designers can clarify aspects that were unclear before, or it can form the basis of the development process of a game.

DESIGNING ONE'S CORE

Game designers can structure their core any way they prefer. After all, the game core is an opportunity to envision your final game and set a starting point for your game design workflow. I prefer structuring game cores for my games based on the game triangle that we saw in Chapter 2. We previously presented the game triangle, consisting of three main axes: the game, the player, and the learning aspect. The concept of the game triangle aims to provide designers with an overall perspective of the three main elements of educational game design. Throughout this book we will try to analyze and examine this triangle, its axes, and their attributes through various perspectives and examine how they are interrelated, offering us intrinsically motivating learning experiences.

Each axis of the game design triangle, game, player, and learning aspect, consists of individual attributes that give a particular texture to the final game. The axis of a learning aspect, for example, consists of learning objectives, learning approaches, the aspect of feedback, evaluation, and several other attributes that we will explore throughout the book. The game core consists of attributes of each of these axes that are important for designers to be clear about from the very beginning of the game design process and may guide game designers toward creating their final gaming experience.

Let's imagine that a game design team was asked to design an outdoor treasure hunt game to teach players about the Olympic Games. In a case like this, three elements forge the team's game core. The first one is the genre of the game, since the team was asked to design a treasure hunt game. On top of this, the team needs to take into consideration that the game needs to be played outside of classrooms. The third element of the game core is related to the learning aspect and more specifically, it provides the learning aim of the game: the Olympic Games. The nature of players is not specified in this case, providing the game design team with the opportunity to decide on their audience. By figuring out their game core, game designers establish a concrete starting point that will help them to avoid future issues like technical restrictions, communication problems, finding materials that will affect deadlines, budget, member motivation, and the final impact of the designed game.

Imagine that you wake up in the morning and have a craving for apple pie. Your mind is set toward a specific taste: The magic smell of caramelized apple inside a nicely baked crust. In order to satisfy this need, you can either buy a cooked apple pie or bake your own. But there is not just one way to get or bake an apple pie. There are many different recipes out there or bakeries that offer different kinds of homemade favorite. The concept of the game core is not very distant from the idea of a great apple pie! If we consider that you are a baker, the minimum characteristics of the dish you are making is that it should be a pie that contains apples. Details, such as the rest of the ingredients, baking tools, the method of cooking, and so on are up to you. All other elements of completing the recipe are yours to decide. This is also how the game core works as a tool.

Creating one's game core is only the beginning of the design process. The game core represents only a small fraction of one's game elements. Its initial purpose is to serve as a starting point for the creation of a game. Inevitably the structure of the core will change, evolve, and grow as designers continue working on their games. During this process new rules will be added or modified, winning conditions will change, or game player interactions will be altered. By adding new elements to their games, game designers actually expand the core of their games, leading to their final game.

But building on a game core is not always straightforward. New game elements might not be in line with existing ones. For example, if a game core targets an adult audience, a later change of the audience to include children might create a conflict in the design process, since that might affect the final game experience. I find there are three ways of working with one's core to facilitate the game design process. I call them the unbreakable core, the flexible core, and the hybrid core. Let's dive in!

Approach No. 1: The Unbreakable Core

As its name suggests, the unbreakable core is the approach of working on your game design project with a game core that does not change as the design process proceeds. It is like it was set in stone. This means that the priorities and elements that the game designers envisioned at the beginning of the design process remain the same throughout.

In some cases, unbreakable cores may be the only option game designers have. Let's imagine that a client comes with a game project and asks you to design it. Whether this client is a multinational company that wants to train its employees, an academic institution that has developed a particular pedagogic approach for a certain subject, or a group of your peers that has a vision, you are presented with a set of requirements, priorities, and restrictions that were already predefined by someone else and, possibly, you cannot change.

But is this a good approach toward designing games? It depends on the structure of the core. There are cases where game design teams want to make sure that their games will fulfill a number of standards, such as targeting a particular audience or addressing specific learning objectives. In this case, unbreakable cores act as a mechanism of ensuring that those conditions will be met.

The use of unbreakable cores, though, comes with a price. Cores that are unbreakable need to be small. The main reason for this is that big cores of this kind are very difficult to work with later on in the design process. As expected, if a great number of elements are predefined and not prone to evolution or change, due to sticking to this way of work, incoming feedback and evaluation are not integrated in the developed game, which in most cases can lead to catastrophic results. Taking into account that educational games always require game designers to consider the particularities for the particular audience and instance in which their games are presented, the inappropriate use of this technique can lead to games that may fail to appeal to their audience. So, if you opt for this way of working, make sure that the elements that you wish to keep the same throughout the design process are few and important.

Approach No. 2: The Flexible Core

Flexible cores are the exact opposite of unbreakable cores. If unbreakable cores always stay the same, adopting a flexible core approach means that the game core constantly changes throughout the design process. Someone may ask: If the core changes, why was it proposed in the first place? The main use of the flexible core is that it offers an initial starting point for the design process. This is very helpful if you consider that educational game design teams without an initial starting point may waste considerable amounts of time trying to define their scope.

Flexible cores may consist of any number of elements that designers consider crucial for the shaping of the gaming experience. During the design process, the elements of the core will be prone to change based on the brainstorming sessions, the ideas of the team, the players' feedback, and playtesting. It is even possible that designers who adopt this approach will finally end up with games that are ways off the initial game core. For example, in a game design workshop once, a team of teachers wanted to come up with an educational game. They had not settled on any topic, game genre, learning approach, or anything else. This team had no initial restrictions, so they could work with a flexible core. They started their design with an educational game about history. As their design process continued, they realized that their game would fit another learning topic better. So, in the end they presented a game about geology. Of course, not all designers have this freedom or possibility to change subjects, but when it comes about, the use of a flexible core is a viable option.

Flexible game cores offer great maneuverability, as they do not have particular restrictions later on. However, this great flexibility and freedom may shift the focus of a team from their learning objectives or any other priority they might have. So, flexible cores are not always the best solution to approaching game design. I find flexible cores to be handy as training exercises for aspiring game designers.

Approach No. 3: The Hybrid Core

There are many situations where a combination of firm reference points and some flexibility is required. Think of a client coming with an idea about a game. Some aspects of the game may have already been defined by the client, but it's also possible that a number of decisions will be up to the game designer. Here, despite some restrictions, several decisions will need to be made at the beginning that could be integrated into the game core. These proposed elements should be able to change during the design process. In a case like this, you can use a hybrid core.

The hybrid core consists of two types of elements: some that cannot change and some that may change during the process. For example, if you are asked to design a game to teach Japanese to native English speakers, you already have a set of defined learning objectives. The game will focus on this area but the structure of the game is entirely up to you. So, let's say that you come up with the idea of a digital board game. Your decision at this phase gives shape to the game core. Later on, though, the feedback you receive from your prototypes and initial testers may lead you to reconsider and change the game genre to a digital card game. In this example, designing a game about teaching Japanese to English native speakers is an element that cannot change. On the other hand, the game genre can be changed.

REFLECTION POINTS 🔍

- What are the absolutely essential elements that define your game?

- By this point do you have an understanding of your audience, learning objectives, and the gaming experience you want to create?

- If you are working in a team, are those elements shared and understood by all its members?

- Have you settled upon a way of using your game core? Will you use any aspects of

  - The unbreakable core?

  - The flexible core?

  - The hybrid core?

GAMES ARE BUILT USING RESOURCES

A group of high school teachers once approached me with a game idea. It was a very ambitious outdoor game, organized throughout the whole city, played by thousands of students at the same time, and aimed at teaching players about environmental sustainability. The idea was very interesting and their learning objectives were quite clear and concrete. There was just a big problem: They had not seriously considered how the game could be implemented. Excited about their idea, they put great effort into trying to make it a reality. However, the great demands of this enterprise finally caused the project to be aborted. Those educational game designers failed to anticipate the resources they needed in order to implement their game.

The implementation of any game needs resources. Whether games are physical, digital, or mental, their proposal and implementation require some type of materials. Those materials may vary from pens and paper for the design of a tic-tac-toe board to highly advanced software solutions for the creation of 3D graphics. Physical games require a great deal of preparation and identification of materials for their implementation. Board games, such as **The Settlers of Catan**, **Cranium**, and **Ticket to Ride**, come with carton boards, dice, cards, wooden or plastic pieces, and tokens. On the other hand, video games require the use of software tools, such as graphics engines, 3D modeling solutions, or animation packages.

Resources are not only restricted to the use of materials. They also include the people and the know-how that are necessary to create games. Video games, in the majority of cases, cannot be created without game developers. Even if a game developer may not be hired, at the end, the designer or a member of the design team will have to do some programming in order to implement the final game. In the same way, technical teams that want to design educational games will at some point need the expertise of an educational expert about the topics they want to present.

It goes without saying that successful game designers can comprehend technical restrictions. Technical restrictions delineate the limit that games can reach with the technology that exists at a given time. In other words, they are what can and cannot be done with one's available resources. An example of technical restrictions can be found in game graphics. Even if modern graphic engines can offer high-quality images, the graphic cards of several computers, smartphones, and tablets cannot accommodate those functions. Technical restrictions can be related to any aspect of the game, such as the printing house's color limitations and costs for a game's board and cards, the hardware and software infrastructure required for an online game to be played by a great number of players, or the number of facilitators required to guide and manage thousands of players for a city marathon.

I believe that being ambitious is a great asset for aspiring educational game designers. However, I try to distinguish ambition from ignorance. Ambition is related to one's positive attitude toward challenging tasks and understanding their complexity and difficulty. Ignorance, on the other hand, is related to the lack of perspective over an issue and it can be catastrophic in our field. Ideas that are proposed without research into the necessary resources may cost money, personal time, or prevent the creation of other, more feasible, opportunities.

On the other hand, it is almost certain that no matter how much designers have done their research, there will always be issues that were not foreseen or that spring up during the design process. This is normal and relevant to the process of game design. It is also important to emphasize that when you start designing your game, you are not expected to know programming, chemistry, or working with burs and lathes. You should, though, be able to find answers to the questions that will come up by asking the appropriate people.

Throughout the book, game design will be explored through the perspective of its individual elements. Consequently, every chapter will be an opportunity to identify materials that will be required for the implementation of your games. In any case, after working on your core, it is a great opportunity to start checking the resources you have at your disposal and to start planning ahead.

REFLECTION POINTS 🔍

- Do you have a perspective on the resources at your disposal?
  - Do you know what materials or software solutions you can use?
  - Do you know what kind of experts you will need in order to implement your game?
- Can you identify possible technical restrictions in your initial concept?

PERSPECTIVE

Q&A with Francesco Mondada

Professor of Artificial Intelligence and Robotics, EPFL, Switzerland

What do you think is the most important aspect of interesting and engaging educational experiences, and how can robotics help toward this?

I think that if you really want to engage people in the process of learning, the need for motivation and attracting their interest toward the learning matter is important. For me, robotics is exactly one of those tools that create motivation. Robotics is strongly perceived as something extraordinary by students. It is still considered exceptional, interesting, and as something from science fiction or the future. So, I think that this is one of the key elements for me about robotics: The fascination it generates. Another key element is the fact that robotics is extremely multidisciplinary. This means that robotics can motivate to study electronics, computer science, or mechanics in many learning activities; hence, there are several fields where robotics can be used as a learning tool. So, from one side there is motivation and from another there is multidisciplinarity.

How we can facilitate game experiences in education through the use of robotics?

I think that robotics can bring into that field a kind of tangible meaning. Game design is often seen as a static track or a virtual experience. I have the feeling that robotics can bring motion into reality and vice versa. It can also help combine reality with virtual worlds. By interacting with robotics, designing, and constructing, children find a bridge between the fantastic and the real. This connection is important and constantly built through their interaction with robotics in games. Let's consider that a robot is used in a game. From one side, it is an object in the real world. It interacts with the world and is bound by the laws of physics. From other side, it is a game object, with a digital presence in the virtual world. So, a key element in using robotics in game design is that it brings another value to games.

How do you work with prototypes? Do you think they are important in developing and learning experiences, and how do you structure and develop them?

Prototypes are key elements in design. There are many things that cannot be done without them. They are key components to evaluate the approaches we use. Otherwise, we base our design on mere assumptions. The prototyping phase is a crucial phase. We often resort to careless prototyping, which can prove to be a mistake. Whether this is engineers, artists, or someone else, prototyping can be used to examine different aspects, such as the visual or implementation ones. It is key also to validate how the designed system can perform, how people can drive it, and its impact on the users.

If you are limited to only engineering, in some occasions, prototyping may not be that interesting. But when it comes to systems related to education, prototyping is very important. Those systems are going to affect children going to school. They are complex structures, created by several experts. It's a multidisciplinary field. You need to validate every step. You cannot theoretically speak with teachers about concrete implementations and it's expected that iterations will happen until you find the optimum solution between the several disciplines that are used in the design process.

How do you work and how you structure these teams? You talked already about an iterative approach, but how does this actually work in practice when designing learning experiences?

In practice it is very hard to work in a truly interdisciplinary way. Having teachers, computer scientists, or mechanical engineers creating something new together with designers is extremely complicated. It is very hard to find a harmonious way to work together, or even simply to communicate. So this is why I think those people should work in parallel and in iterations. When they come together on a concrete system, they could perhaps start to communicate. If you put an engineer together with a designer, the engineer will apply an engineering methodology and will not understand what the designer presents. This is a great mistake. Some goals need to be put in place. Based on those goals, the game will be designed and produce some results. In order to be able to coexist, common design tools and a common language is important. If you are a teacher, a designer, a psychologist, or an engineer, you don't have common tools with the other experts. So, it is very important that each one of them work separately applying his or her own methodology, then iteratively exchange the results and get new input based on concrete systems and experiments.

SUMMARY

So, what topics did we cover in this chapter?

- There is no magic recipe for the perfect game.

- The game core is a helpful tool in order to start and facilitate one's game design process and anticipate several issues and obstacles that may appear on the horizon.

- There are different ways of using the concept of the game core. Game cores may be used as a list of inflexible guidelines among which games need to be structured or may be prone to change, depending on the direction of the design of games.

Game designers need resources in order to design their games. Having a good perspective of one's resources can help designers make better decisions toward their games' completion.

5 Where to Start?

This chapter covers:

- The different approaches to designing educational games.
- The combination of learning and gaming elements.
- Working on brainstorming and idea generation for gaming concepts.
- The structuring and organzing of prototyping sessions.
- Different ways of planning and facilitating game development processes.

Finding balance among learning and gaming elements is a challenging task. There are several ways of approaching this great game design challenge. This chapter aims at providing a holistic overview of the different ways of combining those elements in order to create intrinsically motivating learning experiences, customized for different situations and audiences. The chapter also offers different insights and practical information on the structuring of your game design process.

THE CHICKEN OR THE EGG: LEARNING OBJECTIVES AND GAMING ESSENCE

Every great journey starts with an interesting destination in mind! In this case, the destination is the creation of learning experiences for your players. But is it clear where you want to get to and, more importantly, how? By now you should have:

- Identified your resources.

- Set your mind on a particular pedagogic approach and learning objectives.

- Chosen the elements vital for your game, creating your game core.

What now remains is to decide how to combine these elements to create the learning experience you imagined. At this point, it is important to come to grips with one of the greatest challenges of educational game design:

Educational games need to be both fun and educational. Is this too much to ask?
Absolutely not!

Educational games need to be effective in helping players learn, but is this enough?
The answer is no. There are many effective and cool educational games that never make it to the classrooms as teachers, administrators, or parents do not consider them to be educational. So, the games that you design need to be effective and also able to make people aware of how good they are. At the same time, games also need to be fun in their own right.

Players prefer games over other activities because they find them pleasurable. But is this enough?
The answer is no again! Modern players have already been exposed to dozens of casual and educational games. Their standards are high and as they have already been presented with educational games in the past, they can easily sense when a normal activity is just being presented as a game or whether it is actually a game they will enjoy. So, the proposed game should be fun but also be appealing and attract learners' attention.

In Chapter 2 we were introduced to the educational game triangle, consisting of three main aspects: players, game, and learning aspect. The learning aspect is defined by the designer's pedagogic approach, the learning theories that influenced them, their experiences, the information they want to present to players, the way the game addresses and interacts with players, and the way it offers feedback and learning objectives. So, the learning aspect explains how learning content is presented in games, how game elements behave in order to support players' learning, and how game mechanics are bound with learning aspects in order to produce a particular learning outcome.

On the other hand, the game aspect consists of elements like rules, interactions, object relations, aesthetic representation, narrative, and technologic implementation. It is responsible for the design of game mechanics, the way games are presented to players in terms of theme, world, story, and how all these elements will be constructed or developed in order to create a particular experience. Both aspects are equally important for an educational game and both affect the other one directly or indirectly. But should either of them be leading the other?

- Are the experiences that you are going to create based on pedagogic approaches or on gaming essence? Do you first start to envision your pedagogic objectives and then build your game around those, or do you design a game and then try to infuse it with learning elements? When making a decision, do you value more the gaming or the learning aspect of your game?

All these questions resemble the famous question of which came first, the chicken or the egg?

Obviously, the answer depends on the game designer's personal perspective, ideas, and way of approaching learning and games. As we also saw, there is no perfect recipe that works for every audience or situation. All design decisions come with their own benefits and have a cost in terms of the final learning experience, the project budget, and development time. In fact, there are countless ways of approaching game design. An approach that I find interesting concerns the main driving force in educational game design. So, what is this approach about?

The conception of educational games, like any game, begins from a starting point. This starting point in educational games is usually either the learning or the gaming aspect. Usually one of these aspects drives the design process and dominates the process of decision-making, at least for the first phases of game design. Consequently, we find that there are two approaches to educational game design from this perspective:

- The learning aspect as the driving force of educational game design.

- The game aspect as the driving force of educational game design.

LEARNING ASPECT AS THE DRIVING FORCE

Transforming educational ideas into games is the most common use of gaming in education. In fact, very often, even if they don't realize it, teachers present their courses with a playful attitude or use gaming elements in order to diversify their teaching tools and attract the attention of their students.

In this approach, game designers start designing their games after they have a clear idea of their learning objectives. In other words, game design follows the prior establishment of learning objectives and the selection of a teaching approach. It's a common practice, especially if game designers decide to design games based on previously created learning content such as audiovisual material, exercises, activities, or textbook information. Since the learning aspect has a dominant role in this approach, in most cases it will have already taken a final form before the game design process even begins; thus, the final game will be built based on this form.

As we saw in the previous chapter, there are various reasons why a well-defined learning aspect is helpful in the design process. Firstly, the proposed game ideas can be understood more easily by members of the game design team. Since teams may consist of game designers; developers; artists; and clients such as schools, academic institutions, companies, and national organizations, this structure can help them all to understand the learning aspect and elaborate on it in a more efficient way. As we will see in Chapter 13, designing one's game from the learning aspect makes the assessment of the game's impact on players easier, as game designers know from the very beginning the elements they need to evaluate.

Another important point is that game designers are often asked to create games out of existing learning materials. It is quite common that either you or your potential clients (academic institutions, organizations, and learning specialists) already have considerable amounts of learning content cached away. Often, due to budgetary reasons, time management or the fact that this content is still considered effective and up-to-date, game designers are asked to use this material as the main basis of their games. So, game designers are given the task of analyzing this learning content and coming up with gaming experiences based on it.

Let's imagine a company that, in order to train its employees about new health and safety guidelines, has already spent a considerable amount of resources on the design of learning materials regarding this subject. After this learning material was created, it was observed that employees didn't spend much time reading it, rendering it useless. The company decided to build a game that would present this information in a more interesting manner. The game designers who take on this task will begin with an existing and well-defined learning aspect that they will change very little. So, they will proceed with building a game based on this learning aspect.

Even if transforming educational ideas into games comes with some advantages, it also comes with several restrictions for game designers. Beginning a game design process with most of the learning aspect already predefined leaves less space for proposing a game structure that would be both fun and educational. This is because the whole game structure will need to be an exact fit for the predefined learning objectives and the way they are intended to be presented through a particular learning approach. However flexible the game aspect may be under those circumstances, the form and style of the final game will be heavily affected by the inflexible learning aspect. This leads to the risk of games or activities being created that focus more on learning and much less on fun, or to activities being called "games" only by their creators.

One of the most popular ways of transforming educational ideas into games is gamification. So, let's see what it is and how it has been used in educational settings.

REFLECTION POINTS 🔍

- Why do you wish to begin your game design from the learning aspect?

- Are your learning objectives already defined or is there any existing set of materials that you need to use in order to design your games?

GAMIFICATION IN EDUCATIONAL CONTEXTS

Samantha is a geography teacher who wants to make her course more appealing to her students. After several years in the field, Samantha found her own way of presenting her course using her own personal approach while respecting the priorities set by the official curriculum. But Samantha wanted to add a playful aspect to her teaching process. Initially, she would challenge her students by proposing riddles, the solution to which could be found after research on the Internet, school books, or by collaborative work. In order to keep track of the status of challenges, Samantha proposed a point system, according to which students would be able to review their performance related to their activity during the course. Students could review their points on a leaderboard that was specially conceived for the geography class. Additionally, students who succeeded at some challenges would be awarded badges as rewards.

Samantha actually integrated game mechanics into her teaching process. By doing so, she kept her teaching approach and learning objectives almost intact. At the same time, she created an atmosphere that could foster mechanisms that exist in games, such as collaborative and competitive situations, beating someone else's performance, mastering particular skills, solving problems, or following narrative paths based on a theme created by her. In other words, she applied game design techniques to a nongaming context, trying to make it more immersive or fun. This is gamification.

Gamification as an approach is used to transform learning concepts into activities with a playful atmosphere. Of course there is not just one way of making this happen. So, a gamified activity can function as a novel way of presenting a course, organizing its delivery, and increasing the motivation of the learners participating in it. Even if there are various ways of applying game design techniques and using gaming elements in someone's learning content, the most common mechanics encountered in gamification approaches in educational contexts are:

- **Points**, which present a numeric record of someone's performance at a given time. Points can be used to represent a great variety of attributes, such as the number of homework assignments students delivered, frequency of use of an online platform, one's participation during the delivery of a course, student performance over a test, or the amount of materials a student or an educator has shared on their online profile of a learning platform. Points can also have different formats. They can be integer positive or negative numbers. For example, there can be an infinite number of learning materials that educators may want to share with their peers. If the number of materials is aligned to a point system, those points could take the value of zero to infinity! On the opposite side, driving licenses are given a point system, where points can be subtracted if drivers show inappropriate driving behavior. Points can also be a fraction, especially in cases where a specific and finite procedure needs to be counted. For instance, a multiple-choice test score can always be measured on a percent scale, as the number of correct responses is a fraction of the total number of questions.

- **Badges**, which are visual representations of specific and well-defined objectives during a game, usually called achievements. With the use of badges, game designers can shift learners' focus to particular aspects of an activity or pay greater attention to a particular item. Let's consider an online course about Android development. The course consists of a set of lessons explaining the subject and a final test, the completion of which is required to pass the course. After its release, the game designers of the learning platform observed that a number of learners preferred taking the test without going through all the lessons set for the course, affecting their final performance. In order to put greater emphasis on participating in all the lessons, the designers created a badge, awarded to those who completed all the lessons before taking the test.

- **Leaderboards**, which offer a way to compare players' individual scores. Leaderboards are connected with points as they offer a means of comparison among peers. We have all been in a situation where we succeeded at something and wanted to share it with our peers; this is what leaderboards do. Leaderboards can be about a great variety of elements. Some examples are a leaderboard about the educational community members who contributed the most material and advice, or for players with the highest scores in the activities presented, or one about the number of activities completed by learners.

- **Levels**, which offer different difficulty scales depending on players' mastery over a skill or topic. Leveling is a mechanism that helps game designers provide players with challenges relevant to their skillset. The difficulty of many games can be intimidating, which can make people switch them off and try something else. The use of levels helps in two ways. On one hand, game designers can organize their delivery more easily since players will be presented only with activities and content that they can deal with. On the other hand, levels work as extrinsic motivators, setting landmarks for players during a game, the reaching of which can offer them more power, abilities, new items, or content that was previously unavailable.

Even if the use of gamification has been a matter of great debate, under certain circumstances it can be an interesting tool for creating nice and fun learning environments. Using gamification, though, is not as simple as it sounds. In fact, the most frequent and greatest mistake made by designers who use it is that they underestimate the effort required for it to be effective and meaningful. Gamified activities still need to be interesting, fun, and have meaning for the participants. So, the integration of gaming elements in learning contexts requires the designers to have found a way for those aspects to work harmoniously together and create meaning for the players.

The use of any gamification tool without proper integration and relation to the learning aspect will most likely fail to appeal to your audience. If, for example, you decide to integrate a point system in a biology course for primary school without proposing interesting outcomes related to it, the students won't have much reason to work hard to get points. Consequently, your point system will be an additional, possibly boring, task in the teaching process that will soon be forgotten, instead of being an integral part of classroom life.

Gamification requires great effort, not only to be implemented, but also to be maintained. This is because successful gamification is not a superficial layer that functions in parallel with a teaching course but is infused directly into its delivery, being an integral part for its presentation, implementation, and assessment. Let's consider, for instance, that you propose the use of leaderboards without consistently updating them, discussing them, and connecting them to your course delivery. These will become just tables with no meaning or interest for your students.

Every gamified activity you design should have a particular and considerable value for learners. You should pay great emphasis and effort in understanding the background of your audience and also understanding the elements you want to teach and how you can present them to your audience. In order for your gamification to have an impact you need to propose activities that are based on actions that attract attention and create enjoyment by themselves. Success requires great dedication and resources (i.e., personal time), effort, and money. So, before deciding if gamification is the right tool for a learning situation, try to consider the following reflection points.

REFLECTION POINTS 🔍

Does gamification offer the impact you expect? Even if gamification comes with several advantages and seems easy to use and integrate in several learning contexts, its impact on learners varies in different situations. Efficient gamification is the result of thorough analysis of learning objectives and integration of game mechanics within these objectives, creating a bidirectional relationship.

What effort should be invested for the gamified activities you wish to be created? There are many successful examples of gamified learning environments. Platforms like **Duolingo**, **Khan Academy**, and **Classcraft** are some of them. But there are many more cases where gamification was not such a success. Often what separates successful from unsuccessful gamification attempts is the effort of designers to make an activity appealing and the connection between gamification and learning content. The language teaching platform Duolingo, for example, has bound the delivery of its language courses with gamification techniques. Without doubt, the platform would be different if gamification was not applied. Classcraft, on the other hand, is an advanced gamification platform for schools, offering a variety of game mechanisms that could be integrated into learning concepts with attention to its visual design. It becomes apparent that using gamification correctly doesn't necessarily mean less effort or fewer resources than other approaches to creating games.

GAME ASPECT AS THE DRIVING FORCE

Another way of approaching educational game design is through starting one's design by defining the gaming aspect and integrating learning aspects later on. Since inspiration can come from anywhere and at any point, it is possible that instead of having a particular learning concept in mind, game designers can begin creating learning experiences by having an idea for a game as its starting point.

Inspiration is the result of constant exposure to new stimuli. How many times after playing a game, watching a movie, or reading a book does a new idea strikes us? Ideas like this appear all the time and as we usually find them in contexts we like and choose. They are aligned with our mentality, preferences, and, possibly, pedagogic perspectives.

In several game design sessions, I had the opportunity to witness the creation of games by educators, the mechanics of which would be based on already known games. On top of this, those games' mechanics were altered to integrate their learning objectives and adapt them to the priorities of their learners. Just a few examples include the following:

- A variation of **Monopoly**, where instead of buying streets, primary school students could buy fruit and vegetable fields as well as animal farms and explore the nutritional pyramid.

- A shape **Bingo**, where kindergarten students could explore and identify the defining elements of geometric shapes and develop their mathematical competence.

- **A Guess Who**? game designed to make the citizens of a local village reflect on intercultural learning and diversity.

These are just some of the countless examples of designing educational games based on existing game concepts. I call this **process infusion** as the game design process starts from a concrete game base into which educational elements are added. This mix of games with educational concepts and ideas can vary in nature and intensity. Examining such games, we can identify three major categories of learning concepts being infused into the nature of the games: low, medium, and high infusion.

In **low infusion** of educational ideas, existing games are used in learning contexts. These could be games like **Minecraft**, **Angry Birds**, or **Pokemon GO!**, also referred to as **commercial off-the-shelf games**, but can also be other games that were developed for educational purposes by educators or academic institutions. In this case, designers do not actually design new games, and their impact on the elements of those games is minimal. Instead, their role is more about identifying the proper learning context where the use of those games would be an interesting tool for either introducing or diversifying the presentation and delivery of a learning topic. An example of low infusion would be use of the game **Assassin's Creed Unity**, the story of which takes place during the French Revolution period. The game could be used to introduce players to the historical context of the time. Even if the teacher doesn't modify the game itself, the way it was used and introduced was adapted to the needs of the classroom. In cases with low infusion of educational ideas, game designers need to have a broad knowledge of existing games in order to identify the appropriate game for the specific teaching situation.

In **medium infusion** of educational ideas, game designers start designing their games based on an existing game concept that they are able to modify in order to present the learning aspect. The game mechanics of the initial game may or may not change, depending on the needs of the designer, but its content will be altered to correctly present the learning aspect. Let's take, for example, the game of **Memory**. In Memory players are presented with pairs of cards, arranged in a grid, facing down. At each turn, players have the opportunity to flip two cards. If they form a pair, they win and take the cards. If they fail to form a pair, the cards are flipped back again facing down and another player can play. The contents of the deck in Memory is unimportant to the game itself. In other words, someone could propose that the cards could depict pairs of animals, shapes, elements of the periodic table, or mathematical formulas. The elements of each pair do not even need to be identical. They could form a pattern or have particular similarities. However, whatever the content, the game we are playing is still Memory. This example is rather simple. But the same principle can be applied to any game structure, from board to video games, and target players from the early childhood to university level and lifelong learning.

In **high infusion**, the game design starts from an existing game concept, the elements of which will drastically change in order to integrate the game's learning aspect. In cases like this, the initial game concept acts as a starting point for an iterative design process where integration of learning objectives will strongly affect game mechanisms, aesthetic representation, and narrative elements in order to provide a particular learning atmosphere that is aligned to the teaching approach of the designer. Since game designers can perform any change or modification they deem necessary, the high infusion approach offers great integration of learning objectives as well as endless possibilities in the final form of the educational game. On the other hand, such an approach requires great dedication and caution, as well as increased development effort and, consequently, greater resources.

Designing one's game from the gaming aspect comes with several advantages and opportunities. The most important ones are as follows:

- **Artist's point of view.** There are many cases where novel and innovative game ideas come to someone. Those ideas could be an opportunity for game designers to express a particular point of view, make a statement, or pass the sensation and experience they envisioned on to their players. As creativity is an indispensable element of game design, spontaneous new ideas, based on games, keep pouring into designers' minds. Thus, through this perspective, designers have the opportunity to adapt these ideas to fit their learning contexts.

- **Use of successful practices and patterns.** Starting from a familiar game idea, game designers have the opportunity to base their designs on existing and successful formulas. As mentioned before, being able to identify which mechanisms work and which don't for a particular audience and situation is an important virtue of game designers. By choosing to create a 2D platform game, for example, where players need to collect specific objects, game designers already have several references, like **Super Mario Bros.**, **Braid**, **Rayman**, and **Sonic the Hedgehog** that they could analyze in order to see which patterns and mechanics work better for their players. Game design is a form of art, influenced by and influencing the cultures of a society, so it is highly possible that your games will be influenced by other existing games.

- **Focus on game mechanics.** By starting to design games from the gaming aspect, the produced games will have greater possibilities of interesting gameplay. The possible side-effect of this, however, is that game designers risk shifting focus from the learning aspect to the gaming one, impacting the final learning experience.

- **Use of already developed games to teach a topic.** Not every game needs to be constructed or developed from scratch. There are cases where existing games can be used for learning purposes. In a case like this a game, or a part of a game, can be used as a tool for learning with the designers of the experience taking advantage of the game mechanics of the existing game.

- **Taking into account development or construction.** There are cases that proposed game projects are difficult or very hard to bring to life with one's own resources and budget. In situations like this, estimating the development and production resources, through the examination of previous case studies, offers a better understanding of the effort, cost, and impact of a game idea.

Infusing game concepts with educational ideas can be an interesting tool for the creation of intrinsically motivating learning experiences. There are several examples and applications of this approach in learning contexts. Games like **MinecraftEDU**, **Rayman Brain Games**, and **SimcityEDU** are just some of them. The concept of those games was primarily based on existing game titles, like **Minecraft**, **Rayman**, and **SimCity**. The educational game designers who created those games developed learning experiences by modifying and extending their game mechanisms. This is not an easy challenge, though. In fact, similar to infusing learning with gaming elements, this approach comes with several risks as well.

Putting great emphasis on the gaming aspect and disregarding the game's learning value can lead to games with no educational impact. Such games may be interesting and appealing to players, but they will never make it to the classroom as teachers and parents won't consider them to be educational material. More importantly, they won't actually help players learn or may cause misunderstandings and confusion. An interesting example of this case is edutainment.

Edutainment started as a design approach where entertainment was used as a means to educate. In the majority of edutainment application, games are used as a means of making learning materials appealing to students. A usual metaphor used for this is the chocolate broccoli, where chocolate represents games and broccoli the learning aspect. However, edutainment applications have been criticized a lot for their superficial approach to learning. First of all, we have already seen that the process of learning is not necessarily boring at all. It is the way that information is presented that can make us feel bored. So, even the chocolate broccoli metaphor oversimplifies a highly complex and challenging field. On the other hand, several edutainment approaches presented one solution for various learners, not taking into account that we all learn in different ways. On top of this, players are not passive while playing. On the contrary, they interact with the game world, they reflect upon it, and they construct their knowledge based on the tools they are provided with.

Beware of the risks! If you decide to start designing your games beginning with the gaming aspect, you should take heed of the following potential risks:

Learning objectives might be harder to integrate. Where design starts with a particular game concept or an already complete game in mind, the task of integrating and infusing it with your learning objectives can be difficult. The first reason is linked to the fact that predefined concepts or existing games have already established concrete mechanics, which are the main reason why those games are considered interesting or fun. This can lead to inflexible situations, where either the game or learning aspect could be partially sacrificed. The second reason why infusing games with learning objectives can be tougher than it seems is that not all concepts addressed by your learning objectives can be expressed through a particular game situation. Obviously, trying to teach poetry using **Jenga** or calculus through a special modified version of **Candy Crush Saga** would pose more challenges than help to the delivery of your course. Not that those would be impossible, though!

Superficial approach to learning. In several learning contexts based on gaming the learning aspect can often be neglected or presented in a superficial or ineffective way. Paying greater attention to gaming aspects and caring only about attracting the interest of students, without creating environments that help them to develop particular skills or reflect on new ideas, is a frequent mistake in educational game design. There are several games or applications that adopt this approach and are heavily based on highly polished visuals or gaming elements but put little emphasis on players' learning. If you aim toward this direction, it is highly possible that your games will have little impact on your players.

Monitoring and assessment might prove more difficult. As seen already, teaching is strongly connected with observing and monitoring student actions and performance. It is through constant interaction and understanding of learners' needs, desires, and style of learning that educators can help them reach a better understanding of a concept. By having a good overview of both their players, their learning environment, and its impact on them, educational game designers can make modifications that will create a particular learning atmosphere that will help players to evolve. This is an application of the Zone of Proximal Development proposed by Vygotsky. There are several ways for an educator to assess the effectiveness of their teaching intervention, which we will cover in a separate chapter later on. But any type of assessment needs to be integrated into the game mechanics as well, which requires the extension or modification of its existing form. Beginning the game design process with a strong focus on a particular game idea or an already defined game in mind could lead to a learning experience without the necessary monitoring and assessment mechanisms. This can be a key factor in a game's failure, since you will not be able to look at the appropriate analytics later on in order to improve your game.

Adapting game mechanics to individual player learning profiles might be more difficult. One of the most important principles of modern pedagogy is that not everyone learns in the same way. Each individual has a different and unique mindset that can flourish under the appropriate learning environment. A fundamental argument in support of using video games in the classroom is that they offer this possibility. The ability to change game mechanics and focus on the individual needs of each player is not an easy task and requires special care and reflection, from the very first steps of game development. For example, players with some physical or sensory impairment may require special modifications in order to play a game. If game designers know that there is this possibility, they need to anticipate it from the beginning of the design process. When starting the design of your game, consider what the dynamic and adaptable elements of your game are and if or how it would be possible for them to change according to the individual needs of players, as it might be too late if you change your mind later.

In Greek mythology, after designing the labyrinth, the great engineer Daedalus and his son Icarus were forbidden from leaving the island of Crete for fear that they would reveal the labyrinth's designs. In order to escape, Daedalus created wings made of wax that would help him and Icarus fly away. But he warned Icarus not to fly too high, as the sun would melt his wings. While flying over the Greek seas, Icarus loved this freedom and wanted to go higher and higher. He flew so high that his wings eventually melted and he fell to his death in the sea. Apart from the fact that using the wrong materials can get you killed, the point of this story is to remind you not to get carried away. Game design is an amazing and highly creative experience, presenting several opportunities for you to experiment on different elements and create amazing experiences. It is true that you can keep adding impressive and fun mechanics to your game, and you should, but don't forget your primary aims. Try not to get too carried away by the game aspect or you risk losing track of your learning objectives and, consequently, creating games with no educational value.

REFLECTION POINTS 🔍

- What are the reasons for starting your game design from the game aspect?

- How do you intend to combine your learning aspect with your game aspect?

- Will your design help you later assess your game's learning impact?

PERFECT BALANCE

So, we have seen two approaches to beginning the process of educational game design: on the one hand, the game design starts with clearly defined learning objectives, and on the other, it is based on game concepts that have already been defined. There is also a third way: Starting to work on both aspects at the same time. In this case design starts with nothing predetermined. Of course this is easier said than done! Without doubt, even with the most agile design approach, a few aspects will be predetermined and revised later with the participation of players.

Educational game design is similar in many ways to tightrope walking, where a skilled acrobat performs on a suspended rope. When performing this activity at great heights, walkers use the support of a large pole in order to maintain balance. This sport requires constant focus, experience, a lot of practice, and the ability to shift your body weight in different parts in order not to fall over. In many different ways, educational game design resembles tightrope walking. But what is the main premise in both fields? All the skills, experience, and equipment of the tightrope walker, as well as the continuous iterations, reflection, and assessment of the gaming and learning aspects of an educational game are about the same thing: balance. So, how can game designers maintain balance in their games?

Balance is not a static state of matter or mind. In fact, several mechanisms need to be put in place in order to achieve balance. In the case of a tightrope walker, attention, body posture and form, weight shifting, and use of the pole are just some of the mechanisms that need to be in place. All of these mechanisms do not function in the same way at any given time, they adapt to the optimum state that will assure balance. The same principle applies to balance for educational game design.

Game elements need to adapt to various situations in order to offer the optimum learning experience possible in a given situation. It is highly improbable that all your players will have the same academic background. You don't know if they learn in the same way just like you don't know their emotional state when they play your game. There are lots of factors that you cannot anticipate when designing a learning experience. Obviously, the same recipe doesn't work in any given context and this is where educational game designers are asked to intervene.

By starting games from scratch, you aim for the highest possible interconnection between learning and game aspects. As both aspects of the produced game will be mutually influenced from the very beginning, learning objectives will be presented, monitored, and assessed in a unique way that would serve the game's atmosphere and style, while the game elements will be structured in a way that will serve the learning objectives of the game. By following this approach, you actually consider both the learning and game aspects as part of the same experience. Game elements become the materials through which learning objectives are achieved and learning objectives become part of the core game mechanics of the game. In other words, games that successfully follow this approach offer experiences where players cannot easily distinguish learning from game elements. We could say that the game core consists of many elements of both the learning and gaming aspect of the design triangle.

REFLECTION POINTS 🔍

- Is it possible to start designing both your learning and game aspect at the same time?

- Are there any potential restrictions that you need to take into consideration?

- What is your priority in designing your game?

IDENTIFYING GAMES IN THE SAME FIELD

In programming, one of the first pieces of advice a junior developer usually receives is not to try to reinvent the wheel! However simple and obvious this may sound, this often comes up in educational game design. It goes without saying that many ideas about educational games that come to our minds have been proposed by other people in the past. I do not suggest that there are no such thing as unique and novel ideas; we can have those as well. But in any case, it is certain that for any field, you will find educational games with elements relevant to the ones you want to propose. So, finding and studying them will definitely save you the trouble recreating them from scratch. This is also the main reason why you should be playing games yourself.

More importantly, you should play games that are related to the subject you want to teach. Identifying games and activities in the learning field you want to address is one of the first steps in the design process. In fact, as soon as you identify your learning objectives, you can start your research on existing games and activities in the same field. Thorough research on this aspect can be very help-ful, since it can save you a lot of trouble in the future and help you to identify trends, preferences, and expectations related to your audience.

Finding and playing games related to your topic of interest will give you a perspective on what has already been proposed. In this way, you can avoid proposing something that has already been cre-ated. More than once or twice I have been in situations where someone tried to describe a game concept that already existed without knowing of its existence. Imagine now someone describing to you a game concept where you are responsible for the management of a city and its habitants and where your decisions affect its development and prosperity—without having heard of **SimCity**. Or imagine being presented with a game where one character will jump between platforms, avoid obstacles, and destroy enemy characters without knowing of the existence of **Super Mario**, **Kirby**, or **Rayman**. Research on games in the same field can help you to avoid awkward situations like this and understand your audience better. On top of this, it is possible that by finding existing games that you like, you can become inspired or find cases that you want to extend and build upon in order to achieve your learning objectives.

Playing games that focus on the same learning field will also definitely help you anticipate devel-opment-related issues and plan your budget better. In several cases, where a game's delivery requires technical implementation, such as board games, card games, or video games, designers need to anticipate the problems that may arise during the development process. Implementation also requires engineering skills. Engineering is based a lot on experience, observation, and assessment of previous experiences in order to optimize a process. In other words, you can always be prepared, but without studying and analyzing previous situations, you always risk missing something. Research into existing games in your field allows you to analyze implemen-tation issues from similar contexts. In this way, you can gain a better perspective on potential risks and issues.

Apart from identifying what you like in existing games, by studying and playing other games, you have the opportunity to detect design and implementation mistakes to avoid in your own games. Incorrect representation of the learning content, nonintuitive or boring gameplay, confusing instruc-tions, a non–user-friendly interface, or just a feeling that the experience you entered does not fulfill your expectations are very important reflection points for you and the structuring of your game design process.

Finding and playing games in the same genre and field as the game you want to create is an impor-tant first step toward the creation of successful learning game experiences. Try to play as many games as you can to find what you like, what you don't like, and what you should pay attention to later on during development. Consider that creating games without knowing the market is like try-ing to cook Chinese food without ever having tried noodles or sweet and sour chicken.

REFLECTION POINTS

REFLECTION POINTS 🔍

- Are there other games in the field for which you want to design your game?

- Are there other games with similar mechanics or atmospheres to the game you want to create?

- Which elements do you find interesting after examining games in the same field as yours?

- Which elements should you try to avoid after examining games in the same field as yours?

PERSPECTIVE

Q&A with Nick Winter

CEO of CodeCombat

What do you think the impact of the learning aspect is when designing games? How did this affect your game design process in CodeCombat?

You definitely have to design the game so that the skill you are trying to learn is the game mechanic that you used to play the game. So everything has to be built around that skill. For example, in **CodeCombat**, you run code to control your hero and solve puzzles. For the game aspects, you are leveling up, you are getting items, or you are defeating monsters. All those are game design decisions you make to design great game mechanics, but none of that can save you if you design a game where the skill and the way you play the game are different. For example, imagine that the skill is speaking Spanish and the way that you play the game is like a platformer where you are jumping around and maybe every once and a while you get to a kind of challenge where you are supposed to do some Spanish flash cards. In this case, the gameplay is completely detached from the skill of speaking Spanish, and it's not going to work. You are gamified, but you don't have game-based learning. People will do this a lot: They have their lessons for teaching the subject and they are going to put badges and points and competitions and challenges, but these are added on after the fact. They can only add a little bit of engagement and motivation. However, you can't really get real game-based learning out of that. So, if you design your lessons and materials first and then want to make a game out of it, it is not going to work; you have to do it together. The process has to be one.

How do you start and structure your educational game design process?

It is definitely iterative. You will fail horribly if you try to do a big design up front like in a waterfall model. I see this all the time. So people will try to use an existing game design but they intend to change its game mechanics so that it teaches this thing they know. Almost all education games fall into some trap like this. With CodeCombat, we initially decided that we needed to make a game that teaches coding. We were not exactly sure about it, so we tried the craziest things that we thought and iterated. We tried to find a game genre that would work for this purpose and might be amenable to playing the game by coding. A tower defense might be a good case because you can write the code that controls your tower. Then, for the game design, we would spend a couple of days prototyping it very vaguely.

While prototyping we realized that it is actually fairly complicated to write code that controls your towers, and there are not a lot of things you can do to maintain the progression of strategies used to protect the towers. Players would write some code—they might even make it more efficient, but there was no point playing the game more. And so the tower defense turns out to play actually really well, but it does not give us a good game progression and doesn't give us a good education progression. There is no scaffolding between the game levels. So we came up with a totally new game genre. You can call CodeCombat a dungeon-crawling puzzle adventure game, but it doesn't really capture it. Most of the mechanics are aspects we have never before seen, and this is because we used a very iterative approach.

If you are going to make an educational game, this is actually very important. You are going to need to do something like that because there are very few examples to look at; you don't have good educational coding games outside apart from a few typing games. Typing games are actually really easy to do because there are a lot of game mechanics to hook up just for typing—it's a very easy skill to teach. If, for instance, you want to create a first-person shooter for math, you have to figure out what that means. Probably you are not going to call your game a first-person shooter for math when you are done with it; you'll have created your own genre.

How do you approach evaluation when designing your games?

There are actually two competing forces with your game: engagement versus effectiveness. So you can say fun versus learning. You can always have the kid learn less and make it more fun until you've gone to a completely noneducational game. You can go all the way in the other direction and say that you're not specially focusing on fun at all but you are going to make sure that it is extremely effective. That is the approach that we took with **Skritter**, which is a tool for learning Chinese and Japanese characters; it is actually an app where you write the characters and practice them.

Coding should also be learned like a foreign language; it should be a conversation between the computer and the student and everyone should be talking in computer languages, such as JavaScript or Python, as much as possible. But the student does not know that at the beginning. So when they may make a mistake, they need to be able to read the computer's JavaScript or Python error messages; the computers should respond with just enough English to tutor them. The transition between students' and computer language happens continuously. It's really simple but also very fast. Every area of the educational game needs to have very quick feedback and very quick mechanics. If you are learning something, you are going to be practicing the thing 100 times an hour. You have to. You cannot do it slowly. Every educational interaction has to go fast, and it has to be active learning. The student has to produce and actually use the skill. So, how can you actively practice the skill? The computer needs to offer the correct feedback for this. It is like computers scaffold you for the right knowledge. But this is not easy. It took us several years of developing CodeCombat to offer this type of feedback to players.

What is the most important virtue of an educational game designer?

My one piece of advice would be to set out to build something that is by far the best in the world, that nobody is trying to do, because almost everything out there is not good enough. So if you don't really aim really high, your educational game will not be good enough. It will probably not be any fun at all; it may be either not fun enough or it may be not effective enough. In any case, you will need to iterate.

There are so many things you need to do right; I guess the virtue would be optimism. You are setting out to do this nearly impossible thing and you have to have a firm vision of how the world can become a better place. You have to believe you can do it; you are not going to succeed if you are driven by your mission and almost recklessly overconfident. If you are, maybe you can change the world. So be optimistic.

EDUCATIONAL IMPACT ON GAME DESIGN AND USE

Deciding on the starting point and direction of your game design approach is just the beginning. As educational game designers, your task is to create intrinsically motivating learning experiences based on games and, to achieve this difficult task, you need to be part of every step of the development process, from the conception of an idea to its implementation to its application until its evaluation and restructuring. Before we proceed with presenting and examining every element of educational games separately, we will examine educational games through the prism of broader element categories that help designers gain an overall perspective of the design process, laying some groundwork for the later analysis of educational games.

ELEMENTS OF A GAME

Trying to identify the fundamental elements of games, game designer and scholar Jesse Schell in his book **The Art of Game Design** proposed the schema of the "elemental tetrad" [1]. His analysis consists of four basic elements: technology, mechanics, aesthetics, and story. Every element of the elemental tetrad has a very specific role in the creation of a game experience. The following is a small presentation of each element.

Mechanics: Mechanics represent all the game rules, number of players, interactions among players, interactions among players and the game, winning conditions, and any other element that is essential for the game logic to exist. As Schell notes, through an examination of other, more linear, forms of entertainment such as books or movies we will notice that even if story, aesthetics, or technology may be there, mechanics will be missing, making it an element that primarily exists in games.

Aesthetics: Aesthetics are related to the look and feel of a game. Aesthetics can indulge any of our senses and they are a key ingredient that characterize experiences and the emotions they cause. Aesthetics are also connected with culture; a very important factor in the design of learning experiences as the symbols, styles, and representations of games may have particular meanings in different contexts.

Story: Story is a sequence of connected events. Games can tell stories but also stories can be created through players' interactions with games. Stories can be told in different ways. They can be linear, nonlinear, or spatial; they can have different themes, tone, and objectives. Like all elements of the elemental tetrad, story is connected with mechanics, aesthetics, and technology in order to help game designers create the experiences they want.

Technology: Technology represents the set of tools, resources, and know-how needed to bring the game to life. Technology is related to any form of these elements, from crayons and duct tape used in your first prototype to the advanced graphics engines and animation software required to realize a game. Without doubt, it is through technology aesthetic elements or gameplay elements are implemented. So, the decisions around it have great importance for the final outcomes of the game.

By placing each element in that particular order, Schell also wanted to show that there are elements that are more visible to players than others. Aesthetic and narrative elements can be perceived more easily than game mechanics and technological implementation. Also, all elements are related to each other. There is no single element that is developed separately from another, since they are all interconnected and any change in one will have an impact on all three others. If, at Halloween, for example, the aesthetic element was to change in order to offer a darker atmosphere, that would possibly have an impact on the story element, as the story would change to support the new aesthetic direction, while game mechanics and technology would also be impacted in order to integrate and highlight the change of theme in the game.

It is likely that not every game will have all four elements evolved. Obviously games like tag or hide-and-seek do not have a particular story element or an aesthetic direction. Game designers develop these elements that are important in order to create a specific atmosphere or offer a particular experience. That means that games that focus on narrative elements, such as adventure games, must present a developed story element that would be supported by visuals that highlight the particularities and essence of the game's world, and game mechanics that would facilitate the progression of the storytelling process, such as quests or challenges, implemented through the use of technology.

EDUCATIONAL IMPACT ON GAME ELEMENTS

Any game with a learning impact is still a game. Consequently, the schema of the elemental tetrad is an interesting way to reflect upon your designs. What is missing from the schema in this case is the aspect of learning. The aim of educational game designers is to create environments that foster learning experiences so this analysis schema should include the aspect of learning as well. But what is the role of the learning aspect in an educational game?

Educational impact varies greatly from game to game. As we have already seen at the beginning of this chapter, games can have different directions, and learning objectives and be used on various occasions. These attributes are influenced and formed by the designers' pedagogic approach, methodologies, perception of the learning context, and the target group. Two educational game designers that create their own game about the same topic will probably create two totally different games, both in terms of gameplay, aesthetics, narration, and implementation, but also in the way the game interacts with players and helps them learn. All these interrelated factors of the learning aspect need to be taken into account. The result is a new schema, which adds one more element to that of the elemental tetrad, making it an "elemental pentad!"

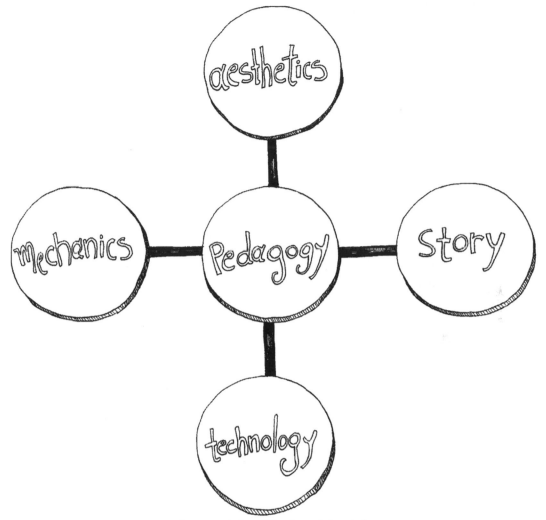

A representation of the elemental pentad.

Let's take a moment to reflect on this schema. The elemental pentad maintains Schell's analysis about the four game elements, while the element of pedagogy is presented in the middle. As we saw before, the element of pedagogy can have greater or lesser impact on the game itself, depending on the priorities and intentions of the designer. Its placement in the middle of the cross suggests that it affects the development of all other elements. As we have seen, there are different ways of designing educational games and there are also different levels of impact among the different elements of games. Games with a weak learning aspect, such as recreational games or games with a superficial layer of learning, present a pedagogy element that is less developed, and its impact on other elements is small or nonexistent. On the other hand, games with a strong learning aspect present a pedagogy element that has a great influence on all other elements, being a key part during the development of any mechanism of the game. In order to understand this concept, let's take as examples two different situations for which we could design learning experiences based on games:

Example #1: The City Hunt

The municipal authorities decided to design a treasure hunt game to encourage the exploration of cultural heritage of their city. The learning objective of this game is to help city visitors to explore its most important buildings, monuments, and sights, and to understand their cultural impact on the city's history and life. Players can download a mobile app that presents them with a map of the city. The app features several markers, corresponding to points of interest. Each of the markers represents a city landmark that players need to find. By locating and visiting those points, the application is automatically activated, presenting players with informative content about the landmark they visited. This content is essential for players to complete challenges, helping them to unlock hidden information. By unlocking all the hidden information, players win. This game was structured upon the need to present and facilitate the exploration of city monuments. The design of the game started with a game core and focused on the learning aspect, which is the presentation of the city's cultural heritage and the need for the game to be played outdoors. The game was also designed from scratch, with no clearly defined learning objectives or gaming aspect. The game mechanics, its aesthetic direction, and the story and its implementation were greatly affected by the pedagogic element, while the latter was greatly affected in turn by the other elements.

Example #2: The History Course

A group of teachers is interested in presenting a course on Roman history by using the real-time strategy game **Total War: Rome II**. In this case, teachers intend to introduce their students to Roman history by getting their attention through presenting the game, the theme of which covers the period of the Roman Empire. Teachers know that they cannot affect the game elements of the game since it is a commercial off-the-shelf game. The game elements in this case were developed separately from the learning objectives and, thus, there was no impact of the pedagogy element in the development of the other elements. However, the way the game is going to be presented and used in the classroom to create the particular learning experience that the teachers envisioned is affected by pedagogy.

Whether or not games were designed to be educational, they can be used as part of learning environments in various ways, as a means of introduction for learning topics, a means of exploration, or for the facilitation of work or assessment. Actually, it is rather common that commercial games are used as tools for learning at the discretion of every educator. Also, from the analysis of the two previous games, we can see that even in cases with already developed games, their use and thematic use can vary depending on the way that educators introduce them to their delivery. From the perspective of the elemental pentad, the element of pedagogy can have an impact on any game. From the examples of the creation of a treasure hunt game and the use of **Total War: Rome II**, we could also say that this impact can vary depending on when the educator becomes involved in the game design process.

Analyzing all these cases leads to the **funnel of pedagogic impact**. The funnel is a representation of what we have already analyzed so far about the impact of the element of pedagogy in the design and use of educational games. Depending on the phase when the element of pedagogy is integrated into the game design process, its impact on the game elements as well as the impact of the game elements on it changes. If the pedagogy and game elements are worked on from the beginning, their interconnection and mutual impact is strong. Games like **Slice Fractions** and **DragonBox Algebra** are like this.

There are other occasions, though, where either the pedagogy or the game elements are already defined when the design process starts. In those cases, game designers need to come up with solutions that fit those prerequisites. Consequently, the impact among those elements is smaller. Such cases include the design of educational games using a specific technical platform or game engine, or the need to design a game according to a specific approach and learning objectives as defined by a client or a curriculum. Last but not least, the use of commercial games, which is always an option, comes with several possibilities for adapting one's learning objectives, using those particular games, to the particular requirements of their course delivery. In such occasions, however, there is little space for changing or adapting game elements to particular learning objectives or expanding one's learning objectives outside the scope and capabilities of the existing game. So, the sooner a game designer starts designing an educational game, the more the interconnection between all five elements of the pentad and the bigger the integration between learning and game aspects.

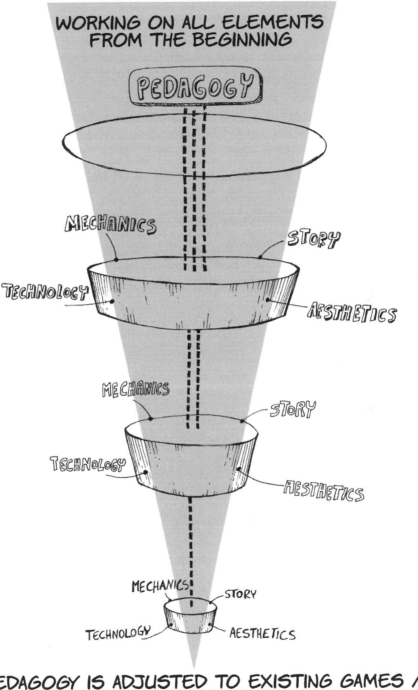

The funnel of pedagogic impact.

Let's take the city hunt game, for example. The game's learning aim is to create an experience through which players will acquire a greater perspective of the city's history and life by getting to know its most notable landmarks. If game designers start designing all game elements from the beginning, the learning approach and methodologies, which are addressed by the pedagogy element, will be affected by game mechanics, technology, aesthetics, story, and vice-versa. At the same time, the game aspect will evolve in order to highlight and present the learning aspect and at the same time the structure, presentation, and interaction of pedagogy elements with players will be integrated into the game mechanics, creating a seamless learning experience.

If game designers start designing the learning experience with a predefined game or pedagogy elements, the impact of one upon the other will be considerably less. It goes without saying that if the designers had to implement the city hunt game using an existing game or a game engine that came with technical restrictions, their options would be much more limited and the learning aim might not be fully fulfilled. On the other hand, if the manner and approach of presenting the learning aspect is already defined before the game design starts, it is possible that game elements, under the resources of the game designer, may not be able to evolve in the optimum way to present and highlight the pedagogy element.

There are occasions where the use of an existing game would be enough to help educators to achieve their objectives so the design of a new game would be unnecessary. Those games could be integrated into the delivered courses and adapted to the needs of learners. If this is not possible, either because the materials cannot cover the necessary subject matter or because the existing games cannot be adapted to the needs of your audience, then the sooner you start working on connecting the elements of the elemental pentad, the greater the interconnection and efficiency of your final games.

INFINITE SOURCES OF INSPIRATION

One sunny day around 300 years ago, Isaac Newton was enjoying the view of the British countryside under the shadows of an apple tree. As he was relaxing, an apple fell on his head, making him ponder upon why objects fall toward the earth. This was a pivotal moment for the proposal of Newton's theory of gravity and some of physics' most influential works. Whether or not this is an anecdotal story about how Newton conceived his theory is true, it makes a very compelling point about how inspiration can arrive from anywhere.

Inspiration is a key ingredient for designing games. Inspiration and the way we find it also define our games. But how do we really find inspiration? The answer is simple: by living and interacting with the environment we live in. Game designers, like all artists, produce games as an expression of the stimuli they receive. The more stimulation we receive, the more information we collect and process and the more personal resources we have to make our games. What makes games magic is their ability to present situations that elicit particular emotions in players: happiness, anger, sadness, empathy, and so on. In order for this to happen, your games need to present elements to which players can relate. And in order for this to happen, the universes you create need to be based on real experiences—your experiences.

HARVESTING IDEAS

In 1951, while living in the Bahamas, Ernest Hemingway wrote his novella **The Old Man and the Sea**. Hemingway, living on an island and being part of the life there, was inspired by his environment. He felt the calm waves on his feet when they trickled up to the shore and their destructive power on a windy day while out in his boat. In this way, he could present the glory of the sea and the struggle and respect of human beings for it, giving us a masterpiece of modern literature. In the same way, encountering new experiences helps game designers get inspiration and produce new and novel ideas. If you feel that you do not have enough ideas to make a game, the first thing you need to do is get out and explore the world around you. Our environments can be constant sources of inspiration if we know how to look at them properly.

The interesting part about educational game designers is that their diverse backgrounds lead to a wide range of inspirations, leading to endless possibilities for proposing new learning experiences. This is also a reflection point for your games. If you see that the elements you propose resemble games or ideas that have already been proposed, you should reconsider your sources of inspiration and search for new ones. The following is just a selection of opportunities to do just that. Feel free to find new ones or identify which ones work better for you.

Meet and talk to people. Games are tools that indulge people's feelings. They are built around the needs of human nature and thus there is no better way to get a good perspective on this than by meeting and getting to know new people. Each person is different and comes with a particular set of experiences and a unique understanding of the world that can also expand your horizons.

Go out, travel, explore. Like all artists, game designers need to constantly update their images of the world. If we consider that a great number of game designers have reasonably similar backgrounds, we might expect the vast majority of games to be very similar. But this is not always the case. There are games with different stories, gameplay, aesthetics, implementation, and learning aspects. A reason for this is that designers seek to make unique games and so they explore the world around them and try to get as much new information they can.

Read and listen. Successful game designers are good listeners. Everybody has a story to tell and stories are always inspiring. It might be a personal problem, a happy moment, a strange event, or a fight. Some stories may be boring but some of them are gold! But apart from this, by listening to other people's stories game designers get a better understanding of their problems, their fears, their priorities, their needs, their misconceptions, or understanding of a learning topic. These are great sources of inspiration.

Participate, don't just teach. Some years ago I was a participant in a training event in Belgium. It was one of the worst experiences of my life! The activities were terribly boring, interaction with trainers was completely absent, and the tension and frustration among uncoordinated participants reached a boiling point. At the same time, it was also one of the most educational moments of my life. As a participant, and thus a learner, I had the opportunity to identify all the things I would never want to happen to me when I participate at a training event. So, it's always interesting to switch places once in a while and live gaming and learning experiences from the role of players or learners.

Observe your peers. The human touch in any educational aspect is unique. This is also the main reason why machines do not design games. Game designers have their own unique style of designing games and educators have their own unique styles of teaching. This is the value of observing your peers. Whether you agree with them or not, there is always some aspect that you find interesting and could use in your designs. Observing your peers can help you expand your perspective on education, game mechanics, narratives, or life itself.

Rest a lot. While it may be good to focus and dedicate one's time, attention, and effort on a project, giving your brain time to rest is part of the thinking process. It often happens that an idea or solution that had eluded us during an intensive session pops into our heads after a good night's sleep.

Why? Why not! This philosophical statement has proved to be rather helpful in educational game design. Educational game designers should be able to experiment, break boundaries, and find the most efficient ways of educating their players. We all have personal inhibitions and restrictions that stem from our views and perspectives, but trying new things can lead to endless possibilities.

BRAINSTORMING

Brainstorming is usually a collaborative technique during which a group of people propose various solutions or ideas for a particular problem or situation. Brainstorming is an interesting way to start when designing a game, as it can reveal new ways of examining and approaching your games while also giving everyone the opportunity to express their thoughts and considerations on various aspects of the game. Through this creative process, you have the opportunity to come up with concrete ideas based on every set of materials, ideas, objectives, and perspectives that have been gathered. Brainstorming can be helpful in so many ways. In some cases, even the fact that we get to talk and express our thoughts can be helpful not only for the greater good but also for us. Often we might find that an idea that is later verbally expressed does not sound as good as it did in people's minds, or vice-versa! Just try to facilitate and manage this process as there can be brainstorming sessions that literally can take days!

There are different ways of handling the outcomes of brainstorming. You can start brainstorming without many elements in place or you can start the process after you already have a draft idea of what your learning objectives and game aspect will be. Usually having the elements of your game core clear in your mind comes in handy! Try to avoid seeing brainstorming as a moment to create final ideas and to be open to any idea that pops out. Filtering creativity later is better than suppressing it from the beginning. There are several activities or tools for brainstorming. In the section Activities for Game designers, you can find a selection of those.

IMPORTANCE OF PROTOTYPES

Game designer Tim Schafer once said that designing games is like cooking waffles. The first ones are always burned! It takes time to be able to design nice games, and nobody is an exception to this. So, you should be aware that your games will not be intriguing and appealing masterpieces from day one. Games are the fruit of a lot of effort and constant evolution of both your designs and yourself. No one expects your first ideas and designs to lead to amazing games. On the contrary, when designing games, you need to know that **the vast majority of everyone's initial proposals will not reflect the final game**. This is natural in many ways. First of all, games are designed for particular audiences. This means that it's highly unlikely that your first ideas will reflect the needs of your audience completely. You will need to tweak your design in order to create experiences that players enjoy. Your games also need to be fun. There are many times that ideas in our heads seem fun but when put together and implemented, we actually realize that they were only fun inside our heads!

Another point is that your initial ideas have not been assessed for their impact on players' learning. You might create games that are fun to play but if they lack the ability to facilitate your players' learning process, you're only halfway there. Additionally, you cannot always fully estimate the development cost of your games without trying to create them first. This means that initial ideas may be amazing and could have a potential game impact, but their implementation may be practically impossible if you do not have the resources to achieve them. In the end, you need to be prepared to discard ideas that do not work the way you expect, however emotionally attached you are to them. This is a great virtue of educational game designers and this is the reason why we need prototypes.

Prototypes are simplistic versions or representations of games whose main objective is to prove the validity of a concept. We use prototypes to see if our game logic makes sense, if players can understand our rules, if the game is interesting or if it's boring, if there are technical implications hadn't been considered, if we offer learning value, or if there is an actual impact on players. The sooner these issues are identified and your concept is revised, the fewer problems you will encounter later on.

Sometimes educational games that are released may not be that interesting or may fail to have an impact on players. With prototypes you can assess almost every aspect of your game concept and anticipate those issues.

Prototypes are very efficient at shedding light on aspects that we are unsure about. In order to be able to do this, you will need to have concrete questions answered:

"Does my game clearly address its objectives?"

"Can players easily maneuver the character by pressing four buttons on a smartphone screen?"

"Can I use dice in my outdoor game activity?"

Prototypes have a greater meaning if used like this.

What I try to remember every time I'm in a game design session is that prototypes are not final products. This means that no one else apart from you and possibly some testers are going to play or even hear about them. So, pay more attention to their functionality and learning impact rather than their appeal. In fact, trying to make a prototype look nice could cause more problems that it would solve. The main reason is that it may absorb the focus of your testers or even you, causing delays, which usually cost money, time, or both. A great piece of advice is to avoid presenting poor or half-made implementations when asking for someone's feedback, especially when the games you want to design are educational. You don't want your testers focusing on the aesthetic issues of the prototype and forgetting about its educational aspect, which was the primary reason for the prototype in the first place. So, try to create simple and quick examples so that you can later dedicate more time to your actual implementation.

Prototypes are also a nice opportunity to reflect on the learning impact of your games. Through prototypes you can see if your games are appealing to their audience or whether the proposed experience has a potential learning impact. We will also examine this aspect in Chapters 6 and 13, when we examine game assessment. Depending on the materials and technical complexity, prototypes can be categorized as low-tech or high-tech.

Low-tech prototypes are created using everyday materials such as paper, pencil, crayons, cartons, or clay. The huge advantage of these types of prototypes is that they can be designed by everybody and they do not require any particular technical training in order to start working on them. Low-tech prototypes can be used to:

• Test the concept of a board game, using just markers and some piece of paper.

• Experiment on different ways of designing a platform game, using action figures and boxes.

• Present a game concept about a third-person video game, using a member of your team as the main character.

• Work on the mechanics of a puzzle game and ensure that your logic is correct.

A low-tech prototype for an adventure game, using paper and stationery. The designers printed a tiled board and tested the logic of their games.

High-tech prototypes are more advanced implementations, in most cases requiring the use of some hardware or software. These prototypes can be developed on the final game engines that will be used for the creation of the game or other ones that may be easier to use. High-tech prototypes are used to test game concepts that are closer to the final product and they offer designers and developers the possibility to test their ideas and check to see whether the technical resources (programmers, artists, software platforms, game engines) they have at their disposal are enough for them to build their games. At the same time, high-tech prototypes offer a first insight into the final gaming experience, helping game designers see how players will experience the game and if their software and hardware equipment is enough for the game to be played. High-tech prototypes can be used to:

- Check whether a particular game creation platform can create the game the team wants to create.

- Experiment on the different visual styles of a game, offered by a particular game design platform.

- Test the controls of a game played on a mobile device.

- See if players can understand how to navigate inside a virtual reality environment game.

REFLECTION POINTS 🔍

Prototyping is a very helpful process in game design. It can save you from very serious trouble down the line. Try to experiment as much as you want both with low-tech and high-tech prototypes.

- Are you going to work with low-tech prototypes? What are the materials you will use?

- Are you going to work with high-tech prototypes? What are the platforms and tools you will work with?

- Which game elements will you test through your prototypes?

WHEN IS THE CONCEPT READY FOR IMPLEMENTATION?

There always comes a point where you need to stop preparing and get into action. In your case, this marks the transition from collecting materials, defining your learning objectives, setting your mind toward your game core, and considering your game elements. The truth is that it is possible that you may never feel ready to move from preproduction to actual production. It is like the first time you tried to ride a bike or addressed an audience. You are never ready until the moment you try!

In fact, the implementation phase does not mean that you will finish developing the game soon. On the contrary, the implementation phase marks a new era for your game design creation since it includes a number of steps, some of which you will need to repeat several times in order to make sure that you create a particular learning and gaming atmosphere. The only thing that is sure when you start designing an educational game is that many things will change along the way. Your audience may change, the environments may change, even your mentality and pedagogic direction may change. This is expected and natural and it's why educational game designers exist: to monitor the game creation process and help a game project evolve so that it becomes both fun and educative.

There is no general principle on when your project is ready to be implemented. Situations and learning objectives vary for different projects. There are some tips, though, that can give you a better perspective on this matter. First of all, you need to avoid two basic situations: Being very premature or too mature in your game design process. Being very premature means that you start implementing the game without taking into consideration several of the elements that we have mentioned previously. This risks not having reflected on your game core, your learning objectives, or your elemental pentad; not having made a prototype; and not having a clear idea of the learning experience you want to achieve. Beginning implementation prematurely comes with the risk of not anticipating problems that will arise during the development process and knowing if your game can actually offer a learning experience that's both intrinsically motivating and educative. Often inexperienced game creators start designing and developing their games only to realize that the game they envisioned was difficult or impossible to make with their current resources. Cases like this could be avoided through the use of prototypes.

On the other hand, a very mature concept also comes with several risks. Concepts that are very mature in the designers' minds are not necessarily the best options to teach something. Whether your teaching tools are effective will be evaluated after your players are exposed to your games. The sooner you enter the implementation phase and have a concrete deliverable to show to your players, the easier it will be for you to assess your tools and adjust them to your learning objectives and your players' needs. In other words, if you try to evolve your game too much without getting your hands dirty, it may lead to a situation that can render your efforts moot. Let's imagine the case of a game design team that wants to create a PC game focused on improving the soft skills of an international company. The team takes several months to develop the perfect concept, testing the validity of their ideas through prototypes and finally deciding to proceed with the game's implementation. After one month of implementation, the team realizes that many employees don't have access to a PC or laptop but use a tablet instead. Since the proposed game requires a keyboard or a gamepad, the game will probably not be used in training events for the company and the game design team needs to reconsider their design to propose a more context-appropriate game. This team entered implementation with a very mature concept, causing them to lose time and money due to elements they would avoid if they started implementing their game earlier.

WORKING ITERATIVELY

At the beginning of every autumn, wine producers harvest the grapes of their vineyards, crush them, and preserve them in special spaces where fermentation takes place. During this preservation period, the sugars of the grapes are turned into alcohol with the help of yeast, giving birth to wine. At the end, the produced wine is bottled and served up at our tables and parties. Every step of this process is interesting! More importantly, when all those steps are completed, they give birth to a new product. In the same way, game development has its own pipeline.

An interesting aspect of game creation lies in the way teams or individuals structure the development process. First of all, let's take a moment to consider what **process** means in this context. Let's say that an educational game design team comes up with an idea about a video game. After doing some research on the learning aspect and having a more concrete idea about the elements of their game, they switch to the development phase, where artists, programmers, sound engineers, composers, and beta testers need to work together in order to produce the final game. But how do all those professionals work together? Do artists start designing graphics before programmers start coding? Do educational game designers interfere in the development process, and if so, how? There are several questions about the way the game development pipeline is structured and what the role of each team member is. This is the reason why processes are needed.

In the early years of software development, engineers came up with a linear process for creating their products. Every step would take place in a sequential order; initially a team would assess their software requirements, then analyze them, design the appropriate architecture, and then continue on programming. At the end, they would test and release what they had created. This sequence sounded logical and effective to most members of the design process. After completing one step of the process, teams could not go back. They needed to be prepared and anticipate situations, but also they would move forward and deliver in a timely manner. This sequential process was called the waterfall, since it resembles the way water flows in waterfall: from top to bottom, with no exceptions—at least on this planet!

There are several issues with the use of this model. These issues are more obvious in teaching contexts, where we seek a particular learning impact. In order to identify those issues, let's have a look at two real examples about games that used waterfall development processes. Since both games were not officially released, their names were modified.

Case 1: The Hundred Faces

Inside the framework of a national project on immigration, an Estonian nongovernmental organization wanted to create a game that would inform about and interest players in immigration and human rights. Since their objective was to involve as many people as possible, they wanted to create an outdoor activity that would captivate the interest of people passing by, who would either play themselves or observe other people playing. The designers wanted to create a learning situation where players would question themselves about their prejudices and reflect on the rights of immigrants who arrived in Europe by presenting situations that could happen to anyone, no matter their origin, color, or gender.

Their team, consisting of members of the organization's office and volunteers, proposed a bigger version of a board game eight by eight feet long, played by a maximum of four players, whose pawns would be manipulated by the throw of a dice. By throwing the dice, each pawn would move for an equivalent number of steps. Each tile of the board corresponded to an audio recording or text, presenting the testimony of a person who shared a positive or negative experience of their lives. After listening or reading about that experience, players needed to say if the person related to the story was from Europe or not. By guessing correctly, players could play one more time. The first one to reach the finish line won.

Following a waterfall development process, the team came up with a game design document, found the necessary materials, built the game, and presented it on a Saturday morning at a local park. The interest of people was quite high, so they formed a big circle around the game board. The designers then realized that not many people could actually participate and listen to the testimonies at the same time because of the power of the speakers that the team had bought, taking into consideration the open space of the park and the noise of the audience. Additionally, the size of the board and pawns proved to be rather small for the number of people attending the activity, causing problems for the observers who were interested in seeing what was going on but were not able to figure out what the game was about.

The game proved to be rather effective in attracting the attention of people passing by, yet it failed to have the impact the designers expected, as several points were not taken into account.

Case 2: *Brick Master*

In order to teach programming for the creation of 3D graphics, a university engineering faculty wanted to create an educational game. The objective of the game design team was to help students develop their coding skills and understanding of the C++ programming language while creating primitive stereometric objects, like spheres, cubes, pyramids, and so on.

Following a waterfall design method, the team proposed **Brick Master**. In the game players needed to construct specific structures using their programming skills. The game interface presented two different views: one showing an empty 3D world and another one where players could use a command line and review the history of their actions. By using their coding skills, players could create the 3D shapes and move them around the empty 3D space, helping them to build the expected object. Upon completing a level, players would be introduced to new tasks with higher complexity and difficulty.

After its development, the game was presented to the students of the faculty. After a week of testing, it became apparent that students were not interested in playing the game. Additionally, the game's interface was so complicated that it caused frustration for students who preferred to use traditional coding tools instead of **Brick Master**. The game lacked fun elements and it offered no challenge, suspense, collaborative, or competitive attributes, making it no different than any other software used to teach or simulate the craft of 3D programming. In the end, the only ones who actually completed the whole game were its designers!

In both of these cases, the main problem is that the game design teams followed a linear development process. Consequently, they arrived at several stages where they could not anticipate upcoming problems, the perspective of their audience, or technical restrictions that would only become apparent after starting to develop their game. Another issue in this case is that when those teams arrived at the testing phase, using a waterfall model, the development was already complete, which means that changes were difficult, expensive, and sometimes impossible.

It is natural and part of an educational game designer's role to understand that not everything can be anticipated. Some issues only reveal themselves when the development of the game starts and some others may arise later due to unexpected turns of events. Whether you are an expert or not, no one expects you to know the de facto correct way to teach 3D programming to university students or how to motivate the entire population of a local community to reflect on prejudice and immigration. What is expected from you, though, is the ability to continuously adapt your designs to whatever new information that arrives regarding your environment, audience, expectations, or client objectives, in order to create learning environments that help your students evolve while keeping them engaged.

Working iteratively was the result of designers' reflection on this need. Instead of completing each of the development steps one at a time, in singular consecutive pipelines, designers work and rework all those steps over small periods of times, called **iteration cycles**. Iteration cycles offer the possibility of working on small deliverables, the continuous improvement of which will eventually lead to a final game. By finishing and testing them, designers can make adjustments to their course of development and design for the next iterations to come. At the end, the final game is the result of a process where all elements are developed at the same time, tested, and continuously modified in order to reach the expected learning atmosphere.

Iteration cycles should be kept small and effective. Their duration depends on the complexity of a game and could be from one week to several months. Effective iterations focus on clear and measurable outcomes, which always offer a greater perspective of what you want to achieve and how to get there. You can organize your iterations in any way that's most convenient for your project. You could, for instance, dedicate one or several iterations to your prototypes. After completing your prototypes, you could continue your iterative work on specific aspects of your game, building up on your final product. Being able to gradually evolve your game elements together will provide greater coherence to your learning experience and help you to structure your way of thinking, while dealing with new issues.

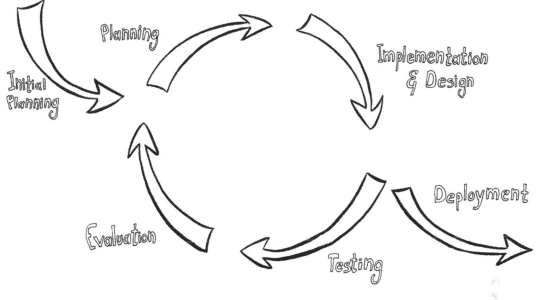

Iterative design consists of the following phases:

Planning: During the planning phase, the available resources for the creation of an educational game are identified. This is also the phase where alternatives or problems are solved if materials, tools, or people are missing from the design process. During the planning phase, all game requirements are listed and a plan for their completion is compiled, leading to the design phase.

Design: During the design phase, games are proposed based on the existing requirements and available resources. Educational game designers examine their learning objectives, their audience, and game aspect and come up with designs that will later be implemented.

Implementation: During the implementation phase, games are built based on the instructions of the educational game designers. The implementation phase does not only consist of programming but also the graphics design, sound effects, creation, and music composition.

Testing: Following the implementation of a game is the testing phase. All game elements are tested during this phase: The game logic is examined for its consistency, the technical aspect for its robustness, the game interface for its simplicity, and so on.

Evaluation: Since educational games are designed around learning aims, it is important that the completion of those aims is evaluated. The final phase of the iteration cycle is the one of evaluation. As we will see in Chapter 13, there are different ways to evaluate educational games, depending on the priorities the educational game designers have.

These phases do not need to be necessarily sequential. They may also overlap, depending of the needs of the team that designs the game. In fact, for every occasion, every project, and every audience, the design process needs to be adjusted in order to deal with the individual challenges of the given situation.

PERSPECTIVE

Q&A with Benjamin Huynh-Kim-Bang

Game Designer at WeWantToKnow

What is the process and approaches you use when you design educational games?
It depends on the situation. Sometimes we may have an intuition. For example, our founder may come with an idea that we haven't done before that might be with learning value and fun. It is then that the designers (because we are all designers!) try to refine this initial idea and see if it is possible. For instance, one day the founder came with this idea of fingers put on the screen to jump with a height equivalent to the numbers of fingers. So the kids would see, in real time, the results of their decisions. The rest of the team worked several weeks on this initial intention and, finally, we get a runner gameplay using the number of fingers to jump and make additions.

Another way is when we are working on a new topic and then want to address the learning aspect. In these cases, we deconstruct the knowledge and information of the domain we target. And in this process, we examine the connections and goals, priorities, and mistakes that learners perform and try to address them. Then we try to find mechanisms that would allow players to better learn. When I was working on my PhD, we worked on a new methodology that we called the six facets of serious games. And the idea was that to merge learning and fun, you are at the core of the game. So, you needed a simulation of the domain you want to learn and to teach; for example, in **DragonBox Numbers**, our characters have mathematical properties. You can cut them, you can make them eat each other. This is addition, subtraction, and decomposition. So, it is a kind of simulation of arithmetic directly integrated in the core of the game.

So, when we start for a new project we start to deconstruct the domain and which ones are more interesting to target.

How do you evaluate your games' effectiveness?
First, and most importantly, when we observe kids playing we observe if they are motivated and if they understand what we want them to understand. Evaluation happens in different phases. It depends on the situation. Sometimes you can prototype something on paper, like in the kind of board games, or you may use any other type of prototyping material so that you observe very fast the results you want to examine.

Recently, I was interested to see how we could teach chess with our current approach. So, for example, in this case I could simulate the game using a chessboard. Through this simulation I conducted a test to see how it feels, how the kids react, and what type of misunderstandings they could have. But some other games rely on more digital experiences. So, for example, if you want kids to catch something on the screen, you cannot simulate this behavior without a computer. Hence, it depends on several aspects, like the experience and behavior we observe when we present our prototypes.

About the assessment, there are several ways to do it. It can be theoretical, for example, but we would like to focus on the needs of teachers, for example. At the same time, we know that if we focus on what they say they want, we wouldn't innovate. So, I will take an example from the autobiography of Steve Jobs: Where if you ask people whether they want an iPad, they would say they don't need it—until they got their hands on it. So, it's very sensitive when you take feedback. Maybe it's not that good to take feedback from the very beginning or wait to get feedback from the final user.

How important do you think that prototypes are, and how do you use them?

This is not even a question! Prototypes are vital. We have killed several projects because after prototyping, they weren't convincing enough. But it is complex process. In our company we have a word, **tension**. Everybody in the company is encouraged to have a unique, particular point of view, and everybody is happy to express it and disagree with others. Hence, we have hot discussions, and this is important for creativity. As a result, there are different opinions and perspectives even before the design of each game. So, prototyping is a very interesting tool that facilitates this process and helps us clarify and filter ideas; see which ones work and which ones don't. Prototypes have helped us many times work with such issues and also challenge our own way of thinking about how we design games and how players learn.

SUMMARY

- Maintaining balance between the learning and gaming aspects of games is not easy. There are occasions where learning aspects or gaming aspects are stronger in educational games.

- We examined the pros and cons of creating games with a greater focus either on learning or gaming aspects and emphasized the importance of balance between those aspects.

- Having an understanding of the gaming market and games that already exist in the same field can be a very helpful starting point for educational game design.

- We analyzed games through five elements: aesthetics, story, mechanics, technology, and pedagogy, and we examined the connections among those elements and their impact on the design process.

- We examined different approaches to getting inspiration for game design.

- Prototyping is crucial to game design in the same sense that cooks test their food while they prepare it. There are different ways of prototyping. One way is to categorize based on the technological complexity utilized, leading to low- and high-tech prototypes.

- There are different ways to structure and facilitate a game design process. Iterative design can be particularly helpful since it provides the opportunity to design, test, and evaluate one's games constantly.

REFERENCE

1. Schell, J. (2014). *The Art of Game Design: A Book of Lenses* (2nd ed). London & New York: CRC Press.

6 Let's Make a Game!

This chapter covers:

- An overview of the game possibilities that can be created by game designers.
- An initial introduction to game mechanics, and more specifically:
  - An introduction to game spaces.
  - An introduction to game objects.
  - An introduction to designing and analyzing game rules.

This chapter offers an initial introduction to game mechanics and their connection to players' learning. More specifically, this chapter examines the design and impact of game spaces; the different types of approaching and creating game objects; and elaborates on the analysis, design, and expansion of game rules.

A common topic of discussion in educational game design is the type of games that can be used in learning contexts. What are the possibilities, options, and limitations on the games that can be designed and presented in order to help players learn?

Let's start the chapter with this point:

There is no limit to what educational game designers can create.

There are no boundaries to creating games, and consequently, there are no restrictions to creativity, personal beliefs, or people's passion for the topics they want to share with their audience, as long as those games capture the essence of the game designers' pedagogic approach.

WHAT GAME CAN I MAKE?

As we already saw, there is not a single recipe for designing intrinsically motivating learning experiences. Each audience or occasion has specific needs and expectations and not all environments offer the same prospects for the facilitation of learning processes. Games are powerful learning tools but they need to be selected or created with those particularities in mind. One of the first steps in doing this is by actually selecting the type of game you want to create. As we have seen, this is not always a sequential process. In fact, most of the time this is the result of a continuous and iterative examination of one's learning objectives, game core, and player needs.

Another important aspect of selecting the genre of an educational game is its unique appeal and interest to players. The more technology infiltrates our daily lives, the more people discover new video games and consequently their skills and expectations keep rising. Demanding players tend to lose interest in games they have already played or find unchallenging. Those expectations keep raising the bar for game designers who, on their side, must try to come up with novel concepts based on existing genres, or proposing new ones. Of course, the best way to deal with this is to constantly keep exploring and playing new games! Educational games are not always board games or puzzle games, even if we see lots of those. Thus, they can be based on any existing, or not yet existing, game types. But what types of games exist? Let's have a look at some of them.

Board games are usually played on desks or flat surfaces and feature environments where players need to manipulate pieces and other objects over a defined area, called the board. Some of the most famous games we know are board games like **Monopoly**, **chess**, **The Settlers of Catan**, or **Dame**.

Card games use cards as the main means to facilitate the game process. There many types of card games, spanning from blackjack to solitaire to **Uno** or **Magic: The Gathering**.

Dice games use dice as the main functionality in the game process. Dice games can be as simple as throwing a set of dice, where the higher number wins, to rather complicated games, where the random aspect of throwing the dice plays a central role in the gameplay. Examples of dice games are **Yahtzee**, **backgammon**, and **Boggle**.

Role-playing games present fictional settings, where players make decisions and take roles as certain characters. During those games players may need to interact with other characters and the environment and make decisions that will lead them to victory under the particular rules of the game. There are several successful role-playing games, like **Dungeons & Dragons** and the **Final Fantasy** series. Role-playing games that are played online and can support a large number of players are called massively multiplayer online role-playing games or MMO RPGs. Examples of MMO RPGs are games including **EVE Online**, **Wakfu**, and **World of Warcraft**.

Conversation games are games that are based solely on conversation skills. **Mafia** is an example of a conversation game.

Platform games are video games that are based on characters jumping between platforms. Platform games can be both 2D and 3D. There is a huge list of successful platform games, including **Sonic the Hedgehog**, **Super Mario Bros.**, **Donkey Kong**, and **Crash Bandicoot**.

Strategy games are video games where the application of strategic thinking leads to final victory. Strategy games can take different forms, from real-time strategy games, where the outcomes of players' decisions appear in real-time, to turn-based strategy games, where they make their decisions in defined game turns. There are countless examples of strategy games, such as the **StarCraft** series, **Age of Empires**, **Total War: Rome**, and **Total War: Civilization**.

Adventure games are based on the unfolding of a story through the interaction of players with the game. In adventure games the story may be predetermined or emerge from players' interaction with the game. Players also assume the role of a character who is usually presented with a set of puzzles, the solution of which brings them closer to the game's end. Characteristic games of this genre are **Monkey Island**, **Myst**, and **Life is Strange**.

Location-based games use players' locations as a key aspect of their gameplay. Location-based games can take place outdoors, such as with **Geocaching**, **Pokémon Go**, or **Tactileo Map**, but they can also take place inside closed areas, such as with museum tour games.

Puzzle games are video games where the main component involves solving puzzles. Puzzle games can target any type of problem and can vary in form and style. Examples of puzzle games are **Dr. Kawashima's Brain Training**, **Cut the Rope**, **Bejeweled**, and **Portal**.

Traditional games are informally played games and require minimal equipment. Traditional games include several well-known games such as hide-and-seek, marbles, limbo, or tug-of-war.

Simulation games are games that try to simulate whole or fragments of reality or fiction. Simulation games can be about business, physics, chemistry, war, sports, human behavior, or pretty much anything else and can portray (nearly) anything the designer wishes to present.

Escape games are physical or digital games where players need to escape from a closed and secluded area by solving puzzles in a fixed time frame.

Sports games are games that recreate existing sports games, such as soccer, baseball, basketball, or tennis. There are several examples of sports games, such as **Pro Evolution Soccer**, **NBA Live**, or **Wii Fit**.

It makes sense that there are types of games whose structure and style are more convenient for the creation of particular learning experiences. **Risk** or **Ticket to Ride**, for example, are played on a board that depicts a map. The components of those games themselves are convenient for subjects such as geography or history. Those design decisions, along with the way educators integrate those games in their classroom, training, or personal lives, play a tremendous role in the games' impact on players' learning.

REFLECTION POINTS 🔍

Being able to identify the elements and possibilities offered by a particular genre to the design of your learning experiences is an important aspect of your design decisions.

- What game genres do you consider incorporating into your game's design and why?

- How does your game genre help you or restrict you from achieving your learning objectives?

- Are there any technical, logistical, or design aspects that are affected positively or negatively by designing a game of this genre?

AN INTRODUCTION TO GAME SPACE

In 1884, Edwin Abbott Abbott, a teacher, published a novella called **Flatland: A Romance of Many Dimensions**. The book presented a two-dimensional world, named Flatland, which was inhabited by geometric shapes. Even if Abbott's intention was to create an allegoric presentation of the social structure of his era, he vividly described the practicalities and particularities of living in a two-dimensional space, the experience of which is very different from our three-dimensional one. For instance, the attributes of a two-dimensional world do not allow shapes to recognize one another easily using sight. So, circles, polygons, or lines recognize each other either by sound or by feeling each other and understanding each other's shape.

Space has always fascinated human beings. Every moment of human history has been marked by the importance of space, from architecture to the art of war and from the exploration of the galaxy to the spatial arrangements of living cell components. In the same way, space is indispensable for games. But it is in specific spaces that games acquire meaning. Chess pawns have no use without a chess board, in the same sense that seeing a player just holding a ball does not immediately suggest that they are playing basketball. In this section we will examine the impact of space on educational game design.

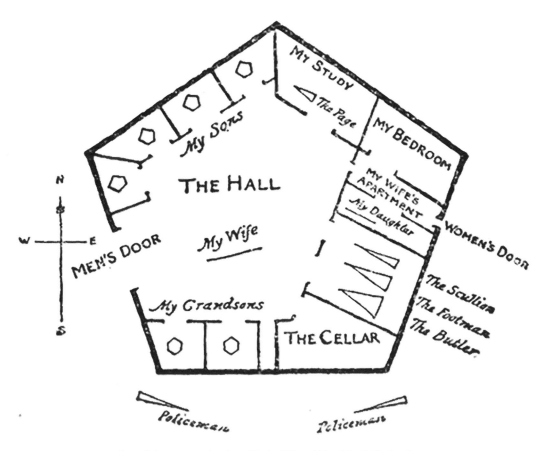

A spatial representation from Edwin Abbott Abbott's book Flatland.

Importance of Space in Games

Whether they are digital, physical, or mental, games take place inside spaces. Space is an indispensable element of games and thus, it plays an important role in the design of game experiences. Even slight changes to game spaces have an impact on how players may perceive games. **Trivial Pursuit**, for instance, is a physical board game. However, there are also several electronic versions of the game. Even if the same game mechanics apply in all cases, the experience is not the same. What changed? Space! The physical arrangement of players around the board and the dynamics that arise from this interaction are not the same when the game is played in front of a computer screen. This does not necessarily make the game more or less fun but it definitely impacts the experience.

The nature and experience of educational games affects and is affected by game spaces. Let's take, for example, shooter games like **Counter Strike**, **Overwatch**, or **Battlefield**. Those games require players to explore virtual spaces and eliminate their opponents, acquire control of particular territories, or take possession of specific objects. Those games, however, present a virtual space where game characters are controlled by players. Equivalent games, played in physical spaces, like paintball or laser tag, bring a totally different approach to the notion of space. **Paintball** and **laser tag** require players to have stamina, the ability to be stealthy, and acute senses of sight and hearing compared to those playing comparable video games. In both cases, the games present similar goals, but the spatial situation has a great impact on their game mechanics.

It becomes obvious that creating game spaces should not be taken lightly. Space defines the nature of games and can prove to be a powerful tool for the facilitation of learning experiences. If not designed properly, it can add unnecessary difficulty to your games and cause more confusion and frustration. The best way to approach space is by considering various perspectives. Let's examine some of those.

Space should facilitate the gaming process. As an indispensable element of any game, space should ease and facilitate gameplay instead of making it more complex. This means that the structure of space and the arrangement of objects inside it should be designed in a way that is easy for players to perceive and understand. Let's take checkers, for example. **Checkers** comes with a clearly defined board space and a concrete arrangement of pieces. When the game starts, players know how to place their pieces and move around the defined areas of the board. Consequently, space acts as a delimiting and facilitating means for the gameplay of checkers. On the other side is an outdoor game of hide-and-seek in the forest. If game designers do not define the boundaries where players can hide, players might go too far, making the game last longer. In this case, some players might get bored because they were found early, while others may become frustrated because they were hiding for a long time and nobody found them. In any case, the choice of space on this occasion was not successful.

Game space can consist of discreet and non-discreet positions. The way that players can explore and interact with space is not the same for all games. In games like **Reversi**, **backgammon**, **Monopoly**, or **Minesweeper**, space offers a set of finite positions that can be reached. Those game spaces consist of discreet positions, the arrangement of which is usually important for the logic of the game. In backgammon, for instance, after throwing the dice players have a limited set of movement options, based on the arrangement of pieces on a board consisting of 36 sequential positions. This spatial arrangement needs to be taken into account from the beginning, since it is a component that may affect the final outcome of the game. On the other hand, there are game spaces with infinite, non-discreet positions. In games like **Need for Speed**, **Starcraft**, or miniature wargaming, players can move in any way they want while each new position is unique.

Space can be fictional, virtual, or physical. Space is not necessarily a physical concept. Every time that we read **The Lord of The Rings**, the fictional world of Middle Earth is created inside our heads. In many situations we need nothing more than our imagination to create new worlds and this is the case in many games, with **Dungeons & Dragons** as a very characteristic example. Technological advances have given birth to digital spaces that are generated by computers, smartphones, or virtual reality devices. These spaces do not follow the same rules and principles as our physical world. They may pose less or more restrictions on players and accordingly they may be used to create experiences with a particular theme or purpose.

Geocaching presents gaming experiences that combine attributes of the virtual and physical worlds. (Used with permission of Geocaching.)

Space can be linear and non-linear. Space arrangement is a very interesting aspect in game design. There are spaces where the specific arrangement leads to game progression along a specific logical order or sequence—let's call them **linear**. There are other ones where players are presented with more than one possible position from which to proceed during a move—let's call them **non-linear**. Linear spaces present a more closed and fixed set of options. Games like **Snakes and Ladders** or **Parcheesi** are linear. In Parcheesi, for instance, even if the board presents a cross-shaped path, the same path could easily be presented as a straight line without any impact on the gameplay. The pieces always move in the same sequence of steps in order to arrive at their destinations. In non-linear spaces, on the other hand, there is no specific sequence of moves for players. In chess, for instance, the different pieces can move forward, backward, diagonally, horizontally, or vertically. The possibilities run to billions of trillions. Obviously, linear spaces are less complex to design or play compared to non-linear ones.

Spaces can be preconstructed or procedurally generated. Game spaces can be constructed in advance or be dynamically created while the game is being played. In the first case, game spaces remain the same no matter how many times we play a game. Several famous games are like this: **Angry Birds**, **Monument Valley**, and **Rayman Origins** being just some of those. On the other hand, procedurally generated game spaces are created dynamically in every game. This means that game spaces will never be the same, even if we play the same level several times. Examples of such game spaces can be found in games like **Canabalt, Temple Run**, or **Doodle Jump**. There are cases where preconstructed spaces are preferred, especially when designers want to control as many aspects of the gameplay as possible, such as the location of objects, the freedom of choice offered to players, or the balancing between the complexity of game levels and a player's skills. There are other cases where designers want to diversify their game spaces and where procedural generation techniques are preferred.

You do not need to take all those aspects into consideration when designing your games. It can be helpful, though, to have a perspective of the different possibilities for structuring your games' spaces.

The game Ludo. (Used with permission of Djeco.)

THE IMPORTANCE OF SPACE IN LEARNING

The process of learning acquires meaning when applied in specific contexts. The fact that someone knows how to tie knots is a highly valuable skill when sailing a boat but might not be applicable when doing software development. People develop their understanding of the spaces they live in and learn from interacting with them. The importance of space has been identified over the course of history by different pedagogues. Maria Montessori, for instance, considered that space was crucial for the holistic development of children and proposed the notion of the "prepared environment." According to her, learning spaces should be designed in a way that would make students feel comfortable, leaving them free to explore but also with direction toward learning initiatives that had been prepared by teachers.

The notion of space has also been examined through the prism of mathematical thinking. Exploring and moving around space helps people to develop the necessary mechanisms for understanding the world around them, navigating correctly in it, and developing the necessary skills to mentally represent the space. For example, someone's ability to read maps, give or receive directions, or visualize complex shapes in their minds can be developed through interaction with their environment.

World Wide Gaming is a geolocation-based skill game designed by Caroline Buttet in order to challenge players' perception of space and distances. The game introduces a virtual tournament where players use a mobile phone trying to accurately aim at cities presented throughout its duration.

Thus, it is not surprising that in the influential pedagogic philosophy of Reggio Emilia, space is viewed as the third teacher, along with children and adults. Space in educational games should support and facilitate the process of learning. This means that spaces should be designed in a way that has meaning and does not add unnecessary complexity to such experiences. In order to achieve this, spaces should be easily adapted to different learner profiles. Let's consider that part of your audience are people with auditory or visual deficiencies. Those people may have difficulty distinguishing complex shapes, identifying color tones, or hearing sounds. Of course, this is not easy and after some stages of implementation, it can be impossible to achieve. This is the reason why space should be seriously reflected upon from the very beginning.

No matter how great an educational game is, in most cases, it will need to be adapted to the individual needs of a classroom, a company, or a learner. For example, the points of interest for an outdoor game, based on geolocalization, will need adjustments if it is going to be played by children or by adults. Also, it is very possible that not all educators share the same perspective on education and learning. Some may be interested in a tightly monitored environment while others may opt for a more open space. So, if possible, educational game spaces should also be able to adapt to different pedagogical approaches.

Even if I love video games, I don't believe that they are the solution to every educational situation. From the perspective of space, I know there are several occasions where digital spaces are not the most practical solutions for the facilitation of learning experiences. We live in a physical world and ought to be interacting with this physical world and developing skills and competences in order to deal with the challenges that arise it.

There are cases where we need to touch objects and understand their structure, composition, or weight in order to have a better understanding of the world around us. To examine the phenomenon of evaporation through a video game could definitely be cool but it would require great detail in order to simulate it correctly. In a physical game activity, this very phenomenon could easily be observed by boiling water in a kettle, providing a cheaper and perfectly accurate representation of the phenomenon. So, not every learning situation can be presented through the same types of space and the advantages and disadvantages of the selection of different spaces should be taken into account when designing one's spaces.

REFLECTION POINTS 🔍

Try to approach your space both in terms of functionality and learning impact.

- How is your game space going to be structured and what materials are you going to use?

- Does your space represent a physical, digital, or fictional world?

- How does your game space facilitate and support the game's gameplay?

- Does it consist of discreet or non-discreet positions?

- Does your space consist of a linear or a non-linear arrangement?

- Is your space dynamically generated or does it follow a predefined pattern or structure?

- How does your game affect the way players learn?

- Does your space guide players toward specific goals?

- What is the level of freedom provided by the game's spatial arrangements in comparison to players being directed toward specific decisions, activities, and outcomes? Does the game focus on guiding players toward a specific sequence of activities, problems, or challenges, or are players left to explore and interact with the game world in any way they want?

GAMES CONSIST OF OBJECTS

Objects are all the necessary items that are required for a game to be played. Objects can be pawns, dice, cards, tokens, characters, or any other physical, digital, or mental representation that facilitates the execution of a game. Digital game characters like **Super Mario**, **Solid Snake**, and the **Lemmings** are game objects. Human players in the game of **tag**, **hide-and-seek**, and **dodgeball** are game objects. The board, cards, and pieces of **Monopoly** are also game objects. So, if every item in a game is an object, how do players understand their use and purpose in the context of a game?

Objects are defined by attributes. **Attributes** are those unique characteristics that give objects a particular function inside a game space. These characteristics can be related to size, shape, symbolic representation, ordering, intensity of events, or any other aspect that helps designers to realize their games. Objects are not limited to one attribute. On the contrary, they can have several attributes. Endless runner games, like **Doodle Jump** and **Temple Run**, for example, feature a main character who needs to go as far as possible during one round. Each go depends on the character's velocity, responsiveness of controls, and jump range. These are all attributes of the main character object. On top of this, the characters interact with other objects inside the game, such as obstacles, enemies, and power-ups. Each of those elements have their own attributes. Obstacles can be big or small or moving or stationary; enemies can move fast or slow and in defined or random trajectories, and so on.

Chess consists of pawns and a game board. Each pawn is characterized by specific attributes, having a different role, impact and possibilities in the evolution of a match. (Used with permission of Djeco.)

During a learning experiment, young children were playing with the **LOGO** educational programming language, changing the speed of moving elements on a computer screen. One girl was trying to assign different values to the speed of those objects. She started by setting the speed to 100, making the objects go very fast. She then placed other values, like 55, then 5, and then 1. She was excited about the outcome of her actions. She was even more excited, though, when she assigned the value of 0 to the velocity of the object. For the little girl, the object was actually "moving" with zero velocity! So zero, for the little girl, was a number, contrary to the notion of "nothing" or "none" [1]. Such circumstances are always important reminders that learning is a subtle process, where every decision of the educator really, really (yes, two reallys!) matters. Therefore, the nature and attributes of your game objects should be designed with caution.

The nature of objects and the attributes related to them can have a positive or a negative impact on the design of your learning experiences. In early childhood, for instance, the defining attributes of shapes are not always clear. This could mean that young students have misconceptions about what a triangle is. The image below presents two identical triangles. However, the second one has been rotated 180 degrees. Research indicates that there are students at this development stage who may consider that triangle B is not actually a triangle. So, if designers decide to use rotated shapes for the creation of games for this age group, that aspect should be taken into consideration. This is just a small example of the different areas that need to be considered for the design of your objects and their attributes.

Another important aspect is that objects should be designed in a way that doesn't create misunderstandings about the subject being taught concept, or indeed, other concepts unrelated to the learning goals of the game. As we have already seen, a great challenge in educational game design is to avoid presenting a concept and creating misconceptions about another due to incorrect representation of the game's environment. Such representations could lead to a false understanding related to a players' spatial thinking. In any case though, game objects, along with other gaming elements that we will see below, need to be assessed continuously both while prototyping and through evaluation phases with learners.

REFLECTION POINTS 🔍

It is helpful to try and approach your game objects both individually and as a whole. Some research on the objects' structure and impact on players' learning is also very important, both for the development of more interesting and meaningful experiences as well as the prevention of new misunderstandings.

- What objects does your game consist of?
- What attributes do those object have?

GAMES HAVE RULES

Rules are the foundation of game mechanics. Their existence and impact on games is a key aspect of the final game experience. Rules are the set of powers that make games what they are. Johan Huizinga considered each game to have its own rules, but as David Parlett noticed, each game *is* its rules [2]. Rules set the context inside which games have a particular meaning. Hiding and moving while concealed around a neighborhood can make people look weird and suspicious. But if someone told you that those weird people are playing hide-and-seek, their actions take on particular meaning in the context of the game. This context is defined by the game rules.

Rules define games in the sense that they are shared by all players, they are absolu, and they are binding. It is impossible to play basketball if the two teams involved play by different rules. Rules are the only point of reference inside a game context. Actions that make sense outside a game may be forbidden inside the same game. In soccer, for example, nobody apart from the goalkeeper can touch the ball with their hands while playing. This also means that rules are fixed during a game. Even if there are games whose rules may change over the course of time, during a particular moment or period of time, the goals are determined and standard for everyone. The absolute nature of rules also makes them binding. When players step into a game, they agree to abide by the rules. If they do not, they will have to contend with the consequences.

In their book **Rules of Play**, Katie Salen and Eric Zimmerman identify three kinds of rules [3]. Those are as follows:

Operational rules represent the set of rules that are absolutely necessary for the game to be played. These may be the set of instructions that accompany a game that we buy or use to explain a game we know to other players when describing it. For one version of the game of tag, for example, the operational rules prescribe that a player chases another player or a team of players. Whoever is caught is the one who must become the chaser.

Constitutive rules represent what lies beneath the surface of a game. Even if I consider myself a good player in The Settlers of Catan, most of the times when I play my friend Fragi I lose. The reason I lose is because he has a better understanding of the game logic and has developed the necessary strategies to address the challenges that the game presents. Even if we know how a game is played, it does not mean that we will play it well. In order to do so, we need to understand its logic and the problematic situations it poses, and come up with solutions that either solve the problem or solve the problem better than the other players. Constitutive rules are a very important component of educational game design, since they are linked to the problem-solving skills and strategies that players need to address to win the game. Constitutive rules are not always clear to all players: How are warrior characters selected in order to set off on a quest in MMO RPG games? Which civilization can counter the attacks of another in strategy games? These are questions related to constitutive rules. Understanding those rules is also an indicator of development in educational contexts and thus could be used as an assessment tool for the learning impact of the game.

Implicit rules represent the set of unwritten rules that are "implied" in the context of every game. For example, not taking a long time to perform a move in draughts or not throwing the dice at the pieces and houses in **Monopoly** are implicit rules. These rules can exist for general categories, such as board games, video games, and outdoor games, but can only exist within the context of each particular game.

REFLECTION POINTS 🔍

- How can the rules of your game be studied based on the analysis of operational, constitutive, and implicit rules?

- What are your game's operational rules?

- What are your game's constitutive rules?

- What are your game's implicit rules?

RULES DEFINE STATES

Rules, among other things, describe a set of instructions on what can, cannot, and should not happen inside the context of a game. In **Minesweeper**, players are allowed to reveal any hidden tile within the area of the map. However, tiles that hide a mine must be avoided if players want to win the game. In **Pac-Man**, players can explore the virtual labyrinth, but if they get caught by the ghosts, game over. Hence, rules define which decision is positive or negative for the development of the game, an aspect that was raised by Brousseau's definition of games, presented in Chapter 2.

In every instance of games, players are asked to make decisions, choosing from different positions. We can call them states, like Brousseau did. Each state presents a set of opportunities and possible outcomes. Some of them may lead to favorable situations and some of them may lead to the player's defeat. However, not all states are allowed by the game rules. In the 3D first-person shooter **Quake**, for example, players can wander freely around space but falling inside holes is forbidden, leading to players' death. In **Doodle Jump**, colliding with monsters means game over. The fact that some states are forbidden does not always make them unappealing, though. In soccer, for instance, physically blocking an opposing team's players while on offense is forbidden. But if the opponents are likely to score, stopping them is an option. Though the act is likely to be punished, it can be a good move for your team.

Permitted and forbidden states are a helpful tool when designers want to guide players toward particular situations or create situations that focus on their learning objectives. Some years ago, I was participating in a training session about group dynamics and communication. The session focused on ways of giving and receiving information. So, the trainers came up with a game where each player was given a piece of information that only they knew about. The team was asked to reach a conclusion about a question posed to the whole group, the answer to which needed the combination of the different pieces of information that each player had. It was obvious that in order for the team to be able to answer the question they all needed to exchange information. However, the game had one more rule: Players could not speak to each other. This rule created a forbidden state that was crucial for the game's learning objectives. Players had to think of other ways of communicating, come up with a strategy of how to collect and process all the different fragments of information, and come to a consensus on the answer to the posed question.

*In the motion sensor control game **PiBot: Math & Action**, players are presented with two main states, only one of which completes the prealgebraic pattern presented on the top of the screen. (Used with permission of Maskott.)*

RULES PRESENT GOALS

All games have goals. Goals describe specific desired outcomes inside the game context, the achievement of which brings either an advantage during the game or personal fulfillment. Goals can involve getting a better score than others, managing to "survive" in a game environment, escaping from a defined close space, or just creating a beautiful structure that only has a unique meaning and appeal to the player who built it. Goals can be set by designers and they are embedded in the mechanics of their games but can also be set by players themselves, who can view and perceive the game and its world in their own unique way. **Minecraft** is an excellent example for this case, since there are different modes of gameplay, each of which presents a different set of goals. From one side, for example, players can mine resources in order to manage and face different monsters, while the game also offers the possibility of freely wandering around the world and interacting with it in every way possible, finding their own meaning for the world and, consequently, their own private goals.

We could say that goals are a major driving force in games, facilitating the process of gameplay, guiding players through designed or emerging gaming experiences. In educational game design, goals acquire another particular use: They can be used to create situations where learning takes place. This is very interesting because, if designed properly, this development of skills that stems from achieving or trying to achieve objectives is not apparent to players, as for them they are only playing a game. In other words, game goals could be used to incorporate, conceal, or guide players toward the game's learning objectives. Let's see an example.

A high school history teacher wanted to present the city's history by introducing students to local landmarks and monuments. She had already presented the same subject in the past through audio visual content inside the classroom but wanted to create a more engaging experience. She hid small chests inside or near city landmarks and organized a treasure hunt. The students of her classroom were divided into teams, each of which had in its possession a piece of information, leading to the location of the next clue. Clues were located inside the small chests they had previously hidden around the city. By collecting all the pieces of information, teams would be able to find the location of the final treasure.

Through this treasure hunt, students were introduced to all the monuments of the city. If they didn't know some or any of them, they would have to know which monument or landmark was which in order to get directions to it and in some cases, they would need to enter a building and search its premises in order to find the hidden chest, thus gaining a better perspective of the landmark. In this case, the game goals were aligned with learning objectives, creating an interesting learning experience.

So, achieving a goal would, on a deeper level, lead to coming closer to the completion of the game's learning objective. At the end of the game, some students wouldn't realize that they had a better understanding of the history of their city but they would say that they had fun playing a treasure hunt game!

It always helps to see if your goals are:

Specific: There is nothing more annoying in gaming than unclear goals. If players do not understand what the goals of the game are, they will initially feel confused, then frustrated, and then they will not want to continue playing the game. Make sure that you have a clear understanding of what your goals are and be careful in how you present them.

Attainable: Goals must not be very easy to achieve, though they shouldn't be extremely hard, either. Very difficult goals might prove to be intimidating for players and discourage them from following them or demotivate them toward specific parts of the game and, if they are too easy, they lose value and become unchallenging.

Facilitating: Goals should be proposed in a way that offers meaning to the whole gameplay. This means that each goal should be seamlessly integrated inside the game mechanics, atmosphere, and style. Goals that have been proposed for any reason but do not feel natural or add unnecessary complexity are better off removed.

There are different types of goals in games. I prefer to examine goals from two perspectives. The first one is their level of importance for the game's completion and the second is their duration and persistence.

Importance of Goals

The first aspect to consider when examining goals is whether they are primary or secondary to the gameplay. Not all goals have the same impact on the advancement of a game. In **Super Mario**, players can advance through the game by reaching the end of each level, which is represented by a castle. If they want, they can also collect coins, an action that grants additional life points. However, collecting coins is not the main focus of the game. Other goals are instrumental to the facilitation and completion of a game and are called primary; some, the existence of which is important for the atmosphere, rhythm, and style of the game, are secondary. Obviously there can be several primary and secondary goals inside a game. In the board game **Risk**, for example, players are provided with mission cards. In order to win, players need to complete those missions, which are **primary goals** for the game.

Then why do **secondary goals** exist? Well, primary goals can't be infinite, so games with only primary goals usually have either very simple game mechanics like the game of tag or hide-and-seek or are very boring because there is not enough action between the completion of the game's goals to keep players interested. I was once presented with a 3D adventure game where players explored a virtual realm, completing quests in several locations. The main problem of the game was that the designers had created a set of quests in specific areas of the map and had paid no attention to the environment between those areas. The result was that players had to walk for several minutes inside empty forests and fields for no particular reason. The game was boring and players would switch to another game the first chance they got. Of course, this is not always the case.

Another important aspect is that secondary goals should have some meaning for players and the context of the game. It is quite common for games to feature secondary goals with no apparent reason, just to fill space or time. This is a bad design practice for several reasons. First of all, more goals usually lead to more development, leading to more possibilities for error and evaluation later on. Second, players have a natural instinct for understanding game elements that do not fit inside an experience. Let's consider that a game puts forward a secondary goal where players need to collect artifacts on different game levels. To make things more interesting, let's consider that those artifacts were placed in difficult-to-reach areas inside the game. How do you think players will react when they realize that all this effort had no apparent meaning inside the game? Losing players' trust on points like this may have severe costs for the later gaming and learning experience of the game.

During a research project at Maskott, we designed Quest Island, a 3D adventure game aimed at helping young players develop their reading skills. The primary goal of the game was to escape the island. While players tried to achieve this goal, they were presented with secondary goals, some of which were necessary for the game's completion, and others that would unlock new content, provide additional information about the game's story, or offer power-ups.

Duration and Persistence

Another way of categorizing goals is related to their duration, persistence, and time of achievement throughout the game. Some goals can be achieved in the short term. Their completion may require effort, but to achieve them, no other condition needs to be fulfilled. Some others, though, require great effort, a lot of time, and might require players to complete other smaller goals before they actually manage to complete the larger goal. Link, for example, wants to save Princess Zelda. In order to achieve this goal, however, he needs to face enemies, solve riddles, and explore the virtual world of Hyrule. Therefore, we can also categorize goals into short-term and long-term ones. **Short-term goals** can be completed in the very near future while **long-term goals** require the completion of smaller goals. In the **Pokémon** games, a long-term goal would be, as the motto suggests, to catch all the Pokémon in the world. Some short-term goals, though, are to make one's Pokémon stronger, win fighting tournaments, and explore areas for new Pokémon.

The relationship between short-term and long-term goals is an interesting one. Games present problematic situations where the solution facilitates the development of the game narrative. However, there is not just one solution to every problem. On the contrary, the problem-solving strategies applied in such contexts are usually a good indicator of someone's understanding of a learning concept and their development during their interaction with a learning environment. Hence, the short-term goals that players will try to complete in order to achieve their long-term goal may not always be the same. Interesting games tend to offer this freedom to players. **Minecraft** offers a whole world to players and encourages them to use their resourcefulness to advance in the game, while in the board game **Carcassonne**, players need to acquire control of as much territories as they can, with short-term goals emerging dynamically by the placement of new tiles by players.

REFLECTION POINTS 🔍

- What type of goals does your game consist of? Are those goals related to your learning aspect and objectives directly or indirectly?

- Does your game consist mainly of primary or secondary goals? How many goals do you have? Is their number consistent with the game's duration and resources offered to players?

- Does your game present long and short term goals? What is their connection, if any?

RULES PROPOSE PUNISHMENTS AND REWARDS

We can see that rules are absolute and binding and their application throughout the duration of games presents players with a set of states, some of which are allowed and some forbidden. Players do not go through this whole analysis while playing games, however. They understand intuitively which states are allowed and which are not. On top of that, they incorporate strategies in order to select the best sequence of states in order to reach victory. Games have mechanisms that inform players about the attributes of different states. These mechanisms are punishments and rewards.

When players enter forbidden states or break rules, games use punishments. The nature of punishments can vary according to the importance of each rule and the dynamics that designers want to create inside a game. They can have severe consequences or trivial impacts on the game outcome. In the 3D endless runner **Temple Run**, hitting an obstacle or falling into the void leads to immediate defeat, a severe type of punishment. In the 3D first-person shooter **Overwatch**, players who are being shot lose energy points that will eventually lead them to lose.

An expected query about punishment in games would be that they may act as a demotivating factor, making them less fun. However, this is far from accurate. Punishment as well as rewards represent a set of interactions between players and games. When players accept to play a game, they agree to its rules. This also includes punishment. It's not punishment that make games less fun, it is its excessive or too-rare usage that can make them unappealing, intimidating, or less challenging to players. The pleasure of winning games is highly connected to their challenge, which is described by game rules.

Rewards, on the other hand, are related to favorable states, where players receive praise for their decisions throughout the game. Rewards could be additional points, more game time, or advantages over other players. The iconic red mushroom in **Super Mario**, the super bananas in **Fruit Ninja**, and the gaining of experience in role-playing games are different types of rewards.

Both rewards and punishments can be of different types within games. They can be as follows:

Permanent or short-term. Not all rewards or punishments last for the same amount of time. There are some that have permanent effects on players or the environment around them. For instance, in soccer, foul play can be punished by a red card, leading to the dismissal of a player. Getting dismissed is permanent for the rest of the match. This means that the punished team will continue the game one player fewer. If we consider that soccer is played by two teams of eleven players, the permanent dismissal of a player during a match gives considerable advantage to the opponent. On the other hand, short-term punishments or rewards are active only for a limited period. In the game of laser-tag, players may receive short-term rewards, like invisibility, where their vests are not lit up, or super armor, making them invulnerable to other players' attacks. But being invulnerable to other players' attacks on a permanent basis would make the game uneven and, apart from the initial kick, would make it quite boring. Hence, these types of rewards are only allowed for a small period of time.

Used once or used several times. Rewards may be used just once after players activate them. In **Half Life**, this is the case with health kits, in **Quake** this is the case with **Quad Damage**, and in **Fruit Ninja** this is the case with super bananas. On the other hand, there are rewards that can be used several times during a game. An enchanted weapon, a superior armor, or a mountable flying creature in role-playing games are just some examples of rewards that are used more than once.

Applied to characters or the environment. There are lots of rewards that are applied directly to game characters, giving them special abilities. In those cases, characters receive more speed, strength, agility, tools, or any other ability that will help them complete a game. But rewards are not limited only to game characters. They can also be applied to any part of their environment, including space and their opponents. In the board game The **Settlers of Catan**, rolling the number seven gives players the option of using the robber piece to steal their opponents' cards and stop the production of the resources of a tile of their preference. Until the robber pawn is removed from the tile where it was placed, players with settlements around this tile cannot produce resources. Even if the reward was not directly awarded to the players who roll the dice, the outcome ended in a favorable state for them.

A team of high school teachers once came up with the idea to teach equations to their students through a digital board game. They had dedicated a great deal of time both to their teaching approach and their gaming elements but also wanted to give a strict tone to the game. The game prototype that was developed presented several punishments when players moved toward incorrect choices. The game became complex and difficult to play and after a while players were tired, annoyed, and lost their focus. The first chance that players got, they would switch to another game. On another occasion, when we were developing our first platform games at Playcompass Entertainment, our prototypes came with lots of rewards. When we later tested the games, we realized that players lost interest in the rewards after a while. Why? Because we were offering so many rewards that in the end, they lost their value and meant nothing to players.

In both cases presented above, it becomes apparent that punishments and rewards should be proposed with caution and in reasonable dosages. Games with lots of rewards tend to be boring. When rewards are freely given and easily acquired, they lose their value and, most of the time, they do not have a strong impact on the final game experience—thus making the games less challenging. Lots of punishments, on the other hand, add a great deal of challenges and complexity, requiring significant effort by players to complete a level or a whole game. Misusing both of these elements can have unexpected consequences on the final game and its learning impact.

REFLECTION POINTS 🔍

- What states can you identify inside your game and how are they presented to players?

- Is the choice between different game states helping your game to highlight your learning content and achieve your learning objectives?

- What types of rewards does your game offer? Are they permanent or short-term, are they used once or several times, and are they applied to characters or the environment?

- What types of punishments does your game present and for what reasons?

PERSPECTIVE

Q&A Session with Klaus Teuber

Game Designer

How do you approach game mechanics when designing your games?
Each time I develop a game, it all starts with a desire: The desire to experience a story in a game. For example, Patricia McKillip's **Riddle-Master** trilogy was the inspiration for my first game, Barbarossa und die Rätselmeister (Barbarossa and the Riddle Masters), while the Vikings' journeys of exploration and the fact that they settled in uninhabited regions inspired me when designing The Settlers of Catan. During the game development process, the game mechanics simply fall into place, because I resort to game mechanics that I deem most suitable for telling my story in a game.

How do you maintain balance between the elements of chance and skills in your games?
Luck is the seasoning of a game. It makes a game more unpredictable, consistently presents the player with new challenges, and boosts the excitement. A game's luck component shouldn't be too strong, though. A player must not have the feeling that he or she is being played. Ideally, strategy and tactics also serve to control luck or chance, so that the effects of

unfavorable events are dampened or even neutralized. I strive for this kind of balance in my games.

How important are prototypes in your design process? How do you use them?
As soon as I have created a concept for a game and I'm satisfied with it, I craft a first prototype. Making my prototypes as appealing as possible is important to me. In the 80s, I employed my own humble illustration skills for this purpose, but today I use illustrations and images from the Internet. The visual aspect of a game is important. Particularly when I want to tell a story in a game, the prototype must already have a creative setting that draws the players into the atmosphere of the game and, in the best case, captivates them.

What do you consider makes a game fun to play?
There are so many different games that, despite their dissimilarities, can be similarly fun to play. For example, I equally enjoy playing Scrabble and Las Vegas, a game published by Ravensburger. Ultimately, the composition of a game determines whether it is fun to play. The composition must be coherent enough for a ghost to establish itself in a game box. As soon as the box is opened and the game begins, this ghost casts a spell over everyone and makes sure that the gameplay becomes the center of attention and a fascinating experience.

Do you have advice for potential educational game designers (ideas, examples, or suggestions to structure their thinking and work)?
When I started developing games, it relaxed me and gave me joy and satisfaction. It was a hobby I was passionate about. During the first few years, I didn't even know that one can make money developing board games.

From my point of view, wanting to become a game designer mainly for the sake of making a lot of money is the wrong approach. You must feel called to design games, just as you must feel called to paint, write, or sculpt. Game designers must develop their games with passion, and they need to muster a lot of patience, which you can only do if you love your work. Each game designer must find out for themselves how best to proceed when developing their game; it is a very individual process that can't be generalized.

I would strongly advise all my young colleagues not to quit their bread-and-butter jobs until they are successful enough at designing games to make a living. Developing games while in financial difficulties and under pressure has little prospect of success.

What are your sources of inspiration?
As I mentioned before, I was inspired by stories or historic events. If I feel the strong desire to make a story come alive in a game, that desire establishes itself in my subconscious mind. I'm pregnant with it, so to speak. Ideas usually come to me spontaneously, during a walk, a car ride, or when I'm taking a shower. I can't make ideas appear by force; however, the stronger the desire, the better the chances for me to be touched by the Muses.

What are your game influences?
Novels, history, and geography. Observations in the everyday world. I detest war games whose goal is to sweep the opponents off the board.

Rules Define Winning Conditions

Games end with unequilibrial outcomes. In other words, in games, some people win and others lose. But the means of achieving victory is not the same in all games. Each game comes with a unique combination of rules that affect the conditions of games for players to win. These are called winning conditions. Even if winning conditions have a direct connection to the achievement of goals, they are not goals themselves. They specify the necessary circumstances under which a goal or a set of goals need to be completed for players to win. There are lots of types of winning conditions. Each of these types has its own purpose while designing educational games. Let's see some of those.

The winner-takes-it-all condition. In George R. R. Martin's fantasy series **A Song of Ice and Fire**, there is only one ruler of the land of Westeros. This ruler is the one who sits on the Iron Throne. In the same way, some victories are exclusive and can only be achieved by one player or team, and when this happens, the game ends. There are many games that follow this approach. In **Snakes and Ladders**, the winner is the first one to reach the final tile on the board. In **The Settlers of Catan**, the first one to collect the necessary amount of points wins the game, while in **League of Legends**, the team that destroys the enemy team's base, called the Nexus, wins.

The independent condition. Independent conditions do not pose restrictions on proposed goals. Every player can finish the game as long as they successfully complete the existing goals. In other words, the victory of each player is independent from the victory of others. Let's see an example: An outdoor treasure hunt game is organized and players are asked to locate five areas around their city and take a screenshot of the monuments that are located there. In this case, all students can go to the five areas and complete their assignment. The fact that other students arrived at these points of interest first doesn't exclude them from completing their goals.

The first come, first serve condition. In this case, the completion of a goal makes it unavailable for others to complete. Let's look at the outdoor treasure hunt game activity again. If players were asked to find five objects, hidden at each of the five areas of interest, then the game strategy changes. By finding and taking a hidden object, the goal of finding this object cannot be completed by other players. Now players know that if they arrive at an area where the hidden object was already found, they may lose time with regards to finding another one. Hence, the strategy of winning the game may change.

The individual or common goals condition. There are games where players share the same goals. In the **Worms** strategy game series, players need to eliminate the opposing teams' worms. In the online card game **Hearthstone**, players need to eliminate their opponents' life points by using their deck cards. There are other games, though, where not all players share the same goals. In the board game Risk, at the beginning of the game, players are provided with mission cards that need to be completed for them to win. Missions are not the same; hence, players can win under different conditions. Similarly, for traditional games like hide-and-seek or tag, some players are hiding or running and some others are seeking or chasing. The winning conditions for those types of players are not the same.

The task-based or the progress-based condition. Victory does not always arrive in the same way. There are cases where victory is the result of the completion of a task or a number of tasks. In adventure games, for instance, in order for the story to move forward, players need to solve puzzles, locate hidden items, or find their way out of complex structures. The completion of such games, though, requires the completion of specific and concrete tasks presented by the games. On the other hand, there are games that players can win by partially completing the presented goals. In role-playing games, for instance, in order for players to level up their characters, there is not just one single way. If leveling requires the acquisition of experience points, those points can be accumulated by completing some of the provided quests or picking random fights with non-player characters of the game. At the end, the goal can be fulfilled by any combination as long as players have progressed up to a specified point.

The personal condition. Every time that I playtest my games with players, I am reminded that playing games does not have the same meaning for everyone. Also, players do not always perceive game goals and winning conditions in the same way. Players may neglect, pass over, or adapt those conditions to their personal needs, ideas, and priorities. Especially in educational games, where game goals and winning conditions are designed to facilitate learning experiences, these conditions become a big challenge for designers, who can address them mainly through lots of prototyping and playtesting.

REFLECTION POINTS 🔍

- What type of winning conditions does your game present?

- Is your game based solely on one type of game conditions or not? If not, do those conditions combine toward a specific type of experience?

- Do your game's winning conditions help the facilitation of learning experiences in your game?

Rules Define Games' Direct and Indirect Responses

One of the most interesting aspects of games is causality. Causality means that for every cause, there is an effect, or for every action, there is a consequence. Getting a red mushroom in **Super Mario** makes Mario bigger, giving players an extra life. Getting attacked by zombies leads to loss of life in **Resident Evil**. Moving one's piece in chess may lead to a checkmate. For every action, there is game reaction. How is this achieved? Through the use of game mechanics.

Punishments and rewards are not the only means of interaction between players and games. Games, through their mechanics, respond to players' actions. To make this clearer, games react to all player actions or events. This presents designers with countless different options and possibilities and a great variety of options for different player moves. This is also one of the most complex and challenging tasks while designing games. The main reason for this is that rules should clarify the outcome of any situation presented inside a game. If this does not happen, the rules are incomplete or substituted by ones proposed by players.

Games provide players with spaces, governed by specific rules, and give them the freedom to make decisions, the consequences of which are directly or indirectly monitored while playing. Let's examine these two cases:

Direct responses are easily observable and affect players directly. Picking Community or Chance cards in **Monopoly** has a direct impact on players who may lose or win money or go to jail; in Snakes and Ladders, landing on ladders or snakes will result in players advancing or falling back on the game board; in **Bejeweled**, creating combos of lines or columns with the same item makes those items disappear and new ones fall from the top. These events are the result of the game's response to players' choices.

Indirect responses, on the other hand, are game responses that do not necessarily affect players in the short term. This is also one of the reasons why indirect responses are not immediately observable and identified by players. In the strategy game **Worms**, for instance, games that last longer than expected lead to sudden death mode, where all worms' health bars are reduced to minimum, making them vulnerable to even the slightest hit and in each round the game field sinks deeper and deeper into the water.

Direct and indirect responses are answers to the question "What would happen if...?" Though it's not always that straightforward! Being able to foresee all possible outcomes in a game is almost impossible. Even the addition of the smallest of game elements can lead to a whole new set of outcomes.

As we will see in Chapters 7 and 13, only through continuous revisions and playtesting is it possible to identify ways to make games responsive to players' needs.

No matter what the medium, games respond to players' actions. What changes, though, is the way that those responses are presented to players. Let's take a look at some examples:

- Falling down on **Doodle Jump** leads to game over.

- Getting a health kit in **Half Life** offers additional life points to players.

- Specific card combinations in **Magic: The Gathering** or **Yu Gi Oh!** lead to additional damage for opponents.

- Inappropriate behavior by soccer players may lead the referee to give them a yellow or red card.

- In hide-and-seek players who get caught leave the game.

In all those cases, the games responded to players' actions. The difference, however, is that those reactions differed in the way they were delivered. In video games, responses are automatic and part of the game's implementation. Nobody can dispute the game's verdict on whether someone fell into a gap or touched an enemy. Even in retro games, where several obvious bugs existed, the response of the game would be the same to all players and would not be subject to any further discussion. In physical games, though, game responses are delivered by players or external observers. In soccer, for instance, there are four referees observing players' actions and they are entrusted with the task of enforcing the rules of the game and delivering its responses to players' actions.

In the mobile platform game Sugar Roll, players experience direct responses when they interact with enemies or collect coins and power-ups. At the same time, the game's pace and difficulty adapts to the player's performance, responding indirectly to their actions.

Being able to identify your game's responses and the way they are delivered can prove to be very helpful in educational games. By understanding your players and your learning objectives, you can help them to reach conclusions and offer guidance to help them develop particular skills through the games' behavior. Some of those game responses could be direct and others could be indirect. Knowing how those responses can be delivered and the technical restrictions that accompany them is also helpful. There are occasions where in order for the game rules to be enforced, several resources may be needed, like a number of observers or a particular development in the game which need to be anticipated in advance.

REFLECTION POINTS 🔍

Being able to anticipate all possible outcomes when designing your games is a challenging task. However, the more prepared you are, the easier it will be to deal with situations that were unaccounted for later. Continuous playtesting and discussions with your peers and players will prove to be very helpful in order to overcome the challenges of this aspect. You can also try to give answers to the following questions:

- How does your game respond to players' actions?

- Are those responses direct or indirect?

- Do your game's responses offer clear information and feedback to players so as to help them clarify issues related to the learning aspect?

SUMMARY

So, what topics did we cover in this chapter?

- Being able to identify the elements and possibilities offered by a particular genre to the design of your learning experiences is an important aspect of your design decisions.

- Space plays a key role in the design and nature of all games. It's advised that space is approached both in terms of functionality and learning impact.

- Games consist of objects. Objects can be pawns, dice, cards, or any other element that is necessary for a game's implementation. It is helpful to try to approach your game objects both individually and as a whole for the facilitation of gameplay.

- Games present rules. Rules can be analyzed in several ways, one of which is in three kinds: Operational, constitutive, and implicit.

- Rules also present goals. Goals need to be specific, attainable, and facilitating. Goals can also be examined as being primary and secondary, depending on their impact and importance for the game's completion, or as short- and long-term, depending on the amount of time required for their completion.

- Rules define ways of punishment and rewards, winning conditions, and direct and indirect game responses.

REFERENCES

1. Clements, D. H., & Sarama, J. (2004). Learning trajectories in mathematics education. *Mathematical Thinking and Learning, 6*(2), 81–89.
2. Parlett, D. (1999). *Oxford History of Board Games*. Oxford: Oxford University Press.
3. Salen, K., & Zimmerman, E. (2004). *Rules of Play: Game Design Fundamentals*. Cambridge, MA: MIT Press.

7 A Closer Look at Game Mechanics

This chapter covers:

- Designing interesting and challenging puzzles.

- Examining the impact of challenge in gaming contexts.

- Presenting different ways that players approach games and make decisions.

- Presenting different cases and elaborating on the balance between chance and skill.

- Studying the different ways of using competition and collaboration in educational gaming contexts.

This chapter offers an advanced examination of several game mechanic aspects in educational gaming contexts. In this chapter we are going to examine several important aspects, such as the design of challenging situations, the notion of flow, the way that players approach games and make decisions, and how learning objectives and gaming elements should be seamlessly blended. Also, the chapter examines the importance of balance in several aspects of game design.

EDUCATIONAL GAMES AND PROBLEM SOLVING

As we saw in Chapter 3, games are excellent environments for the presentation of problems. A very common means of problem posing that one encounters in games is that of puzzles. There has been a lot of discussion about the nature and definition of puzzles. According to designer Scott Kim, in order for an activity to be considered a puzzle, it needs to be fun and have a right answer [1]. There are two aspects in Kim's definition. The first is related to the aspect of fun and the second to the number of solutions that can exist in a puzzle. Obviously, the element of fun is up to the individual and personal opinion of each player, subject to one's preferences, current state of mind, and attitude towards the presented puzzle. But the element of a "right answer" demonstrates that puzzles are problem situations that are solvable. This does not mean that puzzles only have one exclusive correct answer. Puzzles can be solved in many different ways. However, they do have at least one possible way of being solved.

Let's take tying someone's shoe laces, for example. Tying laces is a problematic situation that can be solved in at least one way. In most cases though, the activity itself is not very fun. Consequently, it does not qualify as a puzzle. The definition from Scott Kim allows significant space for interpretation in the classification of puzzles and thus several cases can be considered to be puzzles or not, mainly because of the subjective aspect of fun and pleasure. In his book **Players Making Decisions**, Zack Hiwiller presents a similar, but narrower perspective, considering that puzzles are types of games that require players to use cognitive effort to arrive at solved states from unsolved ones [2]. In his definition he also identifies four features that are necessary for **puzzles** to exist:

• **Puzzles cannot be trivial**. Flipping a coin, boxing a punching bag, and rolling a die are activities that do not require players to actually apply any cognitive procedures in order to achieve them. Puzzles, on the other hand, require players to put some effort in to solve them. This point raises another issue: not every learner perceives the difficulty, challenge, and triviality of an activity in the same way. Tasks that are considered difficult or challenging for some players are not to others, and this is an element that needs to be taken into account when designing puzzles.

• **Puzzles should involve reasoned effort to go from unsolved to solved**. Like in most gaming activities, player actions are the result of meaningful decisions that lead towards a preferred outcome. These outcomes are defined by the rules of the games. Consequently, situations where brute force is the only driving element do not make good puzzles. If we ask a player to pick a card from a deck without any reason, their decision will be based only on luck and brute force, which does not leave much space for thinking or decision-making. Such situations do not usually qualify as puzzles.

• **Solving the puzzle must be the same as winning the game**. There is a difference between being able to come up with a solution that solves a problematic situation and actually winning. Let's see an example: A crossword puzzle presents a situation where filling in all blank squares with the correct letters, in response to specific questions, leads to winning. There are other situations, though, where figuring out the logic behind a game does not necessarily mean that players will win. In **Othello** or **tic-tac-toe** players may understand what strategy is needed to win but applying it does not always lead to victory, as other players can also apply their strategies and claim victory. This is an interesting criterion for the definition of puzzles and it is also one of the main reasons why puzzles are generally viewed as parts of bigger or broader game sets.

• **Even if puzzles may be generated randomly, they must be deterministic once players encounter them**. There can be puzzles with the same logic and set of rules. Using this logic, different versions of puzzles can be created. There can be different types of labyrinths, for example. But after a puzzle is created, a specific set of actions always leads to the same set of outcomes. In a randomly generated labyrinth, the exit is always located in the same location or a puzzle box can be opened with the same movement sequence every time. But playing the board game Carcassonne will produce different outcomes every time the game is played.

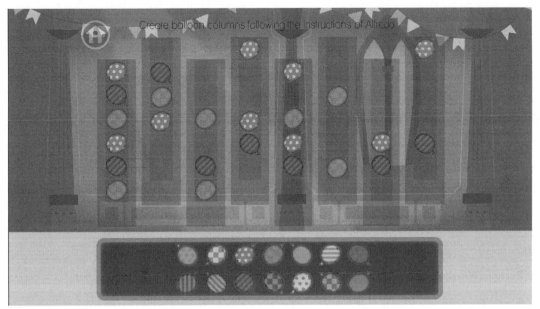

A puzzle level in the mobile game The Fantastic Adventures of Max Squared. (Used with permission of Maskott.)

So, do mathematical problems constitute puzzles? Is the problem: "What is 35 – 5" considered to be a puzzle? Probably not, as most of the times the question itself is not very fun. However, puzzles themselves are problems. So, the main question in educational game design is how we could structure problem-based situations, based on puzzles, that can be presented to players inside games. These are some tips that have proved to be helpful in creating interesting educational puzzles:

• **Puzzles should be clearly presented**. One of the most commonly encountered issues in presenting a game to players is that they have difficulty understanding what they need to do. A game with too much information, lots of givens, lots of demanded elements, and complex elements, or, indeed, if the whole games itself is complex, are some of the possible reasons for this phenomenon.

• **Puzzles should offer players the ability to experiment and discover**. When it comes to education, the most common way of dealing with problems is in the form of problem activities. Activities like this are easy to present and explain and do not require additional work in order to be presented. So, one of the first decisions for educators when it comes to game design is to try and replicate those problem activities inside their games. Even if this is not necessarily wrong, in the end, many games end up becoming quiz activities, which may be useful for assessing what students already know, but in most cases they lack the elements of experimentation and exploration.

- **Puzzles should offer alternative options**. Let's consider that at some point in your game, a puzzle is so difficult that players cannot solve it. After a couple of efforts, it is highly likely that they will be bored, unmotivated, and eventually leave the game. There are many reasons why players may have difficulty completing a puzzle. From one side, the puzzle may be presented incorrectly, and from another side, it's possible that players have not yet mastered the topic you intend to teach. In order to avoid this, one possibility is that your game might offer alternative methods of advancing through the game if players fail to complete a puzzle. These possibilities can vary from just skipping a puzzle and moving forward to being presented with another one.

- **Meaningful hints are always helpful**. Through a challenging puzzle, game designers intend to help players develop their problem-solving skills and get closer to understanding the concept that is being presented. Advice and guidance in the form of hints is always helpful as it can facilitate a player's learning process and clarify possible misunderstandings about the game's elements or learning aspect.

- **Puzzles should be presented with increasing difficulty**. Successful puzzles are the ones that must be solved with some or considerable effort from the player. However, puzzles are not created to give players a hard time or to punish them! Very hard puzzles will frustrate or, even worse, demotivate player and make them lose confidence in their abilities. On the other hand, very easy puzzles don't present a challenge and will make players feel bored easily. This is why puzzles should match the skillset of your players and be presented in a sequence of increasing difficulty that matches the development of a player's skills.

- **Puzzles should consist of a logic, based on learning objectives**. The greatest advantage of puzzles in educational game design is their ability to indirectly present problems that are related to the given learning objectives. The best way to use puzzles in educational game contexts is by using them this way instead of basing them on brute force or luck. The solution of a successful puzzles should be deduced from the underlying logic, presented by the puzzle's given parameters. Let's consider a puzzle with a lock and where players have four key options to use. If the game gave no other hint, players would need to try one key at a time until the lock opened. This puzzle, though, doesn't help players to develop any particular skill. Apart from offering some type of atmosphere or narrative coherence to the game, it's not an efficient learning tool. If, on the other hand, over the lock players could see a pattern with a missing element and the keys presented potential elements to fit this gap, then automatically the focus of the problem shifts towards mathematical problem solving.

- **Good puzzles have meaning in the context of a game**. As we saw before, puzzles are convenient ways of presenting problem-based situations. This means that educators can often love puzzles too much and even overuse them! I have seen puzzles appear in the middle of platform games, adventure games, shoot 'em up games, and even in racing games. The most important point is that students understand when puzzles make sense at a specific point of a game and when they do, they point that out. The point of this tip is not just to suggest that puzzles should be used in a way that builds on the game's experience, but also to highlight that games should not be used as a way to sugarcoat the presentation of puzzles.

- **The number of correct paths**. Successful problems have more than one way to be solved. They challenge the solver's way of thinking and can have multiple solutions, each of which comes with a toll, for example, time or mental effort. In the same way, puzzles do not have just one correct way. More importantly, don't expect that players will think in exactly the same way as you do. Remember that puzzles are used as a way to help students learn, extend their horizons, and develop their problem-solving skills; and for this to happen, they need to be presented with flexible learning environments that help them experiment and explore.

REFLECTION POINTS 🔍

Successful and efficient puzzles that help players evolve and develop particular skillsets and understanding of a learning topic require continuous playtesting and revisions.

- How are your puzzles structured and how do they serve your game or learning objectives?

- Are your puzzle's instructions clearly presented and correctly understood by players?

- Does this puzzle provide players with a sufficient amount of resources in order to experiment and come to a conclusion on the best strategy to find a solution?

- Does your game offer hints, instructions, and feedback to payers concerning their choices on solving the puzzle?

- How does your puzzle connect with the game context? Is it properly integrated into the gameplay or does it stand alone and feel unnatural, being oddly bolted on to the other game elements?

- How does the puzzle completion affect and support the player's development of skills, use of strategies, and understanding of your game's learning content?

GAMES OFFER CHALLENGE

Educational games are powerful learning tools because they manage to captivate players' interest and attention. However, not all games succeed in winning players' interest. A key reason for this is challenge. Challenge plays a very important role in successful games and is also an instrumental factor in why some games may be unsuccessful. Let's have a look at some examples:

Example 1: The Electricity Game
An electronics manufacturer, after releasing new electricity boards, wanted to train their client's personnel on the new devices. In order to do so, they developed an augmented reality game. The game presented a real booth, full of different preinstalled devices. Players would need to use the manufacturer's new devices to replace the existing ones. At the end, they should be able to accurately measure the electricity consumption. The problem was that players, in this case the engineers, found the instruction set of the new devices very difficult. On top of this, the tasks presented by the game required the players to perform complex tasks that they had not previously been trained for. So, during the game, a great number of players would feel frustrated and lose interest, stopping the game and leaving the booth. The game posed a set of extremely difficult challenges and acted counterproductively to the development of players' skills in the use of the manufacturer's devices.

Example 2: The Teamwork Game

A team of trainers organizing an international youth exchange seminar with high school students from different countries wanted to build a game that would introduce participants to the notion of teamwork. They came up with a card game. Players would be divided into teams. Each team would be given five cards, each of which gave one challenge. The players on each team would need to cooperate in order to complete all five challenges. The first team to complete their five challenges would win the game. Since this would be one of the first activities with the new participants, the training team decided not to make the challenges too difficult. However, when they actually played the game, teams found the challenges too easy and completed them very quickly. As the answers to the challenges were easy to find, the teams did not actually need to cooperate in order to come up with solutions to the problems. In the end, the lack of challenge did not lead to a final discussion where teamwork would emerge as the main learning topic.

In the first case, the game presented was highly challenging, causing players to lose confidence in themselves winning the game and finally deciding to leave and do something else, while in the second case, players may have become bored as the game presented almost no challenge. These observations lead to the conclusion that games need to contain the right amount of challenge to attract players' attention and maintain their interest throughout the game. This is related to the notion of flow that we examined in Chapter 1.

THE FLOW STATE

Flow, a concept proposed by psychologist Mihalyi Csíkszentmihályi, describes a state of mind, characterized by intense focus and pleasure, where players are immersed in a task that is intrinsically motivating [3]. In order to enter the flow state, players need to find themselves in situations where there is a great balance to avoid becoming bored, anxious, or frustrated. In order to achieve this, gaming environments need to make sure that:

- Clear goals are provided in order to help players stay focused.

- There is direct feedback and no distractions.

- It is continuously challenging.

Csíkszentmihályi considered that challenge presented by games should be encountered by players with the necessary set of skills. Novice players, with no particular experience playing a game, start by playing levels with little challenge. As the difficult of the levels increases, the challenge gets bigger. Consequently, players find themselves in a state of anxiety, as their current skills are not enough to play the game. They can either develop their skills or reduce the challenge of the game. Csíkszentmihályi, however, considered that players who are aware of existing challenges cannot disregard them for long. So, they will enter a process of developing their skills in order to find some balance between their capacity and the challenge presented by the game. Developing their skills will later lead them to a state where the current challenge of the game is not enough for their skills, making the game boring. Consequently, the game needs to become more difficult again. This is a continuous process, where an equilibrium is constantly sought between the challenge offered by games and the level of skills required by players. If we could draw a diagram of this process, it would look like the one in the following figure. Csíkszentmihályi named the margin where equilibrium is achieved between Anxiety and Boredom the **flow channel**.

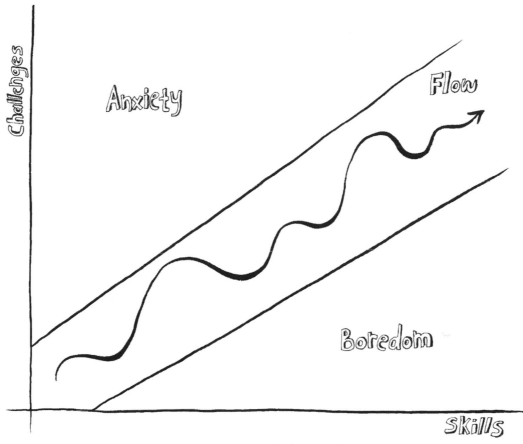

A representation of the flow channel.

In the game **Slice Fractions**, for example, players need to help a mammoth cross to the other side of the platform by clearing all obstacles that exist in between. In order to do so, they need to slice square- or triangle-shaped lava stones and throw them onto ice objects of the same shape. The game aims to introduce players to mathematical thinking and working with fractions. As the game offers a particular gameplay, achieving the flow state is a challenging task, consisting of both introducing players to the gameplay and the notion of fractions. If the game started on a level with complex structures where the problem presented was very difficult to solve, players would become anxious and might lose focus, wanting to quit the activity. If, on the other hand, the challenge presented was trivial for the players' skills, they may choose to quit the game anyway and do something else. The game, though, starts by gradually introducing players to each one of the necessary elements on every level. Players discover the different game possibilities and develop the necessary cognitive and game skills in order to gradually progress through the game.

There are several tips for achieving flow in educational games. The most important ones are as follows:

Tip 1: Challenge should be adapted to players' individual needs.
Not all players learn in the same way and not everyone has the same needs. Players with dyslexia face different challenges from players with movement deficiencies. Players with a more technical background have different needs from players with a more theoretical background when it comes to teaching programming, while the opposite would happen if the course being taught was poetry. Successful flow is the result adapting the game mechanics and the challenge presented to the individual needs of each learner.

Tip 2: Challenge can be presented in different layers and various ways.
Challenge can and should appear in different ways in games. Challenge could be related to mastering the game controls, developing player reflexes, solving problems, applying previously acquired knowledge, understanding new information, transferring knowledge from one context to another, and so on. In this way, games become more interesting and mastering one aspect makes players want to play more in order to master another one.

Tip 3: Challenge lies in both learning and gameplay.
Educational games come with the great challenge of seamlessly combining educational and game elements. If games challenge only within the learning aspect, they are perceived as merely educational activities and if they only have challenge in the game elements, they are perceived as non-educational games. So, challenge needs to come from the combination of both elements, where game mechanics are set in place in order to create the necessary circumstances for the game designer's learning objectives to be fulfilled.

Tip 4: Challenge can be scattered in the space–time continuum.
Not every moment of your games needs to present a challenge. However, when the opportunity comes, those challenges need to facilitate the channel of flow. As we will later see, what makes special moments unique is that they are infrequent. Otherwise, they would not special! So, try to spread the challenges you design throughout the course of your game. This arrangement can be set in time but also in space. There can be areas that present greater difficulty than others and if people know this, they can choose the area of preference depending on their skillset.

Tip 5: Each success leads to a new level of difficulty.
The fact that a level, a quest, or a quiz ended successfully could potentially signal that players have already acquired a specific skillset. In this case, players might need to be presented with more challenging activities in order to match their current skills.

Tip 6: Flow channel is not a straight line.
When it comes to human nature, nothing progresses in a straight line. The same happens with the flow channel. It is impossible to always perfectly match your players' skills with the game elements you propose as it is also impossible to know if players have truly and deeply understood the concepts they are being taught. So, the flow channel is a constant effort of the game as a learning environment to maintain a balance between players' skills and the level of challenge presented to them.

Tip 7: Playtest, playtest, playtest.
You are never sure whether your game is effective until you test it. But how many times do you need to test a game to understand how useful it is? I believe that even if you playtest your game a billion times with a billion different players, you will always discover something new: An aspect you didn't

think about, a new way of completing a level, or a situation that was not clear enough. All of these cases affect the game's challenge and the way that players approach your game. So, the more you test, the more you will know about your game.

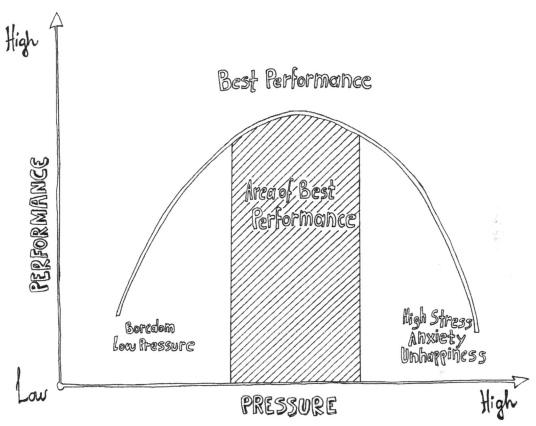

Graph of the Yerkes-Dodson law.

Another aspect that I find very important when designing educational games is the relationship between stress and performance of players while playing games. Have you ever felt that a little stress actually made you more efficient in performing tasks or delivering your work? Have you felt that being a little anxious about performing well on an upcoming test ended up having a positive impact on your final performance? This feeling is expressed through an empirical relationship between performance and arousal that in psychology is called the **Yerkes–Dodson law**.

The Yerkes–Dodson law actually explains that learners' performance can be improved when the challenge presented (otherwise called arousal) is elevated [4]. If this challenge is too high, the level of pressure and stress on learners becomes intolerable, leading to decreased performance. The same happens when the challenge is too little from the game side. In educational game design, performance is related to both playing the game and conquering its learning objectives. In other words, for educational games to be successful, players need to be presented with enough challenge, difficulty, and tasks in order to keep them occupied and active throughout the duration of the game, but avoid situations where anxiety and pressure become so intense that players lose focus.

REFLECTION POINTS 🔍

- How does your game present challenge to players?

- In what ways is challenge presented during the game?

- Is challenge adapted to a player's individual needs?

- Does your game present challenges throughout its entire duration or is there uneven distributions of it? If this is the case, is this intentional? Does it serve specific purposes?

- How is difficulty used as a means of facilitating challenge?

- How much stress is felt by players who play your game?

- Did you consider the development of players' skills and knowledge regarding the game's challenge as a tool for learning? How is this achieved in your game?

DECISION-MAKING

For every problem that is presented, a solution is created. Solutions are the result of players' cognitive processes. As we saw in Chapter 3, in order to solve problems, players enter an iterative process of understanding problems, devising plans, carrying out those plans, and looking back at their solutions. But not all players approach problematic situations in the same way. There are players who get right to the premise of the game, others who like to have a great understanding of the big picture before making any decisions, and others who prefer to let games guide their decisions while they play without trying to get very deep into the logic of the game. In any case though, their decisions and, thus, the development of the game narrative, is related to the ways that games construct meaningful situations where players need to make their own decisions.

A common mistake in educational game design is that several games try to present existing learning content through gaming worlds without altering the content or the initial course delivery. This means that the nature of teaching those subjects does not change, no matter what the medium is, rendering the powerful aspect of games weak. This leads to simply dressing up existing teaching techniques in game's clothes. But let's consider the side-effects of those actions.

- First of all, a great amount of time, effort, and money will be spent to create games that will have little or no effect in helping players conquer the game's learning objectives.
- Secondly, the word "game" loses its meaning in educational contexts, since learners will connect it to activities that they consider far from being actual games. But what makes educational games what they are?

Interesting and engaging educational games offer players intrinsically motivating environments where their decisions have meaning. Players are not idle observers of the events and information flowing in front of them. They are the main driving force in the game world. Games present them with a set of situations, each of which leads to short-term and long-term outcomes. By understanding those possibilities, players make decisions where the consequences affect them and those around them. This very fact gives players the opportunity to propose their own solutions to problems that arise, either by developing particular skills or developing and discovering strategies that will help them to overcome the obstacles presented by games. Effective educational games present the right number of obstacles, create problematic situations that facilitate the development of players toward learning objectives, and help them to clear up misconceptions about existing perceptions by offering the feedback at the right time. In any case, game designers are faced with the task of creating problem-posing situations that will guide players through the gaming experience. These situations present players with a set of options from which they need to take decisions. In his relevant work on decision-making in games, Zach Hiwiller discusses the different attributes that decisions may or may not have [2]:

Blind decisions are made without players actually knowing the outcomes of what they are choosing. Several role-playing games, for instance, start by asking players to create their characters. Their characters can be dwarves, elves, or any other creature that may have particular abilities inside the game. At this stage, though, players are not aware of those abilities.

Obvious decisions are decisions where the outcome is obvious from the beginning. In other words, obvious decisions are decisions where informed or skilled players would always make the same choice. Tic-tac-toe, for example, often presents obvious decisions and that's why experienced players have a great chance of reaching at least a draw.

Meaningless/misleading decisions are decisions where the outcome has no effect on the game. Such decisions are usually presented in adventure games, where game designers cannot account for the infinite possibilities presented by their games. Let's consider that players are locked inside a room and need to find their way out by searching and interacting with its objects. It is possible, though, that game designers do not want or cannot develop content for all the objects in the room. So, clicking on such items would trigger a message, informing players that this item cannot be used or presents a dialogue that has no actual impact on the game.

Handcuffing decisions are decisions that restrict possibilities later on in the game. Losing one's turn, freezing their round, or restricting their abilities are some common examples of handcuffing decisions.

Trade-offs present situations where there are several options, each one with its own benefits and drawbacks. Players need to evaluate their current situation and decide on the optimal way of moving forward. In **The Settlers of Catan**, in each round players have to decide between building roads, raising settlements, or drawing action cards. Each option comes with its own benefits and costs. Trade-offs offer a more meaningful decision-making process, providing suspense to players' choices.

Risk/Reward decisions present different decision options, each of which comes with a different level of difficulty and respective reward. Usually one option offers a difficult challenge with a large reward and others are less challenging but subsequently offer smaller rewards. In several roleplaying games, players are presented with easy quests that offer few experience points and also difficult quests that offer a lot of experience points. Players, depending on their skillset, mood, and style, will choose between those different options.

REFLECTION POINTS 🔍

Every type of decision-making situation comes with advantages and disadvantages, regarding the intensity, challenge, learning impact, or atmosphere that you may want to create during particular game moments. Presenting players with different decision-making opportunities is a matter of design choices primarily.

- What types of decisions are presented during gameplay?

- Are there particular types of decision-making situations that are presented more often during the game?

- Is there a particular reason why specific decision-making situations are presented during the game and why?

PERSPECTIVE

Q&A with Francois Boucher-Genesse
Game Designer/Co-Founder of Ululab

How do you work on creating and setting your learning objectives?
I don't think that games are good for every purpose. If the purpose of instruction is to help students learn a list of facts, then games are probably not the right tool. My assumption is that they are better for intuitive learning, which changes students' perception about specific subjects. To give you an example, when I was a university student, I designed a game about Newtonian physics, which was heavily inspired by existing research on the subject. Scientists had already compiled an exhaustive list of misconceptions that people have on this topic. By playing the game, players didn't learn a list of facts, but their intuition about the subject would change since their misconceptions were addressed through the game. So, what I do is find these lists of misconceptions, helped by experts and scientists in that field, and try to address them.

While teaching math, for instance, we did a lot of research on academic journals; worked with PhD students, researchers, and university professors; and identified the misconceptions that students have in this field. We used standardized tests in order to assess the game's impact on players. The reason we used those types of tests instead of building our own is that building your own tests takes years to do rigorously. If you can find such tests, they can be used from the very beginning and inspire the design of your games.

How do you usually combine the learning aspect and the gaming aspect in your games?
It usually starts with the subject you want to teach. But for me it is also about misconceptions. The reason why I talk about misconceptions instead of just the subject matter is because I find games are a very powerful tool to change players' intuitions about systems. If we were to work only with formulas and lists of facts, which are not really systemic, we would miss out on the biggest potential of video games. In **Slice Fractions**, for instance, children are not yet accustomed to the notions of a half and a quarter when talking about fractions. They don't visualize and they don't have a proper understanding of what those concepts mean. So, we started taking into account the game's subject matter, then identified players' misconceptions

and started building on this. When we were initially designing the game, we experimented with different concepts. Some did not properly address those misconceptions, and some were just not fun. It took several years of testing and prototyping to arrive to the game's final form and it required a great deal of research, work, testing, understanding of the subject matter, and a little bit of luck.

How do you usually work with prototypes in your design?
Let's give an example: At the first phases of designing Slice Fractions, we had already settled on using slicing as a main game mechanic tool. Our intention was to induce states of conflict in our game levels and make players confront their misconceptions. This is where prototyping came in very handy and actually helped to understand several new aspects of educational game design. In order to achieve the creation of this artificial conflict, we came up with individual puzzle levels that were each focused on triggering a single misconception. Players were expected to initially fail, since the puzzle was built to trigger players' misconceptions. After their first failure, players would be surprised, reflect on their actions, confront their understanding of the underlying mathematical concept, and commence some research that would help them evolve. Making mistakes is a great way to motivate players to review their current thinking.

It should also be mentioned that it's a challenge to build highly intuitive puzzles. We initially designed a few levels each with different approaches. For the very first stages, the game presented only shapes that could be sliced. Using prototyping, we experimented with them all and concluded that slicing just shapes was not enough in order to facilitate this learning environment. More skill and options were necessary for the game to be interesting and educational. So, we came up with new mechanics, such as ropes and bubbles that needed to be cut or popped. With those new elements, we could add more freedom, more options, and design levels that could slightly progress the skills and the subject we wanted to present.

When it comes to prototyping, the best way is whatever is cheapest and fastest. Whatever gets you the fastest results. Sometimes it's even better to use existing games as prototyping tools. When designing Slice Fractions, for instance, slicing mechanisms were already developed by several existing games. So, we first examined them. When we wanted to try something later, we would either paper prototype it or use one of the various digital platforms that existed.

What is the most important virtue, the most important skill, that educational game designers should have?
That question is really hard for me to answer. The main suggestion would be to never lose focus of the learning objectives. It's really easy to prototype something and then because of budget constraints, or because of time or some other reason, you have to cut something that will lead to a game that is not ideal for learning. I think that the greatest fight of game designers is not compromising on that learning goal. I think that is the fight of the designer and the fight of the producer against that.

The reason I mention this is because I see lots of new educational games that come out but don't teach you much. They are usually either casual games or gamified questionnaires. A great way to ensure there is educational value is to collaborate with pedagogical experts in the relevant field. So maybe the most important skill for designers is to be great collaborators.

SEAMLESS OBJECTIVES/GAMES

A group of physics teachers, wanting to present the concept of floating and sinking in primary school, came up with an educational game. Excited about their creation, they presented it to their students. But the students didn't react with the same excitement as their teachers. On the contrary, they were easily distracted by other activities, did not seem interested in the game itself, and after a while complained and asked when they could do something else. The learning activity was clearly unsuccessful, even if the teachers had paid great attention in creating a learning experience that would focus on the objectives of their curriculum. It was possible that a simple lecture could have been more effective for the learning outcome in this case. Why did this happen?

The success of educational games lies in the idea that players engage in learning activities, being immersed in intrinsically motivating experiences. It is possible that players can learn consciously or unconsciously in such cases but still, they are having fun. If this criterion does not apply, the offered activities are not viewed as games no matter how they are presented by educators. It's the same as presenting a wonderfully cooked dish of vegetables. No matter how someone presents it to the person who is going to eat it, it is never going to become a dish of cupcakes! I do not suggest that games should merely sugarcoat learning concepts, even if this is very often unfortunately the case. They should always have an honest nature though. Players, no matter their age, can always tell if they are playing games or if they are being presented with activities that are just being called games.

Creating educational games and presenting them in the classroom gives educational game designers a great dilemma. From one side, games that are fun and focus on this aspect are not always received well by teachers, who are afraid of being accused of not sticking to the already heavy curricula. Even if this is not always the case, games that appeal to parents, educators, and other stakeholders in education have greater possibilities to enter the classrooms. On the other side, designing games with a strong focus on learning objectives rather than the game's fun factor risk being received negatively by students. It's important to note that your games won't be the first ones that students are going to be introduced to. This means that it is highly possible that your games will be presented to audiences that have already tried several educational games, several of which were mere activities introduced as games, and players will easily recognize non-fun games as exactly that.

Successful games are those that manage to appeal to both players and parents or educators. Usually, these games find a good balance between game mechanics and the focus on and presentation of learning objectives. Games like this have their game and learning goals connected, if they are not the same. When players play games, they want to complete the goals of those games. They do not view themselves as solving problems or learning history, geography, or business administration. But in educational games those two aspects need to coexist. As we already saw you can't have one without the other. In this case, both those elements need to work together toward the ultimate goal: creating intrinsically motivating learning experiences.

Code Combat is an excellent example of the seamless combination of learning and game objectives. For players to move forward, they need to develop their coding skills, making the learning of coding an integral part of its game mechanics.

But in order for this to become possible, the goals of the game need to be connected to the game's learning objectives. As we saw in Chapter 3, this can happen in various ways: By starting from the game aspect and infusing it with learning objectives, starting from the learning aspect and infusing it with gaming elements, or beginning the development of both at the same time. In any case, though, in the final outcome, the game and learning objectives should not be distinguishable. In **Slice Fractions**, the game goal is to help a mammoth cross to the other side. In order to achieve this goal, players need to use their mathematical thinking skills in order to correctly divide the ice cubes they have at their disposal.

Successful educational games present gaming and learning aspects that are indistinguishable from each other. Concrete and clearly presented guidance before, during, and after game play is a great ingredient for the facilitation of a player's learning. Guidance can clear up misconceptions, emphasize a player's weaknesses, and help them to overcome obstacles that would otherwise be difficult or impossible to deal with. There is, however, a phase where the learning benefits of playing games need to be revealed to the players in order to help them reflect on the skills they have developed while playing the game. As we will see in the next chapter, reflection is an important aspect of playing educational games and can take place in different phases of gameplay.

THE ELEMENT OF CHANCE

Can all outcomes in life be anticipated? At the beginning of the 19th century, French mathematician Pierre Simon Laplace suggested that if there could be a being that knew and remembered the positions and speeds of all the particles in the universe at a given instance, this being could predict their behavior at any time in the present and in the future. In other words, Laplace suggested that future outcomes are already determined and bound by the laws of physics and thus our decisions are also predetermined by this interaction. Almost a hundred years later, German physicist Werner Heisenberg came up with his uncertainty principle. According to him, in quantum mechanics, the more precisely the position of a particle is measured, the less accurately its velocity can be estimated. Hence, the initial conditions of any particle remain unknown, making it impossible to anticipate the future. Whether or not we live in a deterministic world, we cannot fully expect what is going to happen in the future. The same principle applies in games. This uncertainty, however small or large, is what we call chance or luck.

Chance has always fascinated human beings. As an idea, it describes all those countless factors that cannot be foreseen, manipulated, or estimated, but that have some impact on the shaping of a future outcome. Like any aspect of life, chance also exists in games. Its impact on games can vary from tiny to huge. According to Caillois, games where chance plays an instrumental role in their mechanics are based on decisions independent of players, outcomes over which players have no control [5]. In such games, winning is the result of fate rather than triumphing over adversaries. There are several famous examples of this type of game like **heads or tails**, **dice games**, **lottery**, **bingo**, and **baccarat**.

Not all games though are entirely based on chance. In the board game **Trivial Pursuit**, for example, players throw the dice in order to see how many steps they need to move forward, but at the same time they are free to decide which tile they will land on by moving forwards or backwards on the game board. In **The Settlers of Catan**, players roll dice during every turn in order to see which tiles will produce resources in each round. But the final outcome in The Settlers of Catan does not rely so much on chance. The game requires players to come up with the best strategy to increase their points total while also making decisions to face the unpredictable situations that emerge from destiny, which in this case is represented by the throwing of the dice.

As we will see later in this chapter in the section on game balancing, the existence of chance in games does not make them less serious. Chance, like in any other form of art, can be an excellent tool to captivate players' attention and increase their motivation to play your games. Chance represents the unknown. How many times have you watched a movie, read a book, or played a game where the outcome was not obvious to you? This feeling leads to suspense and excitement and keeps players hooked on the game and its progression. Games with obvious outcomes start with an already lost asset, the element of surprise.

Yam Yahtzee, a dice game, is an example of games whose outcomes lie on chance. (Used with permission of Djeco.)

On the other hand, games that overuse chance shift the focus of the game from players to destiny. Educational games aim to create intrinsically motivating learning experiences. Intrinsic motivation requires players to be active during an activity and their participation to have meaning for the outcome of the game they are playing. In order for them to learn as well, games need to create the necessary environment where they can feel comfortable to experiment, explore, and develop the necessary mechanisms in order to construct the knowledge described by learning objectives. Games that heavily rely on chance usually fail to foster such environments. In the card game **War**, a deck of cards is divided between two players. At each turn, players draw a card from their pile and the highest number wins. The game ends when both decks are empty. While playing this or similar games, players use mathematical skills in order to compare numbers and symbols, identify patterns, or perform calculations, but they do not make any decisions. The game mechanics are simple and do not offer enough space for experimentation, decision-making, or the development of any other skills.

REFLECTION POINTS 🔍

- How much does your game rely on chance?

- Is there a particular reason for the existence or nonexistence of elements of chance in your game?

- Does the existence or nonexistence of chance help make a point to players concerning particular learning aspects?

THE ELEMENT OF SKILL

As a kid, every time I would visit a local amusement arcade, I would see other kids playing different types of games and watch them try to finish those games when I was out of coins. Out of all of us who were playing, there were always a few kids who would be able to finish a whole game with one coin. Some of them had such dexterity that they were aiming to beat the high score instead of just trying to reach the end. Those kids had developed such mechanisms in order to face the challenges of the arcade games. Understanding game patterns, getting familiar with the softness or hardness of the joystick's movement, and taking into account the possible lags and bugs of each game, those players were engaged in an interesting learning process. This is skill.

Games that are based on skill make players focused because their decisions affect the final outcome. So, skill is an indispensable element of successful games. But what do we define as skill in educational games? In Chapter 1, we examined skills in learning processes. Such skills can be related to solving problems, understanding the content of text, being able to sketch something we see in our environment, or playing a musical instrument. Those types of skills are defined by the game's learning objectives. But all games require a particular skillset in order to be played. Backgammon requires players to be able to calculate the best positions for their pieces depending on the roll of the dice, pinball entails players being able to instantly repel the ball at the right angle and velocity to get as many points as possible, while in **Splatoon** players need to survive in the game while painting enemy territory using the particular controls of the Wii U.

In educational game design, I identify three points for approaching skill:

POINT NO. 1: THE SKILL

This layer is related to the skills that are required for players to fulfill a game's learning objectives. Games that focus on the mathematic concept of algebraic patterning, for instance, require problem-solving skills, pattern recognition, and reproduction skills. Games teaching the fundamentals of music look for the development of rhythmic skills, musical literacy, harmony, and particular instrument skills. On the other hand, games that are introducing players to digital painting require the development of skills like working with a digital graphics editor, drawing, sketching, exporting one's work, and so on. Every effective educational game addresses a series of concepts through its learning objectives and being able to correspond the expected skills to each of these objectives makes it easier to create the necessary mechanisms to master them.

Apart from the skills that are required in order to fulfill a game's learning objectives, players need to develop skills to deal with the challenges that a game presents. Outdoor games may require agility, speed, and stamina, while video games may require the mastery of a particular logic, being able to deconstruct patterns or getting to grips with particular controls.

POINT NO. 2: THE SKILL BEHIND THE SKILL

Not every skill we acquire through completing tasks are apparent or easily recognizable. In fact, developing some skills will very likely have an impact on other ones. Let's take driving, for example. Driving requires an understanding of how cars are controlled. In order to drive any car, we need to become skilled at maneuvering the car with the steering wheel, regulating gas, and learning how to park. But apart from being able to actually control the vehicle, we develop other skills, like estimating the space around us, performing mental calculations that will help us to estimate our trajectory in a situation, and reading maps. So, the development of a skill can lead to the indirect development of other skills. This is what I call the skill behind the skill.

Games present several occasions of using skills behind other skills. The most common case is the development of skills in order to deal with challenges of the game. Skilled poker players have highly developed mathematical skills in order to calculate the probabilities of the cards in their opponents' hands. In adventure games like **The Room**, **Life is Strange**, **Broken Sword**, or **Firewatch**, players need to control characters and solve puzzles and challenges in order to move forward. Apart from getting used to the individual game controls, players need to develop a particular skillset in solving these puzzles. So, the skill of controlling a virtual character is accompanied by a set of skills related to finding solutions to problematic situations. In the educational game **Slice Fractions**, players need to slice cubes of ice in order to counter lava obstacles. However, slicing cubes is not enough to win the game. Players need to figure out the correct way of slicing those cubes in order for them to make the lava obstacles disappear. By cutting cubes in halves, quarters, or other portions, players are introduced to the notion of fractions and develop their algebraic thinking skills through playing the game.

Skills behind skills offer a great opportunity for educational game designers to present opportunities for players to consciously or unconsciously develop skills related to their learning objectives. If, in step 1 you identified the skills that will help your audience complete your game's learning objectives, step 2 offers the opportunity for reflecting on how those skills can be directly or indirectly developed inside the game.

In Slice Fractions, players slice objects in order to counter obstacles. Even if the initial skill required is the one of slicing, players are introduced to the notion of fractions on a deeper level.

POINT NO. 3: THE SKILL OF USING A SKILL

The fact that players succeed in advancing throughout games does not necessarily mean that they have mastered a given skill. They may have advanced due to sheer luck, used brute force in order to solve a problem, or received help from someone else. It is possible that even if players managed to apply their skills in one context, they may have difficulty doing the same in another. So, educational games should provide students with the opportunity to reflect on the skills they developed and the ways they have acquired them. As we will see in Chapter 8, reflection is a very important process in educational game design.

REFLECTION POINTS 🔍

- What types of skill are required to play your game?
- What types of skill need to be developed in order to continue playing the game?
- What level of each skill is required for the game to be completed?

WORKING ON GAME BALANCE

Balance is important to games in the same sense that the appropriate dosage of salt is important in cooking. Too much or too little could cause the whole recipe to be a disaster. Games that fail to create balance always give a sense that something is not right. Highly unbalanced games lead to even greater inequalities in the games which, if unintentional, will negatively impact the process of learning. For example, games that, intentionally or unintentionally, offer an advantage to some players over others will definitely cause frustrations and internal disputes and shift the focus of the game from learning to endless discussions of whose fault the final outcome was.

In terms of educational game design, balance can be related to many aspects. Balance is required between different game mechanics, like the amount of skill, chance, or difficulty. It can be about the intensity of different elements like narratives, game mechanics, aesthetics, and technology. It can also be about the impact of learning or gaming aspects. So, what kind of balance are we looking for? All of it! Balance is a state where games feel just like they should. The experiences they offer do not bore us but do not frustrate us either. They give us just the right amount of information in order to be able to proceed without feeling lost, they help us to learn but also provide a considerable amount of fun.

Some games can focus too much on the learning aspects and suppress the fun factor, other games may lose their educational focus, and so on. The biggest issue with educational game balancing is that it is very difficult to find the right equilibrium for all elements of games but it is very easy for unbalanced elements to stand out and ruin your learning experience. On top of this, game designers need to strive for balance throughout the whole duration of their games. The fact that a level or a certain situation is balanced doesn't mean that a whole game is balanced. Even if balance is achieved for a specific group of players doesn't mean it is guaranteed for another. Educational games are rather unique in this aspect. Balance is very connected to players and the context which games are presented in. So, how can balance be achieved? The first step to achieving balance is prototyping and continuous play testing. Let's have a look at them.

Progression: Like in any aspect of our lives, we want to feel comfortable with our environment. When players enter a new game, they enter a new experience. Some of them may be familiar with its mentality and some may not. In any case, a game should be able to adapt to players' needs and help them gradually master its mechanics and develop their skills and competences or acquire a broader perspective of a topic. So, a balance between games' difficulty and players' skills should be achieved. This is progression. Games with progression should present players with levels that push their boundaries enough to help them evolve but do not make them feel lost or intimidated.

Skills vs. chance: We already examined the elements of skill and chance in designing games. A question that always bothers game designers is what the right balance between skill and chance is. From one angle games that are heavily reliant on skill may prove to be too intense or intimidating for some players while games that rely greatly on chance may be considered boring or unchallenging by others. Balance between these aspects brings an equilibrium between the great demand for physical or cognitive skill development required from the skills aspect and the unpredictable, yet always challenging, aspect of chance.

Intensive vs. relaxing: Like in any form of art, in games, not every moment is the same. Experiences are shaped from the combination of different moments, each of which builds on a particular message and set of emotions. Hence, there are moments that are intensive where players need to focus, thoroughly examine their resources, and come up with solutions to problems; or reflect on presented situations, creating deductions, and drawing their own conclusions. Those moments are accompanied by less intensive moments, where players have time to reflect on their actions or just relax. Structuring such sequences with intensive and relaxing moments is crucial for the successful progression of your games, as we will see in the next chapter.

Fair vs. unfair: We can all agree that nobody wants to feel treated unfairly. A magical aspect of games is that all players are subject to the same set of rules. So, when players behave or misbehave a referee or the game itself will intervene and enforce the rules of the game. When this doesn't happen, due to bias from the referee or game, the experience is damaged and players feel excluded and annoyed.

Those feelings can also stem from an incorrect estimation of provided resources or the creation of unequal states for different players. For example, if the characters of two players in an RPG game come from different classes, they will have different abilities. If the abilities of those characters give considerable advantage to one over the other, then the game is unbalanced. This may lead to one player feeling frustrated and confused and, in the long-term, will probably render this character class unused by players. So, a great question concerning this aspect is whether your game gives a fair advantage to all players for different states and possible outcomes throughout its duration.

There are also cases in which designers intentionally want to give advantages to some players over others in order to make a point. In simulation games, for example, game designers have made some groups of players considerably wealthier than others in order to emphasize the social and economic differences between groups in the teaching of economics and sustainable development.

Guidance vs. freedom: We have already examined Vygotsky's Zone of Proximal Development and the proposal of scaffolding mechanisms to help people learn. Educational games are expected to directly or indirectly offer some guidance and support to players to help them learn. However, there is a lot of discussion about how this can be achieved. From one side, there are players who do not want to be restricted by specific routines or prechosen paths and want to explore a game world and take their own time conquering its objectives and challenges. From the other side, there are players who want or need some guidance from games in order to proceed. Games should be able to adapt to both those cases. Successful games maintain balance between freedom and guidance. Games should be able to offer guidance and instructions where needed while not restricting players' choices. It is also important to emphasize that guidance does not necessarily mean explicit instructions but could consist of any type of information or indication that could help players clarify a particular game aspect. There are games that offer great flexibility and freedom to players, like **Minecraft**. Even in such games, though, the selection of tools and resources for players gives them guidance toward specific directions.

REFLECTION POINTS 🔍

Achieving balance in educational games is a highly challenging task and requires a global and holistic perspective of the game design process. Some helpful questions are:

- Does the game offer progression related to challenges presented and the players' skills? How is this progression achieved?

- Does the game offer balance between chance and skill? If yes, how is this achieved? If no, what was the reason for this design decision?

- How is the balance between intensive and relaxing moments in the game achieved?

- Does the game offer equal opportunities and resources to all players? If not, is this a design issue or was this done intentionally? If it was intentional, what were the reasons, regarding the game and learning aspects?

- How does the game intervene in players' decisions and guidance? Are instructions provided and to what extent?

ALL FOR ONE AND ONE FOR ALL

There are certain moments where people want to be alone, take some time for themselves, have their own space, and take their own time completing the tasks they set out to do. There are other moments, though, when people have the need to be with others. They long for discussion, company, or common action. Those two needs have been clearly depicted in game mechanics. We can find games for one player and we can find games where several players are involved. No matter what the medium, from digital to outdoor to board and card games, we can find games that are both single and multiplayer.

There are several **single player** games. From **Angry Birds** to the **Legend of Zelda** and from solitaire to pinball, there is a great variety of games that are designed for one player on their own. Those games are not necessarily digital. There are several reasons why educational single-player games exist. From one side, they appeal to players' needs for personal space and to self-regulate their own play process. The fact that modern players have their own personal game devices, such as handheld consoles, smartphones, or virtual and augmented reality equipment, bring single-player modes into the spotlight for their effectiveness and ability to be personalized to players' needs and preferences.

Multiplayer games, on the other hand, appeal to players' need to be part of a group. In multiplayer games, players interact with each other collaboratively or competitively but are all still part of the same learning experience. Multiplayer games involve more than one player who may act as individual entities or as teams. Those players may share the same goals or not. In some cases, their goals may conflict, as we will see later on. In any case, these players are part of the same game world, are bound by the same rules and, whether they are playing with or against each other, will become familiar with each other's way of acting in the game world. This leads to the creation of player communities.

Being part of a community is a strong emotion. This can easily deduced by observing fans of sports teams. Being part of a community fulfills players' needs to be members of a group and to identify themselves as such. Group members interact with each other and communicate, discuss, and express their feelings. They may develop some sort of emotional connection by sharing common memories and interests. In many cases, players feel committed to communities and share an emotional stake in their success or failure.

As social beings, humans want to be part of groups and learn from their interactions with their peers. So, playing multiplayer games can be used as a great opportunity for the creation of learning environments. However, like any tool, multiplayer games may be difficult to organize or implement, let alone to help create the necessary circumstances for learning.

Multiplayer games may be highly entertaining and helpful when several learners are involved, but the increase in player numbers comes with some costs. The first is related to the practical aspect of how all the players are going to get to play and enjoy a game without feeling bored or excluded. As we have seen before, everyone wants to get some part of the action and this can be achieved by feeling involved and active during the playing games. If we take board games like **Monopoly** or **The Settlers of Catan**, for instance, the number of players is limited as players play in terms. This is because a large number of players would mean participants would have to wait a long time for their turns, making them feel bored. This does not mean that games with many players are necessarily impossible to happen.

There are several games played by hundreds or thousands of people, like **Ingress**, **EVE Online**, or **World of Warcraft**. But the studios that developed those games created great infrastructures in order to support their massive demands. Almost always, multiplayer games require logistics and technical consideration. I tend to see game designers getting really excited when creating games for a great number of people. Who wouldn't? It is, however, important to remember that big player numbers require a very good understanding of one's audience and technical restrictions that their resources present.

In order for players to learn from their peers, they need to be able to monitor other players' actions and decisions and reflect upon them. In some cases, where players play individually or in teams, this can be achieved by internal team discussions and later discussion with other teams to see how others approached the same challenges and what strategies and skills they applied to find solutions. There are cases, though, where discussion is not possible. Especially in video games and platforms where players from different regions of the world come together to play, facilitating reflection discussions or being able to monitor other players' actions is not always easy. In cases like this, educational game designers have previously used communities in order to raise discussions around the games by using forums or blogs through which they present pivotal moments in other players' sessions.

REFLECTION POINTS 🔍

- Is your game single player or multiplayer?
- If the game is multiplayer, is it played in teams or by individual players?

COLLABORATION AND COMPETITION

Two aspects that influence multiplayer games are those of collaboration and competition. Both aspects offer educational games a particular spice, contributing to the creation of intrinsically motivating learning experiences. From one side, games with collaborative aspects are considered to provide players with the opportunity to learn with others. This does not mean that players do not learn from their opponents, as we have already seen. So, the question is not about choosing between collaborative and competitive aspects but how they should be used and combined in order to create more powerful learning experiences.

COLLABORATION IN EDUCATIONAL GAMES

Several learning theories have emphasized the importance of **collaboration** in learning. Players can learn by observing their fellow players, discussing issues with them, and sharing common responsibilities and tasks. Players collaborate better when their process of work is facilitated. Facilitation in games can be achieved through the design of game mechanics. There are cases where players assume different roles in order to contribute to the team effort, like in **League of Legends**, and there are other times where players take on the same role.

Players that collaborate have common goals, the completion of which is easier when they work with others. There are times when players who happen to work together take more time to complete a task than they would take being alone. This problem may stem from two reasons. The first is related to the inefficient facilitation of players' work. Facilitation requires good communication among team members. In the first stages of designing the game platform **Tactileo Map**, we realized that communication among different teams was not so easy to facilitate when those teams were playing games outside. The teams were usually situated in distant locations across large areas and communication would be practically impossible. On top of this, the first-level prototypes did not give much incentive for teams to cooperate. Since it was possible for teams to achieve their objectives without collaborating, players would avoid it. In the end, we designed an internal chat function that would help players communicate with each other better and we came up with levels where completion would be very hard without collaboration. The second reason is that, in some cases, games may present situations that do not allow players to work simultaneously on the same task. This may happen due to several reasons, such as limited resources offered or the selection of an inconvenient location where not all players can be present at the same time.

COMPETITION IN EDUCATIONAL GAMES

Competition, on the other hand, rises when players' goals conflict with each other. In this case, the completion of one or more goals deprives other players from achieving them. Competition is very common in games. Some players cannot even define games without including the element of competition. Competition is connected with the element of conflict which in turn is linked with action and suspense.

Similarly to collaboration, competition can lead to several learning opportunities. Even if competing players may not exchange information and ideas, they interact with each other. They observe their opponents and learn from their mistakes and get inspired by the correct choices and techniques they used to find solutions to their challenges. For this to be possible, though, educational games should be able to facilitate visibility of opponents' actions and reflective discussion. Visibility allows players to examine their opponents' decisions and reflective discussion helps them to reach conclusions through their participation.

Collaboration and competition are not mutually exclusive in games. There are several games that present both collaborative and competitive elements. Again, one the most characteristic examples of this are sports. Baseball, rugby, soccer, and basketball are played by competing teams, the members of which need to collaborate in order for their teams to win. On other occasions, competing players may need to collaborate in specific situations in order to overcome a common enemy or obstacle, helping them all to move closer to their final goal. Collaboration and competition can be used in countless combinations in educational games. So, game designers need to decide which mix of collaboration and competition is going to help learning and gaming elements emerge and give birth to experiences that are both entertaining and educational.

REFLECTION POINTS 🔍

Collaborative and competitive aspects can take on great dimensions in game design situations and lead to very interesting gaming experiences.

- Do your game's players or player teams collaborate or compete during the game?

- Are there moments where your game's players or teams need to compete and others where they need to collaborate? How is this achieved in your game?

- Considering that your game is played in teams that either collaborate or compete, do all the team members share the same objectives? If yes, the teams internally collaborate; if not, it's possible that team members may need to compete in order to achieve their personal goals.

PERSPECTIVE

Simon Egenfeldt-Nielsen
CEO of Serious Games Interactive

How and where could games be used in educational contexts?
I think that in general games can really be used pretty much in any context and for many learning purposes. Their use is similar to any other medium. So, you can use a game in the same sense and aspect that you could use a book. Of course, there are several situations where it makes more sense to use games, mainly because of their nature compared to other media forms. In general I would say that if you look back over the last 50 years, you will see that games have been increasingly used in education.

What is the process you apply when designing educational games?
This is a pretty big question! I wouldn't say that we stick to one theory or approach. However, we have some templates that we tend to follow. Initially, we try to frame the learning concept, and this is very much about who our games' learners are, what our objectives are, what the expected impact of playing educational games is, what the context of use is, and how much support there is during play those games. We also try to identify deadlines and technical limitations. We also put great emphasis on the overall learning experience of our games. We elaborate on the atmosphere and results we want to achieve, identify internal resources that we can use, and take into account parameters that will help us achieve this experience.

There are occasions that we are asked to design games and the graphics or contents of which already exist. In cases like this, we may rework those aspects in order to achieve the experience we want. But the experience could also be associated with information and knowledge that we need to provide and communicate. This is the reason why we work very closely with some of our clients. We speak with them, we identify their needs, and we work on anything that is related to the overall game experience, such as the game genre or the complexity and the nature of the experience. This can be about the game's interface; sometimes it can be more about navigation, interaction, or mechanics. So, typically after those steps, we can work on digital or physical prototypes and work on it again and again. Of course, in this process, we take into account the development of those games as well.

You have been designing educational games for a long time. Do you have any advice for potential educational game designers?

I think the first important aspect to really understand and remember is what type of learning experiences you are designing. Even if the mechanics or an idea behind a digital or physical board game may seem the same, they are really different designs due their educational contexts. The second thing that I would emphasize is to make sure that designers know the learning and gaming goals of the projects they want to design for. It is very easy to be suddenly seduced by either a specific learning or gaming goal that is not that important to the bigger picture. You need to be able to design engaging and interesting games that are also aligned with the learning style and objectives that you want to achieve. There are several things that you can forget in the process and it's very important to keep asking those difficult questions during the design process. There are times that when you design, you detour and lose focus of the objective. Or you design something for students and at the end of the day teachers can't use it because it is too complicated, difficult to understand, or not aligned with the elements they want to teach.

Sometimes during the design process you also realize that you might as well be reading a textbook or watching a video—there is no reason for using a game format. Also, never underestimate the power of known and efficient patterns to work with. You do not need to reinvent the wheel every time. There are also times when the teams you are working with don't like compromises. They may insist of maintaining a specific gaming or learning trajectory without taking into account the final impact on the learning and gaming experience. In this case, the design process is difficult, and the final game is likely to fail. Any good educational game design process requires you to be agile and make compromises—you can't get everything. Also, never underestimate the importance of making games that are polished and appealing to players. There are several occasions that designers underestimate the importance of nice and polished games, which may lead to unwanted outcomes.

SUMMARY

So, what topics did we cover in this chapter?

- Games present puzzles. Successful and efficient puzzles, which help players to evolve and develop particular skillsets and understanding of a learning topic, require continuous playtesting and revisions.

- Games present challenge. Designing challenging activities, though, is not that simple. Games need to be challenging enough to meet players' skills and knowledge. Games that are not challenging enough are boring and games that are too challenging become intimidating.

- Players make decisions while playing games. Every type of decision-making situation comes with advantages and disadvantages, regarding the intensity, challenge, learning impact, or atmosphere that you may want to create during particular game moments.

- Games may be based on skill and chance. The use of each of those aspects can have different impacts on the final gaming experience and the way that players learn.

- Game balance is not limited only to one gaming aspect. On the contrary, balanced games present a harmonic combination of elements in every aspect that describes them.

- Games can be single and multiplayer. Additionally, games may present collaborative and competitive aspects. Deciding what type of games you will design will greatly impact the way that players will learn, interact, and approach your games.

REFERENCES

1. Kim, S. (n.d.). *What Is a Puzzle?* Retrieved from http://www.scottkim.com.previewc40.carrierzone.com /thinkinggames/whatisapuzzle/index.html
2. Hiwiller, Z. (2015). *Players Making Decisions: Game Design Essentials and the Art of Understanding Your Players.* Berkeley, California: New Riders.
3. Csikszentmihalyi, M., Abuhamdeh, S., and Nakamura, J. (2014). Flow. In M. Csikszentmihalyi (Eds.), *Flow and the Foundations of Positive Psychology* (pp. 227–238). London: Springer.
4. Yerkes, R. M., and Dodson, J. D. (1908). The relation of strength of stimulus to rapidity of habit-formation. *Journal of Comparative Neurology and Psychology, 18*(5), 459–482.
5. Caillois, R. (1961). *Man, play, and games* (M. Barash, Trans.). Urbana & Chicago: University of Illinois Press.

8 Games as Reflection Tools

This chapter covers:

- The impact of reflection on educational game design.

- Tools and best practices in order to facilitate reflection in educational games.

- Introducing interest curves as a means of assessing and improving one's games.

Reflection and debriefing are crucial to efficient learning in gaming contexts. This chapter is dedicated to the design and facilitation of reflection moments and sessions for players in educational games. Additionally, we will examine interest curves as a tool for monitoring players' engagement and interest during gaming experiences.

I find it remarkable how specific moments, not necessarily noticeable or lengthy in duration, can define the final feeling of an experience. There are cases where a teacher's funny comment or presentation can turn a boring class into a memorable moment and there are others where a miscalculation or the lack of anticipation of some factors can lead to disaster. In the same way, there are particular moments in game-playing that are instrumental for the presentation and understanding of learning concepts. I prefer to refer to those moments as match points, since they can be so critical for the impact of an educational game.

THE IMPORTANCE OF LOOKING BACK

As we have already seen, learning is an individual process and happens differently from player to player. So, even if we had the luxury and ability to replicate the conditions of an effective moment for one person, it would not be guaranteed to have the same effect on someone else. But as educational game designers our aim is to create the necessary conditions, space, and timing that will help each individual learner examine, approach, and conquer a learning concept in their own unique way and at their own pace. Let's consider that by now you have come up with your learning objectives and game mechanics. You have worked on your game attributes, rules, winning conditions, balance, and technical implementation. You may already have a working prototype of your game or a more advanced implementation of it. But is your game actually providing players with the opportunity to conquer a learning concept?

In order to give some more thought to this question, let's have a look at some cases that I happen to have experienced in the past:

- After playing a video game focused on teaching about the gravitational forces among planets, some students showed difficulty explaining the concept of gravity and the rules governing it.

- One month after a video game about teaching fractions was introduced into a primary school classroom, the majority of students were able to successfully finish the game, making the right choices while playing the game, but during later assessment it became obvious that the concept of fractions was not clear to them. From one point, students had learned the exact sequence of moves and choices that would lead to the completion of a level and from the other, they showed difficulty applying the skillset they were supposed to have acquired to another context related to fractions.

- The employees of a company were introduced to a card game about communication. The game was based on giving each individual a missing piece of information and required communication channels to be created between people solely through handwritten messages. After playing the game, the employees thoroughly enjoyed it but did not realize the real purpose of the activity.

In all the cases described, there was something missing from the games proposed. The games did not offer the space and time for players to reflect on the learning process taking place in those games. They did not have the opportunity to evaluate their decisions and either proceed with them or change them. Subsequently, those games did not give players the opportunity to think on their thinking process or, in other words, they didn't help them to reflect on what they had learned.

When students reflect, they engage themselves in a cognitive process of examining a learning concept and the techniques they used to master it. In his book **How We Think**, philosopher John Dewey did not consider reflection to be a mere sequence of ideas but a consecutive process through which each discovery, observation, or hypothesis leans upon the experiences and logic of the student. He also proposed that reflective thinking is an active, persistent, and careful consideration of any supposed form of knowledge in the light of the grounds that support it. What Dewey suggested is that students who have developed reflective thinking have critical skills and are consequently more efficient at making sense of the information they receive.

In Chapter 3 we saw the relationship between playing games and problem solving as well as Polya's problem solving analysis. While playing games, players need to find solutions to problems presented through the game environments. In order to analyze the process of problem solving, mathematician George Polya proposed an iterative approach consisting of four steps: Understanding the problem, devising a plan, carrying out the plan, and looking back over the process. So, we can see that the last step of Polya's problem-solving process is the solver's reflection on dealing with a problem.

By looking back at their performance while playing a game, players have the opportunity to:

- Assess the validity of their choices during gameplay. It is quite possible that during specific game moments players won't have the necessary time to examine their choices. Whether players were able to complete a level or a whole game doesn't mean that all their decisions were correct. By looking back on their actions, they can identify some of their mistakes and address misconceptions they may otherwise have.

- Examine the effectiveness of their decisions and come up with alternative strategies and solutions to problems. We have all encountered situations where we finished a game but did not complete all its quests, did not collect the total number of badges, or just managed to get through with the minimum possible performance. Being able to complete a game is very different from doing so in the most effective way possible. By looking back, players have the opportunity to assess the effectiveness of their strategies and compare them with the strategies of others or new ones they come up with.

- Go deeper in the taught subject. Playing games is always a good opportunity to attract someone's interest in a topic. Players can be motivated to discover more about a concept or idea and looking back is a very good opportunity to provide them with additional information.

- Arrive at generalizations and transfer knowledge they received while playing a game. Especially in the fields of math and science, it is possible that not all scopes of a concept can be taught in one game. Additionally, due to particular artistic or development choices, game objects may be represented in a particular way. Without reflection, it is possible that players may not have the opportunity to grasp the general idea of the concept and stay within the boundaries of the proposed game.

I consider looking back to be the baking process of creating a cake: Even if educational game designers deliver perfect gameplay and mechanics, great graphics, and an interesting narrative, and robust technical implementation have only achieved 50 percent of creating an educational game. All the ingredients are there, they have been blended expertly, they smell great, and they are on the tray, but they are not ready yet. In order for those ingredients to become a perfect cake, they need to be baked at the right temperature for the correct amount of time. This is looking back!

TOOLS FOR REFLECTION

From the previous analysis, we can see that there are two reasons why educational games should facilitate reflection:

1. Since educational games are complex systems that affect players in various ways, players may require further consideration of the gameplay and its underlying concepts in order for the game to achieve its teaching objectives.
2. There is a need for facilitating the process of considering one's decisions throughout a game and the concepts it teaches.

To better understand how to structure moments with meaningful reflection, it is interesting to take into consideration two processes of reflective thinking. Those processes, analyzed by Dewey [1], are (1) doubt, hesitation, and perplexity, and (2) the act of investigating in order to clarify the facts related to a learning experience. When players encounter situations that challenge their existing beliefs and perceptions, they momentarily feel doubt and confusion. This feeling is accompanied by a series of mental or physical actions that aim to shed light on the situation and confirm or reject the hypothesis that players wanted to test.

Reflection sessions usually follow learning activities and aim to facilitate players' discussions and thinking processes to help them develop the necessary skills and understanding of the presented concept. However, poorly structured reflection sessions risk adding complexity to a game, making it more difficult to handle or boring to play. On top of this, they may not have the necessary learning impact on players. The following are some criteria proposed for more effective reflection sessions:

- **Type and nature of reflection tools**. There are occasions where a set of meticulously selected questions could help players to clarify and own the experience they live. At other times a collective discussion among various players can help them make the necessary connections between games and learning concepts. Sometimes activities, related or unrelated to the played games, can be used as reflection tools. The main point to keep in mind is that reflection tools should help players to reach conclusions, make connections, understand topics, and be able to use the knowledge they acquired outside the context of the game.

- **Depth of reflection**. Moments of reflection are great opportunities for players to focus on more than the superficial aspects of the games they play and their learning aspect. These are great opportunities to think further and address deeper weaknesses and misunderstandings. An effective reflection moment raises questions that target those weaknesses and misunderstandings and creates connections with the games to help players acquire a greater perspective of the subject and better understand the learning topic.

- **Right timing**. Like in any aspect of our lives, correct timing is important for reflection. If reflection starts too soon, players may not have the necessary information, experiences, and interest to find solutions to the problems presented by educational games. If it starts too late, players may not be able to actually connect their previous experiences to the ones presented in the game. So, reflection should be facilitated at the correct time. Some designers create sessions after each game level, after particular milestones, or after the end of a game session. The correct timing depends on the type of game, your audience, and the resources you have to facilitate such sessions. So, the only appropriate way to find out what works best for you is through experience and experimentation.

- **Duration**. Reflection sessions should provide players with the proper amount of time to reflect, find solutions to their problems, and reach their own conclusions. This time is different from player to player and from situation to situation. In any case, though, reflection sessions should not be conducted and facilitated hastily just to make them happen.

- **Collaborative and individual**. There are many players who prefer to work alone and others who look forward to working with their peers. So, reflection sessions can be conducted individually and collaboratively. Both cases offer different advantages. In the first case, players can regulate the rhythm of the session since they are the only ones participating in it; in the second case, players interact with their peers, see their perspectives, and learn from them.

REFLECTION POINTS 🔍

- Does your game present players with the opportunity for reflection?

- How does your game present and facilitate player reflection?

- What are the nature of your reflection tools?

- Which particular aspects of your learning topic do you want to address through reflection sessions, and how deep do they go?

- When are these reflection opportunities organized during the game? What is their duration and are they seamlessly integrated into the gameplay?

- How many players do the reflection sessions include and are there the necessary resources to facilitate possible discussions?

WORKING WITH INTEREST CURVES

In his book on screenwriting, **Save the Cat**, Blake Snyder elaborated on the importance of being able to explain one's story in less than 30 seconds [2]. His main argument for this was that when people go to the cinema and need to make a decision on which movie to watch, they are open to suggestions but they have a short attention span. Imagine a company of five friends entering the cinema. Several posters are hanging up, some feature famous actors, and some of them display totally new concepts. To propose a new movie to their friends, people need to able to sell them on the movie that they like within a very short time span, probably less than 30 seconds. The point that Snyder wanted to make is that getting someone's attention is not easy. So, you need to be able to master the art of winning it and working with it.

Getting a player's attention is a key point for a game's impact. But even if this sounds rather straightforward, it is a challenging state to achieve. This is mainly because that attention must be kept throughout the whole duration of the experience. For example, a game with a cool intro or exciting first level can be very attractive at the beginning but doesn't guarantee that players will actually finish the game. Players seek constant excitement, challenge, and exploration. They look for experiences that will indulge their curiosity and help them fulfill their needs. But how would this be possible?

Why do games of the same genre have a different appeal to players? Why are some more successful than others? They incorporate similar mechanics and require an equivalent skillset, but still some games are more efficient at captivating someone's interest and keeping them hooked inside their world. The best way to answer this question is to analyze what elements make learning experiences, and consequently learning games, interesting.

In his book **The Art of Game Design**, game designer Jesse Schell identified three factors that impact the interest of any activity [3]. These factors are:

Inherent interest. Some activities or events happen to be more interesting than others. A game about a scientist having to escape a strange experimental accident and facing aliens from other dimensions is likely to be considered more interesting than a quiz. Or an outdoor game, where players need to hide, chase each other, and use their resources to find solutions to problems may be more exciting than sitting inside a classroom and listening to a lecture. So, the nature of each experience plays a great role in a player's interest.

Poetry of presentation. As we will also see in Chapter 12, a nice presentation creates a positive predisposition to players about one's game. This is not only limited to the polished quality of graphics and sounds, but can be related to the way the game is presented to players through game mechanics, story, or technical implementation.

Projection. Have you noticed that some experiences affect us more deeply than others? One great reason for this is that sometimes we can project ourselves onto them. There are situations where we could not imagine given events happening to us or connecting them with our daily lives, so they seem distant and thus, less interesting. On the other hand, if those experiences are even distantly related to us, we approach them in a very different way. Interesting games succeed in making us feel connected to their characters, events, and situations. We feel compassion for characters; we want them to get what they need and feel happy when they do.

When we started discussing the role of interest in designing one's games, one of the first points that came out is that interesting games are not characterized by a single instance but, instead, are the result of sequences of moments that result in an overall interesting experience. This is where an interest curves come in handy.

> **REFLECTION POINTS** 🔍
>
> Working on making every aspect of your games interesting to players is a challenging task and is a question that should pop up often in the game design process. A first step could be in responding to the following questions:
>
> - How interesting do players find the challenges, obstacles, and activities that are presented in the game?
>
> - Are there particular aspects of your game that stand out more than others and what is the reason for this?
>
> - Are your game elements presented in a way that highlights your design and learning objectives? What aspects of your elements could be improved and how?
>
> - Does your game present compelling aspects and arguments for players to try them out, and how much do players relate to the game's characters, world, and atmosphere?

AN INTRODUCTION TO INTEREST CURVES

Like other art forms, games are tools that manipulate information to create interesting experiences. But, as we have seen, whether a game is considered interesting does not depend only on one particular instant but the overall feeling caused by each and every moment of the game. In fact, games that succeed in getting players' attention take advantage of every moment in order to work on a particular aspect or emotion that gradually builds on the game's experience.

Even if some would expect successful games to be sequences of intensive moments, this is definitely not the case. Let's imagine a platform game where players need to constantly face enemies, jump across to distant platforms, and constantly run against time. In a case like this, it's highly likely that instead of feeling constant excitement, players may feel stressed or frustrated. Why? Because these intensive moments that made the game unique are not unique anymore! Similar examples can be found in any aspect of human life: Even if someone may love a particular type of food, eating it every day would certainly lessen its charm.

So, successful games are not about constant action or excitement; rather, they build on the audience's interest. They lay the ground for highly exciting moments that, when they occur, are actually special. Even if there is not one single recipe for success, building up an audience's interest has been studied since the dramatic writing of ancient Greece. The general principle is that the player's interest should increase gradually while allowing the necessary time and space for the audience to process the information provided and create the necessary atmosphere for the climax scenes to have an even bigger impact.

In educational game design, interest curves can also be used to identify and create opportunities for reflection on learning objectives. Interest curves are an excellent tool for monitoring and visualizing these reflection moments both in relation to one's learning content and the game experience.

As we saw at the beginning of this chapter, effective reflection depends on several factors, like timing, game atmosphere, or the state of players. Games that do not allow space for reflection risk a superficial presentation of their learning content without ensuring that players had the opportunity to understand what the game wanted to help them learn. So, can interest curves be used in order to improve reflection through one's games? Let's answer this through some study cases.

Case Study 1

While I was working on a research project in France, we were trying to introduce games related to the promotion of cultural heritage in school classrooms. One of those games was a prototype virtual reality exploration game. The game actually required players to wear a head-mounted display and explore an area full of volcanos. Even if the premise sounds very cool and the players were introduced to, at that time, a very innovative interface, the game offered almost no challenge. Players would walk around the virtual area and interact with a few elements, trying to find answers to some quizzes. In this case, they easily lost interest and wanted to play something else. The interest curve was like the one that follows.

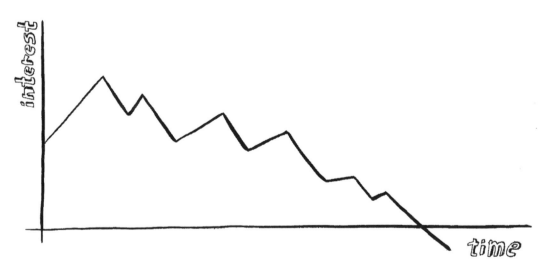

So, after noticing this, we tried to find ways to fix this issue. We shifted our focus from creating more levels and adding more details about the virtual area and worked on the game's mechanics in order to increase players' engagement and meaningful interaction. We discussed the possibility of adding virtual characters and what their interactions with players would be. We designed a set of quests, presenting players with additional problem situations that they would need to solve. But to help players create the necessary connections between the game and learning more about the area and its cultural significance for the region, we arranged these quests in a way that would challenge players but also offer them time to reflect on their actions. This led to an interest curve like the one that follows.

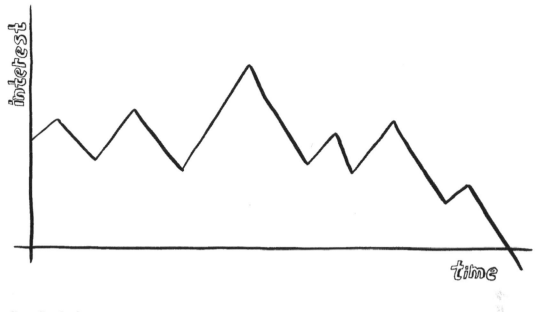

Case Study 2

Another game we used was an augmented-reality outdoor activity called **Tactileo Map**. The game would actually allow teachers to create treasure hunt games based on a real area through the use of tablet devices and geoinformation systems. In other words, teams would be equipped with tablet devices that would use their location and give them relevant information on how to arrive to their next point of interest. During this continuous process of finding points of interest, players would need to discover artifacts, find answers to riddles, and assess the information they already had in order to decide on their next moves. The game would have an interest curve like in the following:

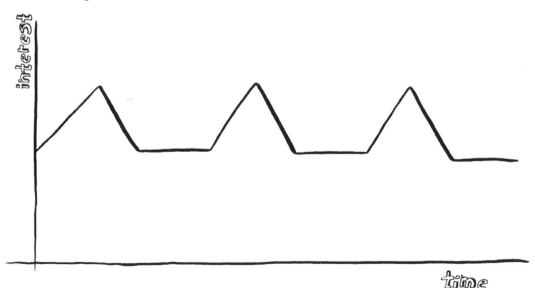

After reviewing the game's interest curve, the teachers who designed these particular levels realized that in some cases, interest points were far away from each other, creating frustration or loss of focus in the players. In some cases, the teachers also revisited the content of the riddles presented.

As we see in both cases, interest curves are a very helpful tool to identify possible issues related to the overall game experience. In the case of the first game, game designers would probably need to revisit the nature of the game by working more on the game mechanics and adding more interaction to their game, while in the second game, game designers resorted to modifications of their design in order to increase players' engagement.

SUMMARY

So, what topics did we cover in this chapter?

- Games without reflection time are like an amazing cake batter that has not yet been baked. Reflection is very important in educational game design and special care should be paid to this process.

- We examined different approaches and tools to facilitate reflection in educational games.

- We examined the use of interest curves and their value in helping game designers evaluate and reflect on their designs.

REFERENCES

1. Dewey, J. (1997). *How We Think*. Mineola, NY: Dover Publications.
2. Snyder, B. (2005). *Save the Cat!: The Last Book on Screenwriting You'll Ever Need*. Los Angeles: Michael Wiese Productions.
3. Schell, J. (2014). *The Art of Game Design: A Book of Lenses* (2nd ed). London & New York: CRC Press.

9 Knowing Your Audience

This chapter covers:

- Techniques and tools in order to better understand your audience.

- Insights on approaching your audience's needs and making them comfortable inside your game's space.

- Elaborates on the creation of player personas.

Games that fail to accurately and efficiently target their audiences have a very high possibility of being boring and providing minimal learning value to their players. This chapter focuses on understanding one's audience. It offers different perspectives and tools to approach and critically examine the needs and expectations of your audiences and create experiences that better address their needs and help them to learn.

While studying in university, I used to earn some money by working as an entertainer at children's parties. On many occasions I would work with a good friend of mine, performing a set of routines. So, when one day we were called to host a party at a local venue, we were excited to do so. The organizers told us that it would be a big event, with more than 200 people attending. Being excited about the opportunity, we rehearsed, worked on a few tricks, and were ready to blow their minds with our amazing performance. It was thus quite surprising when we arrived at the venue and realized that the audience were not kids but elderly people. It goes without saying that the performance ended up being rather awkward as we went ahead in presenting a kids' show to a much older audience and they could not believe that the organizers had hired us to host the event. Could this have been avoided? Definitely! However, I learned a valuable lesson: **Before you make any decisions, know your audience!**

UNDERSTANDING YOUR PLAYERS

Knowing one's players is crucial for the design of an educational game. As we have seen, designing experiences is immediately connected to the way humans perceive and respond to the environments we create. Specific events may be received differently by diverse audiences, different emotions may be triggered, and different conclusions will be produced. In other words, games are designed to affect players and players affect the design of games.

Even if it is not always that apparent to game designers, the nature of a game's players can drastically change its form. Let's imagine that you have been asked to create a game about presenting the negative impact of smoking on the human body to:

- Five-year-old children.
- Teenagers.
- A class of 15-year-old students who are blind.
- Adults, aged from 18 to 35.
- Adults, aged from 45 to 65.
- A university classroom in a medical faculty.
- A university classroom in an economic faculty.

It is apparent that each of those groups offer particularities in the way the subject of smoking could be presented. Five-year-old children are highly unlikely to smoke. But they see their teachers, parents, or friends of their parents smoking. So, presenting the negative impact of smoking to five-year-old children will be different from presenting it to teenagers, who may choose to try smoking or adults who are chronic smokers. But even in these cases, not everyone has perfect knowledge of the human body or the problems caused by smoking. For instance, a student of medicine may be interested in the mechanisms associated with how the lungs process tobacco smoke, contrasted with students of economics, who might be interested in learning more about the social or economic impact of using tobacco. But audiences are not restricted to learning content and its representation. For example, in the case of smoking, one of the groups has visual deficiencies. This should lead game designers to find the necessary means to create a game to address this audience and inform them about the negative impact of smoking.

So, what are the elements that game designers should know about their players in order to design games that interest them and help them learn? Let's have a look at some of those:

- Players' age.

- Players' language.

- Players' cultural nuances.

- Players' idiosyncrasies.

- Players' understanding of the subject matter.

- Players' skills related to the learning context.

- Players' skills related to the presented game.

But is this information enough? The truth is that there is not one absolute list of elements that can help define one's players. Different learning contexts call for a different understanding of a particular audience. So, the more you know about your audience, the better impact your games will have on them. What I find more helpful than making a list of the attributes that help me to identify my players is a set of challenges that game designers face when trying to understand their audience better. So, let's have a look at those.

Educational Game Designers Should Give Players a Stake

During the 1950s, theater practitioner Augusto Boal presented a series of theatrical forms called the Theater of the Oppressed. Through these techniques, Boal presented a type of theater where the audience could interact with the actors, change the course of the presented play, and express their views [1]. A typical performance would feature a story of a situation where a person or a group of people would be oppressed by another person or group of people. After the story was presented once, it would be played again. During the second time, however, the audience could stop the flow of the story and intervene, taking the position of the oppressed or the oppressor. Through this process, dialogue was facilitated and audience members had the opportunity to express their views and ideas about the topic of the play. Among its many contributions, the Theater of the Oppressed is an excellent example of the power of involving one's audience in the creation of amazing and life-changing experiences.

In educational game design, the number of players has a great impact on the final games. Let's examine why that is through the following cases:

- A game designer organizes a game activity on the stage of an event with a 500-person audience, involving five players.

- A game about human rights consists of a discussion section, where a 30-player team need to talk, exchange ideas, and reach a conclusion.

- A game design team is asked to design a game about teaching literature for a particular class-room of 12–13-year-old students of the Caribbean island of Guadeloupe.

- A game design team is asked to design a game for any student of early childhood about mathematics.

All four of these cases present situations where the games' audiences are very different from each other. In the first two cases, the selection of games is most likely problematic. In the first case, the designer came up with a game that will only be played by five players, while the audience is 100 times larger. This will lead to many of the spectators getting bored, annoyed, and losing interest in the activity. In the second case, a game where discussion is a central element was selected for a group of 30 players. Imagine a classroom full of students (the age does not matter in this case), where they need to talk about something in order to win the game. It is likely that some people will dominate the discussion, others will occasionally join the discussion if they don't lose focus, and some others will just talk with each other about something irrelevant to the game. Even if it's possible for a discussion session with big audiences to be successful, the game designers have already put the success of the venture at risk, which could have been avoided by evaluating the number of players better.

The truth is that nobody wants to be left out from the action. There may be players that approach games in different ways and interact with them differently, but still in their own way, they all want to play. So, game designers are presented with the great challenge of creating the necessary circum-stances for everyone to be able to play inside a game. This does not necessarily mean that everyone needs to have the same role inside a game. It doesn't even mean that they should play for the whole duration of the game. However, they should feel involved in the process and have a stake in the final outcome. We will examine this aspect more thoroughly later on when we look at the single and multiplayer modes of games.

Another important aspect of this challenge is the one of learning impact on players. When it comes to game impact, I have one rule of thumb: **The more players a game tries to address, the smaller its impact on those players becomes**. If we examine the last two out of the four cases above, the one about designing a game for a particular classroom in a particular setting and the one of creating a game for all players in the world of the same age, one thing is certain: game designers can have a much better idea of the players in the former than the latter. Without doubt, educators who want to create games for their own classrooms or instructional designers who need to create games for the companies they work for know exactly what the needs and particularities of their learners are. They know their learners individually, they understand their background, they have a good picture of their strengths and weaknesses.

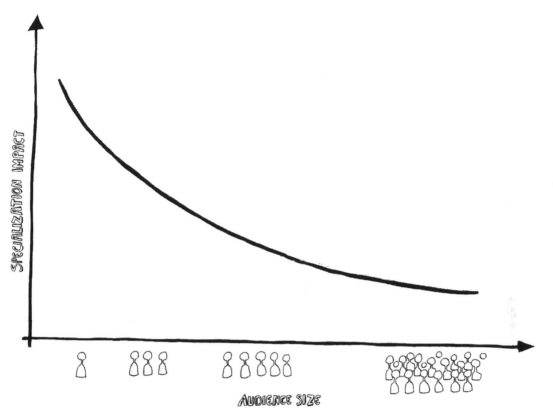

The specialization of a game to players' individual learning needs is inversely proportional to its audience's size.

So, games that are designed for those learners will address the particular issues that those learners have. On the other hand, designing games for a broader audience does not come with this luxury. In this case, players could be in the thousands or millions, they may not speak the same language, they may not even be from the same part of the world. So, game designers will need to adapt their design to a more general approach that will try to address as many players possible.

Communication and collaboration among players becomes more difficult to facilitate as the group number increases. This means that if a game requires collaboration, exchange of information, or expression of ideas, the task becomes more difficult while the number of players increases and it might become almost impossible to achieve if the number is too great. So, designers could consider breaking players into teams or find game mechanisms that could bring balance between the activity and the number of players.

REFLECTION POINTS 🔍

- How well can you define your audience?

- What is your audience's size?

- If more than one player is involved in playing the game, what is their relationship and the resources provided by the game and how do you ensure that they will all be engaged during the game?

EDUCATIONAL GAME DESIGNERS SHOULD MAKE PLAYERS FEEL COMFORTABLE

Even if we expect that all players are super excited to play our games, this is not always the case. There are in fact several reasons why players would not be interested in participating in our games and those can be personal (they could be shy, tired, or not confident enough) or intrapersonal (they might not like to collaborate or compete with other players, they might have difficulty socializing and communicating with a team, or they might want to avoid friction and conflict during play). In any case, though, it is always helpful to assume that even if you have created the best game in the world, there will still be some players who may be reluctant to try it. Let's see two examples of such cases.

Case 1: The ice breaker. In a game design workshop, before starting my session, I asked all participants to stand up and form a circle. Then I presented an ice-breaking game, where each player would need to find a very special gesture and perform it a couple of times so that the other players would learn and remember it. Later players were asked to repeat the gestures of their teammates. However, not all participants wanted to play. The audience consisted of university students from 22–50 years old and some of them were not comfortable participating in this particular ice-breaking game. After a small discussion in the group, everyone participated in the game, but this could have been a pivotal moment for the success or failure of the workshop.

Case 2: The soundscape game. A team of game designers were asked to design a game focusing on helping players to develop their understanding of their environment through identifying sounds. The game would target young children and would try to help them find connections between physical areas and the sounds associated with them. For instance, the ambient noise that is produced in a train station, in a forest, or in a classroom are different from each other. The team came up with an interesting game, that would, however, have complex controls. When the game was presented to players, they felt intimidated by its complex controls, and would not spend the extra time necessary to try and master it. So, at the end, the game did not have the impact it was expected to have.

Even if those two cases took place in different contexts, one aspect remains the same: Some players did not feel comfortable playing the games in the way they were presented. It is certain that not everyone will respond to your games in the same way. But good games manage to make most players feel comfortable when they play them. When players are comfortable, then the possibility that they will learn something increases. It is natural that players who are not interested in playing a game or have problems playing it will focus on those aspects and not on the game's learning aspect. In order to examine this design challenge, I find the comfort zone model helpful. The comfort zone model approaches human comfort in three spaces: the comfort zone, the growth zone, and the panic zone.

In the comfort zone, players feel comfortable. When they are in this zone, it usually means that they are familiar with the situations they are in and that their skills, knowledge, and ideas are not challenged. Players like being in the comfort zone for a while, but as we will see in the chapter on game mechanics, always being in the comfort zone is boring. When players play a new game, though, they enter unfamiliar situations. These situations will require them to use their skills and knowledge, bringing them into a less comfortable situation. When this pressure is manageable by students, it can help them to grow and evolve. They will also enjoy the presented challenge. However, if the pressure and discomfort gets out of hand, players will panic and will not want to participate in the activity anymore.

Of course, those spaces are not visible and defined. Additionally, they are different for each player and for players' interactions with different game aspects. There are players who love interaction with other players and are open to others entering their private space, while there are also players that want to keep their distance from other players while playing. There are cases where players may feel comfortable with the learning aspect of a game but uncomfortable with the game's implementation and vice versa. Since every educational game is designed for particular audiences with specific needs, the comfort zone model is just one additional tool that helps educational game designers to build games that make players feel open and comfortable.

REFLECTION POINTS

- Does your game create the necessary circumstances for players to feel comfortable throughout its duration?

- How does your game push players toward evolving and developing their skills and understanding of the topic you want to present?

- Are there possible situations where players may feel uncomfortable or that conflict may arise, and how are those handled by your game?

GAME DESIGNERS NEED TO HAVE A CLEAR IDEA OF A PLAYER'S SPACE AND RESOURCES

Not all players have access to the same resources or the same spaces. There are players, living in rural areas, with access to vast forest areas and there are others living in cities where the facilitation of outdoor games would require more caution or might be difficult. There are player groups that, due to the context and circumstances they are in, can only play games within limited areas. For instance, games that are designed for museum exhibitions target museum visitors and will probably be played inside or around the museum areas. Space can have an impact on the final gameplay. If, for example, an outdoor augmented reality game requires an Internet connection, playing the game in a forest might interfere with the final experience, since signal might be weak or not exist at all.

Also, not all players have the same resources in terms of technology or materials. Playing mobile games requires players to have access to smartphone devices, playing virtual reality games requires players to have access to virtual reality headsets, and playing games designed for interactive tables requires classrooms to be equipped with the necessary equipment. The fact that some companies, schools, museums or, indeed, parts of the global population have access to those technologies does not mean that this is the case for all players. Game designers should design games that all players can play and this requires some previous research and understanding of the materials and technologies that players possess.

So, there are situations where some types of games could be played more easily than others, there are situations where playing games becomes impossible in specific contexts, and there are cases where there may be no difference between audiences. Each of these present several pros and cons that need to be assessed by game designers in order to have a greater impact on their players.

REFLECTION POINTS 🔍

- Does your game account for the different resources that players may have?

- Does your game take into account differences in the hardware and software that players may use?

- Does your game provide the necessary resources for players to play it or will they need additional equipment in order to organize and start off?

EDUCATIONAL GAME DESIGNERS SHOULD KNOW THEIR PLAYERS' NEEDS

In educational game design, knowing your players' needs is crucial. There are very interesting educational games that don't manage to help players learn. They may be presenting learning content in a particular way, but this doesn't guarantee that players need those specific aspects to understand a topic better or develop their skills in that particular area. A better understanding of players' needs could come about by clarifying the following aspects:

- **What do players know about the learning content?** Do players have an idea of what the learning aspect of the game is? If they do, this provides game designers with a base upon which to structure their games. Starting from familiar concepts and moving forward is a helpful technique of presenting an educational game.

- **What do players think they know but don't?** This question is rather critical in educational game design. There are several occasions where we think we know a topic but in fact we may have a false perception about it or only know fragments of the whole picture. Games are excellent opportunities to address those misconceptions and misunderstandings. By actually presenting players with situations where their knowledge and current views of phenomena and situations are challenged, they have the opportunity to critically examine their ideas and come to new conclusions about the presented subject.

- **Which are the areas that players do not know anything about?** Areas will always exist that learners do not know about. By identifying those new areas, game designers can put greater emphasis, attention, and resources on those elements in order to help players gain a greater understanding of the presented learning aspect.

- **What skills do your players have?** Skills can be related to both learning and gaming aspects. It should be expected that players who are familiar with specific technologies have more developed skills than others who are not. This could mean that presenting a highly advanced game to players with no experience of using a particular medium could make them feel insecure, confused, or skeptical about playing it. If the same game was presented to an audience that is used to playing such games, it could be a challenging opportunity compared to less complex games that this audience might find boring or less challenging. On the other hand, skills could be related to the game's learning aspect. Being able to identify the skills that relate to the presented context, designers can design games that require a skillset relevant to players' competences, helping them to gradually develop those skills and master the game.

- **How do other experts approach an audience for a particular learning context?** Being able to see how other experts approach the same audience or the same learning content is always very helpful and strongly encouraged. It doesn't matter if you agree or disagree with those experts. You also don't need to follow the same learning theories, use the same tools, or share the same views. You can be inspired by the aspects you find interesting, learn from their mistakes, and enrich your perspectives by learning more about their practical and theoretical analysis of previous situations. This knowledge could come from studying previous case studies or research papers, asking friends to share their experiences, or studying relevant curricula. It is also important to have in mind that your audience may have already tried some of those games, activities, or approaches before. So, you can use this previous experience as an advantage when designing your games.

REFLECTION POINTS 🔍

- What are your players' needs with regard to the game and learning aspect?

- What are your players' understanding of the topic you want to present, and what are their weaknesses? How do you intend to help them deal with those weaknesses?

- Are there any particular requirements of your audience that you need to take into account? Any type of disability, personal expectations, or sensitive topics?

EDUCATIONAL GAME DESIGNERS SHOULD KNOW THEIR PLAYERS' PREFERENCES

Sometimes I consider game designers like Santa Claus. In the same way that Santa Claus knows which games kids (or adults) wished for, game designers need to know what their players want to play! The first step to achieve this is by understanding what their players' preferences are. Those preferences may be related to cultural or regional characteristics. A great example is sports. Sports preferences differ from region to region. European audiences prefer to watch soccer rather than baseball or American football, in contrast to North America. In Japan, people are interested in sumo wrestling, while in India, cricket is the most popular sport.

Games with structures that are familiar to players are easier for them to grasp, present them with previously encountered challenges, and have a better chance of meeting players' expectations in terms of what they expect from games that they play. This does not mean that players are uninterested in new experiences. On the contrary, players are always interested in playing something new, exciting, and amusing. The problem in this case is that experiences that are totally unrelated to a player's previous background have a greater risk of not being received well, making players lose interest or feel uncomfortable or frustrated. So, some balance should be found between combining already familiar and totally new elements in order to design intrinsically motivating learning experiences through games.

REFLECTION POINTS 🔍

- How well do you know your players' preferences and expectations?

- What do your players prefer to play?

- What types of games do they find boring or do not like to play?

- What elements fascinate them and what doesn't?

- What types of games would they prefer to see and how could those types be used in order to attract their interest?

PLAYER TAXONOMIES

During a presentation of a game on communication and collaboration to the members of a company team, we observed that not all of the players were participating in the game in the same way. Some were focusing a lot on the rules and requirements of the game, some others would be very energetic, some others would be distant, some players would try things just to try them, and some others would only focus on achieving the final result. At the beginning, our team was rather skeptical about the game's impact and whether it was interesting for players. So, when we asked for the players' opinions at the end of the training event, we were surprised to see that the majority of them had found the game interesting. This was a good reminder that since all human beings are unique, it should be expected that they don't learn, enjoy, and approach games in the same way.

Similar to how people don't eat the same food, listen to the same music, or respond in the same way to other people's actions, they also don't approach games in the same way. This is also the reason why different players prefer different games or game genres. There are players who are interested and need some social aspect in a game; there others who try to avoid it. There are players who want to know every rule and aspect of the game in order to feel in control of their decision-making, and there are other players who just want to jump straight in and learn the rules through trial and error. There are players who are interested in knowing every detail of the game's world and history and would spend lots of time reading manuals and watching cinematics, and there are others who will skip the cinematics or extra information right from the start, wanting to get to the game action faster.

There are various ways of examining how players interact with games. I strongly suggest trying to find your own way of understanding how different personalities would react before designing your games. In the end, every learning context and audience is different and requires special understanding of its needs and preferences. One analysis aspect can happen through understanding how players receive pleasure from playing games. An interesting analysis of different player types is the one by game researcher Richard Bartle, called the **taxonomy of players**. According to Bartle [2], players can be classified into four types. Those types are:

Achievers are players who focus on measurable outcomes when playing games. They prefer advancing levels, gaining experience points, and collecting badges or inventory items. Achievers find pleasure in accomplishing goals while playing games.

Explorers are players who find pleasure in exploring and getting to know more about the game world. They may be fascinated by unlocking new playable content, discovering new or hidden areas, or learning details about the history of the world, its species, and cultures. These players usually want to have a lot of freedom to wander around the game maps and tend to have negative dispositions toward games that have a fixed way of moving forward or expects them to proceed in a specific and binding way.

Socializers are players who most enjoy socializing with other players or game characters. For socializers, games are a tool for getting the opportunity to meet new people and interact with them. These games can be MMO RPGs; strategy games; card games; outdoor augmented reality games, like **Ingress**, **Geocaching**, or **Tactileo Map**, or they can be board games and traditional games. In some cases, socializers may also interact with non-player characters, which are virtual characters controlled by the game itself.

Killers are players who like competition and gaining victory over other players. These types of players find pleasure in destroying things and establishing domination over an area in a variety of ways. Killers may try to impose authority on others by trying to harm them or protecting them.

Like many other uses of theories and approaches in this book, Bartle's taxonomy is an interesting perspective to have in mind but not an absolute formula for designing games. Without doubt, we can find players that may be classified in more than one of those categories. Additionally, we could propose more player categories, depending on what we want to investigate and analyze. So, Bartle's taxonomy is an interesting starting point to better understanding one's audience but your exploration process should definitely not end there.

PLAYER PERSONAS

Being able to understand one's audience provides game designers with the invaluable opportunity of anticipating possible issues and designing learning experiences that focus on this particular audience. At this moment it's a nice opportunity to take a look at a design practice that was followed in the past, which software engineer Allan Cooper called "the sum of all desired features" [3]. So, before software solutions were developed, designers would do a survey, collect the needs of their users, and try to combine them in order to create products that would fit those demands. Practice, though, has indicated that users do not always know what they need beforehand and the same applies to playing games. Don't get me wrong, I'm not saying that knowing what your audience needs is unhelpful. It is extremely helpful and important. However, using this information in order to create intrinsically motivating learning experiences through designing games requires game designers to be able to interpret this information in a meaningful way.

A helpful tool in cases like this are players' personas [4]. **Persona** is the Latin word for a person or a role and in this context, personas represent fictional characters that represent a portion of a game's audience. By using personas, game designers try to represent typical players of a game and anticipate their reactions and choices in the game. Since personas are proposed as a helping tool, they should be used to solve problems rather than create them. So, bear in mind the following:

- Personas should represent realistic potential players and not idealistic ones. Idealistic personas will not help you to critically examine your audience and your potential design and they will only result in loss of time, energy, and resources.

- For a typical game, you should not have more than two to four personas. Personas are ways of trying to critically examine your designs for a set of typical users rather than a wide range of rare examples.

- In educational game design, there are some occasions where personas may be useful and others where they may have a negative effect on the final design. If your audience consists of players who are very different from each other and who require special provisions, then it is possible that personas may not be a helpful tool and you should proceed by individually examining your players, especially if their size is limited. If you are designing a game for a large audience with some homogeneity, then personas might prove useful.

- Personas should give as much information as possible about a potential user, related to the topic of a game. Personas should also be constructed based on common patterns among a target audience. For instance, in the design of a game about teaching literacy to high school students on a national level, the age, habits, access to technology, and the development level of literacy skills are attributes that can describe all the potential players of the game and should be listed as attributes of a persona.

Of course, there is not just one correct way of creating a persona. Design situations differ from case to case. What is important, though, is for the game design team to form a set of fictional characters that correctly represent their audience and try to anticipate their actions and reactions to the game events. In some cases, creating personas can prove to be very helpful for anticipating players' interaction with the game's elements, such as its interface, symbolism, representations, learning content, narrative structure, and game mechanics. There are other cases, though, where personas may not be helpful due to the particularities of an audience and the great specialization that may be required to correctly represent this audience. In cases like this, it's best to use another way of anticipating your audience's reaction.

PLAYERS' LEARNING STYLES

Another way of understanding one's audience in educational game design is by understanding the way that players approach learning. Not everyone learns in the same way and not everyone understands the world in the same way. So, it should be expected that players will not learn from your games in the same ways and will not search for the same elements in their effort to play and learn. There are players who prefer to get as much information beforehand and feel uncomfortable not knowing every little detail of a game and its learning content, and there are others who won't pay any attention to the provided instructions and prefer to learn while exploring the game world.

There have been several attempts to examine the way that people learn. An interesting approach is David Kolb's learning styles [5]. In his **Experiential Learning Model**, Kolb suggested that the way people approach learning can be examined in dimensions. The first one is about perception and describes the extent to which learners put emphasis on concreteness over abstractness. The second is processing and describes the extent to which learners prefer action over reflection. So, learning styles express the position of players on those two dimensions. There are learners who prefer taking part in concrete activities while there are others who feel more comfortable watching lectures about the abstract concepts that they study. There are people who prefer to take their time and reflect on a task and there are others who want to get their hands dirty from the very beginning. Kolb identified four styles based on this analysis. These are:

The **diverging** style, which describes learners who approach learning by participating in concrete experiences and use reflective observation. These learners prefer to experience a situation and then reflect on it, learning from their experience.

The **assimilating** style, which describes learners who engage in abstract conceptualization and a reflective observation of an experience. Those learners prefer to collect information from various sources and critically reflect on them in order to learn. Getting into action comes later, after they have examined all the provided sources of information.

The **converging** style, which involves learners who use abstract conceptualization and active experimentation. Convergers approach learning by trying to find practical application for the theories they have discovered. They are also skilled at finding solutions to problems based on their previous problem-solving experiences.

The **accommodating** style, which refers to learners who use concrete experience and active experimentation to process information. Accommodators prefer getting involved in concrete activities and getting right into action. They arc skilled at working with their hands, use intuition, and prefer practice over theory.

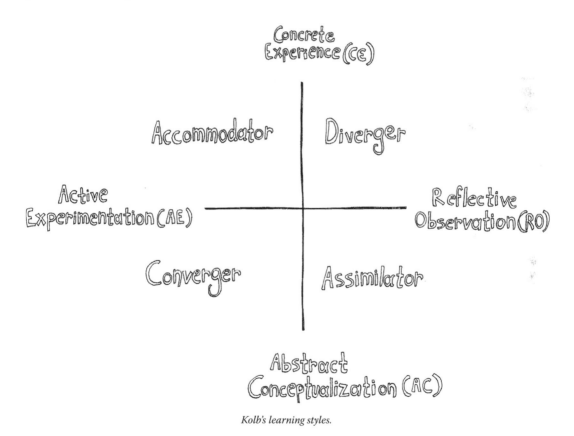

Kolb's learning styles.

Attention! Learning styles in educational game design are just one of many tools that can help game designers to critically examine their players and get to know more about them. Without doubt, not all players can be categorized in only four learning styles, nor do all players need to fit exactly into one of these profiles. So, try to avoid using learning styles in a strict sense when designing your games, but try to reflect on how your particular players approach learning. I prefer to view learning styles more as a reminder that each player is different and unique. Consequently, educational games should be able to approach those individual traits of potential players and help them to learn in their own unique way.

REFLECTION POINTS 🔍

It is important to keep in mind that all players are unique in the way they play, learn, and perceive the world around them. All the tools and points presented above aim to highlight this very aspect. It is up to you to decide how you are going to approach your audience and get to know more about your players.

- How do your players like to approach your game? Does your game present sufficient resources and challenges for players of different backgrounds and preferences?

- Does your game offer a specific way of helping players to learn and master the concepts you want to present or can it adapt to a player's individual way of approaching learning?

- Can you define generic player personas or would your game design not benefit from this?

PERSPECTIVE

Thomas Planques

Game Designer

What is your advice for potential educational game designers?

Make a REAL game!
Many educational games feature very basic gameplay mechanics not reflecting the specificity of the topic they are supposed to teach: The gameplay serves only as a pretext to read or watch educational content. That's the "chocolate coated cabbage" syndrome: The audience thinks they are going to play, but the game elements are actually very shallow and quickly fade in favor of a noninteractive, classic reading/watching content activity.

For educational games, it is paramount to respect the "game" value as much as the "educational" value. The game must be satisfying in itself, or the player will quickly see through the trick. Your game competes for the interest and daily time of the user with other commercial games, from AAA console games to smartphone games, all likely with a much bigger budget than yours. You need to be smart and fit into the codes that built the success of the game industry. Of course, doing this with a limited budget is difficult and you need to maximize the money–game quality ratio by making smart choices, potentially by getting inspiration from the indie development scene that has mastered this art. One thing is for certain: If your game takes the easy solution by being no more than a glorified quiz or a dull pretext to passively watch/read educational content, players will quickly see through it and lose interest.

I recently heard the leader of a university educational game development department say: "Everyone knows that in serious games, you don't play." While this is probably true of many educational games, how can you hope to create something motivating with so little faith in the domain, and such a blatant contradiction with the interactivity that is its heart and soul?

Procedural rhetoric: Align the gameplay with the learning topic
Anyway, this also means the gameplay needs to ask the player to use the skills they're supposed to learn. Indeed, the core grammar of the game medium is interactivity. Thus this "learning" we hope to make happen must come from interactivity itself. By practicing the precise skills, the players are supposed to learn; they will learn much more efficiently than by

playing a game that, even if it's motivating, has no connection with the domain other than a narrative and aesthetic one. This is the notion called **procedural rhetoric**.

Ask for a sufficient budget

Obviously this requires much more design time, and more specific development. This has a price. And there's a good chance your investors will not be familiar with the world of video game development, leading them to not understand the cost of good game development. This means you will need to be able to explain them precisely the cost of making a game worthy of that name. Good luck!

Sacrifices and choices, a designer's usual issues

But money alone does not decide everything, and a lot depends on how you use it. For budget reasons but also for simplicity reasons, and depending on the complexity of the topic that is to be taught, the designer will need to spend a lot of time with specialists of the topic, hopefully available as consultants and advisors for the development team, to have a good grasp on the domain. This way, the designer will be able to select, in mutual agreement with the topic specialist and the client, which elements are key to understanding the domain, and which are secondary and too specific to be expressed efficiently in the game.

Sometimes, the client and topic specialist will want to say everything about the domain. It is understandable, since they both have deep knowledge and interest in it. But it is important to make them understand that trying to transmit everything will end up with transmitting nothing—or at least transmitting many things, but in a hard-to-understand and not enjoyable way. Careful and pragmatic selection of the elements to be addressed allows concentration on design and development efforts; it is the path to quality. Design, in game development as much as in other creative domains, is a lot about selection, and, if I were to use big words, about sacrifice.

Design according to your budget: Any designer's #1 skill

In any case, the key is to design in accordance with your budget, especially in this development domain, which is often characterized by limited budgets. I firmly believe that one of the most important skills of a game designer is pragmatism and being able to project the cost of any feature and asset. "How much will it cost?" is always the first question that I ask of myself or my colleagues. Some great ideas are painful to let go of, but modest ideas can become greatly implemented work, whereas it's never the case for great ideas poorly implemented.

Go further than "gamification"

Nowadays, there are many games and apps that simply add scores, metrics, and achievements to already existing habits and call that "gamification." This is simply adding an extrinsic, artificial, and often meaningless reward for an otherwise boring activity that is seen as uninteresting enough for the players to reward them in itself. Moreover, this "just add a score to it" reflects the alienation with numbers and measures which is deeply rooted in our society, often disconnected from reality and serving ethically dubious management goals. As designers, we have a responsibility to understand the premises our mechanics rest on, and possibly to avoid promoting oppressive instruments. The game is supposed to make the player want to become interested in the domain, not to lock them up in meaningless numbers.

To be clear, there is nothing intrinsically wrong with rewarding the player with scores and achievements—most games do that. But this is not sufficient in itself; thus, it must only come as a minor feature and a side reward for achiever-type players, sustaining the motivation brought by game mechanics that encourages players to engage in a real exploration of the topic.

Adapt to your audience

Like in the mainstream game industry, it is paramount to know your audience and to adapt to it. Perhaps even more for educational games, since many of your players might not be gamers at all, and might not even have chosen to play your game, but have to play it nevertheless for a school/university/corporate training course.

For non-gamers, a very important basis is non-punitive feedback: They are treading in unknown territory, potentially against their will. Feeling that the system might humiliate them for their lack of knowledge may legitimately discourage them. So you'll get better results by positively rewarding good behaviors than punishing bad ones.

This is especially important in learning, since error is a part of learning, and a great feature of games is that they allow someone to experiment with no negative consequences. So let's fully exploit this and present the game as a free and engaging playground rather than a punishing and restraining system.

If you want the challenge to also be enjoyable by more seasoned gamers, you can always add harder goals as long as you keep them optional, so that everyone can tailor the experience to one's own needs.

Graph

Finally, some words about the game's universe. I have a quick anecdote about the educational game I am currently working on, called **Hellink**: the beta version is already used in training sessions, and when the teacher tells the students that they are going to play an educational game, their reactions are rather disdainful, because they have already played educational games before, and those were substandard in terms of graphics and gameplay. But as soon as they see the title screen, they say, "Wow, it actually looks cool!" And simply with that, we have already won a lot of interest and adhesion, which will make them much more willing to take the time to get immersed in the game. What I mean with this short story is that graphics are important: They are the first contact the player has with the game, and have a powerful impact on their perception of it—especially in a time where commercial games, from AAA to indie, deploy so much technological and creative prowess on that side of the development. There are too many educational games with non-imaginative, infantilizing, or bland artistic direction. We need to be just as crazy and creative as in the traditional game industry! Obviously, this probably means hiring experienced graphic designers from that industry. Lucky you: There are thousands of them out there with as many diverse styles as you want, just waiting for a job opportunity.

Aside from the graphic side, the whole game universe must meet the expectations the target audience has from a game: Depending on your topic, do not hesitate to exploit the pop culture exaggerated representations of it that already exist. For example, our game Hellink's theme is freedom and control of information: With that starting point, we chose to use cyberpunk stuff from **Matrix** to **Ghost in the Shell** for reference, firstly because those references are obviously appealing, but also because they are themed both around the current physical support of information (computers) and the use that can be made of information (enslaving people by manipulating them, or giving them power by giving them the knowledge necessary to take decisions). This way, we create a compelling universe that reflects our theme while fully exploiting the exaggeration that makes pop culture so enjoyable.

In one word: exaggerate! Commercial games, movies, and comics do it all the time. "Educational game" just means "learning thanks to the game," it doesn't mean "stay in a boring, academic, institutional zone." Blockbusters actually teach us stuff, and they do so because their creators master the art of triggering powerful emotions in the heart of the audience, making the story a living demonstration of the message, and making the message so much more memorable.

So make it look crazy, shiny, sexy. That's what we all love in blockbuster games and movies, and there's no reason not to do it in your game. Of course, if the investors and clients are not from that kind of culture, you will need to make them understand that it is important to adapt to the codes and culture of your target audience. This might not be easy, but the attractiveness of the game depends on it.

Finally, I found that humor is a good way to generate interest in a game: humor is quite universally appealing, quickly understandable and fun, and does not require a long game session from the player or strong emotional investment to be appreciated—unlike, for example, other emotional moods like horror, poetry, or epicness.

However, good humor is difficult to write. As for all other domains: if possible, ask a professional.

Communication

Educational games are still not well-known and can still generate suspicion. So there is an important need for communication to smooth the process. To some actors, it means helping them to go beyond the preconception that a game cannot teach and cannot transmit anything other than entertainment.

In case the game is supposed to be used in a learning course usually given by a teacher, the teachers might also legitimately show suspicion toward the game. Not only might they see it as something meaningless, but also as something meant to replace them—and in the current economic context, in certain cases, that might even actually be the case. So you might need to invest time to assist teachers and mediators in the use of the game at first, to make them understand that it is not made to replace them, but as a new tool for their work, to appropriate and use as they see fit so as to make their teaching more efficient. The game needs to be a tool for educators to increase their impact, not a dehumanizing means to lower costs.

What are your game influences?

I grew up with story-driven games and especially J-RPGs. Now I turn to any game able to tackle political, social, or educational themes with smart use of interactivity. Here are a few inspirations for my current project **Hellink**:

Ace Attorney: Making one of the most boring jobs on earth (lawyer) look like an epic **Dragon Ball**-like fight. That's what I mean when I say "exaggerate and make it sexy."

Never Alone: Merging gameplay and documentary while carefully managing the game flow to make documentary sessions enjoyable rewards for gameplay sessions.

Papers, Please: Using gameplay to make the player experience the inherent pressure of a position of authority.

Her Story: Discovering a powerful story through innovative gameplay challenging unusual player skills.

SUMMARY

So, what topics did we cover in this chapter?

- Successful games successfully target their players' needs and expectations.

- Being able to identify and describe your audience will bring you a step closer to designing games that attract their interest, fulfill their needs, and help them to learn more efficiently.

- Games should make players feel comfortable throughout their duration.

- You should make your games accessible in terms of technologies and resources that players have.

- Different players approach games in different ways.

- Different players also learn in different ways.

- We explored the notion of personas, a tool that can help you to better describe your general audience.

REFERENCES

1. Boal, A. (2000). *Theater of the Oppressed*. London: Pluto Press.
2. Bartle, R. (1996). Hearts, clubs, diamonds, spades: Players who suit MUDs. *Journal of MUD Research*, *1*(1), 19–42.
3. Cooper, A. (2008). The Origin of Personas. Retrieved from: https://www.cooper.com/journal/2008/05/the_origin_of_personas
4. Cooper, A. (2004). *The Inmates Are Running the Asylum: Why High Tech Products Drive Us Crazy and How to Restore the Sanity*. Upper Saddle River, NJ: Sams, Pearson Education.
5. Kolb, D. A. (1976). *The Learning Style Inventory: Technical Manual*. Boston, MA: McBer & Co.

10 Story
A First Look

This chapter:

- Explores the element of story in educational game contexts.

- Explores the different ways of structuring game worlds.

- Elaborates on the diverse ways of storytelling.

- Introduces principles and best practices for character design.

Story is an indispensable element of several games we love. This chapter examines the art of storytelling through games and introduces best practices and perspectives on designing appealing game worlds and characters that players can feel connected and empathize with.

During recess time, in a kindergarten classroom, I was observing three students playing with some toys in a corner. The students had a few action figures and some building blocks. While they were playing with them, they would create different universes and situations where the action figures live and act. During the fifteen minutes that I observed them playing, they had already created five or six totally different imaginary worlds, inside which they would play. When the recess was over and the students gathered together, the classroom's teacher, out of curiosity, asked the three students what stories they had created during their break. To this, one of those students replied: "We were not making up any stories. We were playing!"

GAMEPLAY, STORY, LEARNING

One great debate among game designers is whether telling stories through games diminishes their gaming aspect. From one side, there are those who consider storytelling to make games less game-like by restricting a player's possibilities and thus making games less fun or intuitive. From the other side, there are those who couldn't consider creating or playing games without there being some kind of story. For them, the relation between story and games is a strong one and indispensable for the essence of play. Both sides probably have some strong arguments. But for the purposes of this book, before forming an opinion on this matter, it is important to consider our most important objective: creating intrinsically motivating learning experiences.

I consider that whether storytelling is a key aspect in designing games depends greatly on one's learning objectives and pedagogic approach. As we saw in Chapter 2, in order to design games that are both fun to play and that help players learn, game designers need to strike a balance among five main elements: Technology, mechanics, aesthetics, story, and pedagogy. Designing successful educational games is related to creating learning environments that help players to understand and master different concepts and there is not always a single correct recipe for success. Consequently, there are some cases where the impact of narrative elements is great and indispensable to the structure of a game and other cases where narrative elements might prove less influential or might even distract players from the game's learning objectives. Let's see some examples of previous experiences:

- **Example 1**: Wanting to introduce students to the history of the classical antiquity era, a history teacher used the strategy game **Total War: Rome II**, a game with strong narrative elements. The students playing the game later worked on particular aspects of this era, based on the elements that had most impressed them while playing the game.

- **Example 2**: While teaching programming, through the visual programming language **Scratch**, a primary school teacher observed that students tended to create games where storytelling was a dominant aspect of the gameplay.

- **Example 3**: For their biology class, students go on an excursion to a nearby forest, where they play a geolocation game using the school's tablets. The game features a treasure hunt, where students need to find a list of herbs they were given in the classroom. The game features a map of the area, along with the location of student teams and hints on the attributes of each herb. The game did not feature any characters or an initial story.

As we see, when structuring learning environments, story can often be an important aspect of a game's learning experience. Though even in games that do not present a story, a story will be created anyway. But does this make sense? Can games that do not come with predefined stories have story elements? When playing **Rayman: Origins**, a game with a strong story aspect, players follow a predefined story, created by the game's designers. But players are also free to play the game in any way they want, by controlling Rayman and completing levels however they please. Similarly, in a game of chess, even if there is not a particular initial game story, players react to their opponents' moves, making each game of chess unique. After the game finishes, those players could narrate this sequence of events to their friends and start a conversation about it. The same happens with other games where the story element is not dominant, like soccer, basketball, or baseball. This is also the reason why it's not surprising that fields like eSports, competitive events based on video games, are becoming more and more popular. Through eSports, players tell their story inside the game they play and viewers are interested to find out more about this story.

Valiant Hearts, a game with a strong narrative element. (©2014 Ubisoft Entertainment. All Rights Reserved. Valiant Hearts: The Great War logo, Ubisoft, and the Ubisoft logo are trademarks of Ubisoft Entertainment in the United States and/or other countries.)

I agree with the approach that Katie Salen and Eric Zimmerman used in their book, **Rules of Play**; that it is not necessary to examine in this context whether games and story are connected, but how! So, we are going to examine how games tell stories and how these can be used to create intrinsically motivating learning experiences. For those with a strong interest in story writing there is already a wealth of excellent material on the matter, from Aristotle's **Poetics** to Joseph Campbell's **The Hero with a Thousand Faces**. This chapter, though, will focus on story as an element of creating intrinsically motivating learning experiences through games.

PERSPECTIVE

Q&A with Gundolf S. Freyermuth

Professor of Media Studies, Codirector of the Cologne Game Lab

How do you consider the element of culture, both from the side of creators and players, as it affects the creation of games?

All media is an expression of the culture in which it was created. Actually, the German sociologist Niklas Luhman once remarked that society is creating media as a means to observe itself. As individuals, we use mirrors to adjust our appearance and our behavior. Societies, Luhman suggested, use media for the same purpose. Hence, there exists a kind of interactive relationship between societies and media—literature and painting, theater, film, television, and, most importantly these days, digital games. Obviously, at certain historical times some media are more popular than others. Also, with each technological push, new media emerge—with industrialization, for example, film and television; and today, with the transition to digital culture, video games. One reason for this emergence and rise in popularity of new media might be exactly that they function as mirrors: that society and culture, when they are changing, are in need of different and better mirrors. Digital media and, specifically, games with their various affordances of participation and interactivity, might very well be the best "mirror medium" human culture has created so far.

Can games and learning exist at the same time?

Most mammals learn through playing—how to hunt, for example. In the same way, humans have always used play as a learning tool. In play, we can train certain skills, behaviors, attitudes. Playing and games offer us a safe way of interacting with the world and with each other. We can try out what is possible and what is not. Thus, playing is one of the oldest "cultural technologies." By definition, playing is supposed to have no serious consequences. Of course, if you play in the real world, even if you just play catch or soccer, you may hurt yourself or get hurt—something that can be avoided now by playing in virtual worlds. In that respect, digital games can be understood as a continuation of old interests and practices with very modern means.

Which of your game influences have had an impact on your work?

I am a pretty old guy … I started playing text adventures in the late 1970s. At that time, I was studying literature and aspiring to be a novelist. From my perspective then, these early text adventures were a new literary form, the dawning of a new age of digital storytelling. Their branching multilinear narratives empowered readers to create their own experiences, partly at least. The turn to graphic adventures in the 1980s and FPS in the early 1990s rather turned me off as both genres reduced the importance of the narrative. I was into storytelling, which is not only an entertaining but also a highly intellectual process. That was the time when I published my first novels. Stories can teach us how to make sense of the world. I loved **Myst**, but I couldn't really enjoy **Doom**. Then, in the late 1990s and early 2000s, digital games changed again radically. They developed into a medium of audiovisual storytelling that soon rivaled film. That was when I decided not just to play, but also investigate games academically.

What is your advice to potential educational game designers?

Generally, as an artist, as a creative person, you should never do something that you are not passionate about. Which is true the other way around as well: If you are passionate about it, then do it, even if chances for big success are slim. If you don't want to work or if you just want to work to make money, then there are better and more lucrative fields. Economics or law or politics come to mind. If you want to create, you have to be so passionate about it that you don't care much for the money anymore. This, of course, applies to the design of educational games as well. Passion alone, however, will not enable you to make a good educational game. You need skills. Actually, you need two very different sets of skills. In this respect, educational or serious games resemble documentaries. I make this comparison because I have written and directed documentaries. To successfully make a documentary or a serious game, you need to be a good artist. You need to know how to make a movie or how to design a game. But you also need to know a lot about the subject matter—the topic and content that the documentary or serious game is supposed to be about. Whether the game is about math or the arts or chemistry, you need to be or to become an expert in the respective field. Of course, in most cases, educational games are made in teams which might include consulting specialists. In any case, as the creative person, you have to not only be on top of your craft, you also have to be a knowledgeable person in the field your documentary or serious game is addressing.

GAME WORLDS

One of the most interesting aspects of game-making is the creation of game worlds. Each game, however abstract, presents a particular game space with specific attributes, possibilities, and constraints. In my experience, game designers tend to spend a lot of their time designing levels for these worlds, from linear endless runner games to complex adventure games. Whether this is instinctive or intentional, all game creators can identify the great impact of creating game worlds on the final game's gameplay and storytelling.

According to scholar Henry Jenkins, game designers do not simply tell stories. In fact, they design worlds and sculpt spaces through which stories are told or created anew. This makes much more sense if we look at two examples:

Example 1: Three games from **Blizzard**, **Warcraft**, **Hearth Stone**, and **World of Warcraft** take place in the same game world, called Azeroth. Even if Azeroth was initially only the fictional world of the strategy game Warcraft, its great detail, along with the history of its characters, led Blizzard designers to create more games, telling stories about this world or giving players the platform to create and live their own stories there, in World of Warcraft. World of Warcraft is now a game played by millions of players. Many of those players may not know the full history of the world, but they can create their own characters, meet other players, and set off on new quests, creating their own stories. Even if there is a predefined narrative around the games, the world itself gives countless possibilities to players to experience their own.

Example 2: **Super Mario** may feature a very basic story in which an Italian plumber needs to save Princess Toadstool, but the world where the game takes place is actually rather big, especially if we take into account all the installments of the franchise. Apart from the particular mechanics and restrictions posed by the world, Super Mario travels through lots of different areas, some of which are underground and some high in the sky. It was also because of this that Nintendo later decided to release **Mario Maker**, a game where players were able to create their own Mario levels, play them, and share them online. The Mario world, created by Shigeru Miyamoto, has given the opportunity for many players to create their own stories.

Math Mathews presents a fictional universe, introducing players to the development of mathematical thinking. Initially a game project, Math Mathews has also become an animated series and is an excellent example of a transmedia universe based on the same world. (©2017, Kiupe/France Télévisions/Les Films de la Decouverte/Big Company.)

In our case, the challenge becomes even greater since our intention is to design worlds that help players learn. As it turns out, it is not that easy. In some cases, game designers get carried away with the process of creating their worlds and do not pay so much attention to their learning objectives. In other cases, they pay little attention to creating their game worlds, making them inconsistent and causing confusion for their players. So, designers strive for balance among all these different perspectives in order to design interesting worlds that facilitate learning experiences. The following are some interesting points that will help you to structure your thoughts when designing your worlds.

Point 1: Game worlds create circumstances for learning.

As part of the learning experience, worlds play an instrumental role in the facilitation of a player's learning. Successfully designed worlds are not just decorative elements with no learning value. On the contrary, efficiently designed game worlds help designers create the necessary circumstances for players to learn. Worlds present physical, mental, and virtual spaces, the structure, composition, nature, and arrangement of which can offer guidance to players, present obstacles that need to be overcome through the use of particular resources, and highlight the use of particular strategies, skills, and techniques in order to give solutions to problems. Game worlds work toward the same direction as mechanics and aesthetics to create intrinsically motivating learning experiences. So, their design and creation should be part of the design process from the very beginning.

The design and structure of a game's world should also be aligned with the game's learning objectives. Even more, game worlds should help important learning aspects emerge from their structures and themes. For instance, adventure and role-playing games that present the horror of war, the stigma of racism, and the need for love and solidarity present characters and situations where those situations are highlighted. Players are part of those situations, they make decisions that affect their characters or other characters inside the game's world, and they form opinions on those subjects.

Point 2: Game worlds tell stories or help players to create their own.

Interesting worlds manage to convey meanings and tell stories without the use of animations or text. The landscape, the laws of nature, the architecture of buildings, and the creatures that live there all tell a story and give additional information about the world's past, offering players insights into what's coming next. There are also worlds that can be customized by players, allowing them to create their own version of the world's past, present, and future. In such cases, players have the opportunity to create their own stories. Sandbox games are rather successful in this aspect, like **Minecraft**, **Skyrim**, and **No Man's Sky**.

Point 3: Game worlds are consistent.

Consistency is the first and foremost element in educational game worlds. Worlds that fail to use the same rules and present the same attributes and behaviors throughout the game may cause annoyance and confusion for players. Even worse, they may cause serious misunderstandings. There are two types of consistency in game worlds.

Internal consistency is related to the connection and relationship between game elements in a game world. Internal consistency, for example, is related to how the world elements act and react to a player's actions. If there is consistency, the same action will lead to the same reaction. However, there are times where this doesn't happen, either because it was not anticipated or because of technical error. In cases like this, players feel confused. They do not know how to react and they may lose focus of other elements of greater importance.

External consistency, on the other hand, is related to how a proposed world is consistent with learning objectives and the content they target. During a research project, a team of educators wanted to create a game for teaching primary school students about how objects flow and sink in water. They designed a game world where players, as pirates, would shoot objects into a water tank and experiment on the attributes of the materials. Some objects would sink and others would float. However, later on, the educators realized that even if the game had a positive impact on the players' understanding of sinking and floating, it also led them to have a false impression of an object's trajectory and movement when shot out of a cannon. The designers had not thought through this issue and had not paid attention to creating an accurate representation of what happens when something is shot from a cannon. So, the game managed to help players to understand a physical concept but also created a new misconception, because its world was not consistent with the learning content's attributes.

REFLECTION POINTS 🔍

- How well and in what extent can you define your game's world?

- How does your world create circumstances for learning and how is it connected to your game's learning objectives? Does it add value to the gaming experience and how is this achieved with regards to other elements of your game?

- How does your game world present information that can help players to have a greater understanding of the game's story or how does your game help players to create their own stories?

- How consistent is your game world concerning the other game elements and your game's learning objectives? Is it possible that your world's design may create misconceptions for players about other topics?

NARRATIVES

It is always fascinating to watch people talk about sports games they have watched. Usually, a sports conversation consists of a presentation of events during a game: "Our team went on defense and then the other team came in a zone formation," "After the goal, the coach changed our system," "After the time-out, the team was more focused," and so on. This representation of events or series of events is called **narrative**. What differentiates narratives from mere descriptions is that narratives consist of events. For example, the phrase "my carpet is red" describes a situation, contrary to the sports discussion which forms a narrative.

In his book **Story and Discourse**, academic Seymour Chatman identified two components of narrative theory [1]: story and narrative discourse. Story and narrative discourse are like two sides of the same coin. From one side, story is related to the content of the events someone is narrating (what happened?) and from the other side, narrative discourse is related to the way this content is communicated to the audience (how is this presented?).

Since educational games differ as a medium from cinematography, literature, and theater, it is inevitable that narrative structures evolve to serve the purposes of this art. Consequently, the way in which "what" and "how" will be presented in your games might differ from previous experiences through other media.

Firewatch is an adventure game, the gameplay of which has a strong connection to narratives. (Used with permission of Campo Santo.)

Following the main question of this chapter, "How are educational games narrative forms?", we will examine narrative and educational game design through different analyses, which I call **prisms**. Not all prisms are applicable to every situation, but having them in mind when designing your games might prove rather helpful in organizing your work.

Prism 1: Embedded and emergent designs.
There are several games where the story is already predefined by designers. In cases like this, players are introduced to a very specific storyline, presented through cinematics, interaction with other players, discovering pieces of information inside the game, and so on. In **Captain Toad**, players need to solve different puzzles in order to advance to the next level, helping the story of the game unfold. But the general story is already predefined and will not change no matter what happens. Consequently, the story was pregenerated by game designers in order to create a very specific experience for players. According to game designer Marc LeBlanc [2], this narrative design is called **embedded**, since the story was already embedded in the game from its creation.

On the other hand, there are games without a predefined story. In these games, the story is created dynamically through the interaction of players with the game world. Let's take, for example, **The Sims** or **Minecraft**. In those games, by interacting with other characters or by raising new structures, players actually set off on their own adventure, where story arises in a unique and personal way. This narrative design is called **emergent**, since story emerges from the interaction of players with games.

As in most cases in game design, not everything is black and white! In most games, there will be both embedded and emergent designs. Even if one aspect will be more dominant than the other, in most games with embedded designs there is an emergent aspect and vice-versa. The location-based game **Ingress**, for example, presents an emergent narrative design, where two factions need to control energy portals. But the game also features a back story. On the other hand, **The Legend of Zelda: The Wind Waker** presents an embedded design where players follow a basic storyline, with defined objectives at each point. However, between the completion of those objectives, players are able to explore the open world of the game, thus helping new stories to emerge.

Both embedded and emergent narrative designs can be useful in educational game design. Through embedded narrative designs, designers can make sure that specific strands of learning content will be presented to players, leading to a particular experience. If, for instance, the learning objectives of a game are the teaching of history, then a prescripted story may help game designers to target players' misconceptions about a certain series of historic events. Embedded designs usually come with restrictions on the adaptability of pedagogic approaches, depending on the needs of each player. Considering that embedded designs already have predefined elements, it becomes unavoidable that students will be presented with the same learning experience, whatever way they decide to play such a game.

Emergent designs, on the other hand, offer a more exploratory approach to the game's narrative, as players need to explore the game world and come to conclusions on their own, through the support of the game. In cases like this, it is important to make sure that the emergent narrative is helping players to master the learning objectives and not shift the focus away from them. The best way to find a balance between embedded and emergent narratives is to constantly test your game concept and prototype. Since there is no single formula for creating educational games, through this process you will see which elements work better for particular occasions.

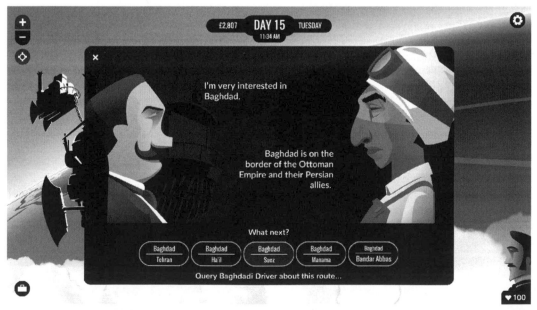

80 Days is an interactive fiction game presenting an embedded narrative design, since players follow a defined storyline. However, players' decisions make varied stories and versions of playing the game emerge. (Used with permission of Inkle Studios.)

Prism 2: Linear and nonlinear storytelling.

It is very common for games to present stories in a straight line. In **Angry Birds**, for example, the piggies have kidnapped the bird chicks and as the game progresses, the birds get closer to getting them back. The sequence of events, no matter how players want to play the game, will unfold in the same way. This chronologically sequential advance of events is called **linear storytelling** as the story is narrated in a defined temporal sequence. Educational games that are based on linear storytelling assure designers that players will follow a specific sequence of events, related to the game's learning objectives.

Let's take, for example, a game about teaching programming to high school students. If the game's designers want to make sure that players first learn the basic concepts of programming, like the notion of constants and variables and then advance to more complex concepts, like algorithms, linear storytelling would be one way to achieve this sequence of events. In many cases, games that use linear storytelling are easier to implement as the structure of the game can be more easily defined and less complex than in games that use nonlinear storytelling techniques. A great challenge with linear storytelling games, however, is the risk of being very closed and formally structured, with a negative impact on the element of fun.

Doodle linear storytelling sequence.

There are other games where story is presented in a non-linear way. There are several ways of doing this. One way is what Jesse Schell in **The Art of Game Design** calls the **story machine** [3]. With a story machine design, stories are generated through players' interactions with the game and because not all players act the same way, different stories will be produced. In **Minecraft**, for example, players are able to interact with the world in order to explore new areas, create their own structures, or interact with other characters. Every interaction event advances their story of playing the game. So, there can be endless stories produced by playing games like this. Hence, we can imagine a story machine like this:

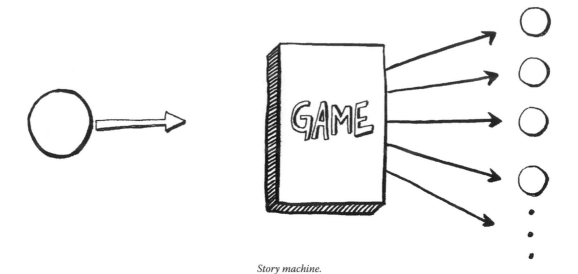

Story machine.

Another way nonlinear storytelling is used in games is through the use of branches. Let's imagine a treasure hunt game where every time players find a clue related to the treasure, they receive instructions about the next clue. Let's then imagine that instead of receiving information of just one clue, players receive information about different locations in the game area. Now, players need to decide which direction to take and which clues to try to find first. This design presents different branches of possibilities, each of which leads to a different story. But this way of storytelling can be more than meets the eye. Let's consider that students start their game with three possible choices, each of which offers a possibility of four new outcomes, each of which unveils the possibility of five new outcomes. Sure, it sounds very interesting and cool, but it also leads to a set of events that need to be designed on a geometric progression. From one side, the development cost of this game will increase exponentially and from another one, designers need to make sure that after all those countless combinations, learning was facilitated. A design like this would be presented in this schema:

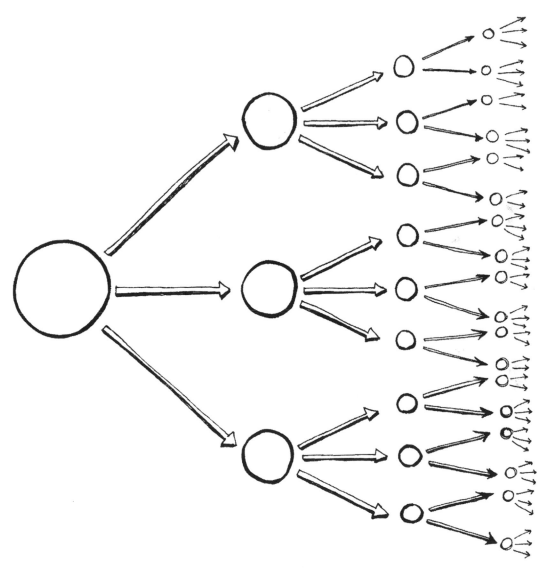

Countless branches.

The challenges and difficulties that arise from the previous nonlinear storytelling design are usually addressed by designers through merging and combining story paths. If we were to represent this design in a schema, it would look like this:

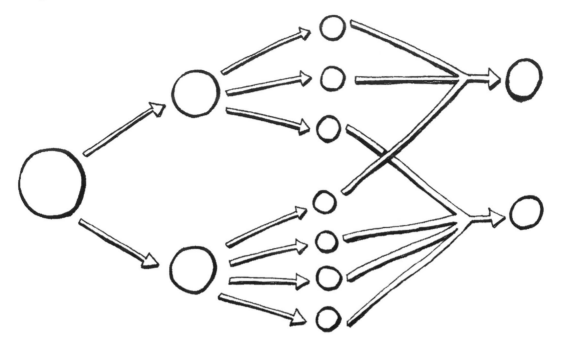

This means that even if a set of options is presented to players at a given point, their final outcome may be the same. This definitely solves the issue of the great number of possibilities arising in the story but makes storytelling much less interesting. In some cases, this choice that is offered to players becomes meaningless and has no actual impact on the development of the story. When players realize this, they lose interest in making decisions and will either focus on another gaming aspect or will leave the game. So, a merged branch design like this should be carefully thought through before getting implemented.

Consequently, games that incorporate nonlinear storytelling are more complex to create. From one point, in some cases their development and design investment is rather high and they need to be very carefully considered in order to actually have a meaningful impact to players. Another issue that arises in this case is that very open worlds do not always guarantee that players learn something. It is very possible that this great set of choices may shift the focus of players toward other game elements rather than help them in understanding the concepts that are presented in the game. Consequently, if you decide to take this direction, it is important to make sure that the game also features the necessary mechanisms that will allow you to achieve your learning objectives.

Games that use nonlinear storytelling can be very powerful learning tools. From one side, such games make it easier to urge players to explore and experiment with the knowledge they receive. Additionally, games that incorporate nonlinear storytelling can be adapted more easily to the needs and pace of individual players, since each player has the freedom and space to play the game at his or her own tempo and pay attention to the elements he or she prefers the most. This is contrary to games with linear design, where all players need to follow the same turn of events.

REFLECTION POINTS 🔍

- Does your game present a linear or nonlinear storytelling design?

- If the game presents linear storytelling, does the story have a strong impact on gameplay and how can it be used to help players learn what you want to present?

- If the game presents nonlinear storytelling, how does the process evolve? Which approach do you use to present players with options? Are there predefined outcomes by selecting particular routes or is every aspect dynamically generated? If yes, how can this approach be used in order to help players learn?

Prism 3: Spatial designs.

Stories can be told in many different ways, one of which is space itself. As we already saw in this chapter, game designers can tell stories through the design of a game world. Additionally, in some games, the main element that helps the story evolve apart from time is space. Theme parks are among the best examples of this approach. Disneyland or the Parc Astérix are designed in a way where space is infused with the history of each of those worlds. By walking around a theme park, people do not just see different games and attractions but also enter the world of each theme.

In the online children's game **Moshi Monsters**, players are free to navigate their way through Monstro City. Navigation around Monstro City is not restricted, and every time players enter a special area, they are presented with a challenge, puzzle, or game. The development of the story in this case depends on which area the players decide to enter in the first place.

Spatial narrative designs are frequently used in educational games when designers want to create thematic areas in their game worlds. In **Dr. Kawashima's Body and Brain Connection**, for example, the designers divided their virtual world into areas with different gameplay, providing players with the opportunity to select the kind of game exercises they want to play each time. Thematic areas can be divided by different criteria like learning objectives, game mechanics, or narrative elements.

During a previous research project, I was asked to design a game for the development of literacy skills for primary school children. After a thorough examination of the learning objectives my team came up with **Quest Island**, a 3D adventure game where players explore a mystical island, trying to find information that would help them complete a set of provided quests. In order to provide players with activities that focused on individual literacy skills, we designed different game areas dedicated to each of those skills. Each area also presented a new story. All the stories in the game were also connected in some way. In this way, players were free to explore the game world and live their own narrative while interacting with game elements and the narrative components we had created in an order dictated by their exploration of the game world.

Prism 4: Narrative designs should be consistent.

I am sure that all of us have encountered situations in games, movies, or literature where the story doesn't always make sense. One of the main reasons why this happens is that the interaction between the characters and the created world are not presented in an established mode, making them consistent. Of course, creating a consistent game world does not mean that game characters can't have particular or supernatural powers. It just means that the same rules should apply for the entirety of the game.

But for educational games, there is an even greater reason why stories should be consistent. This is because inconsistent narratives can cause players to misunderstand learning concepts or create new misconceptions about the elements that are being incorrectly presented in the game. Consequently, in consistent game worlds, it is easier for game designers to monitor game elements that might cause new misunderstandings for players and thus avoid teaching one concept that may cause players to misunderstand another.

REFLECTION POINTS 🔍

- Do the aspects, elements, and events in your game consistently present the phenomenon or aspect you want to present?

- Is your story consistent with other aspects outside the scope of your learning objectives in order to avoid creating misconceptions about other topics?

Prism 5: Hero's Journey.

There are thousands of different ways to tell a story, each of which leads to a different experience for one's audience. After studying folklore tales, myths, and stories from all over the world, mythologist Joseph Campbell identified common patterns in stories that feature heroes' adventures. In his book **The Hero with a Thousand Faces**, Campbell identified a narrative pattern in the form where a hero sets off on an adventure in an unknown realm and encounters great forces that are overcome through a decisive victory, enabling the hero to return back home and use the newly acquired powers to help his or her friends [4].

This pattern can be seen in many games: In **Dungeons & Dragons**, a fellowship of heroes gathers in order to complete a series of quests, helping them to become stronger, face their enemies, and come back with greater experience. In **The Legend of Zelda**, Link sets off on an adventure to rescue Princess Zelda, facing mystical dark forces, which make him a greater warrior. In the **Super Mario Bros.**, Mario is entrusted with the task of saving Princess Toadstool. In order to accomplish this mission, Mario enters the Mushroom Kingdom and faces the Koopa Troopas. There are countless examples where the Hero's Journey is encountered throughout cinema and literature like in **Star Wars**, **The Lord of the Rings**, the Harry Potter series, and thousands more.

Campbell divided the Hero's Journey into 17 stages, grouping them into three acts. Not all stories necessarily feature all those 17 stages or present them in the same order. This analysis was visited and revisited by several scholars and writers, one of whom is Christopher Vogler. In his book, the **Writer's Journey: Mythic Structure for Writers**, Vogler, based on the work of Campbell, presented a more practical analysis of the Hero's Journey for the needs of screenwriting. Vogler's stages for the Hero's Journey are the following [5]:

1. **The Ordinary World**: Offers an insight into the hero's actions in everyday life.
2. **The Call to Adventure**: Where the hero is summoned to the adventure of the story.
3. **Refusal of the Call**: Represents the hero's doubts and inhibitions about setting out on the adventure.
4. **Meeting with the Mentor**: The hero, after encountering a person or group of people with considerable experience, is provided with resources and information in order to set off on the adventure.
5. **Crossing the Threshold to the Special World**: The hero now enters the adventure and is committed to completing it.

6. **Tests, Allies, and Enemies**: After different challenges and obstacles, the hero makes allies and enemies.

7. **Approach to the Innermost Cave**: The hero gets closer to the epicenter of the adventure.

8. **The Ordeal**: Where the hero faces a near-death experience and experiences rebirth.

9. **Reward**: Surviving death presents the hero with confidence and a reward.

10. **The Road Back**: Where the hero's return to the ordinary world is met with problems that have not yet been dealt with.

11. **The Resurrection**: After an even greater challenge than the ones presented before, the hero faces danger and rebirth only to come out stronger and erase all existing problems through the resources and gifts that were gathered during the adventure.

12. **Return with the Elixir**: The hero now returns home with the experience and knowledge gathered during the adventure. The ordinary world conditions have now improved because of the hero's intervention.

Although the Hero's Journey is a very powerful analysis, it is not the solution to every narrative design. I prefer to see the Hero's Journey more like a tool for reflection on writing nice stories. Let's compare it with different chefs that need to cook totally separate dishes. It is inevitable that each one of them will use a totally different recipe, which will be applied based on each chef's individual style and technique. Even if the preparation of a lemon pie or a spicy burrito is not the same, there are general principles and elements of cooking that make them tasty. I believe that this is the best way of using the Hero's Journey when creating your stories.

Prism 6: Story or no story at all!

During a research project, I was part of a game design team that wanted to create a game for the teaching of physics to young children. Even if the game mechanics were interesting in themselves, the team of educators strongly insisted on having a story. They invented a set of characters who were interested in science, and through their curiosity and the questions they raised, players were introduced to the game's different levels. That approach had two problems. First, the questions those characters would ask seemed rather artificial and structured in a convenient way in order to create a logical sequence for the game to advance. Second, apart from presenting the sequence of different levels, those characters and their actions did not offer an interesting story. When the game was presented to students, most of them just neglected the characters and their story. Why? Because the game story was boring and, most importantly, unnecessary for the gaming experience. This story had costs in time and money for it to be written, programmed into the game, and for graphics to be created, but in the end had no apparent effect on the learning experience or the game's fun factor.

In educational game design, I believe that **no story is better than a bad story**. There are several reasons for this:

- **Good storytelling requires a great devotion of time and resources**. In game storytelling it's not only the game designer who is involved. The story will need to be presented in a way that will probably involve artists and developers. This is time, money, and human resources that could be focused on other elements of your educational games.

- **Bad stories can be misleading or create false perceptions on the learning experience of educational games**. Inconsistent stories that fail to correctly present facts and events may become reasons for students to misunderstand particular concepts. In games about teaching history, for example, an incorrect representation of a series of historic events will most likely lead students to false conclusions about how history took place for particular time periods.

- **A typical rule about any experience is that if one element seems unnatural, the whole experience seems unnatural**. Even if a cake is perfectly prepared, bad icing will lead people to think it tastes horrible. Players are very skilled in identifying elements that stand out, negatively or positively. Consequently, a bad story may have a bad impact on the whole game experience.

- **Stories can be biased or polarized, based on the designer's personal perspective**. A common mistake of novice educational game designers is that they try to push a story toward specific outcomes, highlighting their learning objectives. This approach requires great mastery. Otherwise, the story seems artificial, destroying the gaming experience and negatively affecting the achievement of one's learning objectives.

Narrative elements in an educational game should be well–thought-through and definitely not superficial. Superficial storytelling implementations stand out from the game and players will realize this. Consequently, your games will lose their intrinsically motivating nature. This does not mean that all games need to have complex or deep stories. On the contrary, story elements should be used when necessary and at the level that is required for educational games to be effective. There are games where a few strands of a story are enough for the experience and there are other games where the story needs to be deep and consistent. Good stories, though, are tightly connected with gameplay.

DESIGNING CHARACTERS

On one of the very first projects I worked on, I was asked to create a design document for a game proposal. Being very excited about this, I spent days and nights trying to create an amazing game world, full of detail and a deep history. It was a great experience, no doubt about that. However, when I pitched my design internally to my team, I realized that the game lacked a very important aspect: The main character I was presenting was not interesting at all. Interesting game worlds very often come with interesting characters. It is through these characters and their interactions, which are affected by their choices, that stories gain meaning for a particular experience.

In *Her Story, players need to assess the personality of the main character, who is being investigated regarding her husband's disappearance. (Used with permission of Sam Barlow.)*

The design and understanding of a character can in fact be a learning experience on its own. Whether a game wants to promote a healthy lifestyle, intercultural learning, active participation, or any other message with focus on a particular learning area, specially designed characters can definitely help designers move closer to their goals. However, a quick look at existing games will show that many game characters are what we could call "more action, less talk!" Let's explore some of them.

Tomb Raider—**Lara Croft**: A highly skilled and experienced archaeologist, with physical strength and stamina, venturing into ancient ruins all over the globe.

Legend of Zelda—**Link**: A boy entrusted with the task of retrieving a legendary token and saving a princess.

Slice Fractions—**the mammoth**: A mammoth that needs to reach its destination by crossing different sorts of platforms in the prehistoric era.

Ladybug's Box: Early Childhood Mathematics—**the ladybug**: A ladybug, trapped in a stationery box, in search of her family.

Angry Birds—**the birds**: A community of birds, infuriated by the kidnapping of their eggs, seeking revenge.

All these characters do not present an internal struggle. Consequently, they are not characterized by ethical dilemmas, which will eventually lead to what Aristotle called **catharsis**, meaning the purification of negative emotions leading to a new state, a state of restoration. There are two reasons for this. The first one is that this particular character is intentional. Especially in educational game design, there are designers who consider strong narrative elements to act as extrinsic motivation for the main learning experience, shifting players' focus from the mastering of the learning objectives to unfolding the game story and going deeper into the character structure. Games like Slice Fractions and Ladybug's Box are based on this approach. This is the reason why the mammoth and the ladybug are not deeply analyzed and their histories were intentionally omitted, in order to avoid shifting the game's focus onto their background story. The second reason is that designing such characters is usually more convenient for gameplay. Successfully externalizing the internal struggle of game characters requires great skill and in many cases it is not the main goal of a game.

But despite this, there are games whose characters are more dialectic. Those games usually put greater emphasis on their story element and the connection between story and game mechanics is stronger. Let's see some of them.

Valiant Hearts: The Great War—**Emile**: A French recruit during World War I in search of his family encounters the horror of war and reaches his breaking point, leading to his execution.

Tropico—**"El Presidente"**: The ruler of a Caribbean island, using democratic or nondemocratic means, needs to rule over the island of Tropico and guarantee the prosperity of its people.

Papers, Please—**The immigration inspector**: A border checkpoint inspector is responsible for monitoring the entrance of immigrants in the country of Arstotzka.

In each of these cases, the outcome of the game depends on the decisions of those characters and their internal struggles. Emile loses his family, enters the war, and finally, not being able to watch as his fellow soldiers die on the front, he kills his officer, which grants him a death sentence. The horror of war flashes in front of players' eyes through the experience of an old man who could be anyone. In **Tropico**, the prosperity of the island depends on El Presidente's decisions. Players face a dilemma: Choose democratic means of ruling the island or resort to fraud and violence. It is not a given that democratic measures lead to citizens' happiness. The inner struggle of the ruler becomes a moving force for the gameplay and the advancement of the game, which is represented through the character of El Presidente. Similarly, the immigration inspector is responsible for the lives of immigrants crossing the borders of Arstotzka, while still trying to make a living for himself and his family.

So, which type of characters are better to create? The answer depends greatly on one's objectives. If you want to create a story that accompanies gameplay you have created so as to add more power to the initial experience, the "less talk, more action" characters could be more suitable. If, on the other hand, you want to focus on the transformation of characters through their interaction with the game world and initiate a form of player reflection over this event, then dialectic types of characters can prove an effective way of doing so.

The games mentioned before present characters that are very appealing, likeable, and recognizable. However, there are other ones that present characters we do not even remember. In most of those cases, we do not even want to remember them! And this is not by accident. What are those attributes that make characters interesting? Let's have a look at some tips.

Tip 1: Archetypes

Not all characters in a story have the same role or reason to exist. Characters usually serve a particular purpose, affecting the course of a story and helping designers present a particular perspective or create the necessary circumstances for learning experiences. Let's take **The Lion King**, for example. In The Lion King, Simba, a young lion, flees into exile after being tricked about his father's death. Ending up in the jungle, Simba gets help from two wastrels, Timon and Pumba, who help him grow up. Later in the story, Simba, with the support of the shaman monkey Rafiki, returns to face his evil uncle and bring balance to the jungle. The story advances through the interaction of these characters and the dynamics between them.

Russian folklorist Vladimir Propp in his book, **Morphology of the Tale**, analyzed the structure of Russian fairy tales. As with Joseph Campbell, Propp found common patterns in different kinds of stories related to the folk tales [6]. Among those patterns, he identified seven archetypal characters that he called **actants**. Those characters are:

- **The hero**: A character who responds to the call for adventure, faces the story's villains, and restores balance to the world.

- **The villain**: An evil character who is the main reason for the hero's struggles.

- **The donor**: A character who provides the hero with resources or offers advice and information.

- **The helper**: A character with magic powers who comes to the aid of the hero.

- **The princess**: A character, a task, or a goal that embodies the hero's aim in entering the adventure. Usually marrying the princess or achieving this goal signifies the villain's defeat and the end of the adventure.

- **The dispatcher**: A character who presents the hero with the adventure and sets its starting point in the story.

- **The false hero**: A character who tries to take credit for the hero's actions, trying to achieve the hero's goals.

Of course, not every story needs to have all of those characters. The decision of character structure and interaction is an aspect that depends on what you want to achieve with those characters. There are cases where there can be many heroes or many villains. In role-playing games, there are several heroes. If the game has multiplayer features, there could be as many heroes or villains as the players.

Tip 2: Empathy

Great characters need to arouse a player's empathy. Empathy is the human ability to sense the emotion of other people. In other words, empathy could mean "like myself." Without doubt, interesting characters present a human side that players can relate to. This does not necessarily mean that players and game characters have the same personality. However, those characters have something familiar and when players identify this familiarity, they relate to those characters and want them to succeed and achieve their goals.

It is also important to note that empathy is not synonymous with sympathy. Several Pixar characters are sympathetic, like Nemo, Wall-E, and Dory. These are characters that players would like to have around them, to be their friends. Gru from **Despicable Me**, on the other hand, is not sympathetic as he is a supervillain. However, the audience empathizes with him. Consequently, players consciously or unconsciously start relating with him and they want him to have whatever he wants.

A piece of advice that I found very interesting is given by the writer Blake Snyder. Snyder considers that for the audience to empathize with a character, the character needs to do a good deed during the story duration. He called this technique **Save the Cat**, relating to the good deed of saving a cat hanging from a tree. Snyder realized that by doing this, story characters show a human side, a side that players can relate to and project themselves onto.

Tip 3: Characters should be convincing

In his book **Story**, Robert McKee considers that the function of any character is "to bring to the story the qualities of characterization necessary to convincingly act out choices" [7, p. 105]. In other words, characters must be credible and their choices should be consistent with the profile players have created about them.

This is in fact a case that I frequently encounter in educational game design situations, where educators want to present a particular story and lead players to specific conclusions. Once, I was discussing a game story with a team of trainers that wanted to create a board game that would present the story and choices of different teenage characters in order to inform teenage students about sex education. The characters they had created were conveniently designed in order to present very specific arguments. However, those characters and their actions in the stories seemed extremely artificial. It was clear that the characters were created by adults and that their way of talking and expressing their opinion and actions did not correspond to the actions of the age and social group they were supposed to represent. This game was doomed to fail from its inception because its characters were not convincing.

Consequently, players need to be consistent with the profile they represent. Game stories that fail to do so cause players to be confused, frustrated, or indifferent about the outcome of the stories. If you want to convey a particular message through a game story, you need to address the issue on a higher level and not just through the personality of characters and their actions. Games that do not focus so much on story can achieve this through their game mechanics, while games that are strongly based on story elements need to create the necessary circumstances in the backstory for those characters to be convincing and consistent throughout the duration of the game.

Tip 4: The burrito or the pizza

Similarly to cinema and theater, in games, showing players the internal thinking process of a game character becomes a challenge. In order to make my point, try to give an answer to the following scenario. A game character is sitting on a bench. How would you explain to your players that this player internally struggles between going for a burrito or a pizza? The answer would be by using text. A bubble, a comment, or a voice-over might do just fine in this case. But is this really an efficient way of communicating with your players? How many of them actually read texts or pay attention to the voice overs? If you consider this, then you run the risk of a great number of players not even understanding what is going on. In fact, the use of simple text in order to explain aspects inside games indicates weakness in the game's presentation of information, events, and narratives.

So how would it be possible to pass this message to your players? Successfully designed characters have a history, they have a personality, and they are characterized by virtues and flaws. On top of this, characters acquire their traits in specific contexts. How would the characters of Asterix and Obelix be perceived outside their Gaulish village in the era of ancient Rome? Character personalities take form inside particular contexts and give birth to internal struggles and conflicts, which can gradually be understood by players. On top of this, the timing and location play a great role in providing players with information about the game character's surroundings, location, and time of an event. All of these aspects combined together can prove to be more powerful than text alone.

REFLECTION POINTS 🔍

- How have you structured your game characters?

- How compelling are your characters and what connection do they have with your audience?

- What messages or values do your characters convey to your players, if at all?

- How well-structured and consistent are your characters?

- What types of characters does your game have and what is their connection?

- How do your characters affect your game and learning experience?

PERSPECTIVE

Utku Kaplan
Creative Director and Cofounder at KIUPE

What is the impact of storytelling on games?

Not all games need to tell a story. This is obvious to see, and probably points out the fact that we use the same word for **Tetris** or, for example, **The Last Guardian**—which is the last game I played.

I do like it when games have a story, and what I love most is when it's cleverly included directly into the gameplay. For example, a good way to do it are through the reactions characters, player or non-player, can have in response to something you are doing. It can be AI or scripted, such as Nathan Drake screaming when I am running to the edge of a cliff before I jump!

However, storytelling should be something that serves the game. It can have a negative impact when it's not done well. I unfortunately have an example of that with one of my games. During a playtest, there was this nine-year-old girl who sighed every time a dialog cut scene appeared, frantically tapping the screen to skip it. I see storytelling in games as something that gives a meaning to the gameplay, to your actions, to the reason why you are playing this particular game.

There is probably no universal rule on the amount of cut scenes, dialogue, or whatever we think might fit our story and game, but we should ask ourselves why we are doing it and how it serves the game, because it can either enhance it or make it really boring—which is never what you want for a game, right?

How do you design and structure the rules of your games?

Most of my work is trying to get things out of chaos. When I think on it a little bit, I always have ideas that are at first unclear, abstract, and fragmented. It's only when I try to explain them to others do I realize that. But what is often really clear is the intention—either it's something that comes from me or a commissioned work. I have some pictures in my head, or a sentence, or just the aesthetics of what I would like to achieve. This helps me through the design process.

I rarely work alone and I often have brainstorming sessions with my teammates. Working as a team is very efficient for me. I share everything I have, clear and unclear, and we iterate until we have something we think is good enough.

We often try to find inspiration, often in other games—there are so many blogs and developers to discover out there. I spend a lot of time reading them—about board games, animation, and so on. The last thing I can say is that we often rewrite. Really it's amazing to see how much time we spend on ideas, gameplay, and even whole games that are thrown away!

How do you combine learning and gaming elements in order to create your games?

If I look back on games I have made, we always start with the learning objectives we want to reach and work on a game concept that fits. Learning objectives are not always complex and we can easily find a nice concept.

A couple of years ago we worked with an organization for a game about the protection of the environment: **Panache Expedition**. After we read their briefing the idea of the game came quite quickly. The learning objectives were not very hard to implement in the gameplay, but the topic was complex and we were involved with many kinds of scientists and experts who were reading our scenarios and proposing corrections. That was a very good experience and the game had some success on the App Store.

Learning objectives were a little bit more complex to implement in the gameplay of our game about fractions. For this game we had this idea of an adventure game where fractions are used as obstacles in your way. We worked with a mathematics didactician who helped us design all these obstacles based on how fractions are taught in the classroom and which difficulties kids come across. There was some back-and-forth because we had to translate the academic way of acquiring this knowledge into gameplay. Another difficulty was the user experience in our game, with a touchscreen, was quite different than the one the kids had in the classroom—manipulating strips of paper, for example. Strips of paper are used, in some methods to learn fractions, by comparing the length of a strip of paper that equals one to other strips of paper. Most of the time I drew mockups and iterated over them before implementing the module into the game.

To finish this example, another hard part is the progression of difficulty. For that, I have made spreadsheets clearly showing the different difficulty configurations and how they are used in the level design.

In this project, I spent a large amount of time doing my best to help the learning expert understand game mechanics and everything we must be aware of when developing a game. In the end, we both acquired a lot of experience that I am sure we can use on a future collaboration!

How important are prototypes in your design process? How do you use them?

I must say we do not always need to make a prototype. Prototypes are useful when you are not sure of particular features, or the way some game mechanics can work together. And it has a cost.

But we have made a lot of them as well. Most of the time, it is for testing ideas we were not really sure of, and, let's be honest, it helped us realize how bad some ideas were—even those that seemed good at first!

We have a prototype phase in our next game, because this game has some complexity and we have broken down some of the core features in a couple of prototypes to easily test them.

Any advice for potential educational game designers?

I often see educational games that are so boring! I think educational games must keep two promises: Education and fun. Each implemented feature must serve one or another, or, ideally, both. You also need to think about what can be fun about the topic you work on. A game about science can lead to really cool learning situations. If the topic is not very fun, try to contextualize it. Math can be very abstract, so you can think of situations where they can be used in gameplay. For example, **Dragonbox** is a really cool way to contextualize equations.

Also try to work with kids. We work with them early in the project, with participative design sessions, where we try to learn how they deal with the topic, what their expectations are, and so on. And of course, we have a lot of playtesting with kids. That's the only way to know if your game keeps its promise of fun!

What is the most important virtue of an educational game designer?

I think engagement is the key. The game must be engaging all along so the player keeps going. According to David C. Geary, a cognitive psychologist, there are two kinds of knowledge: Primary knowledge, which has an intrinsic motivation, such as recognizing a face or learning how to talk; and secondary knowledge, which is more complex and needs an extrinsic motivation. Games can do that using features that are the keys of primary knowledge, such as exploration or collaboration, to engage learner in secondary knowledge.

Games can be a very good tool to bring about motivation, and they should probably be designed with this idea in mind.

What are your sources of inspiration?

I try to keep in touch with the audience: what they like, and why they like it. Most of the time, I also try to find inspiration in what I like myself. I have some experience in animation and cartoons so there are probably a lot of influences for me there. I really look at the pictures, how they inspire me, the atmosphere they create, and why I think they can be used in the game.

I also try to look at the games kids play. Now, with mobile, you often see kids playing out there, on the bus or wherever. And of course, my own kids—but maybe they are also influenced by me. One thing I noticed and try to keep in mind is that kids often play games that are not designed especially for them. **Minecraft** was not. So, I try to design games that I would like to play too.

What are your game influences?

I am mostly a console game player. I have played a lot of Nintendo games: **The Legend of Zelda, Mario, Mario Kart,** and so on. Really amazing games. I also play a lot on solo games with some storyline. I really enjoyed the **Uncharted series** and **Ueda's games** (I finished **The Last Guardian** in a couple of days…).

I also follow with the greatest interest the indie game scene. I can't play all of them, but I do what I can to play those that interest me most.

I am definitely not a one-type-of-game player. I have enjoyed games such as **Dwarf Fortress**, but I also can't wait to play **Night in the Woods**.

SUMMARY

So, what topics did we cover in this chapter?

- Games present narrative worlds. Those worlds create circumstances for players' learning, tell stories, or help players create their own stories and show consistency.

- There are different way to create narratives. Some types of stories are predefined and always presented in the same way by games. Others are dynamically created through players' interactions with games.

- Stories can be presented in a linear or nonlinear format, and we should examine the different ways that this can happen.

- Narratives can also be facilitated through players' interaction with space and the arrangement of objects and events around game worlds.

- We examined the idea of the Hero's Journey.

- Different games present different character types, each of which has a particular value and impact on the game story.

REFERENCES

1. Chatman, S. B. (1980). *Story and discourse: Narrative structure in fiction and film*. Ithaca, NY: Cornell University Press.
2. LeBlanc, M. (1999). Formal design tools: Feedback systems and the dramatic structure of competition. In *Proceedings of 1999 Computer Game Developers' Conference*. San Francisco: Miller Freeman Game Group.
3. Schell, J. (2014). *The art of game design: A book of lenses* (2nd ed). London & New York: CRC Press.
4. Campbell, J. (2008). *The hero with a thousand faces*. Novato, California: New World Library.
5. Vogler, C. (1998). *The writer's journey: Mythic structure for writers*. Studio City, CA: M. Wiese Productions.
6. Propp, V. (2010). *Morphology of the folktale* (L. Scott, Trans.). Austin: University of Texas Press.
7. McKee, R. (1997). *Story: Substance, structure, style, and the principles of screen writing*. New York: Regan Books.

11 Game Interfaces

This chapter:

- Explores the various ways that communication is facilitated in gaming contexts.

- Offers insights on efficient instruction offering.

- Analyzes existing game interfaces and presents tips and best practices for the design of efficient interfaces.

- Explores the different ways of adapting interfaces to different means and platforms.

Even the greatest games may not be perceived well if they are not properly presented. This chapter is dedicated to the analysis and design of efficient game interfaces that properly present information to players and help them achieve the tasks they wish. Throughout the chapter we will explore different examples and situations of design of successful and unsuccessful interfaces and come up with best practices and tips that will help you design interfaces that speak to your players' hearts and minds.

THE IMPORTANCE OF EFFICIENT COMMUNICATION

During a training event in London about the development of leadership skills, I was asked to be part of the trainers' team. The team consisted of amazing and highly motivated experts and was focused on the creation of learning activities that were mainly based on games. Since everyone in the training team came from a different background, the discussion was fierce and intense! New elements were proposed, modified, and removed constantly. In the end, the team came up with an outdoor game on leadership that everybody was happy with. We were all very excited to present the game to our participants. So, when day one came, we were eager to see how they would respond. The result was terrible! The participants could not understand the game, they felt bored and annoyed, and some of them even argued with each other! The team was surprised and some members even suggested that the problem was with the participants themselves. But the problem was obvious: even if the team had spent lots and lots of time designing the game, we hadn't worked on the game's presentation.

That leadership game was definitely not the first case of bad communication of a game's elements. Moreover, this is a more generic issue that comes up rather often when designing systems where information needs to be shared and diffused. Yes, games are systems of information. When we play Uno, the cards in our hands contain information about the colors or numbers they contain. When we play, draw, or lose cards, this very information is diffused to our opponents, who on their turn make their own decisions. When we play racing games like **Forza Motorsport**, **Gran Turismo**, or **Project Cars**, we need to drive our vehicles and reach the finish line as fast as we can. For this to happen, though, we need to know which route is the shortest, which cars are fastest, and what the current condition of our vehicles is. In order to make this happen, we need to read maps, review vehicle statistics, and drive our cars using racing wheels, gamepads, keyboards, or joysticks. In order for our cars to reach the end of the line, these games need to provide us with information and receive our response, which is also some type of information.

So, we have established that games are systems of information. The main question, though, is how games can present this information effectively to players. Obviously, not all games are effective at communicating all their information to players. In 1982 Atari released the video game **E.T. The Extra-Terrestrial**, an adventure game based on the movie with the same title. The problem with the game was that it was so difficult to come to grips with its controls, visuals, and gameplay that players would feel lost and frustrated. The game did not succeed in producing sales mainly because it failed to effectively communicate the information it needed to provide. Communication and the correct flow of information can consequently help or diminish gaming and learning experiences. In the following sections we will examine several points of games as systems of information and look at best practices in order to maximize the potential of your game.

GAMES OFFER INSTRUCTIONS

The first element of information in games are their instructions. Instructions constitute the initial information that players receive about a game. So, it's not strange for the success or failure of several games to have been decided just from their presentation. Instructions that fail to explain the presented games make players feel uneasy, confused, and finally, look for something else to do. Good instructions, on the other hand, lead to smooth game presentation where players know what they are doing and how their actions have meaning inside the game world.

Instructions are not only limited to game rules. Instructions also consist of any kind of information that builds on the learning experience. So, they can be about game presentation, giving hints, offering feedback on player choices, presenting additional learning content, or any other type of information that is supposed to shed light on any aspect of the game and guide players through learning experiences.

One of the first activities I ask potential educational game designers to do after coming up with a game proposal is to present their game. Believe me, this is not an easy task! We have all been to presentations where, after a couple of hours, we still didn't have a clue what the presentation was about; we have also been in presentations where everything was very clear from the very beginning. Good presentations take into account a great variety of factors: context, audience, game, learning aspect, timing. So, taking some time to reflect on how to present one's game is a complex and crucial process that will absolutely affect players' perception about the game. Whether a game is physical or digital; 2D or 3D; uses augmented or virtual reality or any other means, style, or approach, instructions need to be carefully designed in order to help players understand what they need to do, search for, and how to achieve their goals. I have picked three examples from previous experiences that present interesting characteristics about the use of instructions in educational games.

Example 1: Adventure Story

A game studio developed a 3D "escape-the-room" game to inform players about art history. Players were trapped inside a room and in order to escape, they needed to explore every part of it and identify elements that would offer them hints to help unlock the room's door. Paintings would play a key role in this search as the hints players would get were linked to information about those paintings, their artists, and the movements they represented. Players would need to discuss the connection of these clues with the paintings, review the information they received through playing the game, and reach conclusions that would help them to unlock the room door.

The game, which only reached the prototype stage, started with players locked inside a room and no additional instructions or hints. Players would need to start looking around the room and trying to figure out ways to escape. However, the lack of any information, hints, or advice and the fact that several of the clues were very well hidden around the room led to players not knowing what they should do. Frustrated, confused, and ignorant of their goals, players did not interact with the game. Instead, during test phases, we would see players sitting around computers talking about topics unrelated to the game while the game sat forlorn and ignored on their screens.

The game didn't introduce players to its gameplay or offer instructions to help them understand how it should played and what players needed to do. This led players to wander around the room for a bit, try a few actions and, when they couldn't figure out what to do, leave the game and do something else.

Example 2: Design Madness

A research team, working on the teaching of game design to college students, created a card game to help students better facilitate their design process. The game featured a deck of 60 cards, each of which would address a particular game element that the research team wanted to investigate. Each card would also present a set of questions and actions that players would need to perform when the cards would be drawn. The game would be played by 4 to 6 players, among which the whole number of cards would be dealt. At each round, one player would select a card and place it in the center. All the players would need to read its instructions, answer its questions, and perform the actions described.

Even if the game covered a great number of elements that designers address during the process of game design, it proved to be rather too complex for players to handle. Each card came with several questions and actions, each of which was not very clear about what players were required to do. The players spent a great deal of time trying to figure out what they were meant to do and asking the observers from the research team to clarify the content of the cards. The use of the cards and the unclear and complex nature of their content made several players feel confused about what they were supposed to do. In the end, most teams failed to come up with their own games because they lost considerable time trying to understand how the cards worked and lost focus on their main objective: The creation of a new game.

The game came with lots of unclear instructions. So, the research team failed to propose a game design tool that would facilitate the players' design process.

Example 3: The Great Hunt

In order to inform and motivate young citizens about sustainable development, the members of a nonprofit organization came up with an outdoor game that would be played on a Saturday morning by over 100 players aged 12 to 14 years. The design team, excited about this great opportunity, designed a highly advanced treasure hunt game full of puzzles, outdoor activities, and challenges, all over their local area. The game would be played by teams of 4 to 6 players, each of which needed to finish their race. The designers came up with a great set of rules and information, printed on small booklets, that were delivered to the teams at the beginning of the game. So, in order for players to move forward with their quests, they would actually need to consult their booklets.

From the beginning of the game, it became obvious that players had difficulty keeping up with the complex and numerous rules of the game. Players would constantly need to keep an eye on their booklets even from the very beginning. The fact that they did not know where to go or how to proceed with the challenges they encountered made them lose track of their objectives. From the 42 teams that started the game, only 7 actually finished, and it was discovered that most of the teams completed no more than 20 percent of the game.

In this case, there was too much information. Even if the designers wanted to create an exciting and original experience, they should have found a way of gradually presenting all this information to players and avoided doing this instantaneously from the very beginning.

The cases above present some of the possible issues that may arise when instructions are not presented correctly in educational gaming contexts. Such issues have an impact in every aspect of the final experience: the game may seem frustrating, difficult, and confusing; eventually, most players will abandon it. On the other hand, even if players continue playing, there is no assurance about the game's learning impact on players.

Reflecting on Effective Instructions

It is highly possible that games that do not succeed in presenting the necessary circumstances for players to explore, experiment, identify, and reflect on the elements they encounter, may not lead learners to master the concepts they present. In the worst-case scenario, the games may mislead or create misunderstandings and instead of helping, they might even be harmful as learning tools. I propose three steps that are helpful for reflecting on proper instructions in educational games:

Step 1: What needs to be presented?

The first step for effectively presenting any game is figuring out which information you need to present. So far, you have worked on your educational games and you have a good idea of their structure. It is now time to identify which elements must be presented and in what order for players to be able to understand how to play your games. Figuring out what you need to present so that players can understand your games may seem to vary from genre to genre but the principle remains the same, whether the game is a traditional game or an MMO RPG game. In any case, players need to have enough information to start playing the game. But is figuring out what you need to present enough? In Example 3: The Great Hunt, designers had worked out all the information they wanted to present. They even compiled a booklet in order to present this information. But was this enough? No! Because the vast majority of players do not want to read piles of information before diving in.

But, like movies, books, sports, or other activities, people need space to see if they want to invest more time in the activities put before them. On top of this, they need to be hooked on the presented activity, to feel motivated, interested, and amazed; then, they will want to go deeper.

Step 2: What are the absolute core elements that must be presented?

Thus, the second step to effective game presentation is to reflect on the information designers have in their possession and finding out only that which is absolutely essential for the game to be played. Being able to tell what information is important for players to move forward and what isn't helps in many ways. First, designers are able to better explain their games to players, giving them the possibility to reflect on the experience they are about to present. Second, the instructions are presented in a more effective way, providing players with the purely essential elements of the game. After you are able to isolate these necessary items, you are usually ready to explain your game in any situation. You can do it quickly, you can do it efficiently, and you can do it in varied contexts with different audiences.

Step 3: How is it going to be presented?

The third step to effective game presentation is related to how the game information is going to be presented. We will see later in this chapter, when we talk about interfaces, that there is more than one way of properly presenting games. They all depend on the atmosphere, style, and learning objectives of the game. In games whose learning objectives focus on social issues, designers may want to present and highlight a particular point of view or opinion. In games about history or geography, the ordering of instructions and presentation of game content may need to be aligned with the games' learning objectives. In games about soft skills training, designers may need to emphasize particular instructions and shift the focus of the game towards specific gaming aspects, based on their audiences' needs.

Of course, the most effective instructions are the result of constant revision after playtesting with one's audience. The following is a small set of tips to use so you can present games more effectively.

Tip 1: Keep it simple. Being excited about their game, it is a natural urge for game designers to want to add more and more things to their game presentations. The problem with this urge is that the more information provided, the more complex it becomes. Lots of information may confuse players and lead them away from the game's main purposes. So, always try to keep your instructions simple.

Tip 2: Keep it reasonable. There is a fine line between presenting something in an intuitive and novel way and exaggerating one's presentation. There are certainly people who have a gift for presenting games in innovative ways that amaze their players, but it's very possible that exaggerating and trying to push too many elements about specific game aspects risks making designers and players lose track of what they wish to achieve. Unless you are absolutely confident and sure about going down this path, try to add novel ideas one at a time and study your players' reactions.

Tip 3: Think on behalf of your players. Instructions are put in place to help players. In this case, designers need to anticipate player behavior and their responses to game events and provide instructions that will help them to master the game's environment and mechanics. It's always important to remember that players do not know your game as well as you do. So, nothing should be considered as being obvious or a given for players.

Tip 4: Avoid unnecessary information. A common principle for lifeguards is to avoid constantly blowing their whistle to attract swimmers' attention when tackling inappropriate behavior. The main reason for this is that if the whistle is blown a lot, swimmers will stop paying attention to it, rendering it useless when a really dangerous situation occurs. Information should be carefully filtered and selected. Players tend to skip long texts or continuous information that keeps popping up. So, instead of presenting lots of information, try to focus on important aspects that players will really need to proceed further in the game.

Tip 5: There are no incapable players, there are only bad instructions. I often meet educational game designers who blame their players for not understanding or being able to play their games. Whatever their point may be, I find it difficult to believe that players who can master enormously complex games like **Call of Duty**, **World of Warcraft**, or **Assassin's Creed** have difficulty getting a grip on these other games. So, when something is wrong with a player's understanding of educational games, the very first factor that I question is the game and its instructions themselves. There are no incapable players. There are only games that fail to present their rules and mechanics in a way that can be understood by them.

REFLECTION POINTS 🔍

- What types of instructions do you provide in your games? How much of this information is absolutely necessary for players to understand the game and how much is not? How are the instructions presented and how do you expect players to behave based on those?

- Would you consider your instructions as being simply presented? Do you find any aspects that could be better explained or aspects that may cause players to be confused or overwhelmed by the amount of information provided?

- How effective do you find the game's instructions for your players? Do you anticipate any misunderstandings or confusions to be caused for the players receiving those instructions?

PERSPECTIVE: THE EDUCATIONAL PROMISE BROUGHT BY NEW TECHNOLOGIES

Celia Hodent

PhD in Psychology, Game UX Consultant

Observing people experiencing virtual reality (VR) for the first time is captivating. After putting the headset and headphones on, they often react quite intensely: laughing, or wowing, or keeping their mouth open in awe as they explore a different reality. New technologies, such as VR, have a clear potential to offer powerful experiences. This is why many educators are hoping that this potential can be exploited to help them create compelling learning environments. Using cutting-edge technology in the hope of enhancing education is nothing new, though. With every technological advance came the hope that we could use it to motivate children and adults to learn, and help them learn better.

The rise of personal computers once bore this promise. As early as in the 1960s, Seymour Papert, mathematician and educator, saw in computers a powerful tool allowing children to learn through discoveries, as they manipulate new concepts in contextual and meaningful situations. However, instead of using the computer to teach children, albeit in a new (and then more exciting way than traditional teaching), Papert [1] let the children program the computer. For example, Papert developed the Logo computer language at MIT which allowed children to control a cursor—called "turtle"—that could draw anything they wanted. But they had to tell the turtle how to draw what they had in mind, using geometry rules. For example, if they wanted to draw a house, they could accomplish their goal by drawing a square then a triangle. To draw a square, children needed to understand that it has four equal sides, four 90-degree angles, so that they could tell the turtle to "Repeat 4 [forward 50 right 90]." Instead of being taught what the properties of a square are, they would discover it by themselves, through trial and error, as they manipulated the computer to accomplish a goal that was meaningful to them. According to Papert's constructionist approach, children (and adults) learn more efficiently when they can experiment with the material in a concrete and meaningful situation. The question is thus, can VR, augmented reality (AR), or mixed reality (MR) provide more meaningful environments to enhance learning? They can certainly fully immerse users in any world or environment we want, and allow for safe experimentations of pretty much anything while providing immediate feedback on what users are doing. The potential is certainly here. But the educational potential promised by personal computers, or the Internet, was also already here. Did we truly exploit this potential? Many educational video games, or serious games, are not even trying to place their audience in a meaningful situation in which they can experiment and build their knowledge, although they have the potential to do so. Many are not even trying to be playful or fun, although we know that such experiences are more engaging, which is also important to enhance learning.

Technology can offer us new perspectives and possibilities, but at the end of the day what truly matters is what we do with them. An efficient and meaningful learning environment can be designed with old technology while new technology can be as deceptive as a game of smoke and mirrors. Moreover, developing compelling video games or AR/VR environments is actually quite difficult. Passed the first excitement of discovering a new technology, we do not engage with them as easily as most people might think. In the case of video games, for example, many of them fail to be fun and engaging. Every year, numerous game projects are cancelled, some studios are closed, and too many game developers are laid off. It's not because some good video games can be highly engaging that any video game will be able to engage its audience. This is why adding a basic video game layer on top of an educational content is not enough to change the level of engagement of students, or to make a learning environment more meaningful. And this will be true with the new technologies upon us. In order to enhance education, designers of educational games or environments will have to adopt a user-centered mindset: one that considers the user experience (UX). In the past years, video game studios have increasingly embraced UX knowledge, tools, and methodologies to help them improve the quality of their games. It's mainly about understanding how people learn, how they interact with computers, and how human motivation works. Considering the game user experience entails two main pillars: usability—the ability of a game to be used; and what I call "engage-ability"—the ability of a game to be engaging [2]. When developers have a UX mindset, they constantly evaluate throughout the development process whether their game is usable and engaging, and if the target audience experience it the way they intended. This approach is certainly necessary to ensure that VR or AR environments will be experienced by the audience the way intended, especially when considering education. The purpose is to allow users to experiment with new concepts in a meaningful way, not have them struggle as they try to figure out an interface, controls, or specific mechanics.

While having a UX mindset will be critical to exploit the full potential of new technologies, considering transfer of learning will also be paramount [3]. Making people learn something in the context of a certain game or environment is one thing, enabling them to transfer what was learned to new situations is a much more complex endeavor, although the one that educators need to focus on. This is actually the main flaw of what some call **gamification**, in the sense of adding rewards and a clear feedback on progression: by mostly focusing on external rewards (such as badges), "gamified" educational environments may allow their audience to change their behavior and learn things within the context of this specific environment but not necessarily apply it to new situations. By contrast, learners who developed strategies in the context of meaningful and playful experiences, such as via the environments Seymour Papert designed, seem to be more likely to transfer these strategies to other contexts [4]. With new tools come new possibilities, and cutting-edge technology surely brings exciting and promising potential for education. However, it's not in the tools themselves that the potential lies, it lies in what we design with them.

REFERENCES

1. Papert, S. (1980). *Mindstorms: Children, Computers, and Powerful Ideas.* New York: Basic Books.
2. Hodent, C. (2017). *The Gamer's Brain: How Neuroscience and UX Can Impact Video Game Design.* Boca Raton, FL: CRC Press.
3. Blumberg, F. C. (Eds.) (2014). *Learning by Playing: Video Gaming in Education.* Oxford, UK: Oxford University Press.
4. Klahr, D., & Carver, S. M. (1988). Cognitive objectives in a LOGO debugging curriculum: Instruction, learning, and transfer. *Cognitive Psychology, 20,* 362–404.

THE POWER OF SILENCE

In 1952, experimental composer John Cage created his score named *4'33"* (pronounced "four, thirty three"). The score consisted of three movements during which instrument players were asked not to use their instruments for the whole duration of the score, which lasted four minutes and 33 seconds. He believed that through this period of silence, the audience could listen to the sounds of the environment, which for him was also considered as music. This may sound strange but it was also a statement. Cage wanted to show that silence is another form of expression.

Limbo is an excellent example of how silence can be used as a means of expression in video games. (Used with permission of Playdead.)

Educational game design can become a very powerful tool for shaping values, principles, personal perspectives, and approaches toward life. Players spend many hours of their lives playing games. They interact, they transform, and become transformed through the process of play. On the other hand, educational game designers create intrinsically motivating learning experiences that are characterized by emotions, special moments, and atmospheric spaces. Silence is a tool to achieve these. Silence is not only about sound, it is about actions, about what people hear, see, and feel. Silence can be used to emphasize moments, to create atmosphere, or to point out particular characteristics of a game scene. Popular games like **Silent Hill**, **Alone in the Dark**, or **Limbo** use silence in different ways. In Silent Hill, silence in some cases builds the suspense about what is coming next, giving emotional charge to already tense moments. In Limbo, the intentional lack of colors offers an atmosphere that adds to the game's story, where a little boy searches for his sister.

There are occasions where speech, images, or actions are unnecessary for an experience to take form. There are several occasions, though, where not speaking, not presenting anything, or not taking action says more than doing something. This is the power of silence!

GAMES USE INTERFACES

In order to better explain what interfaces are, let's first start by laying some groundwork. When players play games, they receive information about the game's rules, its world, and the consequences of their actions inside this world. This interaction requires two ingredients: the players and the game. Players see, hear, and feel the information that comes from the games they play and make decisions that affect a game's world. Games also receive information about a player's decisions and present the outcomes of these choices back to the player. But how is this possible? Through interfaces!

If we consider that there are two separate dimensions, one for players and one for the game's world, interfaces are the shared boundary where those dimensions communicate. In other words, interfaces are created to help players talk to games and games talk to players. Let's see some examples. Interfaces are:

- The head-up display, showing lives, points, and score in **Half Life**, **Candy Crush**, or **Ingress**.

- The arrangement of graphics and components throughout the screen of **Math Blaster**, **The Zoombinis**, **Tetris**, and **Words with Friends**.

- The "Are you sure you want to quit?" pop-up message that appears when we press the exit game button.

- The game leaderboards and badge screens.

- A computer's keyboard or mouse.

- A console's gamepad, joystick, motion control device, or driving wheel.

- A computer screen, a smartphone touch screen, an interactive table surface, or an interactive whiteboard.

- A Raspberry Pi circuit featuring LED lights that light up when players activate a proximity sensor.

- The control software platforms for robots and robotic parts like NAO, Bee-Bot, or Lego Mindstorms.

It becomes obvious that interfaces can take different forms and modes, and use different media in order to facilitate the information flow between players and games. Interfaces are used as sources of both input and output between players and games. When players play games, they control their characters, solve puzzles, and perform every other type of action using an input device, such as a mouse, keyboard, joystick, or touch screen. Those choices are received by games as a set of information, processed, and returned back to the players as visual information through their screens, as audio information through their speakers, or as haptic information through the vibration of their gamepads.

So, inefficient interfaces risk misinforming, misleading, or annoying players. In order to be able to efficiently design interfaces, it is first important to examine the notion of interaction.

THE POWER OF INTERACTION

During the mid-1990s, the Japanese toy maker Bandai brought out **Tamagotchi**. Tamagotchi was a pocket-size digital game featuring a virtual pet that players needed to take care of. The Tamagotchi would grow up as players took care of it. They needed to feed it, clean up after it, and play with it on a regular basis. If they failed to take care of it properly, the pet would die. Every time the pet needed something, it would inform players through messages, sounds, and funny images. So, players needed to put effort into taking care of their virtual pet and the virtual pet would, in return, inform them about its condition. This mutual effect between Tamagotchi and players was interaction.

There are different types of interactions in educational games. Let's look at some examples:

- Players interact with shapes as game elements in a game about the development of mathematical thinking.

- Players interact with the pins on a map of a game teaching history and geography to high school students.

- Players interact with a musical instrument in a music-themed game.

- Players interact with game designers or game masters in a live action role-playing game about human rights.

- Players interact with tangible objects in a game training players on a newly delivered piece of machinery.

- Players interact with other players in a multiplayer game.

- Players interact with non-player characters.

- Players interact with game narratives by selecting the course of events that is to unfold.

- Players interact with controls by giving input and receiving haptic responses.

- Players interact with the environment by wandering around and exploring space in a virtual reality game.

So, interaction can take various forms. It can be related to the mutual impact between players and game elements, players and other players, players and the narrative, players and controls, and the list goes on. There is also interaction in educational games without players being present. For example, there is interaction between the learning and game aspect or narratives and mechanics, or technology and mechanics. Even if we have not previously examined games as systems of information, we have indirectly examined several of those interactions through the chapters of this book. One particular and very helpful type of interaction is feedback.

Feedback is any game's response to a player's actions, so if we reflect on what this means, feedback is crucial for players' decisions. Let's take bowling, for example. Bowling presents a number of pins at the end of a lane that need to be knocked over by players who throw bowling balls. Also, there is not just one specific type of bowling ball but rather many variants in different sizes and weights. So, every time players decide to throw a bowling ball, they see it, they estimate its size, they pick it up and feel its weight, then they estimate the distance from the pins and eventually throw their ball. By throwing the ball, players know if their attempt was successful or not. They see the trajectory of the ball, its movement, and how that corresponds to their intentions and, finally, they see if their technique was effective in knocking over the pins at the end of the lane. In this case, players receive feedback throughout the whole course of playing. They measure the weight of the ball instantaneously; they can see if the way they threw the ball was effective by seeing how it spun and moved across the ground and by how many pins were knocked over. But feedback is not as natural in video games.

Video games come with several limitations and advantages. In this context, the greatest aspect, which is both a limitation and advantage, is that video game worlds are limited only by the designer's imagination. On one hand, you can create worlds with any physics, creatures, or dimensions you like but on the other, those worlds do not allow the same interactions and abilities of the physical world. Players that play bowling video games do not lift bowling balls, they do not feel their weight, and they do not throw heavy objects toward the pins, which requires particular technique and strength. So, video game designers need to find alternative ways of offering feedback to their players. But is feedback really that important in such cases? Let's see an example.

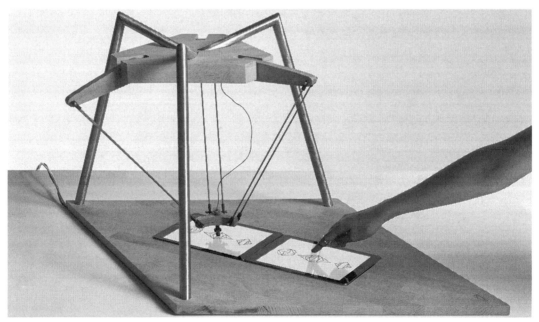

Deltu is a gaming robot that interacts with users through an iPad. (Used with permission of designer Alexia Léchot.)

In the framework of a research project, a team of educators proposed a game to develop the literacy skills of high school students. The game was a 2D point-and-click adventure one, where players needed to help the main character, a robot, complete its missions. The game presented virtual libraries, the books of which contained information about riddles and puzzles that players were asked to solve so that the story moved forward. A prototype of the game was developed and presented to several students. During the testing phase, it became clear that players had great difficulty in identifying the visual components of the game. They were lost! The first reason being that elements which players could interact with were not distinctly marked out from the ones with which they could not. Players would not know which areas to click on and felt confused. The second reason was that after players performed actions during the puzzles and riddles, the game would not clearly inform them whether the decisions were correct. The design team had created a text bar at the bottom of the screen to inform players about their decisions but the text was too small and players didn't pay attention to it.

So, the players' frustration and confusion grew bigger and bigger. A third reason was that even if players managed to complete some game challenges, they did not get a feeling of progression. The game would not inform them of their progress and status apart from presenting their next assignment. So, at some point during the first stages of the game, players would need to request assistance from the designers to continue or just leave the game. When this happens, it's quite a clear indication that something went wrong.

Feedback is crucial in any type of games since it is a game's way of interacting with players and giving them an appropriate amount of information about their impact on the game itself. Interfaces should integrate and deliver feedback when needed. Let's see how.

DESIGNING INTERFACES

Designing interfaces is actually a rather complicated task as game designers need to take into consideration several factors to help them build games that properly interact with their players. In this process, I use a combination of different perspectives that help me to better identify the needs and solutions for creating game interfaces. These perspectives are presented below.

Perspective 1: The Information

This perspective focuses on identifying what information designers want to present at a specific moment or event. This information can vary from a player's current score to the fact that they lost the game. Let's consider that we are presented with a game screen like this one:

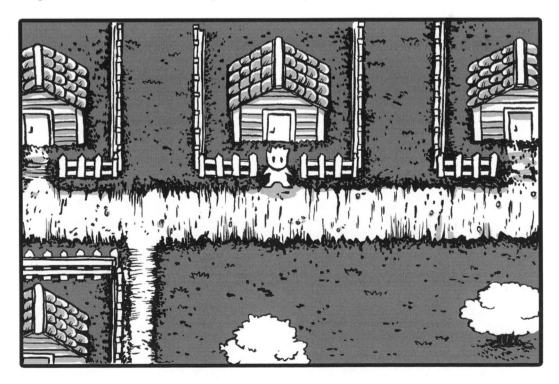

So, there are different types of information that we may want to provide our players with. Some examples are:

• Player score.

• Player lives.

• The achievement of a goal.

• Getting a power up.

• Losing a power up.

• Bumping into obstacles.

• Colliding with enemies and losing life points.

• Losing the game.

• Reviewing players' gear, tools, and weaponry.

• Letting players choose the way they want to develop the skills of their characters.

• Letting players decide the outcome of a story.

These portions of information, though, don't have the same meaning and importance during a game. No matter how important scores are, it is more important for players if they are winning or losing during a game. So, of all the different information that can be provided to players at a given instance, there is information that is crucial for the advancement of the game, there is information that is helpful, and there is information that the game could be played without. Inventories, for example, are important game elements because they allow players to review their current resources, but in most games they do not need to be constantly displayed. Leaderboards, on the other hand, can usually be reviewed after the end of a level, if their use is limited to defining the final performance of players during a level.

The priority and importance of information varies from game to game. In platform games, for example, most of the information is related to spatial arrangement in order to provide players with the best perspective for exploring, dealing with enemies, running, or jumping. In adventure games, on the other hand, there are several occasions where players need to read text, solve puzzles, and focus on visual details in order to move forward. The priority of information in this case is very different from that of platform games. This principle applies in almost all circumstances. Taking into consideration the particularities and requirements of learning contexts, the selection and prioritization of information in educational game contexts needs to be thoroughly considered.

Perspective 2: The Presentation of Information

Identifying the necessary information is not enough. Educational game designers need to take into account how this information is going to reach their players. Information can be visual, auditory, or haptic, and even those forms can be divided into several subcategories. Visual information can be text, video, image, spatial objects, spatial arrangements, darker or lighter, and the list is endless. Auditory information can be music, sounds, or silence, while haptic feedback can be vibrations, changes in size or temperature, or difference in surface textures.

So, the question that is raised in this perspective is, what is the best way of presenting a particular type of information based on its importance? Let's take, for instance, an adventure game, where players need to constantly know the life points, score, experience, and tools they have in their disposal. Let's now consider that the designers of this game want to show some of those elements to players at all times. There are various possible positions where game lives could be placed on the game screen. Could the life points be in the center of the screen? Let's see an example.

Of course they could, but in that case they would make it difficult for players to monitor the main character who will definitely end up moving around this area of the screen some time. Could the life points be placed on the right-middle side of the screen? Similarly, they could, but in this case, players may not be able to see obstacles or monsters coming toward them. So, the life points need to be placed in another position where they will be visible but don't hinder the game from evolving, like this, for instance:

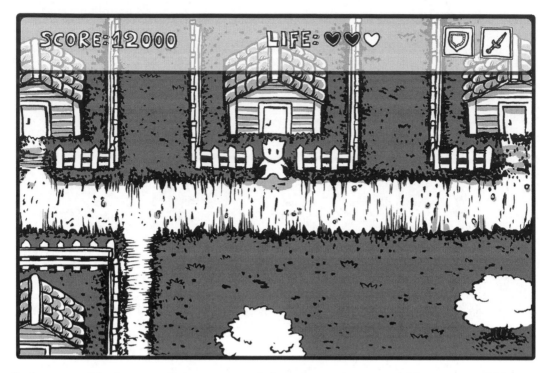

Let's now consider that game designers want to inform players about approaching monsters. This message has temporary value. Monsters come at a particular moment for a particular area. This means that the message might appear only for a limited time period. On top of this, the message needs to be distinctive and grab attention as danger is approaching. In this case, could the message appear in the center of the screen? This would be more of a possibility than in the previous case because the message would only appear for a short time and it is important for the evolution of the game's story.

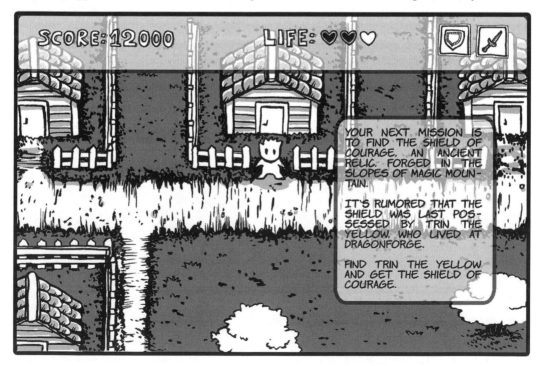

Perspective 3: The Facilitation of Learning

When designing educational games, a very helpful question is whether a game's interface actually helps players to learn. We have seen that interfaces are means of game–player interaction and communication. So, learning content, support, and feedback are provided to players through interfaces. Let's see some examples:

- A special set of instruction screens are presented to players who are playing a flight simulation game for the first time.

- In order to facilitate collaborative learning, a game designed to train employees for a company's new software platform and customer service process presents an online chat interface, where players can interact with each other and exchange information.

- A game offers hints to players who are having difficulties grasping the game logic.

- Examples and help are offered through messages, videos, or in-game character actions to players that show weakness in applying what they have learned in other levels or contexts.

- Information is presented in different ways to players to help them find their most preferable way of approaching the learning objectives of a game. For instance, a 3D adventure game about mathematical spatial thinking could provide a variety of spatial representations, such as maps, compasses, signs, hints, and different camera perspectives.

In all the cases above, interfaces were used as tools to facilitate learning experiences. They presented, organized, clarified, or diversified game information. The facilitation of learning experiences through proper interface design differs depending on the context, audience, and information that designers want to present. A stunning and highly colorful interface will not have the same impact and usability for players with a visual deficiency, while complex and sensitive controls may not be well received by users without finely developed motor skills.

This perspective examines interfaces through the prism of correctly presenting the necessary information so a game experience has the tone, atmosphere, and impact that the designer envisioned. There are several occasions where even if we have a perfect understanding of the games we want to present, presenting them still presents a significant challenge. This may become an issue in educational game contexts, where every word, action, or message may be important for players to correctly grasp the ideas being presented. Information can take different forms, like rules, instructions, game objects, aesthetics, narratives, or any other way that the designer wants to present their game. In any case, though, this information should avoid creating misconceptions or misunderstandings about the game and its learning aspect. Even more, players should be able to feel comfortable; understand the games; explore their worlds; and come out with developed skills, competences, and a greater understanding of the subject the game was about.

Those three perspectives offer a critical glance at the design of educational game interfaces. The best way to assess the efficiency of an interface is by observing how much players feel its presence. Interfaces that are easy to use pass unnoticed. Their use feels natural and players don't have to spend time figuring things out. On the other hand, inefficient interfaces are highly noticeable. Players waste time coming to grips with it and get confused, frustrated, and angry. So, previous case studies and design experience have shown some best practices for designing effective educational game interfaces. Some of those best practices are presented in the following.

Best Practice 1: Interfaces Should Be Self-Descriptive

Interfaces are created to make players' lives easier. They should be easy to use and easy to understand. In order to achieve this, interfaces need to be self-explanatory. This means that players should understand how to use them and their purpose just by interacting with them. Interfaces that are not self-explanatory are prone to creating issues for the game's facilitation of the learning experience.

Let's imagine a game dashboard, full of buttons, each of which is connected to a function. Let's also imagine that the designers of the game decided to put new, wonderfully crafted icons on each button. Now, players need to understand what each button does by seeing these new icons and learning what each of them does. This is not easy and, honestly, might not be worth the player's effort. If the buttons were assigned to symbols already known to players, though, they become automatically self-explanatory. Now, players can figure out what the buttons do without having to read instructions or ask for clarification. The easier it becomes for an interface to be understood and mastered by players, the more seamless the gaming experience will be.

Best Practice 2: Interfaces Should Offer a Diverse Set of Options for the Same Task

It happens rather often, especially when game design teams have limited resources, that interfaces are limiting and binding in terms of possible ways to perform tasks. As we saw before, in a great variety of educational gaming contexts, there can be numerous solutions to problems. In the same way, interfaces should support and encourage different ways of completing game tasks.

Let's consider the possibility of an outdoor exploration game about biology. If players were asked to explore the area outside their schools and take notes about the plants that grow in their area, they can achieve this by using pencil and paper, but they can also do it by using smartphones or tablets. In this way they can take photos and videos, record sounds of the area around them, or get the geographic location of plants. If this whole process was facilitated through a smartphone or tablet game, the game interface should be able to facilitate all those options.

Best Practice 3: Interfaces Should Be Customizable Where Possible

Where possible, interfaces should be customizable to players' needs. Customizable interfaces allow players to arrange the flow of information in ways that suit them best. Of course, there are occasions where players experiment so much with customization, that at the end, they have problems using their final interface. This is also the reason why customizable interfaces should always come with a reset option!

Customizable interfaces may address game-related or learning-related issues. In cases where games present complex controls and information, like MMO RPG games, for example, customizability is offered as a way of better organizing a player's workflow during the game, as they will need to select from the various options of weapons, spells, and combos they will use during a battle. There are other occasions where interfaces need to be customized to support the particular needs of players, like those with disabilities or audiences of different ages.

Best Practice 4: Interfaces Should Be Tolerant to Errors

It goes without saying that not all players will always understand what they need to do at some points. They will try to connect everything to anything; they will press any button; they will collide, destroy, modify, or move everything that you have so worked so hard and passionately on. And this is natural and expected! This is the reason why interfaces should be tolerant of players' errors. Interfaces should be designed in a way that discourages players from performing errors in the first place but also requires minimal effort to resolve if those errors do occur.

So, there are three ways of making interfaces error-tolerant. The first is to try and anticipate players' errors and design your interface so that it diverts players from actually going that way. The second is to pose restrictions within the game that stop players from performing particular actions. In a point-and-click game, for instance, being able to place any game object on another and expecting something to happen might lead to countless combinations that could distract players from the main game objectives. That is, of course, unless the game's premise was based on those countless combinations! The third way is dealing with errors when they happen. After an error, interfaces should offer feedback and support to help players realize that something went wrong so that they can fix it.

Trying to play a movie on a Blu-Ray player without a disc inside prompts a message informing us that "play" was pressed but no disc was inserted in the player.

Best Practice 5: Testing Is the Best Practice
I can list several best practices and analyze interfaces from various different perspectives. However, there is no better way of creating efficient game interfaces than by testing them. It goes without saying that during the design process even the most experienced of game designers cannot anticipate all the possible issues, misunderstandings, and necessary additional clarifications, and that's why everybody tests their games. By testing you will have the possibility to assess your interface's efficiency, analyze its weaknesses, and come up with solutions that are relevant to your learning context and audience.

REFLECTION POINTS 🔍

- What is the information you want to present through your game's interface?

- Are you considering using particular representations in order to offer this information to players, and why?

- Is the information about your game's interface accurately presented so as to avoid any misunderstandings?

- Are the components of your interface self-explanatory? Do players understand what all the interface components are for? Would players need to ask for clarifications about your interface's structure and components?

- How can players achieve the functionalities you provide through your interfaces? Is there more than one way of performing those tasks?

- Can your game's interface be customized when needed and possible by players who have particular needs or disabilities?

- Is there error tolerance for players' actions concerning your game's interface? What are the most common errors that appear and why?

NOT ALL PLATFORMS ARE THE SAME

During a research project, I was a member of a game design team for an educational game about teaching mathematics to primary school students. The project mainly focused on students with motor deficiencies. Based on this context, the team's experts who worked with this audience proposed creating a digital version of an existing game they had previously proposed. The physical game consisted of a five-by-five grid. The grid columns would be assigned a sequential number, while the grid lines would be assigned a letter, like on a chess board. Players would be provided with a set of stereometric shapes of various colors that would fit the grid's tiles. The game would be played by two players. One player would possess a card showing where the shapes should be positioned on the grid while the other player would need to receive instructions and place the items in the correct position. The game was rather straightforward and, in order to be created, designers needed stationery and a few stereometric shapes. So, what was the reason for recreating the game for a tablet device? There was none! It was a bad idea! Let's see why.

Space Invaders played on an arcade table. (Presented at the Ontario Science Center Game On 2.0.)

The team actually decided to move forward with this proposal. However, a physical board game featuring a grid and a couple of shapes can be created with ease. There are no space or implementation limitations. Since the game needed to be recreated for a tablet device, the main issue was that both the game board that presented the grid and the shapes that needed to be placed on top of it had to be presented on the same small tablet screen. This comes with several challenges:

- How much screen space should the grid take?

- How much screen space should the area where shapes are presented take?

- Since shapes need to fit into grid tiles, if the grid is big, its tiles will be big, so the shapes will need to be big as well.

- Would a separate screen or a moving side view create more space for moving shapes?

- If the team goes for a separate screen or a moving side view, what should be the action for moving the shapes? Will players need to drag and drop them? Or select them and make them appear on a specific screen area?

These are just some of the countless questions that came up after the team had worked for a while on this idea. In the end, the idea was rejected for one simple reason. The first implementation of the game offered a better experience than the digital one. This was an excellent example of how different platforms come with their own pros and cons.

Every medium, every platform, and every resource comes with some advantages and disadvantages that need to be considered by designers. There are differences between digital and physical means; tactile and non-tactile devices; screens and head-mount devices; speakers and headphones; and keyboards, mice, and gamepads. Some differences are huge, some are not so great. But still, the final experience will be affected for sure. Those differences can be related to the capabilities of those means, the flow of information, the way feedback is delivered and received during playing games, and the symbolic representation of this information. So, reflecting on which platform you should build your game on should not be taken lightly. When doing this, it is a good idea to take into consideration the following four points.

Point 1: Technology

Every platform comes with its own requirements in terms of technology. This point is not only restricted to digital games. Escape the room games, educational theme parks, and outdoor activities are just some examples of educational games that require the use of particular resources and know-how. An outdoor activity, involving a large number of players in a limited space, may require the use of loudspeakers or even for designers to consult an expert in acoustic design.

There are several attributes that need to be examined when looking at the particularities of platforms as information systems. These are generally its possibilities, its limitations, and its costs in money, time, and resources. The best way of dealing with this aspect is always by consulting an expert in the field. It is always a bad idea to take technology lightly, since it is very likely that at some point the problems you didn't anticipate will come to the surface and disrupt the development of your games.

Point 2: Symbolic Content

Information is not always represented in the same way on different platforms. As philosopher Marshal McLuhan said, "The medium is the message." In its own way, the medium that delivers the information affects what designers want to say. Information needs to be adapted to the capabilities of this medium and conform to the channels that the medium presents.

Let's take, for instance, programming platforms for young audiences, where games can be created. Scratch is a visual programming platform where players can control characters by combining code blocks in vertical or horizontal order. There are also several robots that can be programmed by reading the drawings of students on a piece of paper, like **Thymio**, **Ozobot**, or **Edison**. Players design the robot's movements on large pieces of paper and control their behavior by drawing specific combinations of colors or dots. There are also robots with remote controls. The simplest case is the one of **Bee-Bot**, which presents an arrow on the back of a bee. Players control the bee by creating move sequences using the keyboard. These are three different platforms with three different representations of the information for their controls.

Point 3: Input and Output Methods

We previously examined the analysis and design of interfaces in games. Interfaces are the means of facilitating the flow of information in games. Information is received by games as input while feedback comes out of the game systems as output. Input methods are also called controls. Controls can be of different kinds, such as:

- Keyboard

- Mouse

- Gamepad

- Joystick

- Steering wheel

- Touch screen

- Interactive whiteboard

- Interactive table screen

- Motion sensor controls, like PlayStation Move, Microsoft Kinect, the Wii Remote, or Leap Motion controller

- A digital instrument

- A buzzer
- A device gyroscope or accelerometer
- A microphone

Each of these controls comes with different possibilities and limitations. A keyboard, for instance, offers a great number of buttons, which can be combined in countless ways. On the other hand, it means there are a great number of keys and combinations which players must learn, adding possible complexity to the proposed game. A steering wheel, on the other hand, may be very efficient in controlling vehicles in racing games but prove to be less effective when playing role-playing games where game characters require another type of manipulation. Also, an RPG character would require considerably more buttons in order to be able to take part in a fight.

Output devices on the other hand can be:

- A TV screen
- A projector
- A touch screen
- An interactive whiteboard
- An interactive table screen
- A gamepad, when it vibrates
- A steering wheel, when it offers feedback to players
- A virtual reality headset display, like Oculus Rift or Microsoft's HoloLens
- Speakers, headphones

COSMO is a learning platform, using specially designed buzzers as means of input and output to present gaming experiences for players with disabilities.

As you can see, some input methods are also used as output means as well. Each platform comes with particular input and output methods. Understanding the ways that your game will communicate and interact with players is crucial since it will later affect the way that you design your games.

Understanding the capabilities of your input and output methods makes a big difference in designing games for different platforms. Before the smartphone era, most gaming platforms came with some sort of gamepad or keyboard. Consoles would have gamepads, computers would have keyboards and mice, handheld video game devices like Game Boy or PSP would also have integrated buttons and joysticks. With the development of smartphones, though, a new gamer audience appeared and thus, several games that were popular on other platforms were transported to mobile devices. This was not easy at all. Smartphones, in most cases, have one main control, which is their touch screen. So, designers had to create mobile alternatives to games where the controls were based on pressing buttons, directional pads, or joysticks using only their touch screen. Over time, several implementations were proposed, from using device gyroscopes to creating virtual buttons and directional pads in order to simulate the games' previous controls. This is a very characteristic example of the great impact of controls on the final form of games.

Point 4: Digital and Physical Experiences

A very common exercise about mutual trust is "the guide of the blind." In this game, a player is blindfolded while another one needs to control the blindfolded player out of a room full of obstacles. Players are not allowed to talk with each other and the guidance needs to be given only through touch. The blindfolded players base all their actions on the feedback they receive from their drivers. Even if this is not a video game, the drivers use their hands as controls to guide the blindfolded players through the space. This brings us to Point 4, the discussion about physical and digital experiences in educational games.

Even if the principles of educational game design remain the same, digital and physical means come with their own particular capabilities. We have already examined the example of the grid game at the beginning of this section. In some cases, physical experiences can facilitate learning experiences better, while in others, digital experiences offer other considerable advantages, where creating similar games in the physical world would be difficult or impossible. There is also the possibility of using the best of both worlds. The use of smartphones, tablets, and the continuous interest for applications of augmented reality point to the direction of combining physical and digital elements in the creation of gaming experiences.

REFLECTION POINTS 🔍

- Did you take into account the particularities of the platform or context you are designing your games for?

- Are there any particular symbolic aspects that you need to take into consideration in order to present your interface in a more efficient way?

- What are the input and output streams of your game and how are they going to affect your game's structure?

PERSPECTIVE: IMMERSIVE STORYTELLING IN EDUCATION

Ryan Gerber

UX Designer

Mira steps out into the busy street and turns to wave goodbye to Marcus Vinicius. The older man stands in the doorway behind her draped in the resplendent white toga of a Roman senator, hemmed all around in purple. He drops his stern demeanor long enough to smile fondly and nod as a distinct, pleasant chime plays in the air. This trilling note signals the completion of Mira's current task; delivering birthday invitations to a handful of Caesar Augustus's closest friends. With this task complete, a small, floating interface pops up to her right to congratulate her and display her current quest objectives. Mira ignores it, choosing instead to push through the people before her as they make their way around the corner and through a large series of stone archways, toward the distant calls of vendors and shopkeepers.

She ducks her head to avoid a large bundle of onions hanging from a nearby shop window and skirts her way around a group of teenage girls only a few years older than herself. They carry wicker baskets of fresh flatbread with cheese and garlic baked on top, an early predecessor to pizza, a dish Mira knows will not exist for another 14 centuries when tomatoes are discovered in the Americas. Unlike the senator's toga, their simple tunics are gray with short aprons tied around the waist. More than one of the girls turns to eye Mira's outfit: jeans and a pair of black Converse sneakers. She wears a sweater with the words "Monster Planet" smeared across the top. She could change her avatar to match the Roman garb of 13 BC, but it is not important to her current quest. Like most other students in her school, she likes to feel like herself when she visits these other worlds.

As she steps beyond the series of arches her breath catches. The tight-knit city street gives way to an immense public square full of sunlight, people, and pageantry.
"June," Mira says. "What is this place?"

As she speaks the words she senses the other girl materializing beside her. June steps forward, dressed simply in a long gray shirt and black jeans, one of several outfits Mira has chosen for her AI assistant. Her hair is black to Mira's blond.

"This is the Roman Forum, as it appeared during the Golden Age of the empire. It's the center for commerce, religion, and politics in Rome. Isn't it beautiful?" the second girl says, coming to stand beside Mira with a patient smile.
"It is," Mira agrees.

The immense plaza is hedged all around by vast stone structures: temples, palaces, and places of commerce. These are the vehicles of the Roman Empire. Soaring marble columns hug every facade, above which large pitched roofs pierce the heavens. Giant marble figures rise up across the plaza, above the mobs, born on soaring stone pedestals. Many are flanked with wings or bound in resplendent armor. They bear the names of long dead senators, legionaries, and even gods. Painted and dressed, they are living incarnations of Rome's past come back deified to reside among the living. Thousands of these stone figures crest the distant rooftops, winding their way up the most dominant hill to where a vast stone structure stands, an imposing gray against the darkening sky.

"What is that up there?" Mira asks, pointing past where the road leads upwards at the far end of the forum.

Though the cameras and eye-tracking algorithm built into the virtual simulation to know just where she is looking, June turns her attention from a nearby street performer and looks up to where Mira is pointing.

June considers the behemoth that stands above the city. Distant fires flicker and glow around its base, illuminating a half-dozen colossal columns. "What would you guess it is?"

Mira bites her lip. Such questions are common within the educational quests. The thousands of game designers and educators who work on these experiences encourage ways for students to think for themselves, replacing the older tradition of written tests with a free-form thought analysis.

"A palace, maybe, because of where it is. But it looks like a temple, I think. Like the ones we saw in Athens, like the Parthenon."
June nods.

"It is a temple. Temple of **Jupiter Optimus Maximus**, the supreme god of the Roman Pantheon. He is in many ways the Roman incarnation of Zeus. In fact, the main columns you see in the distance were taken after the Roman armies sacked Athens nearly 90 years ago. The temple is built atop the Capitoline Hill, the most sacred place in the Roman Empire, yet it is largely designed after the manner of the Greek temples."

Mira thinks back on the numerous educational quests she has gone on the past several years. She vividly remembers sitting with her fellow classmates in the restored amphitheater of the Athenian Agora and learning the scientific method from Aristotle. She always enjoyed the way he would stroke his thick white beard and consider the student's questions.

"It seems like they took a lot from the Greeks," she says, somewhat annoyed. "Why wouldn't the Romans make their own gods and design their own temples? Why steal it all?"

"It hasn't always been so easy," June says with a shrug. "Humans evolved slowly early on. The Romans were brilliant in regards to many things; engineering and strategy. But it's said they lacked a cohesive body of myth and religion, they were a people without a story and growing fast. In conquering the Greeks, who had thrived for nearly 1000 years before, they adopted their philosophies and truths and tried to incorporate them into their own way of life. The stability that came with it allowed the Romans to thrive and conquer many lands. It is said that the culture of the Greeks flourished within the Roman Empire."

"Huh," Mira says, chewing on the other girl's words as they walk together. They pass between the chimneys and braziers scattered around the square where bystanders stand warming themselves. Others sit among the tables set up around the perimeter of the plaza, drinking wine from clay cups and playing dice.

"I guess I understand," Mira says. "It's like when you meet other new kids and you try to find something in common with them, maybe they play the same games or something. Because then you share something personal with them. It makes you feel more together. Maybe the same is true with culture."

"I think so," June says. Then, "Would you like to learn more about the influences of Greek culture? Or, perhaps hear a story about the Roman gods?"

"Not right now," Mira says, holding her hand out in front of her, the floating menu system appears hovering a foot in the air before her.

Nobody at any of the tables takes notice as the animated title of her current education quest appears, "Caesar Augustus' 50th Birthday Party." Beneath is a miniature map with the faces of Mira and her classmates plotted around the city, each working on their own unique set of tasks as they hope to earn their next graduation badge. With every badge corresponding to the level of the student, this puts Mira at level 54, a few badges advanced for her age. But then she has never been one to back down from a challenge. Especially considering the perks awarded to good students.

While some quests like this one can take students days or even weeks to complete, Mira has grown up hearing stories from her older siblings of the advanced quests higher-level students are given. Some can take months to complete, each experience uniquely crafted to challenge the students based on their lifetime of learning. It's worth it though, as a student gleans more factual information in a day of playing a quest than a student might otherwise learn in a month from a traditional classroom setting. This being only one of thousands of education quests available for students.

Mira swipes the air with a finger and the menu flips over to reveal a list of her current objectives under the heading of "Help Livia Drusilla Prepare for the Party," the title of their current subquest, of which there are three. At the bottom is her specific list of tasks, all of them now checked off:

- Talk to the head chef to plan out how much food to order for the 500 guests.

- Meet with the **Praefectus aerarii** to convert the cost into Roman coinage.

- Deliver invitations to Caesar's closest friends.

This last task had a dozen names attached to it, of which Mira took three. The other two focused more on math, which Mira has always enjoyed. By working in smaller teams of classmates, students negotiate among themselves which tasks they want to work on, either collaboratively or individually.

There is a notification waiting for her as well, a red dot pulses overtop a floating envelope. She pokes it to find an animated message from her classmates congratulating her on finishing her tasks. Their avatars appear next to hers in the menu and give her a thumbs up as applause fills the air. She smiles and sends a reaction back and glances at the map where her teammates are still at work—Kim having taken on an engineering challenge back at the palace and Tom helping the stone carvers design a statue of Caesar for the celebration.

There is a soft ping and another alert appears.
"It's Mother, letting you know dinner will be ready soon. It looks like you've accomplished all your tasks for the day. Would you like me to tell her you're coming down?"

Mira shakes her head.
"I think there might a side quest around here somewhere," she says. "I need another couple minutes."

June nods and composes a simple message telling her mother that she will be down shortly. Apart from achieving the 100 badges needed to graduate, the education quests students are designed with endless hidden side-challenges created in real time by the AI to push students in their learning. It is an art in and of itself to identify these small side quests, one which Mira is especially adept at. They are especially valuable to students as they reward them with a global currency that they can spend anywhere they want, even in the latest big game releases like **Monster Planet**. For Mira, these extra moments spent learning and problem-solving in the education quests help fund her experiences playing games with her friends. Particularly, she has been saving up for weeks now for a new set of battle armor for her 12-foot-tall monster bounty hunter—and she's only a few credits away.

"What are you looking for?" June asks her.
"It's something Livia mentioned," Mira says, her eyes scanning the market stalls. "Just before I left. Could you play back the last thing she said?"

June waves a hand and Livia, the wife of Caesar Augustus, appears before them just as she had earlier that morning in the royal palace. She is dressed in her customary silken pleated dress that Mira identifies as a **stola**.

"... And if you could find me some ice," Livia says to Mira with a wink, "I would be very obliged. You might be able to find some near the home of Marcus Vinicius. It's not a party in Rome without ice, after all..."

"It certainly sounds like a side-quest," June says. "Iced wine was considered a delicacy in ancient Rome."

Mira nods.
The recording plays once more before Livia Drusilla disappears, leaving Mira standing in the square perplexed. While the late September weather of Rome is not terribly warm, she has no clue where one might find ice. She knows it will be another 2000 years until refrigeration becomes viable technology and by her estimation the nearest place cold enough to find ice is several hundred miles away in the Alps. While there might be some clever way to create ice using chemistry, she assumes the solution is much simpler, as these things usually are.

"It has to be around here somewhere," she says, idly eyeing the distant animal cages being pulled off a wagon on the far end of the forum. They're full of jaguars and bears. "They have everything here."

"It has been said that if it cannot be found in the markets of Rome, it does not exist among the treasures of the earth."

"I like that," Mira says. "I should use that for my oral report. Can you save that?"
"Sure, I'll add the citation to your notebook."
"Thanks," Mira says. Then, "I don't suppose you also know where I can find any ice, do you?"

A barking laugh catches both their attention and Mira turns from her absent-minded wandering to look. Behind them two men stand in front of what looks to be a tavern. The first is tall with broad shoulders and a thick black beard. Older, with a dark sleeveless tunic, he stands in sharp contrast to the younger man standing next to him, clearly a painter judging by pigment-stained gray tunic he wears and the paint supplies stacked beside him. They are sipping wine and admiring the artist's most recent work, a frescoed-mural that covers the entire front of the tavern. Like most of the buildings in the market, this facade is painted brilliant colors. Mira walks closer to see the central figure draped in a crimson red cape and a bronze breastplate and helmet, both in the Roman fashion. In his hands he holds a **gladius**, the short stabbing sword from which the gladiators took their name. Mira knows this from a previous quest that took her through the Colosseum, a structure which, in 13 BC, would not be constructed for another 90 years. Beneath the radiant god is a slain enemy with wild hair and a club.

"Who is it supposed to be?" she asks the painter.
"Quis est ut volo est?" repeats June, in Latin.

Mira heart jumps when she glances down to see that both men are holding glasses of iced wine. The artist gives them a bashful smile and explains that the fresco it is supposed to be the god Mars claiming victory over the Gallic barbarians at Alesia. June patiently translates his Latin so Mira can follow along. The words appear in the air in front of Mira so she can read them as well. Both men stand expectantly with their glasses in hand, waiting for Mira to comment, but she ignores them.

She turns to June instead.
"Does he believe this really that? Does he believe the god Mars is real?"
The other girl smiles and turns to the man and translates the question.
The man nods in the affirmative but gestures to the work, speaking quickly so that June translates his words.

"He says yes, but that this piece is in dedication to the new master of the house, the owner of the tavern." The taller of the two men bows slightly at the mention. "His name is Mars Antonius, a successful former gladiator who retired from his earnings and was able to open this tavern. His final battle before earning his freedom was a reenactment of Julius Caesar's victory of the very same battle."

"I think it's wonderful," Mira says. "How do I say 'I love it' in Latin?"
"Ego amo eam," June says, pronouncing the words slowly. They again appear in the air before Mira.

"Ego amo eam!" she says, trying her best to inflect the early Roman accent.
It's far from perfect, but the larger man pounds the artist on the back and lifts his glass casually. Inside the doorway behind him is a chunk of ice on the stone counter, a metal pick jutting out of its top.

"Quod est perfectum!" he says.
He turns to Mira then.
"Quid vis ut faciam tibi?"
"He's asking what he can do for you," June says.

"Tell him," Mira says, a spark of excitement in her eyes, "that I'm going to need to know where he got that ice."

June smiles. "I suppose I'll go ahead and let your mother know that you'll be late for dinner, as well."

SUMMARY

So, what topics did we cover in this chapter?

- Games, in order to be played, offer instructions. Complex, unclear, or long instructions may cause players to lose focus or interest in your games. As a result, we examined several tips and best practices that can help you propose efficient game instructions.

- Games offer interfaces that allow and facilitate their interaction with players. Being able to present the appropriate information, facilitate its flow, and support players' learning is crucial for the efficiency of educational games.

- We should examine a variety of different technologies, platforms, and means and discuss the different ways that information is delivered through their channels.

12 Game Aesthetics

This chapter:

- Offers insights on how to approach aesthetics in educational game design.
- Discusses the impact of aesthetics in its appeal to players.
- Discusses the impact of aesthetics and symbolism to learning.

This chapter presents insights and different perspectives on how aesthetics impact players' perception of educational games. Aesthetics can have a great impact on educational game design, affecting the way that players approach and understand the game and its components.

THE ENDLESS MAGIC OF THE HUMAN BRAIN

In 1951, social psychologist Solomon Asch conducted an experiment that would later be considered a classic example of social psychology. Asch organized sessions with university students, during each of which participants would be presented with a line. Participants would be asked to estimate its size in comparison to three other provided lines. As shown in the following image, the answer was always obvious. However, what was not obvious was that the sessions were in fact rigged. Among the whole group, only one participant was unaware that all other people in the room were, in fact, part of the experiment and their answers were preselected and would in most cases be wrong. So, for instance, instead of finding similarities among the target line and line C, they would say that they found the target line similar to lines A or B. The unaware students would always give their estimations after everybody else. At the end of several trials with different unaware students, the experiment showed that almost 75 percent of those people would provide a wrong estimation, against all logic.

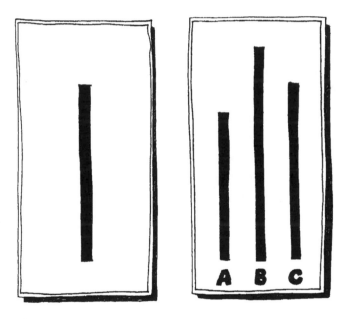

Asch's experiment raises an important question: How do we perceive our world? Is perception only related to our senses? If so, then let's try to figure out what we see in the following picture.

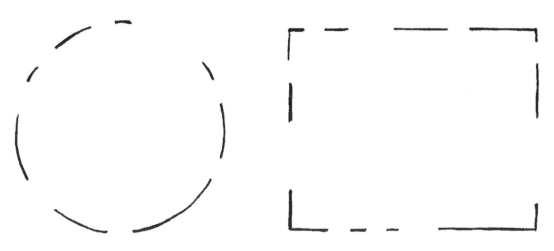

The answer that most people will give is a circle next to a rectangle. But does this picture really present a circle or a rectangle? The answer is no. The image presents incomplete forms, consisting of arcs and lines. However, experimental psychologists of the Gestalt school observed that the human brain has a disposition to identify patterns such as similarity, form, proximity, or continuation, and completes the shapes based on those. So, perception is not only about senses. It is also about memory. In order for our brain to be able to recognize and complete a shape, it needs to have come across this shape before. So, perception is also about learning. This is also the reason why the more we learn, the deeper and more changed our perspective of the world becomes. But since learning is a personal and individual process, perception can also be seen as a personal and individual aspect. Not everyone perceives the world in the same way.

Using this as a starting point, game designers are endowed with the amazing task of understanding, manipulating, and distorting the laws of perception in order to create games that help players evolve by interacting with them.

AESTHETICS IN GAMES

I always found it interesting that the word **aesthetics** derives from the Greek word **aesthesis**, which means sense. Aesthetics is connected to arts, beauty, the perception of our world, and every aspect of how we approach and live experiences that challenge and indulge our senses. Games are no exception to this. Aesthetics are a large component in games. We have all played games and been excited by their amazing graphics, the atmosphere they created, and their impact on other game elements. But how are aesthetics expressed and presented in games?

The most usual and most established aesthetic forms that we encounter in games are audio and visual ones. However, aesthetic forms can be expressed through materials that stimulate other senses, like smell, touch, and taste. Due to the technical restrictions presented in video game design, those cases are few and far between. However, they can be encountered in physical or outdoor games, like in the scouts' game, Kim's Game.

When it comes to audio stimuli in games, there are two major categories.

Music: How often does music play a key role in movies, theatrical performances, or games? We listen to music every day and we create connections between songs and important aspects of our lives. In games, music creates atmosphere, offers context, sets the pace, and builds up suspense when necessary.

Sound effects: An aspect that educational game designers don't often pay so much attention to are sound effects. Sound effects are any sounds in video games that are not music. They can be the sound of jumping, the shooting of a laser beam, the steps of an enemy approaching, or ambient noises. If music offers atmosphere, sound effects offer feedback. Games without sound effects seem unnatural. Players expect to get audio feedback for their actions.

Visual elements in games, on the other hand, can be highly diverse and take different forms and representations, and be implemented through different types of materials. Visual elements can be digital and physical.

Physical elements exist in the real world. They can be paintings, sculptures, or special constructions for the sake of the game. Physical visual elements can be elements of nature, from sand and water to snow and mud. In theme parks, outdoor areas, board games, and card games, physical elements are the main aspect of the game's visual representation.

Digital elements are generated through the use of machines. Digital elements are presented through screens, projectors, or head mount devices. These elements are also called **graphics**. There are two main ways that graphics are designed, processed, and rendered in digital media.

Two-dimensional (2D) graphics are created from two-dimensional forms and shapes that are moved, scaled, or rotated around space. There are many famous 2D games, such as **Super Mario**, **Sonic the Hedgehog**, **Pac Man**, **Angry Birds**, **Cut the Rope**, and a whole lot more.

Three-dimensional (3D) graphics are the result of the manipulation of objects in a virtual 3D space created for the sake of the game. Contrary to 2D games, 3D games offer a broader type of perspective as a whole world has already been constructed and presented through the eyes of players. 3D games are also highly popular, with several very successful examples such as **Grand Theft Auto**, **The Last Guardian**, **Mass Effect**, and **Need for Speed**.

However, deciding what type of graphics your game is going to have is not a simple choice. Deciding between using 2D and 3D graphics requires at least a minimal understanding of the technologies that are required to implement them. For instance, in order to create 3D graphics, a whole team of special artists is required to design the 3D models. This team may consist of one 3D generalist and may also consist of a modeler, a rigger, a texturer, an animator, and a rendering specialist. That's a lot of people! Imagine how much these specialists will cost for a small studio.

On the other hand, 2D games come with the restrictions that two dimensions offer. For sure a shoot 'em up game is more interesting when presented in 3D graphics, where players can move their characters in any way they want and look up, down, and everywhere around them.

Another important aspect related to graphics is that not all devices and platforms can perform the rendering calculations and processes of heavy graphics. It's rather common that games with lots of graphic information may take mobile devices or old computers a lot longer to run, greatly impacting the playing experience. Considering that not all educational institutions have the fastest hardware devices, it is always wise to anticipate such issues and make design decisions that guarantee the greatest device compatibility possible. A graphics decision can have great consequences on the game's development costs and the number of players that are actually going to play your games.

So, before deciding what type of graphics you are going to use in your game, it is important that you consult both the developers and artists of your team and together anticipate the different issues that may come up. Believe me, they will come up!

REFLECTION POINTS 🔍

Graphics, music, and sounds play a key role in the design of learning experiences.

- Have you chosen what type of graphics your game is going to be based on?

- Were technical and platform restrictions examined before making this decision? If yes, are there any potential issues or restrictions in terms of hardware or software that you need take into account? Does your decision affect the number of players that have access to your game?

AESTHETIC IMPACT ON GAMES

I find that the use of aesthetics in games can very often be either overrated or underrated by designers. On one side, there are designers who put all of their efforts and faith into how beautiful their games will look; on the other, there are designers who don't want to make their games look good or don't consider the game's appeal an important aspect, fearing that it may make their games look "less educational." Of course, both those extremes are wrong for different reasons.

Aesthetics is a way of presenting our thoughts and designs to our peers, friends, and players. In many aspects, aesthetics help to make our games more concrete and more easily perceivable when we need to explain them or visualize them. Even designers with mediocre design and sketching skills (like myself!) need to draft some designs in order to explain what they have in their minds. Expressing one's thoughts does not necessarily need to happen with paper and pencil. Other materials, like clay, miniatures, or digital tools can have the same or even greater impact in this aspect.

In any case, though, aesthetics is a distinct and visible game element that affects your learning experience and definitely cannot be left unattended. One of an educational game designer's most usual mistakes is that they may disregard aesthetics, leave their designs unpolished and end up presenting players with games that look bad. Since players' standards keep increasing, it's absolutely sure that when they have the chance, players will leave those games and look for games that are more appealing to their eyes. This is natural and expected. Which bakery would you go into? The one that is clean, comfortable, and looks like great effort has gone into arranging its products in a way that captures your attention? Or would you rather a dirty, dusty, old bakery that claims to have quality bread? First impressions are everything. However, they are not enough to keep players interested forever.

When games are only about graphics, they can often fail to capture players' interest for a long time. Players may feel bored and unchallenged and, consequently, they may also look for other, more interesting and intuitive experiences. Even worse, games like this may not focus on educational aspects or may even create more misconceptions than they were supposed to be clearing up.

Aesthetic elements should be used as an element that facilitates learning experiences through games. Aesthetics should create the right atmosphere in games and highlight the other game elements. In **Valiant Hearts**, the aesthetics are not vibrant; they show a dark and sad vision of war while offering a glimpse of the past. This is harmonically bound with the game's story. In **Monument Valley**, the visual illusions created by the game's level design perfectly complement the game mechanics, creating an excellent puzzle game experience. In **Rayman Legends**, there are music levels where listening to the level's music helps players set the tempo of their movements and understand when they need to jump or duck.

Rayman Legends *presents a characteristic example of how aesthetics can impact the gaming experience. (© 2016 Ubisoft Entertainment. All rights reserved.* Rayman, *the character of Rayman, Ubisoft, and the Ubisoft logo are trademarks of Ubisoft Entertainment in the United States and/or other countries.)*

Aesthetics elements impact and get impacted by other elements. If you are the one setting the aesthetic direction of your game, try to critically approach your designs and reflect on how they interact with your other game elements. If you are working with an artist or a team of artists, try to explain every aspect of the game as clearly as possible and create a mutual understanding of how aesthetics interact with the other game elements.

AESTHETIC IMPACT ON LEARNING

In the middle of the 20th century, psychologist Jean Piaget conducted research on children's mathematical thinking. In one of his experiments, an interviewer would ask children to give themselves the same number of candies as those presented in the top line of following figure. Children would match that arrangement by corresponding candies one by one, creating the bottom line of the figure. However, when the interviewer would spread their objects out, like in the figure below, children would consider that the interviewer had more candies than they did. Children would still think that the interviewer had more candy even if they counted the candies later on.

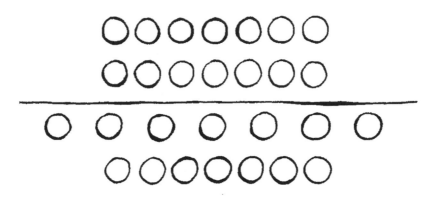

The example presented above raises an important issue: In educational game design every aspect should be thoroughly considered and nothing should be left to chance. Excellent learning situations can come from successfully implemented graphics, shapes, arrangements, and forms. On top of this, weaknesses and misunderstandings can be identified by how players approach and work with representations, spatial arrangements, and symbols.

On the other hand, graphics that aren't well thought out can cause problems and lead players to wrong conclusions. But how can you avoid this? Good knowledge of the previous research in the same field is very helpful in these situations. By knowing what previous empirical evidence has shown so far, you will have an idea of which elements work and which don't. This is also the reason why it is always helpful to discuss your designs with other peers and consult experts in the field you are presenting to, if you are not one yourself. However, it is also certain that, since every learning situation and audience is unique, only after continuous and effective evaluation will you be able to assess your aesthetic aspect's efficacy on your players' learning.

SUMMARY

- Aesthetics play an important role in players' first impressions of your games. Games that are not well-presented risk receiving worse opinions than others with a more polished look.

- Aesthetics and symbols may have a great impact on players' approaches to games. Poor representation of objects and concepts may create misconceptions for players. So, great attention is required in creating the graphics and materials of your games.

PERSPECTIVE: MINECRAFT IN THE CLASSROOM

Stephane Cloatre
ICT trainer at ISFEC Bretagne (Institut de Formation de l'Enseignement Catholique)
Twitter: @StephaneCloatre
Blog: http://www.stephanecloatre.fr

Minecraft in survival mode. (Screenshot courtesy of S. Cloâtre.)

Minecraft, the famous sandbox video game, allows players to journey through a natural landscape made of blocks (stone, wood, grass, etc.). The blocks can be mined and then crafted into other materials or objects. You can meet creatures and animals: some peaceful, some fearfully hostile!

The two main game modes are:

- Survival: You need to collect everything, hunger is possible, and you can be hurt.

- Creative: You have access to all the blocks and you can fly.

Why is this game widely used for educational purposes?

- It's a **very creative** tool.

- It's **social** and attractive: Huge projects are possible if you play with friends.

- It's **open** and customizable (depending on the version): A large number of mods are provided by the community.

Several studies confirm that "supported, educational, and purposeful use of Minecraft can significantly benefit student learning" [1]. Some relevant impacts are:

- Better communication and information technology skills.

- Increased creativity.

- Increased feelings of academic self-efficacy.

- Creation of a positive learning environment.

- Increased collaboration among students.

- Improved computer programming and computational logic skills.

- Improved problem-solving skills.

- Improved informational research competencies.

Versions include the following:

- Minecraft PC (Windows, Mac, Linux)*
  The original version, coded with Java. This is not the best for video performance but is the most widely used (a lot of mods are free). You can connect to many servers (for free) or set up your own easily.

- Minecraft Pocket Edition
  The portable version for iOS, Android, and Windows phones. It is less customizable with limited access to servers (subscription), but has higher performance than the previous version.

- Minecraft Windows 10
  Very close to the Pocket Edition but for PC. Allows use of Hololens or VR helmets (Oculus Rift and Gear VR).

- Minecraft Education Edition**
  Based on the Windows 10 version and offers specific features for teachers:

  - Classroom mode to take control of the game and manage students.

  - New blocks: Allow or deny (building) to protect parts of the map, border blocks to keep students in specific areas, etc.

  - Code connection to program an agent in the game using Scratch, Tinker, or Makecode.

THE UNKNOWN PLANET: HOW THE AVAILABILITY OF MATERIALS INFLUENCE ARCHITECTURE …

I found it quite difficult to make students understand that materials are not available everywhere. Throughout history, humanity has always struggled to find resources: It has a strong impact on architecture and the environment of cities, even today.

Scenario

Scientists discovered a strange planet. Five different biomes cover its surface but are very close to each other: You can travel from a desert to an arctic climate in a few steps! Players arrive in a teleportation hub then go to a train station to be driven to their biome. Their mission: Collect samples of materials, compare them with what we find on Earth, and build an exhibition to explain what they discovered.

Minecraft Version

Minecraft Education Edition.

School Level

Year 8 (12–13 years old).

---

* See www.minecraft.net.
** See https://education.minecraft.net/.

Time Needed

Exploration (90 minutes), planning and blueprints (4.5 hours), building in Minecraft (4 hours).

Objectives

The student will be able to:

- Discriminate between raw materials and manmade materials.

- Identify materials' origins and their availability.

- Draw a 2D blueprint for a building and use it to build in 3D.

- Identify functions for a building and find technical solutions to implement them.

- Work in a team and communicate with others during a project.

Feedback

The original project (the availability of materials) took another dimension and became richer than expected.

The realization of the plans in teams before the construction has helped the students overcome their difficulties in representing an object in 2D and has demonstrated that they meet a real need: Each view was made by a different student, so they needed to coordinate to draw and then build. The limited time for construction forced them to divide the tasks (collecting, crafting, building) and find optimal solutions … using mathematics!

For example, some teams had the misfortune of being assigned to a desert area (sand and sandstone). One of them had the idea to build a glass pyramid (made by melting sand). Students asked themselves, "How many blocks of glass should we make for our pyramid? We can't lose any time!" So, they had to apply the calculation of volume to meet their real need. **Minecraft is always a wonderful tool to make learning meaningful.**

A building in the European biome. (Screenshot courtesy of S. Cloâtre.)

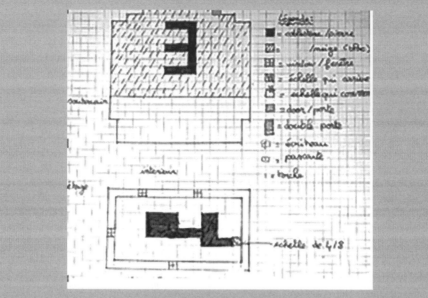

Example of blueprint.

Some students had never played Minecraft before (50–60 percent of them had already played). An introduction to the game was necessary. I relied on expert students to help and advise their colleagues. The groups were then balanced with a good distribution of experienced students (I gave them a special role in their team). Finally, **students discovered that playing Minecraft at home is not the same experience as using Minecraft in the classroom:** There are guidelines and objectives set by the teacher.

A certain level of excitement is palpable during the first sessions. Some students tend to test the limits. Fortunately, the educational version of Minecraft allows the game to be locked, giving the teacher the possibility to block this type of behavior. Nevertheless, this is an opportunity for a discussion about the rules in the digital and physical world (including social media). This phenomenon quickly fades after two or three sessions, and the mood becomes quieter.

I find Minecraft to be a powerful tool for students to express their creativity. Even in the same biome they found their own solutions for lighting, circulation, exhibition, architecture style, and so on.

By comparing the buildings made in the different landscapes the impact of the resources available on the choice of construction became obvious for everyone.

BUILDING OUR CITY IN THE MIDDLE AGES: TIME TRAVELING WITH MINECRAFT

Scenario

After using Minecraft to build our school, a church in our neighborhood, and the medieval castle of our city, a partnership was signed between our school and the town Heritage Service. It gave us access to historical documents, advice, and physical visits to achieve a new project: Building our city in 1450.

A Minecraft map showing the topography of the city landscape in 1450 (to scale) has been prepared with the assistance of the Geographic National Institute (IGN). Three teachers are involved: mathematics (measurement, proportionality), history (research, writing texts for Minecraft books), and technology (research, blueprints, building). Each building is under the responsibility of a team of four to six students.

We participated in various events to present this work: The city's medieval festival, heritage days, and others.

Minecraft Version

Minecraft PC with an online server.*

School level

Year 8 (12–13 years old).

Time needed

Research (4.5 hours), building (7 hours), presentation (2 hours). With more than 110 students involved, 40 percent of the city was built quite fast. We plan to finish it next year.

Objectives

The student will be able to:

• Participate in a project's organization.

• Identify the evolution of a city and its buildings over time; connect it with the evolution of a population's needs.

• Imagine solutions and solve problems to achieve tasks inside a project.

• Work in teams and communicate with others during a project.

Feedback

This activity allowed students to have another look at their environment. They gained a better understanding of how a cityscape evolves over time and found traces of the past that had been forgotten in the modern city. For example, we thought some elements, like the four city gates, had completely disappeared but, newly aware of their locations, we could identify still-existing parts and give them life with our 3D reproductions. Texts on daily life in the Middle Ages were written in history and inserted into the game through books scattered in different places. The map can also be used as a track set by other students.

An element that can save time is to teach students how to identify the repetitive elements of a building and then copy/paste it with Minecraft. Students with academic difficulties have also found a motivation for school (from messages received from the parents) and were among the most willing to come back on Saturday to present their achievements (at the Medieval festival).

---

* fougerescraft.omgcraft.fr:10622 The server is whitelisted: to register please contact fougerescraft@outlook.fr.

The medieval castle. (Screenshot courtesy of S. Cloâtre.)

That kind of project is close to the experience of a school trip: Students are immersed in another world in which they live experiences that mark them and leave with memories upon which the teacher can rely. Thus, students develop an intimate knowledge of a building and of a construction that leaves traces and **positive self-esteem** ("It is MY tower!").

Using Minecraft revealed an **extraordinary collaborative experience**. As a teacher, I enjoyed listening to students' conversations to solve problems, make choices, and coordinate.

More with Minecraft

Minecraft can be considered a **digital platform [2] for learning** that can be used for:

- **Communication and collaboration** (such as for teaching languages).

- **Code learning**. Minecraft Education Edition has an available add-on, Code connection, which allows the coding of a robot or agent with different languages like Scratch or Tynker.

- **Learning sciences**: Minecraft has been used to simulate blood circulation or energy plants!*

- **Making movies,**** as you can create your own setting, change a character's look, and record voices and soundtracks.

- **Print in 3D**: Several platforms allow the conversion of Minecraft constructions for 3D printers.

---

* With the mods Electrical Age or Industrial Craft.
** Movies made with a video game are called *machinima*.

Electrical age mod: Three solar panels connected to a data logger. (Screenshot courtesy of S. Cloâtre.)

ABOUT STEPHANE

I teach science and technology in a French middle school. I'm also an ICT trainer at the ISFEC (Institut Supérieur de Formation de l'Enseignement Catholique) for teachers of the region of Brittany. I discovered Minecraft with my students and my own children: as soon as I put my hand on it, its potential for education struck me.

REFERENCES

1. Karsenti, T., Bugmann, J, & Gros, P. P. (2017). *Transforming Education with Minecraft? Results of an Exploratory Study Conducted with 118 Elementary-School Students.* Montréal: CRIFPE.
2. Wilmot, J. (2016). A space to create: Teaching with minecraft. In C. C. Williams (Eds.), *Teacher pioneers: Vision from the edge of the map* (pp. 143–174). Pittsburgh, PA: ETC Press.

13 Testing and Feedback

This chapter:

- Explores the different ways that games can be assessed in educational contexts.

- Presents tools and best practices for the facilitation of feedback sessions.

- Presents a diverse set of evaluation processes, among which designers can structure their own.

- Describes tools and sessions that will help designers test their games with regards to various factors.

Evaluation and testing is one of the most important steps of educational game design. In the same sense that cooks test the food they are cooking throughout the whole process, testing should happen in various moments of the design process. This chapter offers insights, best practices, and tools in order to help readers better structure their assessment processes.

THE ETERNAL DANCE

A game design team once told me that their game was the result of constant interaction with the game's community of players. In fact, they started off as a small community but it became huge as the game was played by large numbers around the world. However, in our discussion, they were sometimes confused since they were blessed with a very vocal and active community that was critical of new features and functionalities that they added to their game. This reminded me of a scheme I use to describe game design: the eternal dance.

Let's imagine a couple dancing to the melody of a tango. The gentleman leads the way, guiding the couple's movements and proposes the moves they are going to use. But this relationship is bidirectional. The lady, on the other hand, responds to the gentleman's prompts, gives feedback to the gentleman, and sets the tone and style of their dance. In other words, it takes two to tango! Successful and efficient educational games rely heavily on a similar interaction, where the two parties are the players and the designers. So how do these two contribute to the dance?

- From one side, educational game designers create games that will introduce players to intrinsically motivating learning experiences. To achieve this, game designers put players at the center of the design process and create games by taking into account the context and the learning aspect that they want to help players master.

- From the other side, players who are interested in playing the designers' games want to make the games better. By improving the games, they fulfill their needs in a better way and create a more pleasant environment for them to be in. The game meets their expectations and so they decide to spend more time playing it.

But why is the dance eternal? Nice games, games that players want to play and through which they also learn, attract people's attention, they inspire them, and they make them use them more and more. Games that are played and enjoyed by players, educators, educational administrators, or parents attract greater resources. Those resources can be financial but can also come in the form of new people who were inspired by the game or want to be part of something that they find meaningful and want to contribute to the game's development. In cases like this, games enter a continuous iterative cycle where designers present new additions and expansions and players offer their feedback and ideas based on what they have played, leading to a constant evolution of the game. Successful games like **League of Legends**, **EVE Online**, **World of Warcraft**, or **Geocaching** are some of many examples of games that are constantly evolving along with their designers and players.

On the other hand, when either designers do not take their players' needs and feedback into account or players lose interest in the game and do not want to contribute to its evolution, the game may not evolve in the best direction. This is actually a very common scenario. Several designers fail to consider their players' feedback and reactions and prefer to play deaf concerning issues that arise when their games are being tested or released, with catastrophic consequences both for their games' learning impact and appeal to players.

So, the eternal dance is an agreement between two parties, the designers and the players. According to this agreement, game designers create educational games that focus on players' needs and make an effort to constantly meet their players' expectations while players will play them and offer their feedback. With the continuous evolution of technology and the benefits of modern communication media, this exchange has led to the creation of local, national, and international communities, where players and designers can exchange their perspectives on games under development. This raises the discussion about an interesting topic: Evaluation.

EVALUATING EDUCATIONAL GAMES

Often when I introduce a new game that I or a friend have designed, people ask if it is effective. This simple question is actually not very easy to answer. The main question is what is the aspect or element whose effectiveness we are measuring? Is it:

- The game's ability to motivate players to learn more about a topic?
- The game's ability to help players develop a particular skillset?
- The game's approach to helping players learn one concept compared to another one?
- The time that players spend playing the game compared to other curricula activities?
- The game's connection to existing official research and national curricula?
- The game's connection to specific learning theories and practices?
- The game's adoption and use in classrooms or other learning contexts?
- The game's appeal to both students, parents, and educators?
- The game's fun factor?
- The game's capacity to involve players from different areas around the world?
- The game's inclusiveness of people with some sort of disability?

So, the answer to this question requires a greater level of specificity. In fact, evaluation, especially in educational contexts, is a matter of great discussion. In this chapter, we will get a glimpse of this field, as it is indispensable for the design of educational games.

Is Evaluation Necessary?

In 1935 physicist Erwin Schrödinger, in order to express his thoughts on quantum mechanics at that time, presented a paradox called **Schrödinger's cat**. In this thought problem, a cat, a flask of poison, and a slightly radioactive material are placed in a box. The radioactive material has a 50/50 chance of being detected by a radiation detector inside the box. If this happens, the flask is shattered and the cat dies; if not, the cat stays alive. In this way, Schrödinger suggested that in quantum mechanics the cat in this problem could be considered both alive and dead inside the box. Only by actually opening the box could someone know what exactly the case was.

Similarly to Schrödinger's cat problem, you cannot really know if your games are actually fulfilling the goals you have set or appealing to your players. It is only through evaluation that you can get answers like the ones mentioned above. Evaluation can be helpful at:

- **Helping you validate your game's concept, prototype, or final product**, both for its learning and entertaining aspects, and giving you insights about its development. Being able to evaluate a concept, a prototype, or whole game is a crucial task in game design. Apart from saving you a great deal of money, time, and resources through avoiding later revisions, it can help you to focus your efforts on another idea that might have a greater impact on players.

- **Helping you evolve your games.** Great cookies are not created on day one! It takes several attempts before you get that perfect golden brown color, great cinnamon smell, and maintain an excellent chocolate-to-dough ratio. In the same way, great games are not produced on the first try. This is among the first things every game designer will say. Good games are the result of constant assessment and revision, taking into account players' needs.

- **Offering insights and fostering practices that will be used in future games**, related or unrelated to a particular learning topic. Every experience, however painful or cheerful, can always teach us something. From selecting one particular strategy over another or avoiding certain design processes because they are less effective, evaluation can be a helpful tool for creating better games in the future.

- **Providing players with the opportunity to be part of the design process.** Through evaluation, players have a direct and indirect influence on the game's form. Their actions and behaviors can be used to lead designers to conclusions, but they can also directly express their opinion about the game, explaining what they would prefer to be done differently.

It is important at this point to say that, however necessary evaluation is, it is also not really a game designer's favorite moment. This absolutely makes sense as nobody wants to hear that their ideas have flaws or, at worst, are straight-up awful. But, as we will see later, by being able to receive feedback, manage it, and use it to evaluate your games later is a great virtue of educational game designers.

Evaluation Tools

Like in any situation, being able to identify and use the proper tools to achieve an objective is very important. In the context of evaluation, there are different tools that can be used, each of which comes with particular advantages and disadvantages and focuses on different aspects of educational game design. Probably, during your design process, you will not use all of these tools. It is certain, though, that knowing their nature and focus will save you a great deal of time, as you will be able to identify which tools are the most effective and convenient for particular situations. So, let's examine some of these tools:

- **Questionnaires** are a very typical way of getting answers to design questions. Questionnaires are convenient tools when designers want to measure specific outcomes, such as a player's impression of the game's usability or a player's understanding of the presented learning content. However, they don't offer players the possibility of diverting from the asked question or expressing an opinion on an aspect that was unaccounted for by designers. Questionnaires are efficient tools for large numbers of players because they are easy to collect and process through the use of statistical software packages. Properly designed questionnaires can offer great insights to designers. Those that are not well thought out can prove to be misleading for designers to interpret and even more difficult for players to respond to.

- **Interviews** are individual sessions between designers and players. During interviews, players offer their perspective on different aspects of educational games. There are different types of interviews, such as structured, semistructured, and unstructured. The more structured an interview, the more sequential and predefined the questions are. Less structured interviews present players with some questions but let them deviate from the question subject so as to present the particular aspects of games that they deem important. Interviews are very powerful tools and can give great insights into the thought process of players. At the same time, they require a great deal of resources to be conducted. This means that both players and designers need to invest time conducting these interviews. This is why interviews are not usually used as a large-scale audience evaluation tool.

- **Analytics** are among the most standard data-gathering tools in video games. Analytics are bits of information generated from players' interactions with video games. Designers can specify which actions and events they would like to be traced, and at the end of each session, specific log files are created that designers can later to extract information about the game's impact on players and users' reactions to game events.

- **Focus groups** are a type of group interview where people who share some type of connection are brought together and moderated in order to acquire more information on a phenomenon, in this case playing educational games. This connection can be of common interests, location, background, context, or anything else that designers consider to be an important attribute of their audience. In focus groups, players can express their needs, ideas, what they like, what they don't like, and what new things they want in games. Focus groups can shed light on several aspects of game design but also require time and resources to be conducted.

- **Usability tests** are set in place to study the game's ease of use. Usability tests explore if a game's elements and user interface are self-explanatory, resistant to errors, and intuitive enough to help players achieve the set tasks.

- **Quality assurance tests** are used to identify technical problems, usually referred to as "bugs." Quality assurance tests are related to the way games were constructed and designed and are connected to programming, visual, or platform technical failures. Quality assurance helps to prevent games from crashing, not working properly, or working only on limited equipment.

- **Playtesting** are sessions where a game is presented to potential players. During playtesting, players actually play the game, while designers observe them. Playtesting is a highly powerful tool as it presents designers with concrete answers to their questions while players live the experience that the game provided. During playtesting, weaknesses and problems are identified, hypotheses are being validated or rejected, and cracks or unexpected situations are noticed. Even if all the previous tools are very helpful, playtesting is indispensable as a game designer's evaluation tool, from the beginning to the very end of the design process.

It is very important to underline that though these tools can save you serious time and trouble, they can also cause several problems if not used correctly and at the right occasion. Like most of elements in education, tools acquire special meaning in specific contexts. So, it is important that you understand the use of each of those tools, as well as their advantages and disadvantages for different situations.

THE RIGHT TIME

Let's imagine that a game has already been designed and developed and is soon going to be released. The designers are now ready to present the game to players and receive their feedback. Until now there had been no evaluation of the game. So, the team wanted to study players' reactions and make the necessary adjustments to the game. Was that a correct approach? Absolutely not! At this stage, any feedback from players will be very difficult and expensive to integrate into the design, let alone develop from the beginning. The team lost considerable time working on a project without any feedback from players and ended up with a game whose effects remain unknown. So, when should evaluation start?

The right answer to this question is that evaluation starts from day one of a game's design. Every concept, idea, design document, learning theory, or component that is integrated into your games should be somehow reflected upon and evaluated. Of course, this is not always easy or very feasible. So, every person, team, or studio create their design processes and set up their own evaluation procedures. As a general principle, we can identify four phases of evaluation. These are:

Ex-ante evaluation is evaluation that happens before any development of a game and focuses on the assessment of players' needs and priorities, the evaluation of concepts and ideas, the use of learning theories, the establishment of learning objectives, or the identification of the game's core audience. As a result of this evaluation, those aspects are critically reflected upon and revised to ensure the best possible kick-start of the game design process.

Ongoing evaluation is the evaluation that is conducted from the first day of any kind of game development until the game's release to its final audience. This process includes design phases like prototyping and beta testing, which is the release of a non-complete version of the game to a group of players in order to receive information about their reactions to the game. Ongoing evaluation, as we will also see later, can target different stakeholders of the design process, from members of the design team to friends, family, or players.

Release evaluation is the evaluation that takes places after a game has been presented to players. This evaluation aims to assess players' development while playing a game as well as evaluate a game's individual aspects and appeal to players. Release evaluation can take place as long as the game is in circulation, which can be from the first day to a couple of years later.

A posteriori evaluation is the evaluation of the game's impact after a certain length of time from the moment that players first played the game. A posteriori evaluation aims to examine the game's long-term impact on a player's learning process.

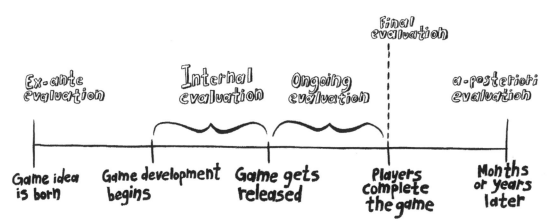

Different phases of evaluation.

These evaluation phases are prone to each designers' individual way of working and approaching their game design process. There are some designers who delay ongoing evaluation until a minimum viable game has been produced and players can actually play something, and there are others who try to involve players and external observers in the evaluation process right from the very beginning of their iterative design process in order to get as much insight as possible from the get-go. There is no right or wrong approach. It's true that unnecessary evaluation efforts can slow down, confuse, and distract designers from their final target, but it's also true that no evaluation at all may lead to irreversible disaster, where a game may lack learning impact or appeal or contain serious flaws in the game logic.

This process is also not always sequential but iterative. Online games that have been around for a long time and are still successful are excellent examples of this case. When games get released, the only way that their appeal and impact persists is when they are maintained, revised, and constantly evolving according to players' needs. Based on the phases presented above, this would be a continuous sequence of ongoing, release, and a posteriori evaluations, where the information from each of those evaluations is used in a particular way to design and redesign intrinsically motivating learning experiences.

THE WHO QUESTION

There are different ways of evaluating your games. There are also different moments where games can be evaluated. Another classic question is, who are you going to evaluate the games with? Without doubt, the best ones to evaluate your games are your potential players. But presenting unfinished games to players is not always easy or possible. So, designers, depending on their resources and design process, may perform evaluations on different groups of people. Those people can be:

- **The design team**: On many occasions, games are evaluated internally by game design teams. In those situations either a part or every member of the team playtest or evaluate the game in any way they can to identify flaws that could be rectified before the game is presented to people outside the team.

- **Friends and family**: Some of the most frequent players of our games are our friends and family. Without doubt, they are easy to approach, they probably have an idea of what the game is about, and can provide their own feedback.

- **Beta testers**: When games have reached a playable level, they can be presented and played by small groups of players that dedicate their time to playing games and providing feedback. Beta testers will play a game, find bugs, report their opinion about the game, generate analytics to identify the game's patterns and weaknesses, and help designers understand the learning impact of their games.

- **Players**: After the game is released, player feedback is invaluable. The more players, the more feedback. This raises the issue of being able to collect and analyze this information in order to acquire a better perspective on the game's efficiency and ways of making it better.

Games are usually presented to all these different categories of players in different occasions and contexts. Each of the types are characterized by some attributes that are useful for designers to get a broader perspective. For instance, it's possible that members of the design team may share the same outlook about the game, making them a polarized and very subjective evaluation audience. So, the more diverse your audience, the more perspectives you are going to examine. On the other hand, friends and family may be very strict or not strict at all. So, being able to identify their way of providing feedback will help you use it in a more meaningful way.

When working on evaluation, there is one point that is always good to have in mind: **Evaluating games with the same audience many times can be helpful but also misleading**. On one hand, players who are familiar with the game from the very beginning know your objectives, the atmosphere you want to create, and the style that you want to create, and they can provide you with interesting feedback from start till finish. On the other hand, people who are part of the design process for a long time are prone to losing their objectivity. This can be because they may evaluate the current game version in comparison to a previous one, meaning that they will find it better or worse than a previous one but will fail to see the big picture. Another point that usually comes up is that players who do not know the design and development pipeline of the game will easily focus their attention on half-finished or not-yet-polished game elements that you know will obviously be fixed and consistently point them out rather than focusing on the whole game experience. So, when presenting versions for testing to players be prepared for such situations.

WHAT TO EVALUATE

Discussing the impact of an educational game during a conference, I asked a game designer her opinion about her game. Excited about her work, she explained how the game worked and what its learning objectives were, closing by saying that the game was very successful. Amazed by her description, I asked her how she measured the game's effectiveness. The answer was simple: She had measured the time players spent playing the game compared to other activities. The results showed a greater engagement time playing the game in comparison with other activities. But was this enough?

Evaluation is an indispensable tool when conducted properly and knowing what we need to measure in order to arrive at meaningful conclusions. However, I strongly believe that **an improperly designed evaluation is worse than no evaluation at all**. So, before starting off to evaluate your games, make sure that you know what you want to evaluate and what the most effective tools to achieve this will be. So, what do we evaluate in educational game design?

The expected answer is everything! But what is "everything"? And how easy is it to evaluate this "everything"? Some questions that pop up when thinking about this are as follows:

- Is the game fun?

- Do players understand the game's goals?

- Is the game easily understood by players?

- Is the game balanced enough?

- Does the game offer different players the same time to play?

- Do players enjoy the game's visuals?

- Is the game's story well-told and does it build on the game's experience?

- Were the game's learning objectives met?

- Which competences specific to the learning aspect were applied by players?

- What types of strategies did players use to find solutions to the problems presented?

- Did the problem situations presented help players to explore different options before arriving at a solution?

- Did the game provide players with a good variety of resources among which they could choose which ones they prefer to use?

These are all valid questions and of course, the more information you get, the better perspective you will have, but it's absolutely sure that more and more questions like this will keep pouring in. So, an effective way of organizing educational game evaluation should be put in place to help you facilitate your thinking and analysis process. The very first question that needs to be answered is what elements should be evaluated. This question takes us back to Chapter 2, where we tried to analyze the nature of games. So, being able to explain what games are for you gives you the first insight into what you need to evaluate.

If, for instance, you are using the model of the elemental pentad that we saw in Chapter 2, you would have five distinct elements that you could evaluate: education, aesthetics, story, mechanics, and technology. However, this analysis may vary according to each designer's perspective of games, play, and learning.

A great discussion about educational evaluation has been on the focus and purposes of evaluation. Do we evaluate in order to assign a rank or a mark to a game or a learner? Do we evaluate at specific moments, usually the end of semesters or trimesters, in order to identify the level of learners after they have participated in a teaching intervention? Do we evaluate to compare learners to each other and create leaderboards? Or do we constantly evaluate the process of delivering learning content and how people learn in order to make it more efficient, personal, and, hence, help learners evolve with it? The first is called **summative assessment** while the last is called **formative assessment**. Even if both of those types of evaluation have their own meaning and purposes, educational game design, being the art of creating intrinsically motivating learning experiences as a result of players' interaction with games, can mainly be examined through the perspective of formative assessment.

Even if designers need to find their own way of evaluating, adapting their tools to the contexts for which they design their games, the following are a set of not-necessarily sequential levels of an educational game's evaluation content:

- **Learning objectives**: Is the message or learning content you want to convey properly analyzed and concrete enough? This level of assessment aims to investigate this aspect and provide you with answers on whether the game's learning objectives were properly identified, defined, and presented as part of the design and delivery process of the game.

- **The learning aspect**: As we saw, successful games manage to seamlessly blend all elements together so that learning and playing become part of the same learning experience. In this level, the assessment focuses on whether the game elements correctly present the learning content and if they successfully facilitate learning experiences in order to fulfill the proposed learning objectives. This aspect is not necessarily connected to the game's impact on players' learning, but focuses on the way that learning theories, methodologies, and approaches are combined with the other game elements.

- **The game aspect**: This level investigates the combination of gaming and learning elements, like the previous level, but through the perspective of the gaming aspect. Educational games need to be both fun and educative. So, this aspect focuses on how gaming and learning elements are bound together in order for the game to present intrinsically motivating experiences for players.

- **The individual elements**: It is always interesting to evaluate both the big picture and individual game elements. Both perspectives offer different insights into the game design process and can help prevent different types of issues. This level aims to help designers evaluate each game component individually for its structure, connection with other elements, and consistency. Elements that can be examined are aesthetics, narratives, technical implementation, goals, winning conditions, game interactions, or any other element that designers consider necessary to evaluate.

- **The play experience**: While all previous levels evaluate games on a structural level, this one focuses on the process of playing the game and the reactions, emotions, and behaviors of players before, during, and after their play experience. This level offers insights into how players approach the game, interact with it in terms of usability, understand its rules and instructions, and also into how much players enjoy the game and want to explore its world or lose interest in it, and why.

- **Learning impact**: Educational games are always expected to have a learning impact on players. This level aims to identify this learning impact, if it exists, by studying players' decisions. Through this study, the assessment aims to find out what types of problem-solving strategies were used or invented by players, what types of skills were developed, and what level of understanding of the presented subject they managed to reach.

> **REFLECTION POINTS** 🔍
>
> Efficient and meaningful evaluation requires great preparation and reflection from your side. Being able to identify what elements to evaluate and which tools will allow you to do so is always a challenge.
>
> - Have you identified what you will evaluate your games for? It is probably going to be more than one aspect. Are those aspects well defined so as to help you easily study them later on?
>
> - What are the tools that will help you to better evaluate the game aspects you are interested in?
>
> - During which occasions are you going to conduct evaluation sessions? Are those sessions going to be repeated?
>
> - What duration will your evaluation sessions be?
>
> - Who are you conducting your evaluation on?

RECEIVING FEEDBACK

Receiving feedback is not always easy. Actually, I have experienced situations where game designers did not receive players' feedback with the grace that might be expected. Extreme occasions include throwing things at each other, cursing, and storming out. As we already said, nobody likes hearing bad things about their creations but you need to always remember that this is part of the job! Players that give you honest feedback are doing you a great service, which you should try to use to figure out how to make your games better rather than arguing or making excuses. In fact, being a good listener and an efficient feedback receiver is among the greatest virtues of educational game designers.

In order to receive feedback effectively, players should feel comfortable and interested enough to spend their time providing you with the information you want. So, creating a comfortable environment where players feel relaxed and secure usually increases feedback quality. For feedback to be efficient, questions need to be asked properly and players need to provide it in a way that can be assessed by designers. So, feedback should be:

Concrete: The more specific the feedback, the more effective it becomes. General comments that do not address particular aspects of the game may still be helpful but cannot be easily used to solve specific issues of the game.

Descriptive: One-word remarks, like yes or no, are not always enough to provide designers with information about the source of a problem and help them find solutions. Descriptive feedback, on the other hand, can be of great assistance to designers.

Clear: Clear questions usually result in clear answers. When players do not understand the questions the evaluators give them, it is normal for them to reply in an ambiguous or unclear way that cannot be used to make the game better.

On time: It is helpful to receive feedback from players soon after playing your game. At that time, memories are fresh and players can explain with greater detail their impressions of playing the game.

THE POWER OF LETTING GO

It is certain that all designers want players to like their ideas and games. It is also a given that this will not always be the case. To be more exact, it is highly possible that in many cases players will not like our ideas. This is the reason why we constantly revise them to create experiences that are nice and enjoyable for our audience.

There are cases, though, where a game's evaluation may not be favorable because:

- The audience might not be interested in a particular concept or approach.

- The resources required for a game prove to be prohibitive for the game's implementation.

- The game's prototype shows that the game does not seem to have a learning impact on players.

- The game is simply boring.

All those cases are possible and should be expected. There are cases where the game can be fixed and there are other ones where that might be impossible, very difficult, or not worth the team's time and resources. It is in situations like this that game designers need to know when to quit pursuing this project and move to another one. Of course, this is not easy and it goes against our ego and dreams, but being able to recognize when it's best to let go is also part of the job.

During every game designer's career, there have been times that ideas, prototypes, or even finished games have failed to reach their own or their players' expectations. This is why you should avoid becoming too attached to a single project. I know it might be difficult and, on some occasions, impossible. But at least try to remember that, especially in the first stages of the design process, you will need to greatly revise your game ideas so as to create games that facilitate intrinsically motivating learning experiences. As a great captain, in order to help your ship find land, you may need to steer a different course than the one you had initially plotted. So, consider evaluation as an indispensable navigation tool toward greater and more effective learning experiences.

PERSPECTIVE

Laura Malinverni

UX Researcher

ON DESIGNING EDUCATIONAL GAMES FOR CHILDREN WITH SPECIAL NEEDS: THE VALUE OF PARTICIPATION

In the past few decades, educational games for children with special needs have been gaining increasing importance. This tendency derives from the interest that children show in video games and the capacity of games to foster motivation and to produce behavioral changes. However, specific concerns have pointed out the challenges related to properly combining therapeutic goals, engaging gameplay, and children's interests. Often, serious games oversimplify game design principles and may have a reduced appeal for children who are used to much more sophisticated commercial games. Furthermore, most educational games for children with special needs do not include children's interests and contributions in the design process, hence running the risk of failing in properly making sense to children.

To address these shortcomings, several researchers are exploring the possibilities of using **participatory design** (PD) to involve children with special needs in co-designing educational games. In this this text, I will focus on the value of participation in designing educational games for and with children with special needs. As a necessary premise, the goal of this text is not to suggest a set of prescriptive guidelines and tools that can be applied in all cases. Instead, it aims at offering instruments to help practitioners to evaluate and reflect on their PD practices.

What Is Participatory Design?

PD has its origin in Scandinavian countries, where from the 1970s a new design approach was developed to better understand users' needs and to respond to the political claim for horizontality and participation [1]. Since then, PD has been an active research field, and today it represents a wide range of techniques for enabling user participation in design.

In the 1990s, PD was also adapted to children [2] by acknowledging that their involvement in the design process would be helpful to design technologies that speak their language and meet their interests. To this end, researchers have started to organize workshops based on different techniques and activities to facilitate children's participation and contributions. Examples of these techniques can be found by involving children in thinking and tinkering around with novel technologies by making them outline their ideas, enacting them, producing storyboards, constructing low-tech prototypes, and so on. The results of these activities are generally analyzed to understand children's interests, values, and ideas, and, therefore, design a technology that fits with their worldview.

Participatory Design and Special Needs

In recent years, research around PD has been expanded to investigate methods and strategies to involve children with special needs in the design process [3–5]. This research has generally pursued a twofold goal. On one hand, it aims to better understand them so as to design better solutions. On the other, it aims to support the empowerment and self-confidence of children with special needs, who are often underrepresented in any decision-making process.

However, despite these promising directions, PD with children with special needs can represent a complex task. On one hand, it requires orchestrating the various contributions, requirements, and constraints within a coherent holistic design (e.g., children's interests, educational goals, therapeutic guidelines, technological possibilities, and so on.). On the other hand, it requires designing activities that can fit with children's skills and know-how (e.g., dealing with preferred expressive modalities or with specific difficulties such as cognitive, verbal, or motor disabilities). Finally, often, the complex situations that these children are facing require particular care for the ethical implications related to the nature of the proposed activities. To address these latter aspects in the following sections, I will present some key concepts to be considered when organizing, planning, and conducting activities to involve children with special needs in PD.

Organizing PD with Children with Special Needs

Before starting a PD process with children with special needs, practitioners need to clearly understand and frame the specificities of the context where the research will be carried out. In particular, I suggest that the following aspects should be carefully scrutinized:

- The specificities of the project (e.g., What are the end goals of the project? Who decided them? How is the design space defined? How much space is open to participants contributions and why? Who is involved in decision-making and at what level?).

- The constraints of the PD process (e.g., How much time can be dedicated to PD? How will participants be involved? What are the benefits that they will have from this involvement? Where will it take place? With whom?).

- The specificities of our populations (e.g., How much do we know them and they know us? What are their skills, difficulties, interests, and preferences? How much time can they dedicate to these activities? Did they choose to join the workshop or did somebody else decide for them?).

- The skills of the involved researchers/designers (e.g., Up to what level is this person experienced/trained to facilitate a participatory and creative process with children?).

Once these aspects are examined and clarified, researchers can start to sketch a plan of the workshop and of the activities that will be used to engage children in the process of co-creating novel games and technologies.

Defining PD Activities: Some Key Considerations

Often, the challenges related to involving children with special needs in the design of educational games end up shaping the activities as decision-making inquiries on accessory features (e.g., whether they prefer a certain character or another) or as discrete units that do not give children the feeling that they are contributing to a bigger project. This tendency does not only run the risk of obtaining inconsistent outcomes, but also, and more importantly, it implies ethical reflections around what we are offering to the participants and what are they obtaining from participation. Often participants in PD do not receive any material compensation; hence, their takeaways from the experience should, at least, be something immaterial. Thus, even if one of the main goals of PD is to better understand children in order to better design for them, we cannot forget that the proposed activities should not only be informative for the researchers, but also relevant and interesting for the children. To this end, I propose the qualities of **meaningfulness, empowering**, and **multisensorial** as cornerstone concepts to examine and evaluate the activities that we are planning.

Meaningfulness: Proposing meaningful activities means proposing tasks that children care about and that are relevant and interesting for them. This implies both conveying the feeling that they are working on a valuable personal project, as well as connecting the tasks with their personal interests, contexts, needs, previous knowledge, and ways of being (e.g., designing ways to improve their space or make a certain routine funnier, designing something for somebody they care about). To this end, an optimal approach is to plan the activities only after having gained preliminary knowledge about the participating children (their skills, interests, habits, etc.). This may be achieved either through participant observation during their daily activities (e.g., in a school setting), through the planning of a set of warm-up activities, or by talking with parents and caregivers.

Empowering: Planning empowering activities means offering experiences and tasks where children can demonstrate, feel, and track their competencies and achievements. This is particularly important when we collaborate with children with special needs, as often the focus on "needs" reduces the attention that can be placed on "skills." It is therefore fundamental to facilitate conditions in which they feel that their capabilities are recognized, that they are skilled for doing relevant things, and that their ideas are valuable. Examples of this strategy can be related to reinforcing their feeling of authorship during the process, allowing children to feel challenged (but not overwhelmed) by the task, fostering forms of collaborative work, structuring the activities to promote a feeling of continuity and progression, and providing concrete supports to visualize the results of their works (e.g., a display wall/final exhibit).

Multisensorial: Defining multisensorial activities means providing children with different media and tools through which they can express themselves. In PD, researchers can employ a wide range of materials and techniques (e.g., drawing, note-taking, low-tech prototyping with arts-and-crafts materials, video or photographic recording, physical enactments, etc.) to foster people's ability to express themselves. Each of these materials or techniques has its own specific affordances and require different skills and ways of working with them. In the context of special needs, particular attention should be devoted to selecting and offering a wide range of materials and techniques in order to offer different possible entry paths to the tasks and enable children to express themselves through the media that they find most comfortable. At the same time, while analyzing and interpreting the results of the workshops, these multiple expressive resources should be carefully considered and analyzed instead of focusing only on verbal outcomes.

Conducting PD Activities with Children with Special Needs

Preparing well-designed activities constitutes a central part of successful PD workshops. Nonetheless, it becomes equally important to be capable of conducting the activity, establishing a fruitful and positive relationship with the participants, and being responsive to the unforeseen flow of the moment-by-moment continuation of the activity. Hence, being a researcher involved in PD requires cultivating a specific mindset. To guide this process, I propose two key qualities that researchers should consider as concepts to guide and self-examine their own practice: **mindfulness** and **reflexivity**.

Mindfulness: Being mindful while conducting a PD workshop means to be actively engaged with the present moment, sensitive to children's affective state, and open to change one's plan. Hence, researchers should approach PD with a flexible mindset, where it is more important to be capable of constantly adapting to the current situation instead of rigidly sticking to the plan. To this end, it is fundamental to constantly observe and evaluate children's responses to the proposed activities and to be capable of empathizing with the different moments and feelings children may go through. Useful strategies include training our observational ability, embedding flexibility in the structure of the workshops, and having a set of possible alternatives available to adjust and refine the session. To this end, a fundamental tool is represented by the documentation of the relevant processes that unfold during the session. This documentation should be generally carried out just after the session combining both visual material and written reflections.

Reflexivity: Being reflective while conducting a PD workshop means carrying out a constant self-analytic reflection on our practice, our attitude, and our beliefs. In particular, I suggest researchers should carefully reflect on their standpoint with respect to PD (e.g., What does PD mean to me? Why do I choose to use it?), their views and expectations about participants (e.g., What do I believe the participants may or may not be able to do? Why? How are these beliefs shaping the role that I assign to them and the way I behave with them?), and their goal with respect to PD and the project (How do I feel about these outcomes? Why?). To this end, I suggest that keeping a self-reflective diary could represent a useful tool to guide self-examination and avoid acting in a sort of automatic pilot mode.

CONCLUSION

Being a researcher involved in PD with children with special needs is not an easy task. It implies carefully planning relevant activities, establishing a fruitful relationship with the children, mediating the constraints and requirements of the specific project, and making full use of one's own design knowledge. Furthermore, it requires a careful self-examination of one's own standpoint and role in shaping the participatory process.

In this text, I presented some considerations and suggestions derived from my practice in this field and oriented them to guide practitioners interested in this research. Nonetheless, these suggestions should not be taken as a comprehensive guide manual to be blindly followed but instead as a reflective starting point to frame one's research.

REFERENCES

1. Muller, M. J. (2003). Participatory design: The third space in HCI. In A. Sears & J. A. Jacko (Eds.), *Human–Computer interaction: Development Process* (pp. 165–185). New York: CRC Press.
2. Druin, A. (2002). The role of children in the design of new technology. *Behaviour & Information Technology, 21*(1), 1–25.
3. Benton, L., Johnson, H., Ashwin, E., Brosnan, M., & Grawemeyer, B. (2012). Developing IDEAS: Supporting children with autism within a participatory design team. In J. A. Konstan, E. A. Chi, & K. Höök (Eds.), CHI '12: *Proceedings of the SIGCHI Conference on Human Factors in Computing Systems* (pp. 2599–2608). New York: Association for Computing Machinery.
4. Frauenberger, C., Good, J., & Keay-Bright, W. (2011). Designing technology for children with special needs: Bridging perspectives through participatory design. *CoDesign, 7*(1), 1–28.
5. Malinverni, L., Mora-Guiard, J., Padillo, V., Mairena, M., Hervás, A., & Pares, N. (2014). Participatory design strategies to enhance the creative contribution of children with special needs. In *Proceedings of the 2014 Conference on Interaction Design and Children* (pp. 85–94). New York: Association for Computing Machinery.

SUMMARY

- Testing your games is very, very, very important (yes, three verys!). Testing can help you identify issues on all game elements.

- Evaluating your game's learning impact on players will help you validate your game's concept, evolve your games, offer insights and practices for future designs, and provide players with the opportunity to contribute to the design of your games.

- There are different ways to evaluate your games, such as questionnaires, interviews, analytics, focus groups, usability tests, playtesting, and quality assurance tests.

- Evaluating your games should happen from the very start of your concept phase till years after your players play your games.

- You can evaluate any aspect of your games you want. The more elements you test and evaluate, the more informed you will be about your decisions.

14 Documenting and Communicating

This chapter:

- Elaborates on the different forms and ways of compiling and maintaining game design documents.

- Examines the different types of contents that are included in game design documents.

- Examines ways of using game design documents in the design process.

THE PERFECT GAME DESIGN DOCUMENT

Game designers need to take into account a great variety of factors and come up with designs for their games. As we have seen, those factors can be related to mechanics, aesthetics, technology, narratives, and learning. But even the greatest ideas amount to nothing if they cannot be properly applied and understood by one's peers. It's not uncommon for great concepts to be poorly implemented because game designers had difficulty communicating their perspectives properly. That's why game designers create game design documents.

At this point I want to clarify a common misconception. Many people believe that game designers draft huge documents, full of every detail about their games, and spend hours updating them in order to support the development process. This is not the case for one main reason: Successful game design documents are written to help everybody, not to create more problems.

Game design documents would not exist if every member of the game development team could magically enter the game designer's brain and understand exactly what they are thinking about their games. Thus, team members need to find a way in order to get the information they need without searching for hours and getting frustrated. So, forget about long documents with lots of details and focus on saying what you want in the best and easiest way possible. Game design documents are not about formalities, they are about action! So, what are the attributes of efficient game design documents? The following are some key attributes of efficient game design documents:

- **Never the same structure**: A common question on game design documents is whether there are specific ways of structuring them. Brief research online will give you several templates or ways to structure your game design documents. However, I would like to emphasize that efficient game design documents do not have a specific structure. Educational games need to be adapted to the particular contexts and needs of learners, in the same way that game design documents need to be able to adapt to the needs of game designers. There is not a right or wrong way of structuring your documents as long as everybody can read and understand them.

- **Simple structure**: Game design documents should be structured in a simple way to make them easy to read through. Complex structures with lots of references to other points are highly likely to frustrate people who are looking to be informed by the document. They may misunderstand what you are trying to say or have to keep asking you about elements that already exist in the document.

- **Clear**: Reading a game design document should clarify points about the game design process and not cause more frustration or confusion. The clearer the content of a game design document, the more effective it becomes. So, instead of trying to write as many words as you can, try to make your statements clear, self-explanatory, and to the point.

- **Descriptive**: Game design documents should be simple, clear, and to the point. This does not necessarily mean that designers should be laconic. On the contrary, designers should give the necessary amount of description and avoid any possible confusion to the members of the design team. Descriptions can be in the form of text, image, video, music, or anything else that works for you and your team.

DOCUMENT FORMS

Another expectation of novice educational game designers is that game design documents take the form of a book. While true that often this structure is used by designers, it's not always preferred by other stakeholders of the development process. Considering that artists and developers of a video game encounter difficult situations every day where they need to find solutions, they don't want to have to search through long documents. If that happens they either won't read the document or will just come to you directly to discuss it with the designer. In the first case, time and resources will have been wasted for no reason as in the end nobody used the document; in the second case, designers risk being constantly interrupted by their peers looking for clarifications. Imagine working in a studio with 10 or 20 people. After some time, it's possible that the designer will become a helpdesk for anybody who can't find what they need in the game design documents.

This fact made designers come up with different forms of presenting their game design documents. Let's have a look at three of those:

- **The classic document**: This is the classic approach of drafting game design documents. All information about the game's design is stored on one or more documents that can be read by members of the design team when necessary.

- **The wiki**: Wikis are a common way of setting up game design documents nowadays. They are online, are accessible to every member of the team, offer a rather straightforward index and search functionalities, and can support different representations of information, from text to audio and video.

- **The forum**: Especially in situations where game design becomes a participatory process, where their elements are reviewed and critically reflected upon, forums can provide an environment where information can be spread across the team as well as where the necessary feedback from team members is received in order to revise the document.

It's always helpful to remember that game design documents are not set in stone. They evolve and change form along with the needs of a game project. Game design documents follow the design process that was set by the team members. So, their form needs to be easily adaptable to the needs and expectations of the people who are going to write and read them.

DOCUMENT CONTENTS

Game design documents offer both a global and thorough perspective of one's games. Some designers prefer creating different game design documents for different situations. For instance, some use short documents to present their games to people outside the design team, such as producers, educators, educational administrators, or potential buyers, intending to present them with just the necessary information that they need to understand what the game is about. The same designers may use longer documents to describe their game and its individual elements to the members of their teams.

At the end, though, the structure and length of your game design document depends entirely on you and your team. In educational game design, the most common aspects that are encountered in game design documents are:

- Learning aims and objectives.

- Learning methodologies.

- Learning theories used and their impact on the game.

- Evaluation of the game.

- Presentation of the game, especially if special preparations are necessary for the game to be introduced to players.

- Audience.

- Audience needs and preferences.

- Learning context.

- Game mechanics, including some or all of the aspects we examined in this book.

- Narrative elements.

- Game characters and their abilities.

- Connection and impact between game elements, like mechanics and story or technology and mechanics.

- Technology features, related to any of the above categories.

This list and arrangement is just an example of aspects that exist in educational game design documents. This list can definitely be expanded or reduced based on the designer's needs for a particular game design situation.

USES OF A GAME DESIGN DOCUMENT

Game design documents can serve as tools for different situations in design processes. The most common one is their use as a means of expression for one's ideas. By being able to write game design documents, designers critically reflect on their own ideas. Often what is in our head may seem easier or different from what comes out when written on paper. Drafting game design documents offer this opportunity to designers. Additionally, this process is also helpful when the game needs to be presented to people who are not familiar with the design process and the game's background. In cases like this, designers need to be able to briefly and effectively explain what the game is about and how it is going to help players learn.

Game design documents are also used as common reference points for the design process. As it is a document that presents and explains the elements of a game, this document can be referred to in discussions and everyone in the team will know what they are talking about. This is a huge asset, especially for medium-sized and large teams, where better communication can definitely make the design process more efficient.

So, game design documents become part of the design team members' common language. Another use of game design documents is that they contain all the information required for the design of a game. As we have seen, members of design teams, such as developers, artists, beta testers, and musicians, are not expected to remember every aspect of your designs. They already have their own challenges to face and it's possible that they will forget or miss elements, which they can access by reading the game design document.

Last but not least, game design documents can be rather useful when evaluating educational games. As they already present important aspects of the envisioned game, game design documents can themselves be evaluated at the beginning as proofs of concept, and can also later help designers define how and which game elements are going to be evaluated.

15 The Final Chapter

I have to admit that when I started writing this book, I had in my mind lots and lots of things to express and talk about. And I did! However, during this great journey of mine and my interaction, communication, and connection with all of the amazing people who participated and contributed to the creation of this book, I challenged my views, I reduced or expanded several aspects of the book, I explored new design possibilities and, through this process, I learnt more about educational game design. Hence, several times I recalled the saying of ancient Greek philosopher Solon:

I grow old but I always learn.

There is always an opportunity to learn, an opportunity to explore, and an opportunity to grow—and this is what educational game design is about.

Undoubtedly, every beginning has an end and so does this journey. It's also inevitable that after closing one chapter, another one, possibly bigger, with even greater challenges may open.

And so, your own real journey begins!

Thanks again for sticking along for the ride!

Bibliography

Abbott, E. A. (2006). *Flatland: A romance of many dimensions.* Oxford: Oxford University Press.

Abt, C. C. (2002). *Serious games.* New York: University Press of America.

Adams, E., & Dormans, J. (2012). *Game mechanics: Advanced game design.* Berkeley, CA: New Riders Games.

Amory, A. (2007). Game object model version II: A theoretical framework for educational game development. *Educational technology research and development, 55*(1), 51–77.

Andresen, L., Boud, D., & Cohen, R. (2000). Experience-based learning: Contemporary issues. In G. Forey (Eds.), *Understanding adult education and training* (2nd ed), (pp. 225–239). Sydney: Allen & Unwin.

Aristotle (1996). *Poetics* (M. Heath, Trans.). London: Penguin Books.

Asch, S. E. (1956). Studies of independence and conformity: I. A minority of one against a unanimous majority. *Psychological monographs: General and applied, 70*(9), 1–70.

Asimov, I. (1986). *Futuredays: A nineteenth century vision of the year 2000.* New York: Henry Holt & Co.

Avedon, E. M., & Sutton-Smith, B. (1971). *The study of games.* New York: John Wiley & Sons.

Bartle, R. (1996). Hearts, clubs, diamonds, spades: Players who suit MUDs. *Journal of MUD research, 1*(1), 19–42.

Bartlett, F. C. (1995). *Remembering: A study in experimental and social psychology.* Cambridge: Cambridge University Press.

Bloom, B. S. (Eds.) (1956). *Taxonomy of educational objectives. The classification of educational goals, Handbook I: Cognitive domain.* New York: Longman.

Boal, A. (2000). *Theater of the oppressed.* London: Pluto Press.

Bodrova, E., & Leong, D. J. (2015). Vygotskian and post-Vygotskian views on children's play. *American Journal of Play, 7*(3), 371–388.

Broadhurst, P. L. (1957). Emotionality and the Yerkes-Dodson law. *Journal of experimental psychology, 54*(5), 345–352.

Brousseau, G. (2002). *Theory of didactical situations in mathematics* (N. Balacheff, M. Cooper, R. Sutherland and V. Warfield, Trans.). Dordrecht: Kluwer Academic Publishing.

Brown, M. (2008). Comfort zone: Model or metaphor? *Australian journal of outdoor education, 12*(1), 3–12.

Caillois, R. (1961). *Man, play, and games* (M. Barash, Trans.). Urbana & Chicago: University of Illinois Press.

Campbell, J. (2008). *The hero with a thousand faces.* Novato, California: New World Library.

Chatman, S. B. (1980). *Story and discourse: Narrative structure in fiction and film.* Ithaca, NY: Cornell University Press.

Clements, D. H., & Sarama, J. (2004). Learning trajectories in mathematics education. *Mathematical Thinking and Learning, 6*(2), 81–89.

Cooper, A. (2008). The origin of personas. Retrieved from: https://www.cooper.com/journal/2008/05/the_origin_of_personas

Cooper, A. (2004). *The inmates are running the asylum: Why high tech products drive us crazy and how to restore the sanity.* Upper Saddle River, NJ: Sams - Pearson Education.

Costikyan, G. (2006). I have no words and I must design. In K. Salen & E. Zimmerman (Eds.), *The game designer reader: A rules of play anthology* (pp. 192–211). Cambridge, MA: MIT Press.

Crawford, C. (1984). *The art of computer game design: Reflections of a master game designer.* Berkeley, CA: Osborne/McGraw-Hill.

Csikszentmihalyi, M., Abuhamdeh, S., & Nakamura, J. (2014). Flow. In M. Csikszentmihalyi (Eds.), *Flow and the foundations of positive psychology* (pp. 227–238). London: Springer.

Csikszentmihalyi, M., & Bennett, S. (1971). An exploratory model of play. *American anthropologist, 73*(1), 45–58.

Cutter-Mackenzie, A., Edwards, S., Moore, D., & Boyd, W. (2014). *Young children's play and environmental education in early childhood education.* Switzerland: Springer.

Dewey, J. (1997). *How we think.* Mineola, N.Y.: Dover Publications.

Dewey, J. (1994). Art as experience. In S. D. Ross (Eds.), *Art and its significance: An anthology of aesthetic theory* (3rd ed) (pp. 205–223). Albany: State University of New York Press.

Dewey, J. (1938). *Experience and education.* New York: Touchstone.

Dickey, M. D. (2007). Game design and learning: A conjectural analysis of how massively multiple online role-playing games (MMORPGs) foster intrinsic motivation. *Educational technology research and development, 55*(3), 253–273.

Egenfeldt-Nielsen, S., Smith, J. H., & Tosca, S. P. (2008). *Understanding video games: The essential introduction.* New York: Routledge.

Friere, P. (1970). *Pedagogy of the oppressed.* New York: Continuum.

Fullerton, T. (2008). *Game design workshop: A playcentric approach to creating innovative games.* New York: CRC Press.

Gardner, H. (1983). *Frames of mind: The idea of multiple intelligences.* New York: Basic Books.

Gee, J. P. (2003). What video games have to teach us about learning and literacy. *Computers in entertainment, 1*(1), 20.

Gennari, R., Melonio, A., Raccanello, D., Brondino, M., Dodero, G., Pasini, M., & Torello, S. (2017). Children's emotions and quality of products in participatory game design. *International journal of human computer studies, 101,* 45–61.

Groos, K. (1976). *The play of animals* (K. Groos & E. L. Baldwin, Trans.). New York: D Appleton & Company.

Hennessey, B. A., & Amabile, T. M. (2010). Creativity. *Annual review of psychology, 61,* 569–598.

Hiwiller, Z. (2015). *Players making decisions: Game design essentials and the art of understanding your players.* Berkeley, California: New Riders.

Hodent, C. (2017). *The gamer's brain: How neuroscience and UX can impact video game design.* Boca Raton, FL: CRC Press.

Hofstede, G. (1984). *Culture's consequences: International differences in work related values.* Berkeley Hills, California: Sage Publishing Inc.

Huizinga, J. (1955). *Homo ludens: A study of the play element in culture* (R. Hull, Trans.). Boston, MA: The Beacon Press.

Jenkins, H. (2007). Narrative spaces. In F. von Borries, S. P. Walz & M. Böttger (Eds.), *Space time play, computer games, architecture and urbanism: The next level* (pp. 56–60). Berlin: Birkhäuser.

Jenkins, H. (2004). Game design as narrative architecture. In N. Wardrip-Fruin & P. Harrigan (Eds.), *First person. New media as story, performance, and game* (pp. 118–130). Cambridge: MIT Press.

Juul, J. (2004). Introduction to game time. In N. Wardrip-Fruin & P. Harrigan (Eds.), *First person: New media as story, performance, and game* (pp. 131–142). Cambridge: MIT Press.

Juul, J. (1999). *A clash between game and narrative: A thesis on computer games and interactive fiction.* Copenhagen: University of Copenhagen.

Kafai, Y., & Peppler, K. (2012). Developing gaming fluencies with scratch. In C. Steinkuehler, K. Squire & S. Barab (Eds.), *Games, learning, and society: Learning and meaning in the digital age* (pp. 355–380). Cambridge: Cambridge University Press.

Kalmpourtzis, G. (n.d.). Connecting game design with problem posing skills in early childhood. *British journal of educational technology.*

Kalmpourtzis, G., Vrysis, L., & Veglis, A. (2016). Teaching game design to students of the early childhood through forest maths. In *Proceedings of 11th International workshop on semantic and social media adaptation and personalization* (pp. 12–127). Thessaloniki: IEEE.

Kalmpourtzis, G., Berthoix, M., & Vrysis, L. (2015). Serious+: A technology assisted learning space based on gaming. In Proceedings of 2015 *International conference on interactive mobile communication technologies and learning (IMCL)* (pp. 429–431). Thessaloniki: IEEE.

Kalmpourtzis, G. (2014). Find the Jackalop: A game enhancing young children's spatial thinking. In *CHI '14- Proceedings of the SIGCHI Conference on human factors in computing systems* (pp. 1165–1170). New York: ACM.

Kellinger, J. J. (2017). *A guide to designing curricular games: How to "game" the system.* Cham, Switzerland: Springer.

Kim, S. (n.d.). *What is a puzzle?* Retrieved from http://www.scottkim.com.previewc40.carrierzone.com/thinking games/whatisapuzzle/index.html

Kloosterman, P., Giebel, K., & Senyuva, O. (2007). *T-Kit 10: Educational evaluation in youth work.* The Strasbourg: Council of Europe Publishing.

Klopfer, E. (2011). *Augmented learning: Research and design of mobile educational games.* Cambridge: The MIT Press.

Klopfer, E., Osterweil, S., & Salen, K. (2009). *Moving learning games forward: Obstacles, opportunities and openness.* Cambridge, MA: The Education Arcade.

Kolb, D. A. (1976). *The learning style inventory: Technical manual.* Boston, MA: McBer & Co.

Kolb, D. A., & Fry, R. (1975). Toward an applied theory of experiential learning. In C. Cooper (Eds.), *Theories of Group Processes* (pp. 33–37). New York: John Wiley & Sons.

Lajoie, S. P. (2005). Extending the scaffolding metaphor. *Instructional science, 33*(5-6), 541–557.

Lameras, P., Arnab, S., Dunwell, I., Stewart, C., Clarke, S., & Petridis, P. (2016). Essential features of serious games design in higher education: Linking learning attributes to game mechanics. *British journal of educational technology, 48*(4), 972–994.

Land, G., & Jarman, B. (1992). *Breakpoint and beyond: Mastering the future today*. New York: Harper Business.

Lapsley, D. K. (2006). Moral stage theory. In M. Killen & J. G. Smetana (Eds.), *Handbook of moral development* (pp. 37–66). Mahwah, NJ: Lawrence Erlbaum Associates Publishers.

LeBlanc, M. (1999). Formal design tools: Feedback systems and the dramatic structure of competition. In *Proceedings of 1999 Computer Game Developers' Conference*. San Francisco: Miller Freeman Game Group.

Maslow, A. H. (1943). A theory of human motivation. *Psychological review, 50*(4), 370–396.

McKee, R. (1997). *Story: Substance, structure, style, and the principles of screen writing*. New York: Regan Books.

Montessori, M. (1949). *The absorbent mind*. Madras, India: The Theosophical Publishing House.

Moran, S., & John-Steiner, V. (2003). Creativity in the making: Vygotsky's contemporary contribution to the dialectic of development and creativity. In R. K. Sawyer, V. John-Steiner, S. Moran, R. J. Sternberg, D. H. Feldman, J. Nakamura & M. Csikszentmihalyi (Eds.), *Creativity and development*. (pp. 61–90). New York: Oxford University Press.

Nolan, J., & Mcbride, M. (2014). Beyond gamification: Reconceptualizing game - based learning in early childhood environments. *Information, communication & society, 17*(5), 594–608.

OECD (n.d.). *Recognition of non-formal and informal learning*. Retrieved from http://www.oecd.org/edu/skills-beyond-school/recognitionofnon-formalandinformallearning-home.htm

Papert, S., & I. Harel (1991). Situating constructionism. In S. Papert & I. Harel (Eds.), *Constructionism: research reports and essays* (pp. 1–11). Norwood, New Jersey: Ablex Publishing.

Papert, S. (1988). The conservation of Piaget: The computer as a grist to the constructivist mill. In G. Forman & P. B. Pufall (Eds.), *Constructivism in the computer Age* (pp. 3–13). Hillsdale: Lawrence Erlbaum Associates.

Parlett, D. (1999). *Oxford history of board games*. Oxford: Oxford University Press.

Pellegrini, A. D., Dupuis, D., & Smith, P. K. (2007). Play in evolution and development. *Developmental review, 27*(2), 261–276.

Piaget, J. (1952). Play, dreams and imitation in childhood. *Journal of consulting psychology, 16*(5), 413–414.

Polya, G. (1945). *How to solve it. A new aspect of mathematical method*. Princeton, NJ: Princeton University Press.

Propp, V. (2010). *Morphology of the folktale* (L. Scott, Trans.). Austin: University of Texas Press.

Provenzo, E. F. (2009). Friedrich Froebel's gifts, connecting the spiritual and aesthetic to the real world of play and learning. *American journal of pLay, 2*(1), 85–99.

Rogers, S. (2010). *Level up!: The guide to great video game design*. Chichester, UK: Wiley.

Salen, K., & Zimmerman, E. (2004). *Rules of play: Game design fundamentals*. Cambridge, MA: MIT Press.

Sanchez, E. (2017). Competition and collaboration for game-based learning: A case study. In P. Wouters & H. Van Oostendorp (Eds.), *Instructional techniques to facilitate learning and motivation of serious games* (pp. 161–184). Heidelberg: Springer.

Sanchez, E., Young, S., & Jouneau-Sion, C. (2016). Classcraft: From gamification to ludicization of classroom management. *Education and information technologies, 22*(2), 497–513.

Sanchez, E., Kalmpourtzis, G., Cazes, J., & Berthoix, M. (2015a). Learning with tactileo map: From gamification to ludicization of fieldwork. In A. Car, T. Jekel, J. Strobl & G. Griesebner (Eds.), *GI_Forum 2015, Journal for geographic information science* (pp. 261–271). Berlin: Wichmann.

Schell, J. (2014). *The art of game design: A book of lenses* (2nd ed). London & New York: CRC Press.

Skinner, B. F. (1948). "Superstition" in the pigeon. *Journal of experimental psychology, 38*(2), 168–172.

Snyder, B. (2005). *Save the cat!: The last book on screenwriting you'll ever need*. Los Angeles: Michael Wiese Productions.

Sylvester, T. (2013). *Designing games: A guide to engineering experiences*. Sebastopol, CA: O'Reilly Media.

United Nations (n.d.). *Sustainable development*. Retrieved from http://www.un.org/sustainabledevelopment/

Vandercruysse, S., Vandewaetere, M., & Clarebout, G. (2012). Game-based learning: A review on the effectiveness of educational games. In M. M. Cruz-Cunha (Eds.), *Handbook of research on serious games as educational, business and research tools* (pp. 628–647). Hershey, PA: IGI Global.

Vogler, C. (1998). *The writer's journey: Mythic structure for writers.* Studio City, CA: M. Wiese Productions.

Vygotsky, L. (1978). Interaction between learning and development. In M. Gauvain &. M. Cole (Eds.), *Readings on the development of children* (pp. 34–40). New York: Scientific American Books.

Vygotsky, L (1978). *Mind in society: The development of higher psychological processes.* Cambridge, MA: Harvard University Press.

Wood, D., Bruner, J. S., & Ross, G. (1976). The role of tutoring in problem solving. *Journal of child psychology and psychiatry, 17,* 89–100.

Yerkes, R. M., & Dodson, J. D. (1908). The relation of strength of stimulus to rapidity of habit-formation. *Journal of comparative neurology and psychology, 18*(5), 459–482.

Index

Keyterms in bold indicate **games** and those in italics indicate *books*.